Exemplary Science
for Building Interest
in STEM Careers

Exemplary Science for Building Interest in STEM Careers

Edited by Robert E. Yager

National Science Teachers Association

Arlington, Virginia

National Science Teachers Association

Claire Reinburg, Director
Jennifer Horak, Managing Editor
J. Andrew Cooke, Senior Editor
Wendy Rubin, Associate Editor
Agnes Bannigan, Associate Editor
Amy America, Book Acquisitions Coordinator

ART AND DESIGN
Will Thomas Jr., Director

PRINTING AND PRODUCTION
Catherine Lorrain, Director

NATIONAL SCIENCE TEACHERS ASSOCIATION
Gerald F. Wheeler, Interim Executive Director
David Beacom, Publisher

1840 Wilson Blvd., Arlington, VA 22201
www.nsta.org/store
For customer service inquiries, please call 800-277-5300.

NSTA is committed to publishing quality materials that promote the best in inquiry-based science education. However, conditions of actual use may vary and the safety procedures and practices described in this book are intended to serve only as a guide. Additional precautionary measures may be required. NSTA and the author(s) do not warrant or represent that the procedure and practices in this book meet any safety code or standard or federal, state, or local regulations. NSTA and the author(s) disclaim any liability for personal injury or damage to property arising out of or relating to the use of this book including any recommendations, instructions, or materials contained therein.

PERMISSIONS
Book purchasers may photocopy, print, or e-mail up to five copies of an NSTA book chapter for personal use only; this does not include display or promotional use. Elementary, middle, and high school teachers may reproduce forms, sample documents, and single NSTA book chapters needed for classroom or noncommercial, professional-development use only. E-book buyers may download files to multiple personal devices but are prohibited from posting the files to third-party servers or websites, or from passing files to non-buyers. For additional permission to photocopy or use material electronically from this NSTA Press book, please contact the Copyright Clearance Center (CCC) (*www.copyright.com*; 978-750-8400). Please access *www.nsta.org/permissions* for further information about NSTA's rights and permissions policies.

Library of Congress Cataloging-in-Publication Data
Exemplary science for building interest in STEM careers / Robert E. Yager, editor.
     p. cm.
 Includes bibliographical references and index.
 ISBN 978-1-936959-35-8
1. Science--Study and teaching. 2. Engineering--Study and teaching. 3. Mathematics--Study and teaching. I. Yager, Robert Eugene, 1930- II. Title: Exemplary science for building interest in science, technology, engineering, and mathematics careers.
 Q181.E84 2012
 507.1--dc23
                          2012026203
 ISBN 978-1-936959-64-8 (ebook)

Contents

Foreword

Attracting More Students to Pursue STEM Careers

Robert E. Yager
University of Iowa

Goal Four, which was included in the 1996 National Science Education Standards (NSES) has attracted few, if any, disagreements regarding its appropriateness. Everyone agrees that encouraging student interest in science and technology careers is a good thing. There have been no objections to its inclusion as one of the goals (reasons) for teaching school science. In fact, most K–16 science teachers endorse the current stated aim for their teaching: to attract more students to careers in science, technology, engineering, and mathematics (STEM).

Interestingly, there are but four Goals for teaching science included in the 1996 National Standards. Everyone especially liked Goal One; it calls for teachers to ensure that students "experience the richness and excitement of knowing about and understanding the natural world" (NRC 1996). Goals Two and Three focus on the importance of science being used for meeting personal and societal issues.

Goal Four calls for instruction to "increase student economic productivity through the use of the knowledge, understandings, and skills of the scientifically literate person in their careers." Interestingly, some of the authors of chapters for this monograph have even indicated that Goal Four may be the *only* important goal! Yet it is the one that seems to be most difficult to accomplish in terms of evidence for success and effectiveness over time. It is rarely included in textbooks or curriculum frameworks with specific ideas for trying and information to use in activities. Further, relatively few educators are able to discuss what they specifically do to meet the goal. Some have argued that if such a career goal were to succeed in terms of actions taken, most of our problems could be eliminated and students would use the experiences to lead them to identifying current problems and considering STEM careers for themselves.

Looking for specific features in submissions indicate exciting efforts by our Exemplary Science Programs (ESPs). The examples of success comprise the chapters of this monograph. They indicate that there are exciting ways to mentor students and to deepen their interest in pursuing STEM careers. This book is all about specific ways that are effective in increasing interest in STEM careers.

Selecting the 16 programs to highlight in these chapters was the greatest challenge, due to the dearth of responses to our call for submissions for this monograph, compared to previous titles in this series. Why? Unfortunately it has been found that student interest in science actually tends to decline each year over the K–16 interim (Ali, Yager, Haciemenoglu, and Caliskan 2011).

Research indicates that enrolling in science classes *decreases* student interest in science careers! It is interesting to note that this continues even at the college level, when a larger percentage enrolls in science by choice. These facts alone should encourage more to try and to report on successes for our ESP efforts.

The hope is that this publication will excite more teachers to try even more creative efforts to portray students as actually *doing* science rather than continuing with typical courses where teachers try to transmit the information they know directly to students and to test for their degree of success (memorization).

The real successes for stimulating more students to aim for STEM careers are eye-opening. One facet of the ESP Careers effort is the diversity of the plans offered. Many have used the help of community members, business and industry representatives, and more current views of what science is and how it indicates the importance of collaborative learning. Often this means experiences with current projects dealing with local and personal problems as well as those that affect and include students in selecting and developing their own ideas (e.g., students as part of leadership teams). Science is the act of humans trying to make sense of objects and events found in the natural world. It is exciting to engage students in resolving problems and issues using their own ideas. As noted, if science is personally experienced, it will attract many more to STEM careers! And, with more enthusiasm!

The 16 chapters that follow report on ideas and experiences representing a large number of career areas; they include scientists, engineers, inventors, and education reformers, all of whom are often aware of the importance of personal, local, and current issues as opposed to merely doing something prescribed (often from a textbook). One exciting observation is the varying forms of collaboration that have been accomplished through the efforts of the author teams. Chapter 1 starts with the inclusion of five efforts and ideas from Bruce Alberts, the editor of *Science*, the official journal of the American Association for the Advancement of Science (AAAS). Alberts's efforts in developing the National Science Education Standards add to the importance of the reforms of school science. He has also been involved with the recent development of a new framework that is to be used for guiding the 2012–13 efforts and the work on new standards that is underway. These new efforts surely are focused on STEM teaching, curricula, and careers.

Some have expressed that there would be more interest in STEM careers if students were simply not permitted to enroll in traditional science courses. But the nine statements from the 1996 Standards call for *less emphasis* on: (1) treating all students alike and responding to the group as a whole; (2) rigidly following curriculum; (3) focusing on student acquisition of information; (4) presenting scientific knowledge through lecture, text, and demonstration; (5) asking for recitation for acquired knowledge; (6) testing students for factual information at the end of the unit or chapter; (7) maintaining responsibility and authority; (8) supporting competition; and (9) working alone. Certainly the authors of the 16 chapters that follow were not doing or advocate such "typical" teaching. Instead they were aware of and interested in the nine *More Emphasis* conditions: (1) understanding and responding to individual student's interests, strengths, experiences, and needs; (2) selecting and adapting curriculum (3) focusing on student understanding and use of scientific knowledge, ideas, and inquiry processes; (4) guiding students in active and extended scientific inquiries; (5) providing opportunities for scientific discussion and debate among students; (6) continuously assessing student understanding (and involving students in the process); (7) sharing responsibility for learning with students; (8) supporting a classroom community with cooperation, shared responsibility, and respect; and (9) working with other teachers to enhance the science program.

When teachers change their teaching, student interest increases—and more students aspire to science-related careers as well. Changes in teaching must occur and typical courses must change to focus more on student efforts with projects, activities, and problem-solving. This is the best plan for getting more students interested in pursuing STEM careers after high school. Unfortunately though, typical college courses, with large enrollments in lectures and cookbook laboratories, provide poor models for K–12 teachers preparing themselves to teach. It is gratifying to see more college science teachers changing the typical mode of their college teaching. Some even label their reform teaching as to be "no lecture, no cookbook laboratories." These are exciting efforts that can result in more students wanting to spend a lifetime with STEM careers!

Reference

Ali, M., R. E. Yager, E. Haciemenoglu, and I. Caliskan. 2011. Changes in student attitudes regarding science when taught by teachers without experiences with a model professional development program. Under review.

Acknowledgments

Members of the National Advisory Board for the Exemplary Science Series

Lloyd H. Barrow
Missouri University Science
Education Center
Professor
Science Education
University of Missouri
Columbia, MO 65211

Bonnie Brunkhorst
Past President of NSTA
Professor of Geological Science and
Science Education
California State University–San Bernardino
San Bernardino, CA 92506

Herbert Brunkhorst
Professor of Science Education and Biology
California State University–San Bernardino
San Bernardino, CA 92407

Lynn A. Bryan
Professor of Science Education
Department of Curriculum and Instruction
Purdue University
West Lafayette, IN 47907

Charlene M. Czerniak
Professor of Science Education
Department of Curriculum and Instruction
University of Toledo
Toledo, OH 43606

Pradeep (Max) Dass
Professor, Science Education & Biology
Department of Biology
Appalachian State University
P.O. Box 32027
Boone, NC 28608

Linda Froschauer
NSTA President 2006–2007
Science Education Consultant
Editor, Science and Children, NSTA
Westport, VA 06880

Stephen Henderson
Science Education Consultant
President, Briarwood Enterprises, LLC
Richmond, KY 40475

Bobby Jeanpierre
Associate Professor
College of Education
University of Central Florida
Orlando, FL 32816

Page Keeley
MMSA Senior Program Director
Maine Mathematics and
Science Alliance
Augusta, ME 04332

LeRoy R. Lee
Executive Director
Wisconsin Science Network
4420 Gray Road
De Forest, WI 52532-2506

Shelley A. Lee
Science Education Consultant
WI Dept. of Public Instruction
P.O. Box 7842
Madison, WI 53707-7841

Lisa Martin-Hansen
Associate Professor of Science Education
Association for Science Teacher Education
    Board Members at Large
Georgia Science Teacher Association
College Board Representative
College of Education
Georgia State University
Atlanta, GA 30302-3978

LaMoine Motz
Science Facilities and
    Curriculum Consultant
8805 El Dorado Drive
Waterford, MI 48386-3409

Edward P. Ortleb
Science Consultant/Author
5663 Pernod Avenue
St. Louis, MO 63139

Carolyn F. Randolph
Science Education Consultant
14 Crescent Lake Court
Blythewood, SC 29016

Barbara Woodworth Saigo
Science Education and Writing Consultant
President, Saiwood Publications
23051 County Road 75
St. Cloud, MN 56301

Pat M. Shane
Education Consultant
1289 N. Fordham Blvd., #266
Chapel Hill, NC 27514-6110

Patricia Simmons
Professor and Department Head
Math Science & Technology Education
North Carolina State University
Raleigh, NC 27695

Gerald Skoog
Texas Tech University
College of Education
15th and Boston
Lubbock, TX 79409-1071

Mary Ann Mullinnix
Assistant Editor
University of Iowa
Iowa City, Iowa 52242

About the Editor

Robert E. Yager—an active contributor to the development of the National Science Education Standards—has devoted his life to teaching, writing, and advocating on behalf of science education worldwide. Having started his career as a high school science teacher, he has been a professor of science education at the University of Iowa since 1956. He has also served as president of seven national organizations, including NSTA, and has been involved in teacher education in Japan, Korea, Taiwan, Indonesia, Turkey, Egypt, and several European countries. Among his many publications are several NSTA Press books, including *Focus on Excellence* and two issues of *What Research Says to the Science Teacher*. He has authored over 700 research and policy publications as well as having served as editor for eight volumes of NSTA's Exemplary Science Programs (ESP). Yager earned a bachelor's degree in biology from the University of Northern Iowa and master's and doctoral degrees in plant physiology from the University of Iowa.

Changes Needed in Science Education for Attracting More Students to STEM Careers

Bruce Alberts
Editor-in-Chief of Science
American Association for the Advancement of Science (AAAS)

Introduction: Robert E. Yager, Editor of ESP Monographs

Dr. Bruce Alberts served as the President for the National Academy of Sciences from 1992 to 2006. In this position he headed the efforts to produce the National Science Education Standards. He was a strong force for ensuring the inclusion of scientists in defining science and exemplifying it in their work. In addition to defining science as something all people do, Dr. Alberts was anxious that the definition also included science education and the importance of all teachers of being aware of these features and to use them in their teaching.

In 2006, Dr. Alberts became Editor-in-Chief of *Science*—the world's leading journal of original scientific research, global news, and commentary, published by the American Association for the Advancement of Science (AAAS). As editor, he has frequently offered editorial statements concerning how science education should become more inquiry-based so students are able to offer solutions to current problems. He has continued to offer personal encouragements for resolving science education problems in collaborative ways.

Dr. Alberts's editorials—Why I Became a Scientist; On Becoming a Scientist; Prioritizing Science Education; Reframing Science Standards; and An Education That Inspires—provide a "setting" for meeting Goal Four of the NSES, encouraging more students to increase their economic productivity through the use of the knowledge, understandings, and skills of the scientifically literate person.

Why I Became a Scientist

As a pre-med student at Harvard University, I took chemistry, analytical chemistry, organic chemistry, biology, physics, and so on. Although I found the content fascinating, after the first semester I could no longer tolerate the required afternoon laboratory exercise. For two and a half years, I had spent two or three afternoons each week performing tedious cookbook exercises:

Measure this, measure that, get an answer and compare it with all the answers your friends got, fudge the data so that you get the right answer, and then turn in your notebook. (Amazingly, the same boring laboratory exercises continue at most of our universities today, nearly 50 years later!)

I finally found the courage to complain: "I love physical chemistry, but I hate this laboratory. What can I do?" My professors told me that if I joined a research laboratory for a semester, I wouldn't have to take the physical chemistry laboratory. So that spring I worked in Professor Paul Doty's laboratory. This was completely different from the afternoon course laboratories. I discovered the excitement of science, and I forgot about medical school (2006/2007).

On Becoming a Scientist

One normally becomes a scientist through a series of apprenticeships, pursuing research in laboratories directed by established scientists. My own scientific mentors were Jacques Fresco and Paul Doty at Harvard, where I learned not only technical skills but also how to think and function as a scientist. Both from them and by making my own mistakes, I learned how to identify important problems, how to think critically, and how to design effective research strategies (2004). Because so much of one's scientific future is shaped by early experiences, it is critical that beginning scientists select their mentors wisely. Unfortunately, what constitutes a "good" choice is not always obvious. Here I offer some personal advice to help young scientists make these tough decisions wisely.

The exact project pursued for a PhD degree is not nearly as important as finding the best place for learning how to push forward the frontier of knowledge as an independent investigator. My first piece of advice for graduate students is to begin research training in a laboratory led by a person with high scientific and ethical standards. It is by talking to people in that lab or those who have previously trained there, and by consulting other scientists in the same field, that one can gain this important insight.

It is also important to find an adviser who will pay close attention to your development as a scientist. Brilliant scientists sometimes make poor mentors. Often, an established leader who has no more than about a dozen people to manage can best nurture a creative, exciting, and supportive place to work. But carrying out research with an outstanding new professor with a very small group can frequently provide even better training.

Students enter graduate school both to learn how to do science well and to discover where their talents and interests lie. Success at either task requires that they be empowered to create new approaches and to generate new ideas. In my experience, beginning scientists will only gain the confidence needed to confront the unknown successfully by making discoveries through experiments of their own design. The best research advisers will therefore provide their graduate students with enough guidance to prevent them from wasting time on nonproductive pursuits, while giving them the freedom to innovate and to learn from their own mistakes.

In my field of biology, two apprenticeships are standard for beginning scientists; first while earning a PhD degree and then in a second laboratory in a postdoctoral position. The choice of a postdoctoral laboratory is best made with a long-term career plan in mind. Scientists at this stage should intentionally try to choose a laboratory where they can acquire skills that complement those they already have. For example, a student whose PhD thesis gave her strong skills as a yeast geneticist might choose to do postdoctoral research with an expert protein biochemist, planning to use a combination of powerful genetic and biochemical tools to attack a biological problem in an area where very few scientists have the same abilities.

But success as an independent scientist will require much more than technical skills. It is critical to be able to design research strategies that are ambitious enough to be important and exciting, innovative enough to make unique contributions likely, and nevertheless have a good chance of producing valuable results. An enormous number of different experiments are possible, but only a tiny proportion will be really worthwhile. Choosing well requires great thought and creativity, and it involves taking risks (2009).

Prioritizing Science Education

We will focus on the connection between learning science in school and the acquisition of language and communication skills, emphasizing the benefits of teaching science and literacy in the same classrooms whenever possible. In the United States, this would be viewed as a radical proposal. Unfortunately, the great majority of Americans are accustomed to science classrooms where students memorize facts about the natural world and, if they are lucky, perform an experiment or two; in language arts classes, students generally read fictional literature and write about it in fossilized formats such as "compare and contrast."

The exciting news is that "science learning entails and benefits from embedded literacy activities [and]…literacy learning entails and benefits from being embedded within science inquiry" (Pearson, Moje, and Greenleaf 2010). Here, it is helpful to distinguish between factual (or informational) and fictional (or narrative) text. Science reading and writing is largely of the former type, and it is this factual, informational text that dominates today's knowledge-everywhere world. Yet, most of the formal teaching in language arts classrooms deals with fictional text. My own failed efforts at storytelling lacked the imagination to do anything more than rewrite Hansel and Gretel in a thinly disguised new context. Without doubt, learning to write and read clear and concise informational text, as in summaries of investigations in science class, is an essential preparation for nearly all of life out of school.

Reconceptualizing science education by closely connecting literacy lessons with active inquiry learning in science class allows one to make a strong argument for greatly expanding the time spent on science in primary school to at least four hours a week. This alone would carry tremendous benefits in places—like the United States—where science has often become marginalized to less than an hour a week.

A second advantage to forging this connection between literacy and science teaching is that a well-taught science class gives everyone a chance to excel at something. It is hard to stay motivated and interested in schooling if one is always in the bottom half of the class. By linking literacy and science education, those who are more challenged with making progress in reading can gain the self-confidence needed to succeed by demonstrating skills in analyzing a problem that stumps the better readers. Or they might excel in the mechanical manipulation of objects required in a science lesson. From this perspective, the penalties for "failing" schools in my home state of California are tragically wrong: Students who struggle with reading or math are given double periods of reading or math drill, and the very set of activities that could excite them about school is eliminated.

I am reminded of the schooling of P. Roy Vagelos, an outstanding scientific leader in U.S. academia and industry. A fellow biochemist and a friend, Roy topped off his career by becoming the chief executive officer of the major pharmaceutical company Merck, with *Fortune* magazine anointing his company as the "most admired in America" for seven successive years (1987–1993). In his biography, he describes himself as a poor memorizer, who nearly failed first and second grade and was largely alienated from school until he was given the chance to demonstrate other skills that allowed him to excel (Vagelos and Galambos 2004).

How many talented young people are we losing in today's schools, driven by test scores that reward teachers for drilling students to remember obscure science words, and by an early reading curriculum based on stories and folk tales? Instead, we should be rewarding teachers for teaching science inquiry skills and literacy together, through collaborative and critical discourse (Osborne 2010; Alberts 2010).

Reframing Science Standards

A promising draft *Framework for Science Education* was posted by the National Academies for public comment and review. Its goal is to define the science that all students should be taught from age 5 through precollege in the United States, building on lessons learned from the 1996 National Science Education Standards (NSES). Will this new effort, initiated to help produce a common core for science education across states (Leshner, Malcom, and Roseman 2010) be more successful than the last one?

In 1989, the governors of all 50 states issued a call for "voluntary national standards" in each of the major academic disciplines. In response, the NSES were issued by the National Academies of Sciences in 1996. The results have been disappointing. In particular, the requirement for students to master a large number of facts and concepts took precedence over the strong emphasis on "science as inquiry" in the NSES. The new *Framework* attempts to overcome this problem in several interesting ways.

First, the *Framework* focuses on only four core concepts in each of four disciplines: life sciences, physical science, Earth and space sciences, and engineering and technology. And differing from the NSES, each core concept extends over all years of schooling. The intention is to leave room during the school day for three important strands of science learning that have been systematically ignored in favor of the traditional content strand, which focuses on knowing, using and interpreting scientific explanations of the natural world. The critical strands that have been missing are (1) generating and evaluating scientific evidence and explanations, (2) understanding the nature and development of scientific knowledge, and (3) participating in scientific practices and discourse (Alberts 2009).

Second, the *Framework* supplements the dominant theme of inquiry in the NSES with a greatly expanded discussion of why any definition of science education must center around active participation in scientific practices and extensive experience with evaluating evidence. The current focus on transmitting only the knowledge that scientists have discovered fails to provide students with the thinking and problem-solving skills that are essential for life in our complex societies, and it also fails to give them a sound understanding of why science has been so successful as a special way of knowing about the world. Thus, the *Framework* contains a powerful chapter with 16 useful tables entitled Scientific and Engineering Practices. (The inclusion of engineering itself represents a major, positive break with tradition.)

The *Framework* also stresses the importance of building coherence into the science curriculum from year to year through reference to the ongoing research on "learning progressions." As an example, the recognition that any object is composed of specific materials, and has certain properties because of those materials, is known to be an important first step toward understanding atomic-molecular theory. To guide curriculum design, the last half of the document presents prototype learning progressions for each of the core concepts to be learned, expanding on the landmark *Atlas for Science Literacy* produced by the American Association for the Advancement of Science.

The Framework was finalized in response to the feedback received on the public draft, and then, because responsibility for education is assigned to each state by the U.S. Constitution, the final standards are being developed through a coalition of states led by the nonprofit organization Achieve. The worst thing that scientists could do would be to insist that the core disciplinary ideas be expanded to include their specialties. Instead, the scientific community should focus on preparing college students to "ask questions; collect, analyze, and interpret data; construct and critique arguments; communicate and interpret scientific and technical tests; and apply and use scientific knowledge"—precisely as the *Framework* specifies for the precollege years (Alberts 2010).

An Education That Inspires

Why is it that children, who enter school at age five, filled with excitement and wonder about the world, often become bored with education before their teenage years? How might the United States produce a more engaging education system, one that allows a child with a specific fascination to explore that interest in depth as an integral part of his or her early education? Here I sketch a possible plan based on science, technology, engineering, and math (STEM) awards that would be largely earned through student activities outside of school.

The idea has been partly inspired by the U.S. Advanced Placement (AP) system of courses and exams, which makes a first-year college-level education in selected subjects available to high school students. As a nationally recognized standard of achievement, passing an AP course is a mark of success for both students and schools. High schools now strive to increase the number of students taking such courses, and this nongovernmental but nationally certified program has been rapidly growing in popularity. Could a nationally validated set of "STEM challenge awards," designed for students at earlier stages of schooling, similarly motivate schools and school systems to value a new type of achievement?

I suggest that the proposed STEM challenge awards be modeled on the achievement badges that youth organizations around the world have developed to promote the active learning of specific subjects in depth. For example, the Boy Scouts of America allows more than 100 different merit badges to be earned, each focused on a specific topic such as plant science or lifesaving.[*] In addition to this large selection, each badge provides a young person with a variety of options. Thus, to earn a plant science merit badge, a scout can choose between agronomy, horticulture, or field botany. Most learning experiences are active ones, such as "Select a study site that is at least

---

[*] *www.scouting.org/scoutsource/BoyScouts/AdvancementandAwards/MeritBadges.aspx*

100 × 100 ft. Make a list of the plants in the study site by groups of plants: canopy trees, small trees, shrubs, herbaceous wildflowers and grasses, vines, ferns, mosses, algae, fungi, lichens. Find out which are native plants and which are exotic (or nonnative)." This is infinitely more interesting than a typical school experience in which students memorize the names of plants and their parts from pictures in a textbook, often without encountering the actual object.

A STEM challenge award program might provide 100 different challenges to choose from at each level of schooling (for example, sets of awards of increasing difficulty for ages 5–8, 9–13, and 14–18), on subjects ranging from reptiles to website design. Scientific and engineering societies in each discipline could create the requirements for many awards, as could industry groups or government agencies such as the U.S. National Aeronautics and Space Agency. But a single umbrella organization would be needed to certify the contents of the award projects, as well as the mechanisms used to judge and record their completion. Such national certification would be critical for the awards to have a substantial positive impact, serving as a widely recognized, valid mark of success for both students and school districts.

The most ambitious and revolutionary part of this plan supplements the teachers in schools with adult volunteers, each serving as an expert for a particular STEM challenge award. To earn a merit badge, a scout must demonstrate to a qualified adult volunteer (a "counselor" for that badge) that he has satisfied that badge's requirements. In a similar way, many thousands of adults with science and technology backgrounds would be enlisted as counselors, both to help teachers and to judge each student's performance, making full use of modern communications tools. A great many scientists and engineers would be willing to contribute to improving science in schools if an efficient and effective way for them to do so could be generated. And their contributions could truly inspire today's students (Alberts 2010).

References

Alberts, B. 2004. Turning points: A wake-up call. *Nature* 431: 1041.

Alberts, B. 2007. Why I became a scientist. *Educational Leadership* 64: 4.

Alberts, B. 2009. On becoming a scientist. *Science* 326 (5955): 916.

Alberts, B. 2009. Redefining science education. *Science* 323 (5913): 437.

Alberts, B. 2010. Prioritizing science education. *Science* 328: 405.

Alberts, B. 2010. Reframing science standards. *Science* 329: 491.

Alberts, B. 2010 An education that inspires. *Science* 330: 427.

Leshner, A. I., S. Malcom, and J. E. Roseman. 2010. Seeking science standards. *Science* 328 (1075): 1075.

Osborne, J. 2010. Arguing to learn in science: The role of collaborative, critical discourse. *Science* 328 (5977): 463–466.

Pearson, P. D., E. Moje, and C. Greenleaf. 2010. Literacy and science: Each in the service of the other. *Science* 328 (459): 459–463.

Vagelos, P. R., and L. Galambos. 2004. *Medicine, science, and Merck.* Cambridge, MA: Harvard University Press.

Designed to Invent: Camp Invention, A 21st-Century Program

Maryann Wolowiec
IEL Education Consulting

Alaina Rutledge and Jayme Cellitioci
Invent Now, Inc.

Setting

Invent Now was founded in 1973 as the National Inventors Hall of Fame, now a non-profit supporting organization, with the mission of recognizing and honoring the great inventors of our time. Over time, we have expanded that mission by creating programs that encourage over 230,000 children, teachers, parents, college students, and independent inventors each year to explore science, technology, and their own innate creativity and inventiveness. In doing this, we not only honor those pioneers whose innovations have built this great nation, but we also invest in the promise of future generations by giving them the tools and confidence to invent, innovate, and create.

Strengthening American competitiveness for the 21st century continues to be one of our country's greatest challenges, and key to achieving a competitive workforce is investment in innovation beginning at an early age. According to the Executive Summary of the American Management Association's 2010 Critical Skills survey, "Critical thinking, creativity, collaboration, and communication skills will become more important in a fast-paced, competitive global

economy." Executives say the 21st century requires more skilled workers. Invent Now's Camp Invention program has been igniting the inventive spirit in elementary children for over 20 years, providing a foundation for tomorrow's workforce.

Invent Now developed the Camp Invention program in 1990 as a one-week summer day camp for children in grades 1–6 with curricula focused on developing creative and inventive thinking and problem solving through science, technology, engineering, and math (STEM). According to the National Science Teachers Association Position Statement, *Science Education for Middle Level Students* (2003), research has shown, "if educators don't capture students' interest and enthusiasm in science by grade 7, students may never find their way back to science." Camp Invention directly addresses this need by targeting young children. The program is currently offered in 48 states to children with diverse abilities, backgrounds, geographies, and economic conditions.

The Camp Invention program is primarily held in schools and taught by certified teachers who are local to the community and familiar to the children. In keeping with our mission, all Invent Now programs are designed to reflect the spirit of invention inherent to the National Inventors Hall of Fame. While curricula are science-based and align with national education standards, all are written in a transdisciplinary approach, incorporating other subject areas such as engineering, mathematics, social studies, literacy, history, art, and 21st-century skills such as creativity, critical thinking, problem solving, collaboration, and communication. The Camp Invention program enhances students' traditional school experience by providing developmentally appropriate science in an informal setting. Evidence that well-designed out-of-school experiences improve student learning is well documented.

> The research warrant for afterschool and summer learning programs is clear: Children and youth who participate in well-implemented programs and activities outside of school are poised to stay enrolled longer and perform better in school than their peers who do not attend such programs. Further, emerging research indicates that when schools and afterschool programs partner to support student success, all parties stand to benefit. (Little 2009)

Key Program Components

Camp Invention curricula contain the following key components:

1. Immersion

2. Create, Test, and Recreate

3. Science, Technology, Engineering and Mathematics (STEM)

4. 21st-Century Skills
   - Creativity and Innovation
   - Teambuilding and Collaboration.

Immersion

Immersion is created by offering engaging challenges that place problem solving into a context. This is accomplished through embedding challenges in fantasy, stories, or real-world problems and using language that allows children to "buy in" and embark upon a learning adventure that unfolds as the immersion experiences deepen. What will be your hook? How will you build anticipation? Where are the opportunities to dive deep and wrestle with ambiguity? What types of new questions and adventures will arise?

Create, Test, and Re-create

Camp Invention curricula employ the "Create, Test, and Re-create" approach, using scientific inquiry or engineering design. After clarifying the challenge or problem, the children begin exploring and investigating. Children move to building models, prototypes, and inventions while thoughtfully reflecting on the strengths, weaknesses, and opportunities of those creations, and then refining the creations based upon what they learned. This approach allows children to refine skills in self-assessment, adaptive creativity, and evaluative thinking. Children also increase their tolerance for and learn the value of failure, especially as it pertains to ideas and/or product development and evolution.

Science, Technology, Engineering and Mathematics (STEM)

STEM comes to life for children through problem solving. In nature and the manufactured world, STEM subject areas are interwoven. Camp Invention curricula use STEM content as a vehicle for the direct application of creativity and innovation skills. Camp Invention curricula are written using an interdisciplinary approach, including other subject areas and 21st-century STEM-focused skills that create engaging, meaningful challenges. Many of the critical challenges facing today's generation of children will require STEM knowledge, keen creative problem solving, and collaboration skills.

21st-Century Skills

Creativity and Innovation

Nearly every modern-day business and education-based publication mentions the importance of developing creativity and innovation skills. But while these skills are recognized as important, there is often a gap between understanding their importance and effectively integrating them into the learning environment. Camp Invention curricula embed strategies that help develop these skills.

The Creative Problem Solving (CPS) process serves as a vehicle and vessel for moving through this process. By using CPS for the invention process, children assess challenges, collect data through testing, generate solutions through trial and error, and continuously refine their ideas and products through evaluation and reflection. In addition, when children use the CPS process through engaging hands-on challenges, they are more likely to internalize the process and use it when they encounter new challenges.

The Camp Invention program is designed and tested as an educational supplement to provide children and teachers with additional resources to augment their classroom learning. Camp Invention program goals include participant learning goals, learning environment goals, and instructor professional learning goals. The learning environment we foster through our programs promotes learning through fun, engaging challenges that are designed to improve children's positive attitudes toward science; to excite interest and motivation to learn about the natural and physical world; to increase understanding of and connections among science, technology, engineering, mathematics (STEM) subjects; and to increase scientific knowledge and skills. The immersive, hands-on learning experiences provide an open, safe environment that encourages risk-taking, creative problem solving, and development of the entrepreneurial mindset. There are opportunities for each child to explore his/her own creative ideas and for children to work in teams in search of solutions.

> The science and math crisis facing our country needs to be addressed at the elementary teacher school level. I personally view the Camp Invention program as a force in restoring America's competitive edge in the fields of science and mathematics by inspiring and rekindling the spirit of invention in today's youth, thereby increasing America's capacity to produce innovative thinkers, engineers, scientists, and entrepreneurs. (Cindy Moss, PhD, Director of Science and Math)

Invent Now's Camp Invention curriculum is designed to promote creativity, and advance the spirit of innovation and entrepreneurship. The National Science Education Standards (NSES) (1996) envision change throughout the educational system and highlight these changes as *Changing Emphases*. The key components of the Camp Invention curricula that align with the NSES Content and Inquiry Standards, specifically *Changing Emphases*, are the following:

- Understanding scientific concepts and developing abilities of inquiry;
- Learning subject matter disciplines in the context of inquiry, technology, science in personal and social perspectives, including history and nature of science;
- Integrating all aspects of science content; implementing inquiry as strategies, abilities, and ideas to be learned;
- Activities that investigate and analyze science questions;
- Process skills in personalized contexts;
- Using multiple process skills—manipulation, cognitive, procedural;
- Using evidence and strategies for developing or revising an explanation;
- Communicating science explanations;

- Doing more investigations in order to develop understandings, abilities, values of inquiry, and knowledge and use of typical science content; and
- Public communication of student ideas and work to classmates, and others.

The Camp Invention program is strengthened through the engagement of National Inventors Hall of Fame Inductees. The Inductees' input and feedback on the programs is invaluable. In addition, numerous excellent instructors have piloted our programs and provided meaningful feedback as to the program workability in actual school or informal settings.

Team Building and Collaboration

Individualization and teaming are present in all Camp Invention curricula. Learning how to work in teams, both locally and virtually, and collaboratively on projects are skills that today's children need for tomorrow's successes. In learning to team, children build tolerance, have respect and enthusiasm for diversity (including differences in creative thinking and problem solving styles), and can move from individual ideas to common solutions that express the group's collective creativity and intelligence. Simply placing children in groups is only one small piece of providing a teaming experience. It is through careful observation, coaching, reflection, feedback, and engaging in numerous opportunities for adaptation that children actually build the skills necessary to be effective team members in the 21st century.

Camp Invention Program

The mission of Invent Now is to be a catalyst for change through recognizing inventors and invention, promoting creativity, and advancing the spirit of innovation and entrepreneurship. Invent Now partners with school districts and organizations nationwide to provide high-quality enrichment programs. Camp Invention is all-inclusive, including cutting-edge curricula, all program materials, promotional assistance, and staff training and compensation for turnkey ease of implementation. Parents/guardians are important partners. A daily newsletter is sent home with information and ideas for extending the child's experiences.

A Camp Invention series consists of a weeklong experience for six and one-half hours each day. Invent Now produces new curricula each year, so multiple weeks of programming can be accommodated. The excitement and wonder children exhibit during the Camp Invention week is exhilarating. The following are descriptions of five modules from one series: Power'd, Hatched, SMArt: Science, Math & Art, I Can Invent: Edison's Workshop, and Game On: Power Play.

Power'd

In the Power'd module, a mysterious scientist is seeking new ways to power robotic creatures in a secret lab. The scientist requests the help of Camp Invention children to explore new types of energy to help bring the robotic creatures to life. Children spend the week investigating alternative energy sources such as wind power, solar power, and hydropower to design and build their own creatures.

On day 1, children explore static electricity and circuits and learn how to power Direct Current (DC) motors. On day 2, children build and power their robotic creatures and explore the strength of the chemical substance phosphor, allowing them to harness the Sun's power. Children create enclosures to surround their creatures and protect them from the dangers inside the laboratory on day 3, and then harness eco-friendly wind power to light their creatures' enclosures. On day 4, children must figure out a way to feed the robotic creatures using a waterwheel as inspiration. On day 5, children use lemons to create batteries that power lights and design a new way to power their creatures when their batteries die. They then design a race track for their creatures and measure the distance that their creatures can travel in one minute.

Hatched

The Hatched module uses a virtual computer world to introduce children to entrepreneurship and economics. During the week, children are presented with the challenge of rebuilding a virtual world for the world's residents and restoring the world's economy.

On day 1, children hear that their instructor has been contacted by a being named Inventar who needs their help in restoring the health of his virtual world. They begin their work by designing a map of the virtual world that details where the avatars live and work, and design their personal avatars for the Hatched world. During day 2, children break into tribes (teams) and build aqueducts to carry water from the Hatched lake to the areas where the avatars live and then hear of their first economic challenge to restore the Hatched world. On day 3, tribes create items to sell to other tribes for their avatars. During day 4, children's tribes create a marketplace in which to sell their items and establish pricing and advertising for their businesses. The week ends with participant tribes advertising their wares and buying and selling with other tribes. The tribe that manages to accumulate the most Hatched money by selling their items is declared the most entrepreneurial of the Hatched world!

SMArt: Science, Math, & Art

Mathematics is a subject that is a part of everyday life. The SMArt: Science, Math, & Art module uses fantasy to introduce exciting mathematics topics that involve very little numeracy. This module uses the mathematical fields of tessellations, topology, minimal surfaces, fractals, and angles to demonstrate that math is a subject involving some of the basic questions and areas of our lives. Children discover that math, at its core, involves patterns and relationships. Each day children explore a new type of pattern or relationship and how this can be translated and used in the real world.

On day 1, children hear that the residents have forgotten about the beauty of mathematics and begin their work to further the residents' understanding by introducing them to the field of tessellations. Children study soap bubbles on day two, forming various surfaces while using singular and multiple bubble forms. Day 3 introduces fractals (shapes in which a smaller piece of the shape is similar to the larger shape) and calls attention to their prevalence in nature—in lightning, blood vessels, or coastlines. On day 4, children explore the varied field of topology while experimenting with Mobius strips and measuring lines using unconventional measurement tools, creating fractal art, and discovering the fractal nature of their own circulatory system. The week ends with children creating games that use a number of different types of angles to move a ball.

I Can Invent: Edison's Workshop

In the I Can Invent: Edison's Workshop module, children walk in the steps of Thomas Edison as they create multistep inventions that they name and prepare to market. Children use science, creative problem-solving processes, and hands-on applications to further their inventiveness and critical-thinking skills. Working in teams, younger children focus on building ball machines that send a ball into one of two ending points, while older children create multistep, Rube Goldberg–type machines that raise a flag proclaiming their successes.

On day 1, children enter Edison's workshop, where they are faced with a challenge to better prepare them for their ultimate challenge: creating, marketing, and selling the next great American toy! The excitement builds on day 2 when children dismantle intricate, wind-up clocks and investigate how the gears and springs inside them make their hands rotate. Using this knowledge, children begin planning their ball-moving toys and Rube Goldberg–type machines. Children put their plans into action as they immerse themselves in full-on construction of their machines on days 3 and 4. On day 5, children name their machines and develop effective advertisements for them. The week ends with children enhancing their Rube Goldberg–type machines by testing, retesting, and making any necessary adjustments before applying for and receiving mock patents.

Game On: Power Play

The Game On: Power Play module scores a home run by combining physical activity and creativity. Children practice teamwork, cooperation, coordination, and creative problem-solving processes during fun, energetic games. Game On: Power Play activities are based on the premise that traditional games can be modified using nontraditional approaches. Employing the concept of upcycling, children use found materials to create completely new games. Unlike competitive games or sports, this module stresses creative problem solving over winning or losing, while boosting self-confidence and encouraging active physical participation.

In this module, each day features new and exciting challenges that vary based on children's ages and abilities. All activities are designed to blend the functions of mind and body while children work collectively in diverse teams. These games facilitate inventive and inquisitive-thinking skills while incorporating 21st-century learning skills such as collaboration, communication, and whole-systems thinking. Children play approximately four games per day that feature nontraditional sporting equipment such as recyclable items, water balloons, and other unconventional materials. Children's curiosity is sparked with a new lineup of wild and wet games that are sure to enrich and energize.

Professional Learning

The Camp Invention program design uses creative teaching and learning practices to develop children's 21st-century learning and innovation skills. With the program offered in classrooms across the country and delivered by local educators, Camp Invention supports these local educators in providing children the opportunity to apply classroom learning through a practical, hands-on approach. The Camp Invention program also provides substantive professional learning for the teachers through their delivery of its inquiry-based curricula. This involves providing hands-on, innovative, and creative experiences that enhance teachers' knowledge and skills in science and engineering, reinforcing educationally sound, evidenced-based instructional methods, engaging teachers in scientific inquiry and the engineering design process, giving teachers experience in delivering elements of creative problem solving, encouraging their transfer of the inquiry-based science experiences into their classrooms, exciting teachers about teaching science, and advancing their understanding of and connections among STEM knowledge and skills.

Each Camp Invention program module contains the written curriculum and all materials necessary for the week. The written curriculum contains information that allows the instructor (teacher) to deliver the curriculum as designed. In addition to having the written curriculum, each instructor has the opportunity to attend curriculum training by the local director, who is often a peer educator. Invent Now hosts a website with videos and more information for the instructors to view and return to as often as needed.

The beginning of each module contains an *Overview* for each of the five days; a section on *Setting the Stage*; notes for *Plan Ahead*; clearly identified *Need to Know*; and *Instructor Background*, summarizing the big ideas in the module. Each day is formatted similarly, designed to allow the instructor to create the learning environment. When the daily activities begin, the instructor finds clear instructions, *Guiding Questions*, and *Discussion* information, all designed to allow the instructor to create the conditions needed to engage the children. Professional learning takes place as the days and week unfold. Using the curricula, the instructors are able to engage children in scientific inquiry. Instructors are amazed at the children's interest in working to solve each module's challenge. They observe excited, creative, self-directed innovators at work. Instructors comment on children doing things not previously considered possible by the instructor, based on his/her experience with the children in the school year classroom. Independent evaluations of instructors confirm that their experience of instructing at Camp Invention has influenced their instruction when they return to the classroom setting.

This is the fourth year that Orange Elementary SD has hosted the Camp Invention program. The impact of programming of this caliber is threefold… children have fun learning 21st century life skills through STEM activities, educators receive quality professional development, and the district as a whole is invigorated—from parent accolades to a shared enthusiasm in the classroom. Invent Now is partnering with school districts to usher in a new generation of innovators. (Tim James, Superintendent)

Other professional learning opportunities for educators who seek to elevate the quality of teacher instruction, thereby transforming student learning in the classroom, are also available. Educators engage in professional learning experiences to explore teaching methods that help develop critical thinkers and creative problem solvers excited about STEM. Modeled after the Camp Invention program curricula, professional learning experiences are created to engage educators in hands-on, inquiry-based experiences that cause them to think critically and to creatively problem solve. This professional learning experience builds STEM knowledge and teaching skills, while emphasizing teamwork, innovation, systems thinking, and self-directed learning. Using reflection and planning tools, participants are challenged to incorporate scientific and 21st-century knowledge and skills into their teaching to foster growth in student achievement.

The curricula, combined with the professional learning opportunities, align with changes highlighted in the *Changing Emphases* portions of the Teaching Standards and Professional Standards of the National Science Education Standards:

- Understanding and responding to individual student's interests, strengths, experiences and needs;
- Selecting and adapting curriculum;
- Focusing on student understanding and use of scientific knowledge, ideas, and inquiry processes;
- Guiding students in active and extended scientific inquiries;
- Providing opportunities for scientific discussion;
- Sharing responsibility for learning with students;

- Supporting a classroom community with cooperation, shared responsibility, and respect; inquiry into teaching and learning;
- Learning science through investigation and inquiry;
- Integrating science and teaching knowledge; and
- Mixing of internal and external expertise.

Camp Invention Program Evaluation

Over a decade of independent evaluations of the Camp Invention program support it as a valuable out-of-school-time enrichment program. Invent Now uses these evaluations to inform program design and delivery of the Camp Invention program.

Invent Now contracted to have the Camp Invention program independently evaluated in 2010. The evaluators designed qualitative and quantitative evaluations to review and appraise stakeholder satisfaction with aspects of the 2010 Camp Invention program. The evaluators collected data as part of regular Camp Invention program protocols throughout the months of May to August. On-site visits took place during the months of June and July when evaluators administered pre- and post-assessments designed to measure creativity. The final report provided anecdotal insights gained from qualitative observations, an overview of survey responses, insights into pre- and post-program test results, and a series of recommendations for Invent Now to consider going forward. In summary, it was determined that Invent Now continues to provide a series of exciting, consistently delivered, satisfying, and motivating programs on a national level.

> As a professional evaluator, I was sincerely impressed at the breadth and depth at which the Invent Now organization requested their program to be evaluated. They are sincere in their efforts to evolve and refine their product in an authentic manner, in order to help prepare youth for success in the 21st century. (AnneMarie Scarisbrick-Hauser, PhD, Professional Evaluator)

Creativity

Several methods of assessment made it clear that the creative abilities of participants increased during the Camp Invention program. This finding came as a result of tracking and analyzing parent and child perceptions, instructor and director perceptions, and pre- and postactivities based on master educator E. Paul Torrance's work in the field of creative studies. On days 1 and 4 of the program week, evaluators administered a series of nonexperimental, pre- and post-creative verbal ideation and figural drawing tasks to program participants at selected sites. This was done to gain informal insights into any changes in idea fluency, quality, and originality from the beginning to the end of the program. The verbal ideation test scoring rubric, based on the Wallas and Kogan Creativity Verbal Ideation test tenets, used four components: originality, fluency, flexibility, and elaboration. Evaluators used SPSS statistical analysis t-tests for matched pairs to generate t-scores among participants. They also used standardized means and standard deviations to provide a more accurate representation of group performance based on total task distribution. Overall, verbal ideation test t-scores indicated a significant difference between day 1 and day 4 participant scores and an increase in performance that did not occur as a random event.

21st-Century Learning

Evaluators observed that all program participants were fully immersed (from day 1) in the daylong experiences of brainstorming, interacting with others, creative problem solving, and using materials to create new solutions. They also noted that the curricula provided an excellent balance for participants to work individually and in teams—something many instructors commented on as well.

The evaluators believe that in addition to serving as an anchor for the weekly program, the quality Camp Invention curricula have the potential to influence the learning and instructional activities of the 21st century.

Professional Growth

During the site visits, instructors reported they benefitted as much from the program (in terms of their plans for future teaching activities during the regular school year) as the participants themselves. They also expressed an interest in incorporating some of the Camp Invention program's team building and creative problem solving methods and activities to foster the sharing of ideas with their future students. In conversations with evaluators, instructors indicated that they felt the major benefit of the Camp Invention program was the strong emphasis placed on team building and negotiation, coupled with the sharing of ideas in a fun-filled atmosphere. Many expressed the wish that mainstream schools would adopt these approaches to learning as a means of increasing creative problem solving and inventiveness.

> Camp Invention was a phenomenal experience. Both students and teachers learned a lot and had wonderful, hands-on experiences. I have also reflected on how I will adapt my teaching this upcoming school year. I need to include more group work, hands-on experiences, real-world connections, and MUCH more creative problem solving. Camp Invention was truly a unique summer experience and I feel fortunate to have been a part of it! (Carrie Monteleone, Instructor)

Parents

Parents surveyed indicated the factors they liked best about their child's participation in the Camp Invention program were: the educational experience, exposure to science and innovation, the opportunity to meet friends, and the enhancement of problem-solving skills. Of those surveyed, 94% of parents surveyed rated the Camp Invention program as a "excellent" or "good," and 86% felt that the program helped their child get better at enjoying science and wanting to learn more; 88% of parents felt the Camp Invention program helped their child become a creative and imaginative thinker; 80%–90% of parents indicated that the Camp Invention program helped their child "find different ways to do things," "play new games," "use imagination more," "work with others to solve problems," and "find different ways to combine and put things together."

Conclusion

With the support of foundations and corporations, Invent Now works to provide programs for all children, including traditionally underrepresented groups such as girls, minorities, inner city youth, and families who lack the financial resources to pay the registration fee. Thanks to over 250 foundation and corporate sponsors nationwide, Invent Now was able to offer 9,974 scholarships to underserved children in 2010.

> I have been an educator in Title I Schools for 28 years, and Camp Invention was the most rewarding experience that I have ever had. (Beverly Stewart, Assistant Director)

References

Cropley, A. 2001. *Creativity in education and learning: A guide for teachers and educators.* London: Kogan Page.

Davis, G. A. 2004. *Creativity is forever.* 5th ed. Dubuque, IA: Kendall/Hunt.

Little, P. M. 2009. Supporting student outcomes through expanded research opportunities. Cambridge, MA: Harvard Family Research Project.

National Research Council (NRC). 1996. National science education standards. Washington, DC: National Academies Press.

National Research Council (NRC). 2008. *Research on future skill demands.* Washington, DC: National Academies Press.

National Science Teachers Association. 2003. An NSTA position statement: Science education for middle level students. Arlington, VA: NSTA.

Puccio, G., M. Murdock, and M. Mance. 2006. *Creative leadership: Skills that drive change.* Thousand Oaks, CA: Sage Publications.

Partnership for 21st Century Skills. 2009. *21st-century learning environments.* Tucson, AZ: Partnership for 21st Century Skills.

Partnership for 21st Century Skills. 2010. *Executive summary, American Management Association 2010 critical skills survey.* Tucson, AZ: Partnership for 21st Century Skills.

Scarisbrick-Hauser, A., and B. Hauser. 2009. 2009 *Camp Invention Evaluation Report.* Akron, OH: H.A. Praxis Solutions.

Science Beyond the Laboratory: The Intriguing Career Paths of 14 Scientists and Engineers

Melissa McCartney, Anne Poduska, Richard Weibl, and Rieko Yajima
Science *Magazine*

Setting

The American Association for the Advancement of Science (AAAS) is the world's largest general scientific society and publishes the journal *Science*, which has an estimated total readership of 1 million. Founded in 1848, the nonprofit AAAS is open to all and fulfills its mission to "advance science and serve society" through initiatives in areas such as science policy, international programs, and science education. These vignettes exemplify the AAAS's support of the breadth of careers that use scientific skills—and AAAS's recognition that one's scientific interests can lead to pathways as diverse as research, public policy, communication, and education. Scientists and engineers working at AAAS offices in Washington, D.C., Cambridge, U.K., and Beijing, China, disseminate scientific research to technical and public audiences, build international collaborations, create curriculum and learning materials to improve science education for all, support human rights issues, and assist local and national political leaders to see the utility and value of science when addressing the critical issues facing us all.

Introduction

A planetary scientist working on human rights issues? A bird brain researcher hosting a radio show? In this chapter, we present vignettes of real scientists who found themselves traveling unique career paths that put them in jobs they didn't necessarily expect. Tracing their career aspirations from childhood through their college years and beyond, the vignettes demonstrate how our lives, educational experiences, and training teach us skills that prepare us for a career path that is uniquely suited for each person. These scientists offer advice for students who might wish to follow in their footsteps. Despite the very different life experiences of the featured scientists, they have one uniting characteristic: They all love what they are doing!

Many of these individuals grew up with a stereotypical view of science: Being a scientist means working in a laboratory, doing research at a bench filled with machines and test tubes.

However, most did not know what "doing research" really meant. After leaving high school, all of these scientists attended undergraduate college or university—typically for four years, earning a Bachelor's degree in science, engineering, or arts—where their vision of science broadened. Some learned firsthand that you can "do science" in a lab or outside of the lab, "in the field." Most learned for the first time what it meant to *do* research: A problem is identified, a solution is considered, an experiment is designed to test possible solutions, new tools and techniques are created to test more and different solutions, data collected from these tests are analyzed, and results are published to ensure that solutions are more than an accident of circumstances. Additionally, and perhaps most valuably, these aspiring scientists learned that science often deals with improving our health or developing a product that improves our everyday life or the community and world that we live in.

Some of these future scientists enjoyed doing research so much that they went on to graduate school, taking more classes and doing more research. They earned a Master's of Science (MS, which takes about two years) or a Doctor of Philosophy (PhD, which can take around 5–7 years). A few scientists did even more training and research after graduate school, either in companies or at universities as postdoctoral scholars (or postdocs), which is usually an important experience needed if you want to be a research university professor. Many also had fellowships or internships where they worked to acquire even more new skills. At each stage, these scientists learned of more ways in which they could apply their knowledge and skills in a variety of jobs. The range of experiences presented in these vignettes illustrates the limitless ways and potential educational pathways that one can be a scientist.

The vignettes are intended to be read and discussed by 9th–12th grade students, although we know others will find them useful as well. To facilitate a classroom discussion and personal reflection, we have included questions at the end of the chapter. We have also included a timeline that accompanies one vignette and highlights crucial decision-making points and events along this particular career trajectory. The following vignettes combine science with:

- Art
- Radio
- Education
- Traveling
- Journalism
- International Studies
- Editing
- Government
- Religion
- Video Games
- Test Question Evaluation
- Human Rights
- Law

Vignette 1: Combining Science and Art

Two people gifted in both science and art followed completely different paths to arrive at the same job. Chris always knew he loved science and eventually combined it with his art. Yana grew up as an artist and never considered science until she was in college. Regardless of the route they took, both Chris and Yana now agree that they were born to be medical illustrators from the start—they just didn't realize it!

Chris Bickel
Yana Hammond
Illustrators at Science *Magazine, AAAS*
Written by Melissa McCartney

Chris:
High School: Patrick Henry High School, Hanover, Virginia
Undergraduate (BA degree in medical illustration): 1 year of Illustration at Virginia Commonwealth University, Richmond, Virginia and 3 years at Rochester Institute of Technology, Rochester, New York

Yana:
High School: International High School in Israel
Undergraduate (BA degree in medical illustration): 2 years at Monroe County Community College, Rochester, New York and 2 years at Rochester Institute of Technology, Rochester, New York

A documentary on sharks is what convinced Chris Bickel that science was for him. "That documentary inspired me to be a marine biologist (someone who studies organisms in the ocean)," he says. "I was so into science that I used to wear a lab coat around for fun." Yana Hammond always thought of herself as an artist. "I wanted to be an artist since I was two years old," she says. "I always knew my path—I just didn't know what the details would be." How did two people with such different childhood ambitions end up working at the same job?

Chris has his mom to thank. "I was drawing pictures of human body organs and bones at age 4," Chris says. "My mom was an artist herself so she not only supported my drawings but helped me to learn more about medical illustration (the field of creating pictures, figures, and diagrams from scientific information) as I was growing up." Yana credits an art history professor who showed her works by Leonardo da Vinci. "da Vinci was one of the earliest medical illustrators," she says. "It was the first time I considered combining art with science."

A degree in medical illustration requires many hours of honing artistic skills, and also includes a rigorous schedule of science classes, including anatomy. "We took immunology, cell biology, and embryology with the science students," Yana says. "It was pretty much a global overview of advanced science with a concentration in anatomy." And what a concentration it was! "We took 350 hours of cadaver dissection as part of our anatomy class," Chris says. "That is twice as many hours as the medical students." The anatomy class also included time in hospital operating rooms, studying what the human body looks like in real life. "Once you train as a medical illustrator, nothing gory bothers you anymore," Chris says. Yana laughs and agrees. "When we were in school it seemed that the gorier something seemed, the cooler it was!"

At *Science* Magazine, Chris and Yana work with scientists who have authored scientific papers that will be published in the magazine. These scientific reports almost always have data accompanying them, and it is Chris's and Yana's job to bring an artistic view to this data by turning it into a scientific figure. "I love this combination of art and science," Yana says. "To me, the best part about my job is finding the perfect balance between making the data visually appealing and keeping it accurate." Chris enjoys earning the respect and appreciation of the scientists with whom he works. "It is great to realize that I have helped a scientist make their scientific paper better by turning their data into art."

While working as a medical illustrator requires a traditional art background in painting and drawing, it also requires the ability to translate this background to digital media. "As an artist, I was trained in traditional painting and drawing," Yana says. "This is still critical, even in the age of computers. An artist has the ability to see things in terms of light and shadows, and computers are not able to do that for you." Chris agrees, adding, "Computer art is still art; the computer is just another tool artists can use."

The science Chris and Yana learned in their scientific training is just as important as their training in art. "When we talk to scientists, we need to understand their research in order to turn their data into art," Yana says. "In this regard, I appreciate my classes in molecular biology." Chris is equally grateful. "In our particular jobs we interact with prominent scientists," he says. "Having a background in science helps us to communicate with them first as scientists, and we can then translate their science to art."

To aspiring medical illustrators, Chris and Yana have similar advice: Be as versatile as possible, with both your science and your art. "To be a successful medical illustrator you should not be too science-based or too art-based," Chris says. "It is important to have a sense of both and to know when to use either." Yana agrees. "I was talented in art as a kid so I geared away from science completely," she says. "I would recommend being more open-minded. Try new things and broaden your experiences as much as you can." A final piece of advice from Chris: "Concentrate on drawing still life or figure drawings because no medical illustrator program will accept you if you can only draw stick figures!"

♦ ♦ ♦

Vignette 2: Combining Science and Radio

For Kirsten "Kiki" Sanford, some unexpected personal circumstances helped her transform her passion for science into a talent for teaching others through popular media. With the help of mentors who taught her how to effectively communicate with audiences less familiar with technical scientific information, Kiki transitioned over to science journalism and now uses her science background to connect with others through her radio program This Week in Science and her online video show Dr. Kiki's Science Hour.

Kirsten "Kiki" Sanford
Host and producer for Dr. Kiki's Science Hour and This Week in Science
Written by Rahman A. Culver

High School: Linden High School, Linden, California
Undergraduate (BS in wildlife, fisheries and conservation biology): University of California, Davis, California
Postgraduate (PhD in molecular, cellular and integrative physiology): University of California, Davis, California

"When I was young, I aspired to be an Olympic gymnast like Mary Lou Retton. But, unfortunately, that's not really something you can have as a job," Kiki says. She also dreamed of a career in wildlife biology and saving the whales. Elementary and high school consisted of a science fair project here and there and a range of scientific subjects, including biology, physics, and chemistry.

As an undergraduate, Kiki had her first laboratory experience. She found a job working in a medical research lab taking care of sheep, and later enrolled in a summer program where she learned about research scientists who work outside of the laboratory, known as field research. The summer program encouraged her interest in birds and inspired her to pursue a job working as a student research assistant in a bird memory lab. It was in this lab that she learned many skills in cell culture, experimental design, and behavioral assessment.

Halfway through her graduate school studies, her advisor took a new job in England. Kiki found herself without a lab and no clear way to complete her research. She decided to take a leave of absence from graduate school to figure out what to do next. It was this break that really changed her career path. While in graduate school, she was doing an online radio program called *This Week in Science* (TWIS). When she left her studies, she also took a leave from the radio show. It was during this time that she realized she missed the radio show more than a collection of bird brains. This insight prompted her to return to graduate school with a new goal of using her scientific training for a future career in science media. In leaving everything behind during her time away, she was able to gain perspective and find her passion.

Kiki first started to explore a career in science communication by reaching out to science writers around the country to learn from their experience. "Their advice was invaluable to me in my decision-making process, even though most of them told me that you don't need a PhD to be a science writer," says Kiki. She explains that she was lucky to have very flexible and understanding graduate advisors. "Knowing my goals, they supported my focus on communication in addition to the research," says Kiki. "Not all advisors will back students who aren't dedicated to a career in academia."

While in graduate school, Kiki applied for and was selected to be a AAAS Mass Media Science and Engineering Fellow. Her fellowship mentor remains instrumental in teaching her how to think and write for a television news audience. She recommends the fellowship to anyone who wants to get into TV: "You learn by doing."

"My job is something that didn't exist when I started graduate school. The internet was really rather new, and online media was just getting started," explains Kiki. In the early 2000s, she and her colleagues made a website for the show (*www.twis.org*) and began posting MP3 files for listeners. That led to podcasting, which then introduced her to a whole community of people excited about this new media world. She started working in video after meeting a video podcaster.

Kiki definitely relies on the basic scientific information she learned in graduate school. And yet, because she has been covering many different subjects for the past few years, she has gained a lot of knowledge about areas she never studied in school, such as astrophysics, robotics and paleontology. Her favorite part of what she does is traveling to all sorts of places to talk to scientists, engineers, and inventors.

"To work in science media, there isn't any one scientific background that is required or that is useful," says Kiki. However, being an expert in something is helpful; it gives you credibility with other scientists and with the audience, and it gives you an insider's understanding of how science works, she adds. "Additionally, it is imperative that you are passionate about whatever you choose to do. Whether physics, biology, brains or a combination of everything, the audience will know if you are genuinely interested in it."

Kiki recommends exercising an insatiable curiosity about everything and a true enjoyment of communicating what you learn to others. Also, it doesn't hurt to learn how to write. "If you want to do things in the online space, start doing it: blog, video blog, podcast, whatever. Or, volunteer or get an internship with someone who is doing what you want to do," she says.

Finally, Kiki found combining her passion for other interests with her scientific pursuits extremely successful. "I have been known to hula hoop with fire!" says Kiki. Many scientists dabble in dancing, playing the guitar, or painting to get their creative juices flowing. Science does not exist in a bubble and is a creative process just like art and music. Her advice to others looking to combine science with other career interests is simple: "Yes, do it!"

Vignette 3: Combining Science and Education

Throughout her career, Melissa McCartney has never been afraid to head in a new direction. Because she asked people for help, tried new things, and constantly thought about what she enjoys doing, Melissa was able to successfully transition from her career in neuroscience to her current position as an Editorial Fellow at *Science* magazine.

Melissa McCartney
Editorial Fellow at Science *Magazine, AAAS*
Written by Anne Poduska

High School: Kenmore East Senior High School, Buffalo, New York
Undergraduate (BS in biochemistry): State University of New York at Binghamton, Binghamton, New York
Postgraduate (PhD in neuroscience): The George Washington University, Washington, D.C.
Postdoctoral research (in neuroscience): Children's Hospital of Philadelphia, Philadelphia, Pennsylvania

As a swimmer, Melissa always wanted to grow up and become a swim coach. However, her high grades in math and science caught the attention of her teachers. "I didn't really have the greatest guidance in high school. I was told that if you were smart and got good grades you should go into science," says Melissa. "And not just any science—it had to be biology so that you could then become a doctor or a dentist. Looking back, I wish I would've had different advice, but at the time all I knew was that I liked science!" Although Melissa was most interested in chemistry, she tried to follow the advice given to her and eventually went for the best of both worlds: biochemistry, a scientific area that looks at how the chemistry of molecules can affect biological organisms.

While in college, Melissa worked with one of her chemistry professors on an independent research project. "I still remembered that I was supposed to be a doctor or a dentist, but I really loved my chemistry research. I remember one day my professor said to me, 'I don't know why the brightest minds always go to medical school when they are equally suited to becoming scientists.' It was then that it finally clicked in my head—I didn't have to be a doctor!" Melissa also spent a summer doing research at a cancer research institute where she decided to use her biochemistry background as a stepping-stone to becoming a research oncologist, someone who does research to cure cancer.

To become a research oncologist, Melissa needed to earn a PhD. Along the way, she took a course in neuroscience—the study of the nervous system, including the brain, spinal cord, and neurons throughout the body. "I found neuroscience absolutely fascinating. It was the first time that I thought of our brains as a mystery to be solved, rather than a bunch of diagrams in a textbook," says Melissa. She enjoyed neuroscience so much that she switched the concentration of her PhD to neuroscience, and continued doing neuroscience research at a hospital in Philadelphia.

Melissa was not completely satisfied being in a lab, doing the same brain research every day. She knew that she wanted to do something different—but she didn't know what. "Almost on a whim I decided to apply for a fellowship doing science policy work at the National Academies of Science," says Melissa. "It was a short fellowship and seemed like a good way to try something completely different from both neuroscience and the lab without making a huge time commitment. During this fellowship, I realized that there are so many different ways to be a scientist. I learned the importance of scientists in policy making when I went to a hearing at the U.S. House of Representatives and scientists were giving advice about how electronics, such as computers and cell phones, could be disposed of without hurting the environment. The politicians knew they had to regulate this somehow and they were relying on the scientists to give them the best advice."

Melissa enjoyed this three-month fellowship but did not have a clear picture of where to go next. Fortunately, her fellowship director told her that *Science* Magazine needed a summer intern to get some educational projects up and running. Melissa applied and has been working as an Editorial Fellow at *Science* Magazine ever since. She currently runs the research and development behind several educational projects implemented through the magazine. For example, she helped to design the *Science* Prize for Online Research in Education (SPORE), recognizing the best science education websites. "My science background is invaluable in this position," says Melissa. "I can understand the science on the websites and find appropriate scientists to help judge the competition. My analytical and organizational skills that I used in research have helped me design and carry out the logistics of this project."

In this job, Melissa loves the variety and the new challenges that arise every day. "Every morning when I check my e-mail, someone has sent a new idea for a possible education project, there are questions I need to answer regarding our current projects, or someone has sent an invitation to collaborate," says Melissa. "I feel more like a scientist than I ever did in the lab because I get to think about all kinds of science, whether it's the science of planets, oceans, or viruses."

In order to make this transition from science research to science education, Melissa found that a valuable perspective to have is that science is always part of a broader picture. "One of my biggest mistakes after high school was that I only took science classes: I didn't take economics, history, or a foreign language. I wish that I would have tried a variety of classes instead of just being focused on science because, in the end, it was very limiting. I think that having more variety in my undergraduate experience would have helped me to see more opportunities for my science interests earlier on," says Melissa.

If you are ever thinking of trying something new in your life, whether it's becoming a scientist or a chef, keep in mind Melissa's advice: "In reality, most people don't know what is coming next. If you feel that way too, that's normal—and you're in good company. Just make sure that you are doing something that you like and the rest will fall into place!"

Vignette 4: Combining Science and Traveling

Rieko's curiosity and dedication helped shape her career to collaborate with scientists around the world, first starting with her undergraduate and PhD research in chemistry and biology, and continuing in her current position as Project Director for the Research Competitiveness Program at the AAAS.

Rieko Yajima
Project Director in the Research Competitiveness Program, AAAS
Written by Anne Poduska

High School: Saltfleet High School, Stoney Creek, Ontario, Canada
Undergraduate (Honours BS in biochemistry with a biotechnology option): University of Waterloo, Waterloo, Ontario, Canada
Postgraduate (PhD in integrative biosciences with a chemical biology option): The Pennsylvania State University, University Park, Pennsylvania

Rieko first became interested in science when she went with her mother to the makeup counter at a department store. She saw a display of sunscreen products and there were pamphlets at the counter to explain what skin cancer was and how sunscreen is important. "I was fascinated by these new products and I knew that science had to be involved somewhere to understand skin cancer," says Rieko. "It seemed like skin cancer would be a problem that wouldn't go away for a while, so I wanted to be a skin cancer researcher."

However, science classes were a struggle for Rieko at first. "I failed my first science test—it was in photosynthesis—in fifth grade because I was bad at memorizing and couldn't remember the definitions," says Rieko. With time, Rieko was able to excel at science because she took extra time to read the science textbooks and put the concepts into her own words.

Rieko started on the pathway to becoming a skin cancer researcher by earning an undergraduate biochemistry degree. "In high school I enjoyed biology and chemistry and since both subjects seemed appropriate for understanding cancer, I chose to study them both," says Rieko. "During my sophomore year I learned what biochemistry was about—and luckily it turned out to be a good decision because this scientific subject was the closest match to my interests."

Rieko also discovered that she could be a biochemist anywhere in the world. She spent one semester in Cuba interacting with other biochemists and learning Spanish. She also did research on plant proteins at a beer brewery in Japan. "This was the first experience where I learned what it was like to do research," says Rieko. "I saw that there are trial-and-error processes in science, and I learned how to design experiments carefully and to make sure you can get the same results many times. I also had really good mentors that taught me a lot about science that was not covered in textbooks."

From these international experiences, Rieko learned she was interested in helping scientists do research in developing countries, even when they might not have the money or laboratory supplies they need. She also learned that she needed more scientific training in order to be a better scientist. Moreover, she found a new area of science that she liked better than her dream of being a skin cancer researcher: she liked to study the shape of molecules and understand what the molecules do in biological systems. "I chose an interdisciplinary research program for my PhD because I wanted to know about a lot of scientific issues but still do biochemistry," says Rieko. She did her PhD in the United States, studying the hepatitis delta virus, which can cause liver damage in humans. "Up until that time, little was known about what this molecule looked like," says Rieko. "Our laboratory had good ideas to address this challenge and I received a research fellowship to examine the virus structure: the research would provide important clues as to how the virus is able to survive," says Rieko.

During her PhD studies, Rieko saw science in a new light. Once a month, scientists would visit her school, eat dinner with students, and talk about how their research can affect science policy (for example, how the government makes rules to protect the environment). Rieko became interested in science policy and was a Christine Mirzayan Science and Technology Policy Fellow at the National Academy of Sciences, where she worked with the Committee on Science, Engineering, and Public Policy and the Board on African Science Academy Development. One of her projects involved helping scientists in Africa provide advice to their governments about human health issues, such as clean water and vaccinations.

After this fellowship, Rieko realized that she would like a job in science policy but still wanted to maintain her interest in research. In her current position as Project Director for the AAAS Research Competitiveness Program, she works with universities to advance science and help states improve their economies by using science and technology. "I work with the scientific community to provide advice on how scientific research can be improved," says Rieko. "We do this with peer review, where scientists analyze the work of other scientists and then explain whether it is good and where it can be improved. Peer review can be used in all sciences and anywhere in the world."

Rieko found that it was initially difficult to look for the right science policy job. "I had to stretch beyond my biochemistry background and show how my science skills could relate to science policy," says Rieko. However, by thinking about what she is good at and how others might appreciate her skills, Rieko was able to make a successful transition from science research to science policy.

Rieko recommends the following to anyone who might be interested in science but finds some aspects challenging: "Keep in mind that science isn't about memorizing vocabulary," says Rieko. "It's really about whether you're asking the question 'Why?' and if you're curious in general—that's the start of being a scientist. Don't be afraid if you struggle with science and find it tough. Just keep in mind that you never stop learning and asking questions when you are a scientist—it's a life-long learning process."

Vignette 5: Combining Science and Journalism

While navigating several career paths, Robert Frederick has always done what he was interested in. Because he was never afraid to try new things and kept in close contact with his roots as a mathematician, Robert was able to successfully transition through careers in business, publishing, and education before landing his current position as the weekly podcast host at *Science* magazine.

Robert Frederick
Podcast Host at Science *Magazine, AAAS*
Written by Melissa McCartney

High School (graduated with an IB diploma): Booker T. Washington, Tulsa, Oklahoma
Undergraduate (BA in math, statistics, and philosophy): University of Chicago, Chicago, Illinois
Graduate (MS in applied and interdisciplinary math): University of Michigan, Ann Arbor, Michigan

Robert Frederick may have been the only person disappointed when plans were announced for the International Space Station. "I really liked rockets when I was a kid," he says. "I thought people should have somewhere to go once they get to space. I was disappointed that the International Space Station was planned before I finished college because I was hoping to be the one to design it." Despite this very minor setback, Robert still made the most of his undergraduate years by receiving degrees in math, statistics, and philosophy in four years. "Thanks to the International Baccalaureate (IB) program, I was well prepared and could test out of introductory chemistry, math, physics, and a language," says Robert. "It freed up a lot of time and allowed me to try out a lot of things."

With three degrees in hand, Robert took his first job as a management consultant in an unfamiliar setting: business. "I programmed computers, but really it was an opportunity for me to check out the whole business world at once," says Robert. "What I learned was that business-world consulting was not for me—I wasn't connected enough with what was being done or made." His next job, as a mathematics textbook editor at a publishing company, brought him closer to his roots. "I was hoping to change the world one textbook at a time," he says. While working as an editor made Robert happy, he wasn't completely satisfied—"It was still too removed," says Robert, so he became a high school math teacher, which he describes as "a chance to redirect my math skills and focus on changing the world 20 students at a time instead."

Spending his days surrounded by math brought back some old memories. About eight years earlier, he was lucky enough to witness a space shuttle launch in person. "As I stood there watching the shuttle head into space, I thought about everything that had gone into this moment, all the math and engineering, and tears came to my eyes," says Robert. "Seeing my students excited about math made me think about this moment and I decided it was time to go back to graduate school."

Robert was able to leverage his teaching experience to earn a teaching fellowship that paid the tuition for his master's degree. "I was happy to be back learning math full time again, but applied math was really different from pure math," he says. (Applied math is used to solve more applied, real-world problems, whereas pure math is used to advance the field of mathematics.) "It took so much time and there were so many things that could go wrong. It was so different from my undergraduate experience." It was during his first-ever "all-nighter" working on a problem set that he saw an announcement for the AAAS Mass Media Science and Engineering Fellowship in the *Journal of the American Mathematical Society*. "I applied and before I knew it, I was working at KUNC Colorado, an NPR affiliate, telling stories about science on the radio," says Robert. "I was hooked!"

Robert found that the best part of the fellowship was "getting to study the art of storytelling like it was a type of math or science," says Robert. "I learned storytelling from my mentors at KUNC." When the fellowship ended, Robert finished his master's degree and became a science journalist. Eventually, he ended up at the NPR affiliate in St. Louis, where he helped start their science reporting and served as their first science journalist. This was the experience he needed to make his next move to podcast host at *Science*. "The favorite part of my job," says Robert, "is being able to talk to scientists about what they are truly excited about when they're the most excited about it—when they are announcing new findings to the world."

Looking back, Robert credits his love for science to his high school chemistry teacher. "He was the first person who showed me that science was not cut and dry. Sometimes things didn't turn out as expected." He also credits his ability to easily move among several professions to one of his history professors in college. "He once told me, 'Mr. Frederick, you are so well-rounded that you will roll in any direction I push you. Try something. If you don't like it, try something else,'" says Robert. "That was the best career advice I ever received, because in looking back, all of my past jobs had an aspect that I really liked, and I made sure all of my future jobs were able to include those aspects."

Science and math remain a part of everyday life for Robert. "Part of my job is to explain to my listeners how science gets done," says Robert. "To do this, I need to constantly rely on my knowledge of the scientific process. Every time I read a new study and prepare to interview another scientist, I know how to pull out the parts of their story that are part of every scientific story, and this makes it easier for me to ask the right questions."

Robert offers the same advice he was given by his history professor to any students who are considering a career in science, but adds: "Don't confuse what you are good at with what you like," says Robert. "Be careful, because this may not be what your parents or teachers want you to do based on your abilities at the time. If you like what you are doing, you are much more likely to become good at it."

◆ ◆ ◆

Vignette 6: Combining Science and International Studies

Throughout his career, Tom Wang wanted to balance his interests in history, political science, and the social sciences with his engineering and technology interests. He found this equilibrium by taking political science and business courses while he did engineering science research, which prepared him for his current position as the Director for International Cooperation and the Deputy Director of the Center for Science Diplomacy at the AAAS.

Tom Wang
Director for International Cooperation and the Deputy Director of the Center for Science Diplomacy, AAAS
Written by Anne Poduska

High School: Santa Monica High School, Santa Monica, California
Undergraduate (BS in chemical engineering, BA in political science): University of California, Berkeley, Berkeley, California
Postgraduate (MS in chemical engineering practice and PhD in chemical engineering): Massachusetts Institute of Technology, Cambridge, Massachussetts

As a child, Tom Wang enjoyed playing computer games and making different colored fires with his chemistry set, so he dreamed of being either a computer programmer or a chemist. However, his middle and high school history and political science classes were also interesting because his teachers transformed the textbook ideas into real-life stories. So, when Tom went to college, he studied both political science and chemical engineering. "I chose chemical engineering even though I had no idea what it was," said Tom. "I liked chemistry, I knew I wanted to build things—and since engineers build things, I thought I should be a chemical engineer!" Tom chose political science because "in history, you learn about the past," according to Tom. "In political science, you look at how the past and present can help you achieve goals."

While he was an undergraduate student, Tom decided to continue his studies in graduate school for several reasons. First, he liked to use his imagination to figure out something that no one else has done before, and he could do that with a graduate degree. Second, he had worked with university researchers and graduate students in laboratories during the school year and interned at engineering companies, and he learned that he enjoyed doing science research in a lab. However, Tom had to decide if he should study chemical engineering or political science; eventually, he decided to continue with science because it seemed like it offered more practical career options.

During graduate school, Tom studied the chemistry and physics of nano-thin films. These thin films can be more than 100 times thinner than the aluminum foil found in kitchens and can be put onto surfaces to change the properties. For example, the nano-thin films can be put on the surface of contact lens to make the lens feel wet in your eye while keeping your eyes healthy by allowing oxygen to reach the part of your eye under the contact lens. While Tom did his thin film research, he also pursued his interest in the social sciences by taking classes in political science, business, and management. Although Tom did continue doing science after his PhD at a company—this time doing drug delivery–related research—and gained experience in the business world, it wasn't until receiving a AAAS Science and Technology Policy Fellowship that he had a career combining his interest in science and political science.

Tom worked for the State Department in the East Asia Bureau for two years on a wide array of international issues. These projects had a scientific component and affected the United States, including disaster management after the 2004 Asian tsunami, agricultural trade issues, and health cooperation. "I found that my science background helped me in several ways," says Tom. "Having a science PhD degree helped me gain credibility when I was negotiating with people from other countries because they often value higher education and science. Getting a PhD is not just about becoming an expert in a very specific area like nano-thin films, but it is also learning how to approach complex questions and problems and finding ways to answer them. This skill can be applied in the policy world as well and I used it to understand the many international issues that I had to address."

After finishing his fellowship, Tom became the Director for International Cooperation and the Deputy Director of the Center for Science Diplomacy at the AAAS. He helps build relationships between the AAAS and organizations abroad, and he is also involved with a field called "science diplomacy," which uses scientific collaborations to promote better relationships among countries. "I enjoy this job because I can work with international organizations on problems that will benefit everyone," says Tom. "I also get to build something new—I get to help define and educate people about what is science diplomacy."

Tom did find that there were obstacles during his career change. "I found that the policy world and the science world were very different," says Tom. "In the policy world, you have to be very good at dealing with many people from many different areas and who might not speak your language. In the science world, you are in a small community and you work on narrowly focused problems." Although it was difficult at times, Tom found that he was able to make this transition because he was so interested in science and policy and had explored these new environments while in college and graduate school so that he could adapt quickly.

When preparing for a career, Tom recommends the following: "These days, you are expected to juggle many things and are pushed to be the best at everything. That's impossible and unproductive. Try your best at everything but pick a couple of things that you like and really master them. Keep in mind, though, that it takes time to develop mastery in any one thing—and it might not be possible to do both things at the same time—so you also need to have patience and perseverance."

Vignette 7: Combining Science and Editing

Nick Wigginton has always felt connected to the environment. Throughout his career, he found many ways to explore this connection by studying geology, biology, and environmental science. Nick's diverse scientific background made him the ideal candidate for his current position as an Associate Editor of Geoscience at *Science* magazine.

Nick Wigginton
Associate Editor of Geoscience at Science *Magazine, AAAS*
Written by Melissa McCartney

High School: Holt Senior High School, Holt, Michigan
Undergraduate (BS in geology): Michigan State University, East Lansing, Michigan
Graduate (PhD in biogeochemistry): Virginia Polytechnic Institute and State University, Blacksburg, Virginia
Postdoctoral Research (in environmental microbiology): Ecole Polytechnique Federale de Lausanne, Switzerland

As a child in the early 1980s, Nick knew exactly who he wanted to be when he grew up. "Indiana Jones!" exclaims Nick. "He was always on an adventure, traveling the world, saving treasures from bad guys, and making sure the artifacts were preserved in museums." Nick had an alternate career plan, just in case. "I did also want to be a veterinarian if the adventure archaeologist plan didn't work out," he says.

In the end, the veterinary career path won out, and Nick entered college ready to take the required biology and chemistry classes. "I quickly realized this choice of a career path wasn't for me," he says. "There was too much pressure and too much emotion involved. I enjoyed the environmental side of biology. Hiking and fishing had always been a part of my childhood, but there wasn't enough of it in the biology I was taking." Nick ended up switching majors to geology: "I didn't really know much about it, but I wanted to know more," says Nick. "I also thought it would help me stay close to the environmental science that I enjoyed." This turned out to be a great decision, as he went to Brazil and studied the environmental effects of deforestation, the cutting down of trees, along the Amazon river. It wasn't quite an Indiana Jones–type adventure, but working to preserve the ecological treasures of the Amazon was pretty close!

In graduate school, Nick wanted to add more expertise to his growing background in geology and environmental science, and decided to give biology another chance. "I decided to study environmental microbiology," he says. "This allowed for me to visit the Pacific Northwest National Laboratory. It was a chance to incorporate biology with my geology to study the impact that the waste coming from nuclear plants could have on the environment."

As Nick started thinking of where to go next, he realized that he did not want to be a professor. "I found that writing about my research was more interesting to me than actually doing the research. I started asking around for advice and networking with scientists who were in non-academic careers. I found that pretty much everyone recommended I do a postdoctoral fellowship before I looked for a nonprofessorial job. So, I started looking for postdoctoral fellowships."

Fresh off a move across the Atlantic, Nick began his postdoctoral research in environmental microbiology in Switzerland. Less than a week later, the networking he had done paid off when a phone call came from *Science* Magazine offering him an interview for an open position as a geology editor. "I was scared to tell my postdoctoral advisor since I had literally just started in the lab," he says, "But she was very encouraging and didn't place any pressure on me to stay and finish the postdoc."

Nick credits his success as an editor at *Science* to his extremely broad scientific background. "I can basically cover three areas: environmental science, geology, and parts of biology," says Nick. "Because my research projects throughout my schooling were so different, it made it easy for me to transition into this position where you are constantly reading scientific studies that are outside of your immediate area of expertise." Nick says his training in several labs under several different professors was also valuable. "When journals are looking to hire new editors, they are really looking to hire good scientists. They will train you as an editor when you get here, but being exposed to a variety of science and publishing your own work in several areas makes you a very appealing candidate for the job."

Even for Nick, who knew he did not want to be a professor, making this career change was daunting. "It felt like I had decided to walk away from science as soon as I was getting good at it," says Nick. However, he soon realized that being good at science helped him do his job well. "At my job, I am constantly learning about a huge range of topics," says Nick. "Every day a paper shows up on my desk and by the time I am done reading it I have learned several new things. It may not be my own research, but it is still cutting-edge research and I am still getting to be a part of it. Plus, some days I am able to accept an author's paper [to be published], and it is such a great feeling knowing that you made their day."

For young scientists looking to follow in his footsteps, Nick does have some advice. "Take as many different classes as you can, because you may take a class you knew nothing about and it could end up becoming your passion," says Nick. "If your passion does lead you to science, make sure you take every chance you get to actually work in a lab because that is the only place to learn how science is really done."

Vignette 8: Combining Science and Government

Jeff's interest in finding the "practical side" of science drew him to do research on computer models of dog hearts, which combined his biology, math, and physics knowledge. It was this same desire to apply scientific knowledge to everyday life that prompted Jeff to work in science policy at the U.S. Department of State, where he currently supports science education activities between African countries and the United States.

Jeff Fox
AAAS Science and Technology Policy Fellow
State Department's Bureau of African Affairs, Office of Public Diplomacy and
Public Affairs
Written by Anne Poduska

High School: Theodore Roosevelt High School, Kent, Ohio
Undergraduate (BS in physics with a minor in cognitive science): The Ohio State University, Columbus, Ohio
Postgraduate (MS and PhD in physics with a minor in physiology): Cornell University, Ithaca, New York

When he was young, Jeff Fox was always interested in science. "I was curious how things worked and I liked space ships, so I wanted to become an aerospace engineer," says Jeff. In high school, Jeff enjoyed his physics courses, especially the math. His teacher showed him how the physics ideas in his textbook can be found in everyday life. "In high school, I thought that if you were good at science and math, you became an engineer," says Jeff. "However, I didn't know what it meant to be an engineer—but I also didn't know what a physicist did!" After taking both physics and engineering classes in college, Jeff realized that he preferred physics because it focused more on understanding how things worked, whereas engineering was more concerned with making ideas work in real life.

During graduate school, Jeff found a new scientific area to combine with his math and physics interests: biology. "I found that you could take physics knowledge and apply it to problems that could potentially have a really big impact on people's lives," says Jeff. He worked with his physics professor and a veterinarian professor to find out what causes dog hearts to beat irregularly, a condition that can cause a heart attack.

Jeff continued to work on this problem after he completed his PhD, working for a company on cancer and heart-related problems. It was during this time that Jeff became interested in other, more immediate ways to help society. One way he did this was as a math tutor for low-income elementary school students. While tutoring, Jeff was puzzled because he observed that some schools and students did not receive sufficient support, even though education is important for getting a good job and being a productive citizen. Jeff shifted his interest to learning more about how government makes rules and decisions, especially about science and education, and hopefully, to help it make better ones.

This interest lead him into an area called "science policy," where he could use his scientific knowledge to help the government make laws, such as ones to protect the environment or improve science education in schools. Jeff sought and earned a one-year Congressional fellowship through the American Institute of Physics and the Acoustical Society of America, which allowed him to work with a U.S. Senator on science education issues. "During this fellowship, I spent a lot of time talking to people from New Mexico to learn what was important to them, especially in the area of science education," recalls Jeff. "I found that having a science background made it easier for me to talk about science-related issues to both scientists and to people who didn't know much about science. I also found that a scientific approach to solving problems was useful and needed in science policy work."

Jeff liked his work in Washington, D.C. and was interested in working in the executive branch on international issues, so he pursued his current position as an AAAS Science and Technology Policy Fellow in the State Department's Bureau of African Affairs, Office of Public Diplomacy and Public Affairs. Jeff currently works on a number of projects, which include supporting science education collaborations between the United States and African countries, such as South Africa, Ghana, and Ethiopia. This effort promotes "science diplomacy," which uses scientific collaborations to build better relationships among countries. He also works on other nonscience projects. For example, the top priority for his office is to engage young African leaders and to support their efforts to improve their country's future.

Although Jeff enjoys his policy work, he found that the career change process was scary. "It was a big risk, a big change," says Jeff. "But I had time to think about my move from physics research to science policy, and I approached the problem in an analytical way, which made me feel less uncertain. I wrote down the list of things I might do, I investigated all of them, and at the end, I felt the most comfortable with science policy."

Jeff believes that his transition could have been easier if he had focused more on his writing and speaking skills during school. "I recommend that students take seriously those classes that involve writing and communication," says Jeff. "I wish I were better at them. In a lot of science communities, people think that communication skills are less important than scientific skills. However, if you can't communicate, you have no chance—people won't understand your ideas and you'll limit yourself tremendously."

Vignette 9: Combining Science and Religion

One question has shaped Peyton West's career: "What would I do if I could do anything?" With some courage and hard work, Peyton discovered multiple answers to her question. Starting with an English degree and work in the publishing industry, she went on to research lion manes in Tanzania and earned a PhD in ecology. Peyton now works as Project Director for the AAAS Dialogue on Science, Ethics, and Religion where she encourages dialogue and understanding between the scientific and religious communities.

Peyton West
Project Director, Dialogue on Science, Ethics, and Religion, AAAS
Written by Anne Poduska

High School: The Brearley School, New York City, New York
Undergraduate (BA in English): Yale University, New Haven, Connecticut
Postgraduate (PhD in ecology): University of Minnesota, Minneapolis, Minnesota

When she was younger, Peyton had many career interests: She considered being a writer, astronaut, architect, and zoologist. During high school, Peyton put aside her scientific interests because she hated science. "Science was my worst subject," says Peyton. "It was too structured and I felt like it wasn't creative. It seemed like you did things to arrive at conclusions that everyone already knew. There was no real surprise at the end and it didn't feel like you learned anything."

In college, Peyton continued to avoid science because she didn't enjoy the way classes were taught, so she studied English instead. However, after finishing college and working in publishing, Peyton started to feel restless. "I worked in a few different fields, such as publishing, but wasn't passionate about any of them," says Peyton. "I went back to square one and thought, 'What would I do if I could do anything?' I knew I loved animals and figured that was a place to start."

Already thinking like the scientist she was destined to become, Peyton decided to test her idea in small steps. "I first volunteered at an animal shelter, socializing stray cats," says Peyton. "Next, I volunteered at a zoo where I helped with the rehabilitation and captive breeding of raptors. All along, I was trying to see if this was what I wanted—and I kept on telling myself that I could turn back at any point." From these experiences, Peyton realized that, if she wanted to have a career working with animals, she needed a science education. "I figured I could give it a try, even though I disliked science," says Peyton. "I took the only science class, physics, that was available at a community college nearby and to my surprise I loved it. My professor was fantastic and the course had a lot of math in it, which I enjoyed. It wasn't specifically relevant to what I wanted to do, but it gave me the confidence to move in a scientific direction."

When Peyton consulted a science professor about her potential career change, she got lucky: He offered her a research job in his microbiology lab, where she helped with basic lab tasks and eventually began a research project. At the same time, she volunteered at another zoo and took more science classes at a nearby state college. "I was required to do an internship for a class, so

I researched what diets could improve muscle growth in young cranes," says Peyton. "This was a fairly anecdotal process and I realized that I was more interested in the rigorous lab research I was doing."

Peyton decided to go to graduate school to study conservation and the preservation of endangered species. "I only had a minimal science background—two years of biology and one year of chemistry—but I applied anyway," says Peyton. "I wrote a passionate letter to an ecology professor who was doing fascinating work about my interest in working with animals but this actually had an unintended effect—he branded me as a 'bunny hugger' and disregarded my letter. Happily, another professor read it and persuaded him to take a chance on me."

Peyton's first year of graduate school was difficult. "I only got through that first year because I was so excited and I knew what I wanted to do," says Peyton. "I had to take so many classes and read journal articles, which I had never done before. I found it exhausting and stressful." Graduate school became easier with time, and Peyton spent the next six years doing research on lion manes in Tanzania, living in Africa for nine months and then studying in the United States for six months. "Nobody knew why lions have manes or why some are darker than others," says Peyton. "I was very excited to find out the answer to this very basic question."

As she was finishing her PhD, Peyton realized that she didn't want to have a career that spanned two continents, so she worked at a zoo, doing research and managing animal care and breeding. After years of observing animals in the wild, though, she found it challenging to care for animals in a captive environment. Peyton decided to leave the zoo to start a family, and after a few years, she asked herself the question again: "What would I do if I could do anything?" At the time, the debate about teaching evolution in public schools had been reinvigorated by a press to teach "intelligent design" in biology classes. Believing this practice to be inherently unscientific, Peyton decided that she wanted to help people understand evolutionary theory.

Peyton is currently the Project Director for the AAAS Dialogue on Science, Ethics, and Religion; she works to deepen societal understanding about science and values. This includes designing resources to help local school boards better understand math, science, and technology education; creating partnerships with seminaries (schools where public religious leaders are trained) to enhance the presence of science in theological education; and helping scientific and evangelical Christian communities to better appreciate each other's interests and concerns regarding science. In this position, "It helps to have both a science and English background because I can straddle both worlds, look critically at the project, and see how I might develop something that both scientists and nonscientists can use," says Peyton.

For students unsure about their interests in science, Peyton recommends that "Even if you don't enjoy taking science classes, be open to different ways you can use science. It can be found in many places, such as in novels or the Bible, and understanding science will help you understand life in general."

Vignette 10: Combining Science and Video Games

In developing his computer programming career, Shawn found few mentors and did a great deal of learning and experimentation by himself. Because he was passionate about gaming and was willing to dive headfirst into challenges, Shawn got an early start on his career as a computer scientist and video game programmer.

Shawn Lindberg
Vehicle and Physics Video Game Programmer, Volition Inc.
Written by Heather McInnis

Undergraduate (BS in computer science): University of Illinois College of Engineering, Urbana-Champaign, Illinois

Although Shawn doesn't remember what he wanted to be when he grew up, he does have a long history of teaching himself computer skills. In middle school, he taught himself how to program video games on his graphing calculator. In high school, with quite a bit of help from books and the internet, he taught himself how to program in three different computer languages.

Fortunately, Shawn also found ways to explore his interest in computer science, both in the classroom and in extracurricular activities. For example, Sean took an independent study class in high school and wrote a 3-D graphics engine, which helps a computer display images in three dimensions. He also participated in two high school computer programming competitions held by the American Computer Science League.

When Shawn entered college, he took as many computer classes as he could and studied the psychology of vision, which is helpful to understand when you make video games. In one of his courses, he and several classmates made a 3-D Asteroids-like game. It was around this time that Shawn received a AAAS Entry Point! Internship for Students with Disabilities (*http://ehrweb. aaas.org/entrypoint/index.htm*) and worked at the Bowie State University/National Aeronautics Space Administration (NASA) Goddard Space Flight Center Summer Institute in Engineering and Computer Application, where he learned how to design software to help scientists and engineers build satellites.

Shawn's game programming and internship experiences helped him when applying for a job at Volition, Inc., a video game company, shortly after he graduated from college. In addition to his computer science knowledge, Shawn uses a lot of math, especially linear algebra and trigonometry, and physics in his programming. Shawn says,

> In video games, we don't have to exactly follow the laws of physics, but they can often be a good place to start. Sometimes we may need to bend physical laws in order to make a certain part of the game more fun to play, but often what we want is somewhat realistic. For example, I had to add airplane physics to one of our games. For our first physical model, I based it off a simplified version of what actually happens in real life. I added several

elements to the aircraft … [and] the aircraft produced pretty believable flying physics! Of course we made plenty of modifications, but the basic idea started with real physics.

He notes that not all video game companies require programmers with physics training, but if their games feature interactive 3-D environments, chances are they have at least one specialist on the team. Shawn's favorite part of the job is "adding a new feature and seeing it in action," says Shawn. "That's one of the reasons physics programming is cool: It's visible."

Shawn says that he only learned the parts of his job that are specific to video game programming after he started working. "To be a video game programmer, a background in computer science is a huge asset," says Shawn. Today, he notes, there are many more options to learn specifically how to make games: For example, colleges are starting to offer video game courses, and "it is becoming more and more common for video game programmers to have a bachelor's degree in computer science," says Shawn.

If you are interested in combining science with other interests or passions, Shawn advises to find a balance between work and fun. "Life is not all about studying and school," says Shawn. "I think people forget to tell the super-motivated students to find a healthy balance. It catches up to you eventually." He also encourages students to "find someone interested in the same things as you, or if that fails, plow ahead solo!"

◆ ◆ ◆

Vignette 11: Combining Science and Test Question Evaluation

Cari Herrmann Abell has always had a methodical mind. While this initially drew her to math and chemistry, she explored materials science and mechanical engineering as well. Because she has a diverse background that is rooted in analysis, she has successfully moved on to a rewarding career in the development of science-based test questions and data analysis.

Cari Herrmann Abell
Research Associate at Project 2061, AAAS
Written by Melissa McCartney

High School: Madison Central High School, Old Bridge, New Jersey and Owings Mills High School, Owings Mills, Maryland
Undergraduate (BS in chemistry and math): Muhlenberg College, Allentown, Pennsylvania
Graduate (PhD in physical chemistry and materials science): University of North Carolina at Chapel Hill, Chapel Hill, North Carolina
Postdoctoral Research (in chemistry and mechanical engineering): University of Colorado at Boulder, Boulder, Colorado

Growing up, Cari wanted to go into medicine. "I alternated between wanting to be a doctor and wanting to be a veterinarian," says Cari. "I couldn't decide if I wanted to treat animals or people." It followed that math and science were her favorite subjects in high school. "I had an awesome high school chemistry teacher," she says. "He really made it fun for me, and even better, he made it formulaic. Once that happened, organic chemistry became similar to a proof in geometry: you had a product you wanted to make and you had to figure out how to make it. To me, this type of analytical thinking came easily and was something that I enjoyed."

When Cari got to college, she started taking classes needed to become a doctor. "I was still set on being a doctor," she says, "but college biology was so much memorization! It was too free-form for me, there were no set rules and everything seemed to have an exception. I really missed chemistry and thinking analytically, so, I went back to it."

In graduate school, Cari studied both chemistry and materials science. She did research with a type of microscope that lets you take images of atoms on surfaces. However, Cari wasn't happy doing this research because she wanted to do something more applicable to everyday life. She chose to do more research after graduate school, but this time in mechanical engineering. She studied microelectromechanical systems (MEMS), which are very small machines (some are as small as the width of a human hair) that can do many things, such as helping ink jet printers put ink on the paper. "My postdoctoral experience made me realize that even adding the "applied" aspect to my research wasn't enough," says Cari. "I wanted a career that I wasn't going to find in the lab."

While researching possible career alternatives to doing laboratory research, Cari saw a position opening at Project 2061, a long-term initiative of the AAAS that conducts research and develops tools and services that educators, researchers, and policy makers can use to improve the

U.S. education system. Cari's application rose to the top and she became one of a select group of Research Associates developing test questions at Project 2061.

Chemistry is still very present in Cari's daily life. "I am working on a curriculum unit to prepare students for high school biology, which targets fundamental chemistry and biochemistry concepts that students will need to understand to be successful," says Cari. In this way, her background is perfectly suited for her job. "I mostly work with middle school students," she says. "I use my chemistry background from my high school and college years all the time. In a way I have learned a new language, as now I communicate science to a younger audience instead of to experts, but the basic knowledge remains the same."

The most difficult aspect of leaving the laboratory, Cari says, is "definitely having a human audience! In the lab it was just me and the machines and I could work anytime," says Cari. "Now, dealing with teachers and students, I am tied to their classroom and school-year schedule. If I have to run a pilot test, there is a small window of time when it is possible and I have to have everything ready to go."

Cari also has not lost touch with her analytical thinking. "When you are involved in writing test questions, you end up with mountains of data from students all across the country," says Cari. "It is up to me to work through this data, to see which ideas different groups of students are struggling with—and to try to figure out why. My analytical brain enjoys every minute of it!"

To any aspiring science education hopefuls, Cari suggests having a multidisciplinary background. "This is helpful no matter what you want to do, whether or not it is in science education," says Cari. "Narrowing yourself into a specific area only limits you, while a diverse background not only gives you more skills, but it makes you unique and able to stand out. This is easily achievable as long as you keep your options open and take classes that you like and are interested in!"

◆ ◆ ◆

Vignette 12: Combining Science and Human Rights

Jonathan Drake enjoys exploring new places, which initially made him interested in planetary science and astronomy. In his position as Senior Project Coordinator for the Science and Human Rights program, he can explore the world from his desktop, using satellite pictures to help people understand where human rights are not being respected.

Jonathan Drake
Senior Project Coordinator, Science and Human Rights Program, AAAS
Written by Anne Poduska

High School: Carlisle High School, Carlisle, Pennsylvania
Undergraduate (BS in physics with a concentration in astronomy): Dickinson College, Carlisle, Pennsylvania
Graduate (MS in planetary science): Arizona State University, Phoenix, Arizona

In elementary school, Jonathan's father gave him a book with space paintings, which inspired Jonathan to want to become an astronaut. "The book showed powerful pictures of people building space stations in the future," says Jonathan. "I knew I wanted to live in those pictures—and I knew that science and engineering were necessary to make those pictures happen."

It was during his undergraduate studies in astronomy that Jonathan was first able to explore space—but with both feet on the ground. "I spent my senior year doing a research project where I took pictures of asteroids with a telescope to see how fast they were spinning," says Jonathan. Although he enjoyed doing research, Jonathan wasn't sure if he wanted to go to graduate school after college. "I really wanted to finish school first and see what the possibilities were. I knew that I could take time after my degree to think about my career, so I did." After graduating, Jonathan says, he "spent one summer doing planetary research in Hawaii. We were trying to find a way to see through all of the dust in Mars's atmosphere so we could look at its surface and see what rocks the planet is made of."

After returning from Hawaii and inspired by the experience of planetary research, Jonathan took a part-time job teaching elementary students science concepts while he applied to graduate school. He entered a PhD program in a different field—geology—in order to continue studying planetary science. However, after a year in his program, he decided a master's degree would be better for him. "It was a big change, going from physics to geology," says Jonathan. "I was learning a lot, but I wanted to see what I could do with a master's degree before committing myself to a PhD degree."

While Jonathan wrote his master's thesis, he found a part-time job at the AAAS where he got to look at a new planet: Earth. "In my research, I had used remote sensing, which is the use of cameras to look at planets or stars," says Jonathan. "I now use remote sensing to look at Earth and document abuses of human rights—rights that everyone deserves simply by being a person."

Instead of taking pictures of Mars's surface, Jonathan now looks at satellite pictures of the Earth and finds out where human rights are being violated. For example, he identified villages being burned in Sudan, homes being bombed in Sri Lanka, and mass graveyards appearing in Afghanistan that could indicate that many people were murdered at the same time. "There are not many jobs where you can see so many different places on Earth in such detail," says Jonathan. "You know that horrible things are going on, but it is satisfying to know that you are doing your best to stop that. By publishing these pictures and doing a scientific analysis of what we see, we hope to make a difference and help stop the abuse of human rights."

In his work, Jonathan uses a range of scientific knowledge every day: He uses astronomy to understand the Earth's rotation beneath the satellite, geography to know what areas the satellites will be able to photograph, physics to understand how the pictures are being made, and computer science to write computer programs to analyze the data he collects. "I believe that human rights should be respected," says Jonathan. "Science provides powerful tools to be used for both good and bad purposes. I am proud to use them to help advance human rights and make this a better world."

Jonathan recommends combining science with another interest: "Science is great because it touches on so many parts of the world we live in," says Jonathan. "Pursue what interests you, because there will always be some way to connect it to science." He also advises: "Work hard and don't be lazy," says Jonathan. "It's easy to get frustrated, but the knowledge you gain in middle and high school will stay with you for the rest of your life, and the more you learn at that time, the more effective it will be later on, in college and beyond."

♦ ♦ ♦

Vignette 13: Combining Science and Law

Unsure of where to start her career path, Anne Middaugh enrolled in a community college, which typically offers a two-year degree. This turned out to be an excellent decision, as she was able to try different things and eventually discover her passion for psychology.

Anne Middaugh
Forensic Clinical Psychologist
Written by Jen Makrides

High School: Madison High School, San Diego, California
Undergraduate (BS in psychology): Mesa Community College, San Diego, California and University of San Diego, San Diego, California
Graduate (PhD in psychology): George Washington University, Washington, D.C.

Anne is passionate about her career today, but she didn't always know she wanted to be a psychologist. "I wanted to run a surf shop," says Anne about her high school career ambitions. Despite having an average high school career, Anne was always passionate about reading and learning. A few years after graduating from high school, she enrolled at Mesa Community College in San Diego, California, where she discovered her interest in psychology. From there, a scholarship to the University of San Diego led to a PhD in psychology at George Washington University in Washington, D.C.

Since Anne is not one to avoid challenges, she is currently a forensic clinical psychologist who works in the criminal justice system and volunteers her time with asylum seekers and asylum-seeking detainees. "I've been doing this for 20 years and it's still fascinating," says Anne. "In this field, you don't get bored with your day because every case is so different."

Forensic clinical psychology bridges the legal system and mental health issues. Anne provides evaluations of alleged and convicted offenders to determine whether they can stand trial, what risk they could pose to society if released, and whether people with mental illness are criminally responsible for their actions. A typical day could involve testifying in court, meeting with patients, and interviewing police officers. Her job demands strong critical thinking and evaluation skills to ensure both the rights of people with mental illness and the safety of the larger community. In the courtroom, Anne relies on her PhD training and research to arrive at evidence-based conclusions.

In addition to her "day job," Anne volunteers her time and her training as a forensic clinical psychologist to ensure that the human rights of asylum seekers are upheld in the legal system. When Anne interviews asylum seekers, she evaluates them for Post-Traumatic Stress Disorder (PTSD), mental illness, and evidence of past torture. Anne also works with children, many of whom have fled physical or sexual abuse, or have been trafficked into the United States for forced manual labor or to work in the sex industry. Anne's work provides a scientific evaluation of the individual's claim for asylum in the United States.

Although it may seem overwhelming at times, this work is also rewarding. "I meet and learn about people from all over the world: China, India, Africa, Tibet, and South America," says Anne. "I learn about what is going on in those countries and what happens during war and ethnic cleansing." In some cases, Anne has evaluated individuals from opposing sides of a conflict and heard both views on what is happening in a country. Through this work, Anne is reminded that changing the world is a large task, and that "on an individual, personal level you can help one person at a time," says Anne.

To prepare for a job like hers, Anne stresses the need to think critically and broadly. A clinical psychologist works with all kinds of people, and understanding a diverse set of ideas will enable one to connect with a diverse group of people. What about students who want to combine their love of science with other passions, like music or literature? "Do it," says Anne. "Education is not about becoming a worker drone, it's about learning. If you're an artist, musician, dancer, hiker, camper—all of those things make you better at the work you do."

For students who are interested in forensic clinical psychology, a field that usually requires a PhD, Anne recommends starting with an internship or volunteer opportunity in college or graduate school—and also to "have fun," says Anne. "Being perfect is overrated." She urges students to enjoy life, become well-rounded scientists, and make their work "a positive piece of the community and the world," says Anne. "In the end, you want your work to matter to the places and the people you live with."

♦ ♦ ♦

Discussion Questions

Please select one vignette and answer the following questions:

1. Pick one job described in this vignette. What does this job entail? Why did the individual accept this job and what else did it lead to?

2. What type of scientific background is described in this vignette? How does it apply to the job(s) described in this vignette?

3. When did the scientist featured in this vignette become interested in science?

4. What kind of education path is described in this vignette? Was this a straightforward path or were there twists and turns involved? This vignette ends with advice from the featured scientist. How is this advice applicable to you now? Are there ways that you can act on this advice?

5. How has this vignette helped you think about what you want to do with your future career?

6. What did you learn from reading this vignette? Please list at least three things.

7. Please identify the point(s) in this vignette where the featured scientist made a decision to try something new.

8. Please list the points(s) in this vignette where the featured scientist took specific actions that eventually led to that person's next career step or job.

9. Pick an area of science that you like and also something non-scientific (for example, cooking or dancing). Think of three ways that you could combine these in a job. Next, ask your teachers, parents, or friends if they have any ideas—and then do some research, either by the internet or by reading books, to come up with three more career ideas. List these six jobs and write a short description of what each job is.

10. Science can happen outside of your classroom. Examples include science fairs and volunteering at an animal shelter or zoo. Can you think of other places where science occurs outside of the classroom?

11. There are examples in the vignettes that show how science improves both the health and the lifestyle of a community. For example, Nick studied deforestation in order to help preserve the ecology of Brazil. Rieko was interested in the science behind sunscreen, which allows us to remain outdoors even when the sun is intense. Can you think of other examples of how scientific improvements can improve our quality of life?

12. The scientists in the vignettes were able to take their scientific skills and apply them to careers outside of the lab. Based on their experiences, can you describe the general workforce skills that they all exhibit, either as a scientist in a laboratory or in their current career?

13. Figure 3.1 outlines a career timeline for Robert Frederick, which shows his educational background and career changes. Select an individual and make a similar timeline from their vignette.

Figure 3.1. A Timeline of Robert Frederick's Career Path

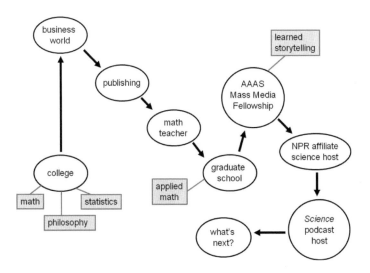

14. Figure 3.2 illustrates when Jeff, Tom, Peyton, and Yana knew that they liked science (indicated by the beaker), changed career paths (indicated by the curved arrow), and had a fellowship opportunity that helped them decide what job they liked (indicated by two asterisks). Pick an adult that you know, perhaps a teacher or a parent, who has studied science or uses science in his or her job. Interview that person and make up a chart illustrating when he or she liked science, changed career paths, and did a life-changing fellowship.

Figure 3.2. A Chart of Career Milestones for Four Featured Scientists

NAME	elementary school	middle school	high school	college	graduate work	post doc	Working life
Jeff	🧪				⌣		** ⌣
Tom	🧪						** ⌣
Yana				🧪 ⌣			
Peyton						🧪 ⌣	⌣

KEY:
🧪   liked science

⌣   changed paths

**   fellowship opportunity

Fellowship and Career Information

Here are some of the fellowships that individuals featured in these vignettes received, which helped with their career decisions:

- AAAS Entry Point! Internship for Students with Disabilities
- AAAS Mass Media Science and Engineering Fellowship
- AAAS Science & Technology Policy Fellowship
- American Institute of Physics and the Acoustical Society of America Congressional Fellowship
- Christine Mirzayan Science and Technology Policy Fellow at the National Academy of Sciences

For additional information about science careers, fellowships, and internships, please consult:

AAAS Careers: *www.aaas.org/careercenter*
Science Careers: *http://sciencecareers.sciencemag.org*

Acknowledgments

We would like to acknowledge the following individuals who helped shape this chapter in a variety of ways: Monica Bradford, Rahman Culver, Edward Derrick, Yolanda George, Pam Hines, Rick Kempinski, Heather Malcomson, Cynthia Robinson, Jo Ellen Roseman, Maria Sosa, Jennifer Wiseman, and Jessica Wyndham.

Educating Students About Careers in Science: Why It Matters

Jonathan Osborne and Stephanie Claussen
Stanford University

Louise Archer, Jennifer DeWitt, Justin Dillon, and Billy Wong
King's College London

Setting

The ASPIRES project is a UK-based research project exploring the formative influences on student engagement with school science from ages 10 to 14. Our work began by measuring the views about science and school science of an initial sample of 9,000 10-year-old students in 2009. We are now tracking how these students' views change until 2014. Our work is driven by the belief that school science is selling itself short. In particular, the one feature of school science that is universally recognized to motivate students—the value of science qualification for future careers—is underemphasized in school science. For instance, the National Science Education Standards (NSES) state that one of the goals of school science is to "increase their [students] economic productivity through the use of the knowledge, understanding, and skills of the scientifically literate person in their careers" (NRC 1996). However, the NSES say nothing about educating students about the enormous range of careers that science qualifications offer both within the field of science and engineering or in other areas, such as management, law, and business. We seek to show why this is invaluable knowledge.

What follows is our analysis of why school science needs to attend more to educating students about opportunities for scientific careers. The arguments of this chapter are twofold: (1) School science education fails to recognize what it is about science education that matters and (2) more importantly, school science gives insufficient emphasis to educating students about the careers that are available both *in* and *from** science. We seek to show that the failure to exploit the value of science for future employment is a missed opportunity to engage students in science. Rather, school science places too much faith in a belief that, for the majority of students, it is just intrinsically interesting. Such a view is unsustainable, in the light of evidence that only a minority of students find school science fascinating (Bøe et al. 2011; Ormerod and Duckworth 1975; Osborne

---

* By this we refer to careers for which science is not a necessary qualification, such as law, banking, and business.

and Collins 2001; Osborne, Simon, and Collins 2003; Sjøberg and Schreiner 2005). Indeed, research would suggest that the standard approach to science education is only successful at engaging somewhere between a fifth and a third of high school students with the further study of science (Jenkins and Nelson 2005; Lyons 2006; Osborne and Collins 2001).

One of the main drivers that motivates students to choose to study science in high school is the value that it has for future careers (Adamuti-Trache and Andres 2008; Lyons and Quinn 2009b; Stokking 2000). Hence, making students aware of the value of school science for their future *is* important. However, the data we have collected for the ASPIRES project show that there is a disconnect between student interest in "doing science" and in "being a scientist" (Archer et al. 2010). While the reasons for this are complex, much of it can be ascribed to the stereotypes associated with scientists that offer little to young people's growing sense of their own identity—particularly to girls and certain ethnic groups. In short, although students may see that science is useful or interesting, they cannot see how the study of science would make them a more valued individual.

There are a number of reasons why this finding should be a matter of concern. First, standard stereotypes of the nature of scientific work and the personalities of those who carry it out are false. Science today is both a creative and intellectually challenging activity done by a diversity of people in a range of different contexts. Moreover, it is very much a social activity dependent on collaboration with others for insight and constructive critical feedback. Second, in contemporary societies, STEM occupations are seen as the foundation of an advanced technological society (European Commission 2004; Hanushek and Woessmann, forthcoming); National Science Board 2010). Student need to know that science qualifications not only enable scientific careers but also are valued in a range of other careers such as law, management, economics, and administration.

School science must take up some of the responsibility, therefore, both to counter the negative stereotypes and to broaden students' knowledge of scientific careers—especially as research suggests that the most useful source of information about careers is subject teachers (72%) followed by adults working in specific jobs and careers (61%) (Engineering and Technology Board 2005; Lyons and Quinn 2009b). Moreover, for the majority of students, interest in pursuing science further, and hence a career in or from science, has largely been formed by the age of 14 (Lindahl 2007; Ormerod and Duckworth 1975; Tai et al. 2006; The Royal Society 2006).

Cultural Capital: What It Is and Why It Matters

One way of identifying the value of teaching about careers in science is to see such knowledge as a form of *cultural capital*—an idea originally developed by the French sociologist Pierre Bourdieu. Bourdieu argues that school subjects have both intrinsic and extrinsic value for students (Bourdieu and Passeron 1977). The intrinsic value of a subject lies in the liberal notion of what it means to be an educated person—essentially somebody who is knowledgeable not just about the cultural achievements of any discipline but also understands how we know and why such knowledge matters (Hirsch 1987). In the case of science, this is much more than a miscellany of facts. Rather, it requires an understanding both of how the processes of scientific discovery and inquiry have transformed our understanding of the material world and the major explanatory theories that have emerged as a consequence, such as evolution, (e.g., the germ theory of disease or the origins of the universe).

In contrast, the extrinsic value of a subject lies in the opportunities it offers its students to careers that are intellectually engaging and well-remunerated. Indeed, research shows that most students recognize the extrinsic value of school science for scientific careers (Adamuti-Trache and Andres 2008; Lyons and Quinn 2009b; Osborne et al. 2003). Our concern here is that science education fails to exploit the career value of science to boost student motivation sufficiently. For instance, aside from the standard scientific careers, any exploration of the broader set of careers that science offers is virtually absent from contemporary textbooks. A search of all the grade 6–8 Prentice Hall textbooks for science found only *one* page that had any explicit treatment of scientific careers. While no curriculum or initiative can transform students' perception of science, the absence of any consideration of what kinds of employment scientific qualifications might enable means that formal science education is simply preaching to the choir, those on the inside, when it could be addressing the congregation.

Bourdieu's concept of cultural capital provides a unique perspective that helps to explain this gap in science education. Bourdieu conceives of cultural capital as the knowledge, skills, and behaviors that are transmitted to an individual from their sociocultural context. Education is important because it is the means by which such capital is acquired (Webb 2002). Those who enter the classroom with cultural capital of the appropriate, dominant type—capital that fits well with the discourse and values of schools—are well-positioned to increase their cultural capital further. In contrast, students who possess cultural capital of a form that is incompatible with the culture of the school, or who lack it altogether, are at a distinct disadvantage. One of the challenges of education, then, is to increase a student's stock of the dominant cultural capital, regardless of the nature of any prior capital they may or may not already have acquired.

Bourdieu proposed three types of capital:

- *Economic capital*, which can be easily converted into money (for example, property rights and wealthy possessions);
- *Social capital*, such as connections with others and formal titles of social position (Bourdieu 1986); and
- *Cultural capital*, which includes, "culturally authorized tastes, consumption patterns, attributes, skills, and awards" (Webb 2002, p. x).

One type of capital can often be converted to another type; for example, possessing cultural capital in the form of a university degree can then be used to increase economic capital through a higher salary. In mature societies, certain forms of cultural capital become entrenched as those who possess such capital defend its value either implicitly or explicitly. Ultimately, its dominance becomes institutionalized in the form of high school diplomas or recognized degrees.

Apple (1979) suggests that cultural capital is such a powerful factor in the classroom partially because schools commonly attempt to treat all students as equal when they are patently not. Rather, many students are handicapped from the beginning. As Jenkins argues:

Those factors which make pupils/students "at home" in an educational institution, which are the product of family education, create or reproduce class inequalities in achievement. Bourdieu argues that the system consecrates privilege by ignoring it, by treating everybody as if they were equal when, in fact, the competitors all begin with different handicaps based on cultural endowment. Privilege becomes translated into "merit" (2002, p. 111).

The problem is that many students come from families who do not have a STEM background and know little of the varied nature of science work. Moreover, in an era of high youth unemployment, obtaining valued qualifications becomes increasingly high stakes. Hence, acquiring institutionalized cultural capital is important for future employment. This is not to say that scientific qualifications necessarily guarantee economic capital. Indeed, there is an ongoing debate about the true nature of the perceived demand for scientists and engineers (Cyranoski 2011; Lowell et al. 2009). Rather, our point is that even though there may be an oversupply in certain STEM professions, science qualifications provide access to an *enhanced range* of employment opportunities. In short, science qualifications make individuals more valued, and hence, more employable.

Acquiring Cultural Capital

Cultural capital can be acquired informally, through *diffuse education*, which occurs through social interactions; through *family education*, which is the greatest source of an individual's embodied cultural capital—so much so that parents' level of education is sometimes employed in research as a convenient indicator of cultural capital (see, for example, Adamuti-Trache 2008); and through *institutionalized education* (Jenkins 2002), which in the case of science is through a formal science education.

For those individuals whose family background does not readily provide access to the dominant forms of cultural capital, school can and should be a vital means of access. As Brown et al. (2009) points out, social mobility without any exposure to the dominant forms of capital would be nearly impossible. Remediating any imbalances, however, requires us to ask, What kinds of cultural capital does a science education offer and which are of most value? In short, how can the science classroom increase its students' stock of this valuable commodity? Commonly scientific knowledge has value both for how it contributes to making an educated and informed citizen (its intrinsic value) and for future employment (its extrinsic value). What does Bourdieu offer that might help to identify the intrinsic value of school science?

Cultural Capital and the Science Curriculum: The Value of Scientific Knowledge

The commonly perceived value of formal education is perhaps articulated most cogently by Hirsch, who has attempted to define the basic elements of what every American should know in order to be "culturally literate" (1987). Hirsch attempted to convey his meaning by creating a list of terms that the culturally literate individual should be familiar with, contending that (a) each of these elements are not simply a definition but a focus for a whole network of interrelated concepts; and (b) rapid change in what aspects or features of culture predominate is "no more possible in the sphere of national culture than in the sphere of national language" (1987, p. 91). As culture evolves only slowly and cannot readily be remade by some act of common will; it is essential for schools to compensate for the "cultural deprivations" of students and ensure that students are provided the basic knowledge and skills of the culturally literate individual.

What, then, does knowledge of science offer as cultural capital? Hirsch argues that the cultural literacy required of today's citizen "includes a larger vocabulary of shared scientific and technical knowledge," especially "when political decisions in our democracy have an increasingly technical element" (1987, p. 108). Thus, being culturally literate about scientific topics enables the individual to at least engage with the policy issues, even if he or she lacks the expertise to make judgments about technical issues. Such a conception lies at the heart of the notion of scientific literacy which is assessed in the PISA tests (OECD 2009).

Hirsch's point, however, is that the nature of the knowledge held by scientifically literate individuals is a network of interrelated concepts. If so, then ensuring that students develop some understanding of a limited set of big ideas and the nature of the achievement required to build this understanding should be a primary goal of science education. However, much science education is implicitly based on a model that fails to place concepts in a context. For instance, does the average textbook make much attempt to explain what question is addressed in each chapter and why such answers might matter? Moreover, any recognition of the achievements of scientific endeavor is virtually nonexistent within formal science education. As a consequence, school science too often fails to show that it is an intellectual creation as creative and impressive as the work of Steinbeck, Twain, and others. Failure to communicate the intrinsic worth of the major ideas of science means that too many students may choose to neglect or reject a body of knowledge that would potentially advantage their future lives. As such this constitutes our first missed opportunity to enhance students' cultural capital.

General Scientific Skills as Cultural Capital

Cultural capital also consists of valued skills and behaviors. In this sense, cultural capital is "more like a style or a set of skills or habits" (Swidler 1986, p. 275). These can be both the traditional academic skills of literacy and numeracy as well as "noncognitive" habits that are not usually assessed, such as completing homework and participating constructively in class. Such skills and habits have been shown to determine school success and levels of educational and occupational attainment (Bowles and Gintis 2002; Duckworth and Seligman 2005). The science classroom offers an arena to develop such culturally valued skills in students—in particular, the commitment to evidence as the basis of belief and an analytical skill that seeks to identify patterns and causal interrelationships (Kirschner 1992). In addition, it provides an environment in which to enhance students' capability to read and produce expository or technical text (Wellington and Osborne 2001), the latter being a highly valued workplace skill.

The irony here is that what the scientist is valued for *outside* of science is the disciplinary habits of mind that science develops—that is, the analytic ability to make logically deductive arguments from simple premises, the ability to identify salient variables and patterns in data, and the ability to critique flawed arguments and numerical fluency (Ford 2008; NRC 2008; Rogers 1948). Yet, *within* science education, such capabilities would appear to be of little value.

For instance, school science tests are dominated by items that test factual recall (Osborne and Ratcliffe 2002), particularly since the advent of No Child Left Behind. This state of affairs exists despite the long and persistent effort that has been made by science educators to argue for the value of teaching science as "a process of enquiry" (Schwab 1962), for developing disciplinary "habits of mind" (AAAS 1993), and to "engage in scientific practices" (NRC 2011). How then can the student develop the skills and habits of mind for which science education is so valued if there is no opportunity to practice? Thus, the reluctance of state, district, and national decision makers to support the development of curricula and assessment systems that value domain-general skills must be seen as a squandered opportunity to endow students with valued cultural capital: the ability to ask good questions, to model unfamiliar situations, to communicate technical ideas, and to argue from premises to a conclusion. Bourdieu would go further and argue that the limited emphasis on developing such skills is deliberate. That is, as far as scientists are concerned, the main purpose of school science is to produce the next generation of scientists. What matters if you are to become a professional scientist or engineer is an extensive knowledge of the domain and the standard algorithms it uses to solve its problems.

A Knowledge of Careers in and From Science

It is the lack of exploration of careers both in science and without science that is the third missed opportunity and which concerns us most. Ever since the beginnings of science in the school curriculum in England in the mid-19th century, the accepted view has been that the role of school science is to supply the next generation of science and engineering professionals required to sustain an advanced technological society. Indeed, the preprofessional importance of school science is such that it is commonly characterized as a "pipeline" supplying the next generation of STEM professionals. Such importance is reflected in the political concern about science education both historically (Dainton 1968; DeBoer 1991), and in the present (Lord Sainsbury of Turville 2007; National Academy of Sciences: Committee on Science Engineering and Public Policy 2005). Much of the focus of all of these reports is the failure of this pipeline to meet the employment needs of society. This argument can be found in the response to the Obama administration's recent investment in its *The Race to the Top* initiative to improve the quality of national education (U.S. Congress 2007). Similar concerns can be found in the European report Europe Needs More Scientists (European Commission 2004). From a policy perspective, the education of the next generation of STEM professionals is a clearly defined and unquestioned goal for science education.

Students, likewise, share such values. In a survey of 15- and 16-year-old students in Australia, Lyons and Quinn (2009b) identified that students held four main conceptions about school science:

1. Science is teacher-centered and content-focused;

2. The curriculum content is personally irrelevant and boring;

3. Science is difficult; and

4. Physical science courses are primarily of strategic value in that they enhance the students' university and career options.

The last of these is strongly suggestive that it is science's extrinsic value (the institutionalized cultural capital) that students value rather than its intrinsic value, which teachers promote. Moreover, this is not an isolated finding, as Stokking (2000) also found that the dominant factor predicting the choice of physics as a subject of study was the perceived relevance for future employment.

The irony is that if the function of school science is to produce the next generation of scientists, why is so little attention paid to exploring the role of careers in science? For example, a search for the word *career* in science curriculum documents for California, New York, Massachusetts, Michigan, and Texas found that the concept was only mentioned in the Texas science standards for high school. Indeed, in comparison, the Texas curriculum could almost be seen as exemplary. The word *career* is mentioned six times. In each case, teachers are asked to explore the relation between the science and future careers.

Our concern is that educational qualifications (institutionalized cultural capital) play a key role (Adamuti-Trache and Andres 2008) in students future life opportunities. However, students from different socioeconomic backgrounds have access to "unequal knowledge about courses and the careers they lead to [and] the cultural models which associate certain occupations with certain educational options" (Bourdieu and Passeron 1979). Knowledge both of the careers in science and the careers from science is then a valuable form of cultural capital. As Adamuti-Trache and Andres (2008) point out, "knowing the current and future worth of various types of academic credentials is key in the transmission of cultural capital from parents to their children."

Some indication of the institutionalized value of science education comes from the fact that many U.S. postsecondary institutions have basic science requirements for admission, a fact that is rarely mentioned in science classrooms yet is relevant to all students, particularly those who lack the cultural capital needed to navigate the college entrance process. Even where such requirements do not exist, as in the United Kingdom, the higher value placed on science qualifications is reflected in the lower grades that are demanded by universities for admission.

As there are considerable motivational problems in engaging students (Lyons and Quinn 2009a; Osborne et al. 2003; Schreiner and Sjøberg 2004) in science, it is ironic then that science curricula do not appeal more to their audience's primary interest—the value of science for future careers—and do more to promote the institutional capital that the study of science offers for careers either *within* science or *from* science (Foskett and Hemsley-Brown 1997; Jacobs and Simpkins 2006; Munro and Elsom 2000; Stagg 2007). Munro and Elsom's research, for instance, showed that students were not aware of *any* explicit links between the science they were taught and its industrial or medical application. In addition, students had no sense that science was developing analytical skills that might be of value in domains other than science.

Munro and Elsom (2000) found, however, that teachers of science do not perceive themselves as a source of career information; rather, this is seen as the responsibility of career advisors or school counselors. Yet very few career advisors have a scientific background, making them potentially even less suited to offering advice about the nature of the working life of a STEM professional (Stagg 2007).

Given that a large body of research shows that, for the majority of students, interest in pursuing a scientific career is largely formed by age 14 (Ormerod and Duckworth 1975; Tai et al. 2006), developing an *early* understanding of the appeal of science careers and the educational requirements required would appear to be essential. As Adumiti-Tranche and Andres (2008) point out:

> The lack of requisite credentials is simultaneously a direct and indirect form of exclusion. Students who do not possess the prerequisites for entry into specific postsecondary programs are simply denied entry…. That is, students eliminate themselves from the full range of educational opportunities or are relegated to less desirable academic programs. (p. 1562)

As a consequence, formal science education needs to take more responsibility to communicate what science qualifications can do for students whose family background does not have the cultural capital to understand the possibilities offered by the study of science. Indeed, Lyons's finding that year 10 Australian students believe teachers to be the most influential figures in their decision to pursue the study of science (Lyons and Quinn 2009b)—more than their parents or a career advisor—provides another reason for the inclusion of the topic of scientific careers in the curriculum.

Sources of Cultural Capital

Learning science is not just a process of acquiring a new form of language. It requires a willingness to develop a new or alternate identity—a process that involves a level of risk as a new way of speaking is trialed and negotiated within different social contexts (Archer et al. 2010). For those whose life-world has not already provided them with such capital, its acquisition is a considerable challenge. The most powerful way of providing students with the cultural capital that enables students to succeed in science is from the support and knowledge the family provides. For instance, using an analysis of a 10-year longitudinal data set of 1,055 respondents, Adamuti-Trache and Andres found that students whose parents had obtained college degrees were more likely to enter STEM-related careers. Science classes in secondary school were seen as "reliable strategies" or necessary requirements to enter the postsecondary system, and were thus often encouraged by parents (2008). This was particularly true of immigrant communities who recognize certain scientific careers as a means of establishing credibility and status within their new community (Archer et al. 2010).

In a study of the college-going culture in a large urban area in California, Brown et al. (2009) showed that the school and its counselors only provided limited information on careers and then, predominantly to Advanced Placement or honors students. Students found themselves reliant on their peers for such information and needed to be proactive in seeking it out. The researchers concluded that the school, its teachers, and its counselors served as "gatekeepers for determining who ultimately [would] have access to valuable resources" (p. 296). Importantly, this study also showed how greatly students benefited from and appreciated the small amount of information related to careers that they obtained from teachers, reporting that students learned a lot from teachers' "little life stories." The latter finding is commensurate with the finding of Lyons and Quinn (2009b) that identified science teachers as a significant source of career information. If relying on one's parents to acquire cultural capital for students from low-income families is "a hit and miss proposition" (Paredes 2011) and "mostly miss," the role of the school as a source of cultural capital becomes ever more important for underrepresented and underprivileged students.

Our analysis demonstrates, we hope, why it is terribly important that some curriculum time be devoted to the study and exploration of the range of careers that science offers both in and from science. As the head of careers of one of the United Kingdom's foremost science and technology universities has stated, all students need to know at the very minimum that the three high school qualifications that make you most employable are math, physics, and chemistry (Simpson 2008).

Indeed, in the past five years, significant resources have gone into the production of websites (i.e., *Icould.org* and *futuremorph.org*), which attempt to communicate the value of science qualifications. Teachers of science do need to be wary of overselling *specific* careers in science as there is good evidence that, for certain scientific careers, particularly those in the life sciences, there is no shortage of supply (Lowell et al. 2009; Lynn and Salzman 2006; Teitelbaum 2007). Rather, there are variations within the discipline. For instance, Greenwood and colleagues (2011) found that the wage premiums for STEM qualifications in mathematics and engineering attract better pay when compared to other occupations. However, science did not. Our view is that students need to be made aware that it is the range of interesting careers both *inside* and *outside* of STEM that the study of STEM subjects offers and that science qualifications offer enhanced opportunities of employment.

Conclusions and Limitations to the Science Curriculum

Our principal contention in this chapter has been to try to show that what students and society value most—the extrinsic worth of science qualifications for future employment—is neglected. Knowledge of its extrinsic value is a form of cultural capital. And those who know this are more likely to be socially and economically advantaged. Therefore, making sure that students are taught about the possibilities that the study of science offers, particularly for students from lower SES backgrounds, is one contribution science teachers can make to social justice.

Moreover, our analysis points to the inherent contradiction that exists between the goals of science education articulated by policy makers and politicians who think that scientific careers matter and the goals of many curricula where little time, if any, is devoted to communicating any understanding of scientific careers. Moreover, there is little emphasis on teaching the critical analytical skills that would provide students with valued cultural capital that could be useful both in and outside science itself.

This state of affairs exists because scientists exert too much emphasis on the school curriculum, framing it in terms of the demands required by the future professional scientist (Millar 2007; Millar and Osborne 1998). The fact that the science curriculum pays scant attention to communicating the role, significance, and value, both to the individual and society, of scientific careers when it is a major policy rationale for its importance is ironic. Our point is not to suggest that providing a curriculum that enables students to become future scientists is wrong. Rather that the lack of discussion about the future career potential that the study of science affords either in science or from science is at best puzzling, and at worst confusing to the student. For, if on the one hand, the value of a subject resides in the potential use and application, then the nature of that use—and the potential rewards it might offer—needs to be clearly communicated. It helps students to see the relevance of science. If, on the other hand the value acquired by a study of science resides solely in its intrinsic merit, why does school science persist in offering a curriculum dominated by the needs of the future scientist? If science education is to be an introduction to the best of what is worth knowing, then what is needed is a broad sketch of the major scientific ideas, the intellectual achievement they represent, and some insight into scientific practices and scientific reasoning. In this confusion, we sense that school science may have lost sight of why it matters to its students. Or, to put it another way, in the gap that exists between the rhetoric of the policy makers and the reality of the classroom, the value of school science has been misplaced.

What then, can school science do to improve the student's cultural capital? Our analysis of the state of affairs, lead us to the view that there needs to be more emphasis on what the overarching big ideas of science are. Second, school science needs to recognize its role in developing the critical spirit of the independent thinker as a force for challenging orthodoxies not only within science but without. By explicitly teaching these skills, and pointing out to students that they are *transferable*, school science offers a means for students to see both the intrinsic value of their science classes for their own thinking and the extrinsic value for future employment. Third, school science needs to sell to its presently perceived strengths, laying out to students the value of the institutionalized capital that it has to offer for future employment.

Acknowledgments

Ideas for this chapter are, in part, a product of work that has been funded by the U.K. Economic Social Science Research Council (ESRC) through grant no RES-179-25-0008.

References

Adamuti-Trache, M., and L. Andres. 2008. Embarking on and persisting in scientific fields of study: Cultural capital, gender, and curriculum along the science pipeline. *International Journal of Science Education* 30 (12): 1557–1584.

American Association for the Advancement of Science (AAAS). 1993. *Benchmarks for Scientific Literacy*. Washington, DC: AAAS.

Archer, L., J. DeWitt, J. F. Osborne, J. Dillon, B. Willis, and B. Wong. 2010. Doing science versus being a scientist: Examining 10/11 year old schoolchildren's constructions of science through the lens of identity. *Science Education* 94 (4): 617–639.

Bøe, M. V., E. K. Henriksen, T. Lyons, and C. Schreiner. 2011. Participation in science and technology: Young people and achievement-related choices in late-modern societies. *Studies in Science Education* 47 (1): 37–72.

Bourdieu, P., and J. C. Passeron. 1977. *Reproduction in education, society, and culture*. London: Sage.

Bourdieu, P., and J. C. Passeron. 1979. *The inheritors*. Chicago: University of Chicago Press.

Bowles, S., and H. Gintis. 2002. Schooling in capitalist America revisited. *Sociology of Education* 75 (1): 1–18.

Cyranoski, D. 2011. Education: The PhD factory. *Nature* 472: 276–279.

Dainton, F. S. 1968. *The Dainton report: An inquiry into the flow of candidates into science and technology*. London: HMSO.

DeBoer, G. E. 1991. *A history of ideas in science education: Implications for practice*. New York: Teachers College Press.

Duckworth, A., and M. E. P. Seligman. 2005. Self-discipline outdoes IQ in predicting academic performance of adolescents. *Psychological Science* 16 (12): 939–944.

Engineering and Technology Board. 2005. *Factors influencing year 9 career choices*. London: Engineering and Technology Board.

European Commission. 2004. *Europe needs more scientists: Report by the High Level Group on Increasing Human Resources for Science and Technology*. Brussels: European Commission.

Ford, M. J. 2008. Disciplinary authority and accountability in scientific practice and learning. *Science Education* 92 (3): 404–423.

Foskett, N., and J. Hemsley-Brown. 1997. *Career perceptions and decision-making*. Southampton: Centre for Research in Education Marketing, University of Southampton.

Greenwood, C., M. Harrison, and A. Vignoles. 2011. *The labour market value of STEM qualifications and occupations: An analysis for the Royal Academy of Engineering*: Department of Quantitative Social Science, Institute of Education.

Hanushek, E. A., and L. Woessmann. Forthcoming. *Do better schools lead to more growth, cognitive skills, economic outcomes and causation?*

Hirsch, E. D. 1987. *Cultural literacy: What every American needs to know*. Boston: Houghton Mifflin.

Jacobs, J. E., and S. D. Simpkins. eds. 2006. *Leaks in the pipeline to math, science, and technology careers: New directions for child and adolescent development*. New York: Wiley.

Jenkins, E., and N. W. Nelson. 2005. Important but not for me: Students' attitudes toward secondary school science in England. *Research in Science & Technological Education* 23 (1): 41–57.

Lindahl, B. 2007. A longitudinal study of students' attitudes towards science and choice of career. Paper presented at the 80th NARST International Conference. New Orleans, LA.

Lord Sainsbury of Turville. 2007. *The race to the top: A review of government's science and innovation policies*. London: HM Treasury.

Lowell, B. L., H. Salzman, H. Bernstein, and E. Henderson. 2009. *Steady as she goes? Three generations of students through the science and engineering pipeline*. New Brunswick, NJ: Rutgers University.

Lynn, L., and H. Salzman. 2006. Collaborative advantage: New horizons for a flat world. *Issues in Science and Technology* Winter: 74–81.

Lyons, T. 2006. Different countries, same science classes: Students' experience of school science classes in their own words. *International Journal of Science Education,* 28 (6): 591–613.

Lyons, T., and F. Quinn. 2009a. *Choosing science: Understanding the declines in senior high school enrolments*. New South Wales, Australia: SiMERR National Centre, University of New England.

Lyons, T., and F. Quinn. 2009b. *Choosing science: Understanding the declines in senior high school enrolments*. University of New England, New South Wales, Australia: SiMERR National Centre.

Millar, R. 2007. Scientific literacy: Can the school curriculum deliver? In *Communicating European research 2005*, ed. M. Claessen, pp. 145–150. Dordrecht: Springer.

Millar, R., and J. F. Osborne. eds. 1998. *Beyond 2000: Science education for the future*. London: King's College London.

Munro, M., and D. Elsom. 2000. *Choosing science at 16: The influences of science teachers and career advisors on students' decisions about science subjects and science and technology careers*. Cambridge: Careers Research and Advisory Centre (CRAC).

National Academy of Sciences: Committee on Science Engineering and Public Policy. 2005. *Rising above the gathering storm: Energizing and employing America for a brighter economic future*. Washington, DC: National Academy of Sciences.

National Research Council (NRC). 2008. *Research on future skill demands*. Washington DC: National Academies Press.

National Research Council (NRC). 2011. *A framework for K–12 science education: Practices, crosscutting concepts, and core ideas*. Washington, DC: Committee on a Conceptual Framework for New K–12 Science Education Standards. Board on Science Education, Division of Behavioral and Social Sciences and Education.

National Science Board. 2010. *Preparing the next generation of STEM innovators. Identifying and developing our nation's human capital*. Arlington, VA: National Science Foundation.

OECD. 2009. *The PISA 2009 assessment framework: Key competencies in reading, mathematics and science*. Paris: OECD.

Ormerod, M. B., and D. Duckworth. 1975. *Pupils' attitudes to science*. Slough: NFER.

Osborne, J. F., and S. Collins. 2001. Pupils' views of the role and value of the science curriculum: A focus-group study. *International Journal of Science Education* 23 (5): 441–468.

Osborne, J. F., and M. Ratcliffe. 2002. Developing effective methods of assessing ideas and evidence. *School Science Review* 83 (305): 113–123.

Osborne, J. F., S. Simon, and S. Collins. 2003. Attitudes toward science: A review of the literature and its implications. *International Journal of Science Education* 25 (9): 1049–1079.

Paredes, M. 2011. Parent involvement as an instructional strategy: No more waiting for Superman. *Teachers College Record*. March 21.

Rogers, E. M. 1948. Science in general education. In *Science in general education*, ed. E. J. McGrath. Dubuque, Iowa: Wm.C, Brown.

Schreiner, C., and S. Sjøberg. 2004. *Sowing the seeds of ROSE. Background, rationale, questionnaire development and data collection for ROSE (the relevance of science education)—A comparative study of students' views of science and science education*. Oslo: Dept. of Teacher Education and School Development, University of Oslo.

Schwab, J. J. 1962. *The teaching of science as inquiry*. Cambridge, MA: Harvard University Press.

Sjøberg, S., and C. Schreiner. 2005. How do learners in different cultures relate to science and technology? Results and perspectives from the project ROSE. *Asia Pacific Forum on Science Learning and Teaching* 6 (2): 1–16.

Stagg, P. 2007. *Careers from science: An investigation for the science education forum*. Warwick: Centre for Education and Industry, University of Warwick.

Stokking, K. M. 2000. Predicting the choice of physics in secondary education. *International Journal of Science Education* 22 (12): 1261–1283.

Tai, R. H., C. Qi Liu, A. V. Maltese, and X. Fan. 2006. Planning early for careers in science. *Science* 312: 1143–1145.

Teitelbaum, M. 2007. Do we need more scientists and engineers? Paper presented at the The National Value of Science Education conference in York, UK.

The Royal Society. 2006. *Taking a leading role*. London: The Royal Society.

U.S. Congress. 2007. America competes act. *Public Law:* 110–169.

Wellington, J., and J. F. Osborne. 2001. *Language and literacy in science education*. Buckingham: Open University Press.

Why STEM? Why Now? The Challenge for U.S. Education to Promote STEM Careers

Brenda Wojnowski
Wojnowski and Associates, Inc.

Karen Charles
RTI International

T. Georgeanne Warnock
R. L. Turner High School

The primary driver of the future economy and concomitant creation of jobs will be innovation, largely derived from advances in science and engineering …. Four percent of the nation's workforce is composed of scientists and engineers; this group disproportionately creates jobs for the other 96 percent. (NAS 2011, p. 4)

Setting

A superpower since World War II, the United States has had the highest per capita income of any major economy, generated the largest share of world exports, and consumed 24% of what the world produces (Center for Sustainable Energy Systems 2005). Central to this prosperity has been a massive investment in science, technology, engineering, and mathematics. Consequently, the United States employs nearly one-third of the world's scientists and engineers, accounts for 40% of all research and development spending, publishes 35% of science and engineering articles, and obtains 44% of science and engineering citations (Freeman 2005, p. 3).

The National Academies' 2007 report, *Rising Above the Gathering Storm,* dramatically called attention to the critical need to reform U.S. science, technology, engineering, and mathematics (STEM) education to remain competitive in a rapidly changing global, knowledge-based economy. China (20% of the world's population) and India (15% of the world's population) are challenging U.S. dominance in science and technology. India has nearly as many young professional engineers as the United States and China has more than twice as many (Freeman 2005).

Rising Above the Gathering Storm pointed out that while we once believed developing nations would specialize in producing low-cost commodities and developed economies would focus on higher-level technologies, South Korea, Taiwan, India, and China have advanced so quickly that they are instead able to produce advanced technologies at costs much lower than those of wealthier nations. The findings were corroborated in the 2011 revisiting of the original report.

The National Science Board collects trend data in science and technology, published as *Science and Engineering Indicators*. The 2004 Indicators report found that of the 2.8 million bachelor's degrees in science and engineering granted worldwide in 2003, 1.2 million were earned in Asian universities, 830,000 were granted in Europe, and 400,000 were earned in U.S. institutions. Universities in Asian countries now produce eight times as many bachelor's degrees in engineering as the United States. Of all bachelor's degrees earned in China, 60% are in engineering, compared to 31% in the United States. Remedying this situation will take years. Students entering the science and engineering workforce with advanced degrees in 2004 decided to take the necessary math courses to follow this career path when they were in middle school. Students making that same decision in middle school today will not complete advanced training for science and engineering occupations until 2018–2020.

Increasing U.S. Concerns

Shirley Ann Jackson, 2004 president of the American Association for the Advancement of Science, has described a quiet, slowly-unfolding crisis in America that "involves the steady erosion of America's scientific and engineering base, which has always been the source of American innovation and our rising standard of living" (Friedman 2005, pp. 252–253). *Rising Above the Gathering Storm* cautions, "The danger exists that Americans may not know enough about science, technology, or mathematics to contribute significantly to, or fully benefit from, the knowledge-based economy that is already taking shape around us" (2007, p. 314). Consequently, business and industry leaders, Congress, state officials, policy makers, K–16 educators, and national defense agencies are concerned that the current education system in America is not preparing students with the STEM knowledge they need to help maintain a competitive edge.

While the general public is not well informed about science, technology, engineering, and mathematics, an incredible shortage of professional engineers and scientists may also be looming. In *The World Is Flat*, Friedman (2005) warns that the generation of scientists and engineers who were motivated to go into science in the late 1950s because of the Sputnik threat are approaching retirement. For example, nearly 40% of the employees at NASA are at least 50 years old and 22% are 55 or older. It is challenging for NASA to recruit employees with sufficient science, engineering, and information technology skills to insure needed advancements in space science, and the situation will only get worse as engineers and scientists continue to retire within the next few years.

Not only is there a growing shortage of engineers and scientists, but there are insufficient numbers of workers trained in STEM fields in general. As traditional manufacturing plants are closing or downsizing, domestic high-tech manufacturing is expanding along with the need for highly skilled workers. On a 2005 questionnaire of American manufacturing companies and human-resources professionals by Deloitte Consulting on behalf of the National Association of

Manufacturers, 90% of the 800 respondents reported shortages of skilled production employees, including machinists and technicians. A 2006 report by the Federal Reserve Bank of New York found that between 1983 and 2002, while low- and middle-skill manufacturing jobs declined quickly, high-skill manufacturing employment rose 37%—an increase of about 1.2 million jobs.

Peggy M. Walton, director of the National Center for the American Workforce, has stated that the new manufacturing jobs require knowledge and skills that schools may not have emphasized 20 years ago. Science-based industries today require scientific thinking and creative problem solving. This is true not only for upper-level managerial jobs, but also for entry-level jobs that do not require a college degree.

Defining the Current STEM Workforce

According to the U.S. Commerce Department's Economic and Statistics Administration (ESA), 9.3 million of the 41.5 million U.S. workers with at least a bachelor's degree have a STEM degree (ESA 2011). So, it stands to reason that to begin to understand the need to prepare a STEM workforce, we need first to understand what the STEM workforce is. Recently, the ESA developed a standard definition for STEM jobs:

- professional and technical support occupations in the fields of computer science and mathematics, engineering, and life and physical sciences
- computer and information systems managers, engineering managers, and natural sciences managers
- science occupations including science technicians; engineering and surveying occupations including engineering technicians and drafters; computer occupations ranging from computer support specialists to computer software engineers.

The ESA list of professions includes 50 occupation codes divided into four categories: computer and math, engineering, physical and life sciences, and STEM managerial occupations. In tandem to the list of STEM occupation, the ESA has developed a list of undergraduate majors related to the identified job classifications. The STEM job definition excludes educators and social scientists, and the list of related degree programs excludes business, healthcare, and social science majors.

Responding to the Need: STEM Education in the United States

As is often the case, the U.S. K–12 education system has been challenged to respond to our country's need to develop a strong STEM pipeline and workforce and to inspire and influence U.S. students to pursue and persist in STEM-related careers. There is no shortage of STEM reports, STEM articles, STEM webinars, and STEM working groups in and around the U.S. education community. Everyone agrees that our future as a nation, our economic growth, and our national security are challenges that our workforce must face in order to compete in a global marketplace. These are nontrivial, well-documented challenges that STEM advocates reference when championing the need for stronger, more robust STEM education in order for our country to produce the scientists, mathematicians, and engineers we will need to create 21st-century solutions to 21st-century problems. But will revitalizing STEM education, especially in America's high schools, guarantee that graduates will choose STEM pathways in college or STEM careers when they graduate? Is it within the potential of the current system to ensure more STEM graduates?

Building a Knowledge Base Around STEM

Agencies, universities, committees, and professional organizations have been reviewing the STEM explosion since the early 2000s in attempts to define STEM education, establish criteria for STEM schools, identify the needs of the U.S. workforce relative to STEM, and determine the links between STEM education and the STEM workplace (PCAST 2011; NRC 2011; NGA 2007).

In May 2011, Harris Interactive conducted an online survey commissioned by Microsoft of 500 college students between the ages of 18 and 24 who were pursuing STEM degrees (IESD 2011). The student survey focused on two areas of interest: how prepared students felt they were for college-level STEM courses and what inspired them to pursue STEM careers. Interesting findings emerged.

- **The influence of school is undeniable.** Nearly 80% students reported developing an interest in STEM in high school or earlier and over half reported that a teacher or class influenced this interest. On the other hand, only 17% indicated that a teacher actually encouraged their choice (this number is even lower for African-American and Hispanic students). This seems to represent a missed opportunity by educators to realize the difference between accidental and incidental influence and purposeful and proactive encouragement. Coursework isn't, in and of itself, a motivator. It is how students experience their classes, how they understand the content in the context of its applications, and how the class deepens their interest and nurtures their curiosity that motivates.
- **Preparation is key to academic success.** Only 20% of students felt that their K–12 education prepared them extremely well for rigorous STEM courses in college. However, almost half (45%) cited their interest and skills in gaming as contributing to their preparation for college work, especially in technology-focused classes. While students recommended more rigorous curriculum offerings in high school, they listed a number of factors as having a greater role in their preparation. Among these were having a passion for their pursuits, studying hard, and having supportive parents.
- **A secure future matters.** Almost 70% of the students indicated that STEM careers represented strong job potential and good salaries to them and motivated their pursuit of STEM studies. They were not motivated by the country's need for STEM graduates in the workforce. This finding points unmistakably to the need for educators to introduce older K–12 students not only to STEM courses but also to STEM career options. If students are motivated by job potential, then they need to understand STEM career options and the importance of informed choices regarding selected degree pathways.
- **There is a difference between having an interest in STEM and pursuing a STEM career in college.** In making this distinction, family still matters. The study revealed that 37% of college students pursuing STEM careers have a parent working in the field. In addition, while over half reported that a teacher sparked their interest in STEM, 36% reported that it was a family member who most encouraged them to pursue STEM as a career.

Further, almost 75% responded that their parents had at least some influence in their decision to study in the STEM field.

It is interesting to note that the survey delved into the students' preparation for college coursework and their interest in pursuing a STEM career but did not question students' direct preparation for a STEM career. This seems to be the point at which many such surveys stop. We are learning more and more about whether K–12 education prepares students for STEM coursework in college, but we know little about the preparation of students for the STEM workforce. There seems to be an underlying assumption that STEM courses prepare students for STEM careers. Perhaps we are surveying the wrong people.

The Rush to Establish STEM Schools

The math-science cycle of influence that repeats itself every 20 or so years has expanded to include technology and engineering and has given us an acronym useful in collectively discussing all four elements of this renewed emphasis. Of particular interest in this STEM age are STEM schools, most of which are self-titled and self-designed. It is this lack of a universally accepted description of a STEM school that has prevented much meaningful research on guiding pedagogy, curriculum design, and student outcomes. Very few self-proclaimed STEM schools are alike, so finding a cluster to study is difficult. In the meantime, this paper attempts to find evidence of practices at STEM schools that do, in fact, influence the STEM career choices of their students at greater rates than non-STEM schools.

We know a lot about student scores and international rankings. We know that American students lag behind other countries in mathematics and science performance on international studies, and we can probably find evidence that students in STEM schools score better than their peers in non-STEM schools. But proficiency is not the issue. One of the underlying premises of STEM schools is that they inspire and encourage students to pursue STEM careers. If this is an explicit goal of STEM schools, then it begs the questions: How do they do this, and do they do it any differently than non-STEM schools? Is there any evidence that students at STEM schools pursue and persist in STEM careers at a greater rate than their peers at non-STEM schools? Even more elusive to study is whether students at STEM schools would have followed STEM pathways *without* attending STEM schools. In other words, did a preexisting interest in STEM lead them to the STEM school?

To examine these questions, this chapter presents a review of several of the most recent reports on STEM education in the United States in an attempt to (a) define a common language around STEM schools, (b) examine attributes common to STEM schools, and (c) determine whether or to what extent STEM schools conduct purposeful activities that highlight STEM career choices for their students.

Goals for Successful STEM Education

In October 2010 the National Research Council (NRC), with support from the National Science Foundation, convened the Committee on Highly Successful Schools or Programs for K–12 STEM Education and charged its members with "outlining criteria for identifying effective

STEM schools and programs and identifying which of those criteria could be addressed with available data and research, and those where further work is needed to develop appropriate data sources" (NRC 2011, p. 1).

In examining the existing research on what defines success in STEM schools, the committee concluded that (1) there is a "limited body" of research on STEM schools, and (2) some findings cannot be "disentangled" from the nature of the students typically found in STEM schools. In other words, these students might have succeeded in STEM classes and pursued STEM degrees regardless of the high school they attended.

The committee fulfilled its charge by using as guidelines the three widely accepted goals for STEM education:

- to increase advanced training and careers in STEM fields
- to expand the STEM-capable workforce
- to increase scientific literacy among the general public

Inherent in these are intermediate goals that include learning STEM content and skills, developing positive attitudes toward STEM, and preparing students to be lifelong learners (NRC 2011).

Linking these goals to the effectiveness of STEM schools is proving difficult for several reasons. First, STEM schools have not been around long enough to have a noticeable impact on the workforce. Second, judging from the surveys reviewed for this report, questions appear to be more focused on the success (or nonsuccess) in achieving the intermediate goals and less on achieving the broader goals. There appears to be an underlying assumption that *preparation* for STEM coursework equates to *preparation* for STEM careers. Most surveys and reports discuss preparation for STEM coursework, and leave the reader to conclude that preparation for a STEM career is a natural consequence.

NRC Criteria for Successful STEM Schools

As the committee considered three criteria for identifying successful STEM schools—measurable STEM outcomes, observable instructional practices, and the design of STEM schools—it found that most studies it reviewed focused on the impact of classroom instruction (NRC 2011). Studies measuring student outcomes focused primarily on test scores and grades, leaving in question whether STEM schools contribute to increasing advanced careers in STEM fields or expanding the STEM-capable workforce.

STEM School Models

The NRC committee also identified and defined a number of differing STEM school models, a variation that also makes it difficult to gather consistent data and reach conclusions applicable to STEM schools in general. Most assumptions about STEM schools are that they offer a more rigorous curriculum, recruit highly trained teachers, and are equipped with better resources. They often target specific student populations. Known by different names across the country, the distinguishable types of STEM schools are:

- *Selective STEM schools*—includes state residential schools, stand-alone schools, and schools-within-a-school, which focus on preparing students for STEM degrees and careers. The committee found no completed study that provided a rigorous analysis comparing the contributions of selective schools to regular schools.
- *Inclusive STEM schools*—includes schools with no admissions criteria but with a focus on one or more specific STEM fields or disciplines. One study on inclusive STEM schools is looking at 51 inclusive schools in Texas, where preliminary findings show students scoring higher on state math and science assessments and enrolling in more advanced courses than their peers. Because students can opt into inclusive schools, students in comparison groups may not have similar interests.
- *Career and Technical Education (CTE)*—includes schools with both career and dropout prevention foci (NRC 2011).

In everyday conversation around STEM schools, most people are referring to some variation of a selective STEM school. Not to be dismissed, however, are "regular" comprehensive high schools, those in which students must meet minimum graduation requirements, which for many states include three or four years of mathematics and science, and for 35% of U.S. high schools includes Advanced Placement (AP) or International Baccalaureate (IB) courses in mathematics and science (NRC 2011).

STEM School Practices

Because of the abundance of rigorous research available on good instructional practices, the committee decided that "the most useful way of identifying criteria for success relates to educational practices;" in other words, it focused on defining "what practices should be used to identify effective STEM schools" (NRC 2011, p. 18). To capture the essence of effective STEM education—that which engages students in investigations, develops their curiosity, and deepens their understanding of core ideas—the committee identified key elements that should be easily visible and identifiable in successful STEM schools. These include:

- a coherent set of standards and curriculum;
- teachers with high capacity to teach in their discipline
- a supportive system of assessment and accountability
- adequate instructional time
- equal access to high-quality STEM learning opportunities; and
- school conditions and culture that support learning (NRC 2001).

These recommendations can guide researchers in developing data collection instrumentations designed to capture the effectiveness of practices most often associated with successful STEM schools.

Implications for STEM Schools

The report from the NRC committee makes the case for studying school practices to determine the success of STEM schools. It states that, "a wide variety of outcomes can be used as criteria to identify successful schools, though it should be noted that outcomes alone do not provide insight into the practices that contribute to success" (NRC 2011, p. 26). A contrary argument is that effective practices alone do not provide insights into the outcomes that contribute to success. The problem is that we still do not know if achieving the overarching outcomes—those related to STEM career choices and a stronger STEM workforce—can be attributed to STEM schools. This may take time to determine, perhaps even a generation.

While we wait, however, one strong argument for establishing STEM schools in K–12 education is that they have the potential to level the playing field for students from disadvantaged backgrounds. Many STEM schools, whether charter or magnet or specialized by some other decree, seek to enroll a diverse and locally representative student population. This has potential to impact the STEM workforce in years to come. Currently, non-Hispanic whites and Asians dominate the STEM workforce, while African Americans and Hispanics comprise only 6% (each) of the workforce. According to the ESA report, these groups are half as likely as other groups to have STEM jobs.

Recommendations for STEM Schools and STEM Researchers

The surveys reviewed for this chapter seem to concentrate on students' preparation for STEM courses in college, not on students' familiarity with STEM career options and their preparation for the workforce. Students aren't being asked to describe how they see themselves in the workforce, what they imagine they will be doing, or how their coursework relates to their potential careers. We recommend the inclusion of questions that investigate what students understand about their career options, the importance of informed choices regarding selected degree pathways, and what their STEM schools did to develop this awareness for them.

While there is no official process or certification necessary, no test to pass in order to be designated a STEM school, it is widely accepted (or expected) that STEM schools provide their students more in-depth curriculum, more advanced courses, more hands-on opportunities, more problem-based learning, more highly prepared teachers, and more innovative experiences. There still appears to be the notion that these alone will prepare them for STEM careers. Remember that the only STEM professionals that many students have seen for 12 years have been their STEM teachers, and it is unreasonable to expect these educators to serve as career counselors to their students. Therefore, we advocate for a more direct approach with frequent and purposeful exposure to STEM careers, STEM employees at all levels and in all categories, STEM workplaces, STEM employers, and STEM degree programs.

To that point, we present a study of a STEM school that does just that:

A STEM Academy Case Study

A Description of the STEM Academy

The particular STEM Academy studied is designed specifically for students interested in an engineering field. The Academy is located as a discrete entity within a comprehensive high school in an urban/suburban setting in a southwest state. The Academy is built according to the small school design with just over 250 students distributed over 9th, 10th, and 11th grades at the time of the study. The school added a fourth class in 2010–11, making it a full 9–12 high school.

The student body is diverse with 68% Hispanic, 22% White, 6% Asian and 4% African-American. Approximately two-thirds of the students are male; approximately two-thirds low-SES.

The Academy is based on the precepts of the New Tech model that began in California and stresses the need for one-on-one computing capability for students. The Academy uses problem/project–based learning (PBL) as its primary teaching strategy while helping students to gain an understanding of career opportunities available in the field of engineering. The intent is for the Academy students to graduate as lifelong learners who will make valuable contributions to society. The Academy's vision is to use innovative ways of delivering science and math education through engineering and technology disciplines and increasing the number of students who enter and complete STEM-related, postsecondary education and enter STEM careers. Through participation in projects, presentations of learning, senior exhibitions, and internships, students complete portfolios that demonstrate their mastery of state competencies. This vision leads to the Academy's mission of inspiring a community of lifelong learners where every student meets or exceeds the state graduation requirements in four years and is prepared to pursue post-secondary ambitions in a STEM-related area. This vision is, in turn, supported by the Academy's goals for its students. The Academy's goals include

- preparing a diverse population of students in math, engineering, technology, and science to succeed in high school, postsecondary education and careers;
- preparing exemplary problem solvers for professional leadership roles through academic and field-based experiences; and
- graduating students who will be thoughtful, engaged citizens.

Through an active pursuit of these goals, the Academy promotes the learning outcomes of:

- Active collaboration
- Presentation skills
- Literacy
- Content skills and knowledge
- Research skills
- Work ethic and effort
- Critical thinking and problem solving
- Social and cross-cultural skills
- Technology skills
- Writing skills

The Academy provides an advisory class for each student each week in order to increase the level of support for students in understanding STEM postsecondary majors and STEM careers. In addition, the Academy assures that students are able to use technology in every class to help them in reaching their learning outcomes as well as in having access to an internet-based learning environment, including a grading system and course calendars. The school's engineering focus is implemented through use of the well-known engineering curriculum model of Project Lead the Way (PLTW). The Academy is supported in implementing its vision, promoting its learning outcomes, and using the problem/project-based learning (PBL) instructional strategy by community and business partnerships, thereby increasing student experiences with people actively engaged in STEM-related careers. The curriculum stresses college preparatory requirements and 21st-century learning skills, including a collaborative work environment geared toward problem solving and critical thinking skills. All students have a required capstone course and a community/work interaction component of learning through STEM-focused community service and career shadowing and/or internships. With sports, clubs, and fine arts available, all students are also required to participate in some type of extracurricular activity. Parents and community members are invited to the school to view and/or critique student work through presentations and showcases.

Goals and Study Questions

The STEM Academy case study was conducted during the 2009–2010 school year. It was designed to collect data surrounding the workings and culture of the Academy and to be nonevaluative in nature. The goal of the study was to describe the current status of the Academy in terms of academic attainment and culture maturity from the perspective of the students, administration, faculty, parents and advisory board members.

The project was designed to answer two primary study questions (1 and 2 below) and two secondary study questions (3 and 4 below):

Study Question	Study Methodologies
1. How do students at the Academy view the current culture of the school?	Walk-through observations, questionnaires, focus groups
2. How do administrators and teachers view the current culture of the school?	Walk-through observations, questionnaires, interviews/focus groups
3. How do parent/advisory board members view the current culture of the school?	Direct interviews, questions on student and teacher questionnaires and during interview of the director and focus groups of teachers and students
4. What is the current academic status of the school?	Numeric data gathering

Methodology

The questionnaires used in this study incorporated elements of instruments used in the 2008 study of the Metro School in Ohio by the PAST Foundation (Hunter and Agranoff 2008). All questionnaires were validated by expert review from three STEM education professionals. Primary qualitative data pertinent to the stated goals for this study were gathered through interviews, focus groups, and field observations. The case study approach was designed to allow the researchers to gain insight into the internal workings and culture of the school from those most intimately engaged in the phenomenon. Data gathering was according to a protocol as described in the approved study IRB.

The study began with walk-throughs to allow the researchers to develop an understanding of the general conduct of the school. Questionnaires were administered to teachers and students.

The director was interviewed alone as were a parent/advisory board member and a nonparent advisory board member. The teachers were interviewed in a focus group setting. Representatives were chosen at random from the students who had parental/guardian permission to participate in the study from each grade level. Each grade level representative group was interviewed as a separate focus group.

Results

Walk-throughs

Two walk-throughs were a part of this study. In each walk-through, the researcher visited each single class or combined class that was in session. During one walk-through, all mathematics students were gathered in the central space to talk with a five-member panel of business/industry representatives about STEM career possibilities. During each walk-through, the researcher visited five groups of students, some being in single class and some in combined class (team teaching or industry panel) situations.

Each walk-through found most classes to have a few more males than females, ranging from a class gender differentiation of 52% male to 65% males on the days of the observations. As noted previously, overall the school has more males than females. Class sizes ranged from 9 to 49 students (2 teachers team teaching). The largest class with a single teacher was 15. Classes were diverse with Hispanic, White, Asian, and African American students.

The culture of the school was seen to be one in which students were actively participating in all classes with evidence of extensive use of technology and collaborative learning. Students were engaged and were being challenged to be creative and innovative through project-based learning scenarios, art projects and reflective writing assignments. The researcher saw evidence of students being mentored by other students who were obviously assuming roles of responsibility.

Data Analysis

Academy student performance for grade 9 and grade 10 state testing in reading and mathematics exceeded averages for the state, the parent independent school district, and 40 schools from across the state determined by the State Education Agency to form a comparable group for comparison purposes. The Academy grade 9 students also matched or exceeded the district and state averages when disaggregated by ethnic subgroup, gender, and economically disadvantaged populations. Economically disadvantaged students at the Academy exceeded similar students at each level of comparison by a minimum of 8% in reading and 17% in mathematics.

The Academy male students outperformed males at the school, district, and state levels by at least 8% in English-Language Arts (ELA), 11% in mathematics, 7% in science, and 5% in social studies. The Academy female students outperformed females at each level of comparison by at least 5% in ELA, 7% in mathematics, and 1% in social studies. Economically disadvantaged students at the Academy exceeded similar students at each level by at least 9% in ELA, 14% in mathematics, 9% in science, and 7% in social studies. The Academy's Limited English Proficiency (LEP) students outperformed subgroup averages at all levels by at least 9% in ELA and 7% in social studies.

Teacher Responses

Questionnaires were administered to all 14 teachers at the STEM Academy. Several responses were particularly reflective of the culture of the school. For example, when asked if the Academy is a safe place to work and learn, 69% of teachers selected "strongly agree," with the remainder of the teachers marking "agree." Similarly, when asked whether collaboration among students is both encouraged and practiced at the Academy, an even greater share (77%) selected "strongly agree" and the remaining 23% selected "agree." The modal response provided by the Academy teachers when asked the question, "What percent of the students in the Academy do you expect to attend college?" was "70–89%" with 62% of teachers selecting this option. Modally, 54% of teachers selected "50–69%" when responding to the question, "What percent of parents request regular feedback from the teacher and/or director as to their child's progress?" When teachers were asked to compare the general reputation of the Academy to other schools, 23% selected "among the best" and the 69% said "better than average." Next, 77% of teachers indicated that teacher attitudes and 62% indicated that teaching methods have a "substantial effect" on student achievement. Finally, when asked how much they enjoy teaching at the Academy, a majority of teachers (54%) responded "tremendously."

Positive Aspects of the STEM Academy

When asked what they thought the most positive aspects of the Academy to be, almost all of the teachers commented on the positive culture/environment of the school with many attributing the culture to the small school/learning community model. Many saw the emphasis on 21st-century skills as a strong positive for the school. One teacher commented, "Students will leave [the Academy] with experience in teamwork, collaboration, and presentation skills that most adults do not have." Going back to the closed response questions, 97% of the teachers stated that the Academy is a safe place to work and over 91% rated the general reputation of the Academy as compared to other schools as "better than average" or "among the best."

Areas for Improvement

In response to the question asking what areas could be improved, several teachers commented on the fact the school-within-a-school design creates additional work for them because they must comply with the main high school's requirements as well as the Academy's. One teacher commented, "There is way too much work for one teacher to do while balancing things with the main building." In general, the aforementioned workload and difficulty in creating professional development specific to the Academy while still tied to a main campus comprehensive high school seemed to be the main concerns. Teachers were also concerned with what they perceived as a lack of parent involvement.

Student Questionnaire Responses

A questionnaire containing a battery of 29 closed-response items was administered during an advisory period to Academy students who had returned forms allowing them to participate in the study. Students were asked to indicate the degree to which they agreed or disagreed with questionnaire statements. The questionnaire also contained a series of demographic and open-ended items. This section of the case study highlights both closed and open-ended student responses to the questionnaire.

A total of 110 students completed the questionnaire for a return rate of 44%. Thirty-nine percent of the students responding were 9th graders, 32% were 10th graders, and 29% were 11th graders. At the time of the study, there were slightly more freshmen than sophomores or juniors (95 freshmen, 83 sophomores, and 72 juniors). Of the 108 Academy students responding to the questionnaire item concerning gender, 64% were male. Concerning post-graduation plans, the majority of students indicated that they are planning to work while attending college (60%) while 38% indicated that they would not be working while attending college. Only one student plans to enter the military and no students responded that they would be working only.

Responses to Closed Items

The bulk of the student questionnaire consisted of a series of 29 items that asked students to read a statement and select one of the following response options: "almost always," "often," "sometimes," "rarely," "never," or "no basis for a response." Selected items are highlighted here. When asked to respond to the statements, "The teachers are available to talk with me when I have a question" and "The teachers provide help outside class time when it is needed," in each case 86% of the students selected either "almost always" or "often." Additional high modal responses included: "Working on projects with my classmates improves my ability to learn" (77% "almost always" or "often"); and "The teachers demonstrate that they are very knowledgeable of the course subject matter" (79% "almost always" or "often").

Students selected the response option "often" most frequently when responding to the statement, "The teacher provides guidance on how to complete each assignment" (47%). The response option "often" was also the modal response for the following five statements: "The teachers present class information in a clear and understandable way" (45%); "I feel my classmates contribute adequately to our group projects" (43%); "The teachers cover the course material at a reasonable pace" (42%); "Students in my classes are encouraged to help one another" (42%); and "The teachers adapt lessons to accommodate different student abilities and learning styles" (41%). "Often" and "almost always" were bimodal responses for the statement, "The teachers make sure everyone in the class is involved" (40% each).

When asked to respond to the statement, "My parents and teachers communicate with one another," students selected "sometimes" as the modal response (31%). Although "almost always" was the modal response for the statement, "I feel comfortable sharing my thoughts and opinions in class," this statement also represented the second highest percentage of students selecting "sometimes" (30%). "Sometimes" was the modal response for the statement, "My parents are aware of what is going on in my class" (30%). The response option "never" was selected as the modal response for the statement, "My parents have been invited to take part in class related activities" (27%). This item also was the most frequently selected item for the option "rarely" at 18% and an additional 6% of students indicated that they had "no basis for a response." Therefore, it is important to note that this item was the statement with which students had the least agreement for those items in this battery. Over 30% of students selected "never" or "rarely" when responding to the statement, "My parents and teachers communicate with one another." An additional 30% of students selected "never" or "rarely" when responding to the statement, "I feel responsible for my classmates' learning" (13% and 17%, respectively).

Responses to Open-Ended Items

In response to the open-ended question concerning whose decision it was for the student to attend the Academy, an overwhelming majority indicated that it was their decision (82%), 11% said it was their parents' decision, and 7% said that it was a joint decision. Of the students who reported that it was their decision to attend the Academy, most said they were interested in a career in engineering or math and science.

In response to the open-ended question asking students what they like most about the Academy, many of the students responded that they liked working together on projects. Many of the students also enjoyed working with computers and related technology. When asked what they liked least about the Academy, several of the students indicated that there were too many projects and not enough time to complete them. When asked what they would change about the Academy, many of the students wouldn't change anything.

When asked, "Does advisory have a benefit to you? If so, how?", 52% of students said "yes" and the remaining 48% responded "no." The students who found it helpful responded that it informed them about college and careers and helped them plan their future, helped them check their grade status, and helped them revise their portfolios.

The final open-ended item on the questionnaire asked students to, "Tell me about your experiences with problem/project-based learning, PeBL, and Grade portal." (PeBL is a data entry system initiated by the New Tech Network for teacher, student, and parent use. Teachers are able to enter assignments on the system, and students and parents are able to access the system to keep up with assignments and due dates. Grade portal is another online system available to teachers, students, and parents. Teachers enter grades on the system and students and parents are able to check the grades in real time.)

Fourteen of the students didn't respond. Among the students who did respond, PeBL and Gradeportal were almost universally loved while project-based learning (PBL) received somewhat mixed reviews from the students, although more spoke favorably than unfavorably. A student who listed PBL as what he/she liked best about the Academy said, "I like PBL. It helps me learn. I can work with new people each project and learn from them. PBL has taught me how to lead a group." Alternately, here is one student's negative comment about PBL: "Project based learning, while fundamentally sound, seems to dissolve upon application … PBL has a tendency to let students specialize far too much in one particular content area." The student who expressed his feelings most succinctly said, "Project-based learning really helps me understand the material. PeBL helps me keep track of what I need to do. Grade Portal helps me decide what I need to do to get my grades higher." Another student who saw value in the tools commented, "PeBL and Grade Portal are the most important factors in [the Academy]. Grade Portal allows for us as students to check our grades any given time and see how we can improve it or if we're missing an assignment. PeBL allows for us to download templates, or other forms and sources we need in order to complete given projects as well as looking into the calendar and see what we've got to do." Another student responding favorably to the question said, "I think PBL is one of the best school programs. It gives you technology and presentation skills. More importantly, though, I think, is the fact that it teaches you how to be able to work and communicate with any kind of person. Grade portal, in my opinion is one of the best tools for a student that cares. It shows me all I need to know about my own grades and learning. I think [the Academy] is doing great and I wish to stay for all of my high school education career." Another student who appreciated the utility of the tools commented, "All these programs have helped me improve my learning throughout high school. Project-based learning has helped me improve on many of my learning outcome skills. PeBL helps me stay organized and on top of my work allowing me to be ready for what's ahead. Grade portal helps me make sure I know what classes I need to improve on, but it just doesn't tell me a grade, it breaks it down to my learning outcome allowing me to improve on a certain skill. Many people will talk negative about these programs just because they dislike them and I am not very fond of them myself but I must admit they are very useful programs."

Interviews and Focus Groups

Interviews were conducted with the director, a parent who is also on the advisory board and an advisory board member who is not a parent of an Academy student. Focus groups were conducted with teachers and with students from each grade level, by grade level. The transcripts were analyzed for recurring themes which are summarized and bolded below:

Student themes across all grade levels included a **sense of school pride** with students often highlighting the differences they saw when comparing the Academy to other schools. **Problem/project-based learning** was also a topic of discussion in each grade level. The majority of students were enthusiastic about being in classes taught using PBL, although a few students did voice objections to that method of instruction. All student groups spoke of the **dedication of the teachers and director.** Some remarked that even when they did not like the decisions of the director or particular teachers, they knew the decisions were made with their best interests in mind. The students indicated that they felt **safe** and were particularly complimentary of the **family-like culture** that permeates the school. The only negative that came up in every class group concerned the **space issues** and what they perceive as overcrowding that will only get worse in their building.

The parent and advisory board member expressed very similar themes talking extensively about the caring **culture of the school** and the use of **PBL** as a teaching methodology. The adult stakeholders saw the **role of community STEM professionals** as critical to the school. They stressed the engineering and architectural aspects of the services community members are able to provide to the school. Both obviously felt knowledgeable of and critical to the work of the school.

Much of the teachers' discussion focused on the **culture of the school**. The teachers have an obvious pride in the family-like culture they have been able to create for the students, including an attitude of respect in a safe, supportive environment. They see the **small school structure** as enhancing the **21st-century skills focus** of the school allowing both the students and the teachers to operate in a **collaborative** manner that builds student confidence. The teachers are clear that they came to the Academy to teach in a creative way that would produce students who are able to act independently, to manage their own learning, and to communicate with their peers and adults.

The director has been with the Academy from the beginning of the design phase in 2006. In essence, the director detailed the history of the building of the culture that students, teachers and community members have described as one of the most unique features of the Academy and one of the aspects of the school that they see as most critical to student achievement and in which they have the most pride.

Summary

The original four questions for the case study were approached through both quantitative and qualitative study methodologies.

1. *How do students at the Academy view the current culture of the school?*

   The students were particularly pleased with the family-like culture of the Academy and indicated this in both their answers to questionnaire queries and in their focus group interviews. The students were seen as actively engaged during walk-throughs (viewed as indicative of a vibrant learning culture by the researchers).

2. *How do administrators and teachers view the current culture of the school?*

   During the focus group session, much of the teachers' discussion focused on the culture of the school. The teachers exhibited an obvious pride in the family-like culture they have been able to create for the students, including an attitude of respect in a safe, supportive environment.

3. *How do parent/advisory board members view the current culture of the school?*

   The parent advisory board member and the nonparent advisory board member both spoke extensively to the caring culture of the school.

4. *What is the current academic status of the school?*

   The researchers found the current academic status of the school based on state testing scores to be above that of averages for the state, the parent independent school district, and the campus comparison group of 40 schools determined by the SEA to be comparable schools from across the state.

The researchers found the current academic status of the school based on state testing scores to be above that of averages for all comparison groups used in the study. Additionally, all study groups (students, teachers, advisory board members/parent, and director) were found to view the culture of the school as a safe, supportive, family-like environment in which students are encouraged to learn using creative problem/project-based teaching and learning strategies.

Conclusion

Based on the definitions articulated by the NRC's Committee on Highly Successful Schools or Programs for K–12 STEM Education, the Academy is an example of a "selective" STEM school, one that focuses on preparing students for STEM degrees and careers. Of the students who reported that it was their decision to attend the Academy, most said they were interested in a career in engineering or math and science. While the case study does not compare the Academy to regular schools with regard to its impact on student decisions about STEM studies and STEM careers, it does demonstrate how a school can do more than provide rigorous coursework to inspire its students to consider STEM career pathways. In summary, the Academy

- provides an advisory class for each student each week in order to increase the level of support for students in understanding STEM post-secondary majors and STEM careers;
- assures that students are able to use technology in every class to help them in reaching their learning outcomes;
- provides access to an internet-based learning environment, including a grading system and course calendars;
- uses a well-known engineering curriculum model, Project Lead the Way (PLTW)
- promotes community and business partnerships, increasing student experiences with people actively engaged in STEM-related careers;
- stresses college preparatory requirements and 21st-century learning skills, including a collaborative work environment geared toward problem solving and critical-thinking skills;
- requires a capstone course and a community/work interaction component of learning through STEM-focused community service and career shadowing and/or internships; and
- invites parents and community members to the school to view and/or critique student work through presentations and showcases.

We began this chapter with two central questions: (1) Will revitalizing STEM education, especially in America's high schools, guarantee that graduates will choose STEM pathways in college or STEM careers when they graduate? And (2) Is it within the potential of the current system to ensure more STEM graduates? Researchers found that the Academy provided a range of experiences for its students that extend far beyond rigorous coursework and directly support one of its primary goals of "preparing a diverse population of students in math, engineering, technology and science to succeed in high school, postsecondary education and careers." The Academy consistently involves business and industry representatives and parents in student activities, a strategy that should increase parental influence in career choices that the Harris survey for Microsoft found to be critical. The Academy also pursues community and business partnerships in order to increase student experiences with people activity engaged in STEM-related careers. In creating a culture that supports student learning and encourages student aspirations toward STEM careers, the Academy serves as a model of the types of activities encouraged by the studies reviewed in the opening sections of this paper. Rigorous coursework does not, on its own, promote interest in STEM careers. It may stimulate interest and deepen curiosity, but students need to experience STEM opportunities, talk with STEM practitioners, and explore STEM career options in order to make informed decisions about their own potential for success in the STEM workforce.

References

Center for Sustainable Energy Systems. 2005. U.S. energy system factsheet. Ann Arbor, MI: University of Michigan.

Committee on Science, Engineering, and Public Policy. 2006. *Rising above the gathering storm: Energizing and employing America for a brighter economic future.* Washington, DC: National Academy of Sciences.

Economic and Statistics Administration (ESA). 2011. *Education supports racial and ethnic equality in STEM education.* Washington, DC: U.S. Department of Commerce, Economic and Statistic Administration.

Keeping America competitive: Five strategies to improve mathematics and science education. *Education Week.* March 26, 2008.

Freeman, R. B. 2005. Does globalization of the scientific/engineering workforce threaten U.S. economic leadership? Working Paper 11457. Cambridge, MA: National Bureau of Economic Research.

Friedman, T. L. 2005. *The world is flat.* New York: Straus and Giroux.

Harris Interactive. 2011. *STEM perceptions: Student and parent study.* Commissioned by Microsoft. Available at *www.harrisinteractive.com*.

Hunter, M., and R. Agranoff. 2008. *Metro high school: An emerging STEM community.* Columbus, OH: PAST Foundation.

National Academy of Sciences (NAS). 2007. *Rising above the gathering storm: Energizing and employing America for a brighter economic future.* Washington, DC: The National Academies Press.

National Academy of Sciences, National Academy of Engineering, and Institute of Medicine. 2011. *Rising above the gathering storm revisited: Rapidly approaching category 5.* Condensed version. Washington, DC: The National Academies Press.

National Governors Association (NGA). 2007. Innovation America: Building a Science, Technology, Engineering and Math Agenda. *www.nga.org/Files/pdf/0702INNOVATIONStem.pdf*

National Research Council (NRC). 2011. *Successful K–12 STEM education: Identifying effective approaches in science, technology, engineering, and mathematics.* Washington, DC: The National Academies Press.

National Science Board. 2004. *Science and Engineering Indicators.* Washington, DC: National Science Board. *www.nsf.gov/statistics/seind04*

National Science Board. 2006. *Science and Engineering Indicators.* Washington, DC: National Science Board. *www.nsf.gov/statistics/seind06*

President's Council of Advisors on Science and Technology (PCAST). 2010. Prepare and inspire: K–12 education in science, technology, engineering, and math (STEM) education for America's future. *www.whitehouse.gov/administration/eop/ostp/pcast*

Using Inquiry-Based Teaching and Kids Inquiry Conferences to Strengthen Elementary Science Instruction and to Encourage More Students to Pursue Science Careers

Paula A. Magee
Indiana University–Indianapolis

Ryan Flessner
Butler University

Setting

For the past 20 years, there has been a push to improve the teaching and learning of science in elementary schools. One strong reason for this was the release of the National Science Education Standards (NRC 1996). The Standards articulated not only *what* K–12 students should know (science content standards), but also *how* science teachers needed to teach (teaching standards) and be continuously *supported* (professional development standards). The Standards also considered ways to support inquiry-based and meaningful science learning for K–12 students (program and system standards). According to the NRC, one of the four reasons underpinning all of this is because "the goals for science education within the school day are to educate students who could increase their economic productivity through the use of knowledge, understanding and skills of the scientifically literate person in their careers" (1996, p. 13). Additional reasons for this push include greater attention to the STEM fields, evolving and expanding global networks, and an ever-increasing list of accountability mechanisms thrust upon schools and teachers (Marx and Harris 2006). Clearly, in order to pursue a career in a scientific field, children need knowledge and skills very different from those traditionally taught in elementary schools. Unfortunately, what occurs in elementary schools is the opposite of what the Standards advocate.

For instance, in many schools across the country, science fairs are held to showcase work completed by students. While science fairs differ in form and function, they generally highlight procedures students have followed to construct hypotheses and collect data to validate or refute the hypotheses. In most cases, science fairs are competitive events with prizes awarded to the most outstanding presentations. Interestingly, these experiences are quite unlike the daily lives of practicing scientists and do not provide students with the opportunities to develop the skills necessary for scientific literacy. In contrast to the children engaged in school science fairs, practicing scientists talk informally on a daily basis; they share their work at professional conferences, and they engage in noncompetitive conversations. Scientists present ideas that are in progress, give and receive feedback, and exchange information in order to move their work forward.

In order for teachers to prepare students to be scientifically literate, we need to rethink the ways we teach science in our schools. This chapter examines the ways we, as educators, engage students in scientific inquiry and the opportunities we provide to children for sharing their work with others. In doing so, we highlight ways that children can experience scientific knowledge, understandings, and skills that align more realistically with the work conducted by practicing scientists. In this way students are able to develop the skills necessary to be more productive in their careers while also inspiring more to try such careers.

We begin with an assessment of the current state of science teaching and learning in elementary schools. This is followed by an examination of our collaborative work with elementary teachers. We describe our approach to professional development in inquiry-based teaching and learning as well as the use of a Kids Inquiry Conference (Saul et al. 2005) as ways for students to engage in conversations similar to those of practicing scientists. We end with an examination of what we've learned about science teaching and learning by creating spaces for professional dialogue between university-based teacher educators and elementary school–based practitioners.

The State of Science in Elementary Schools

Walk into any elementary school and you will see abundant evidence of mathematics and reading instruction. Bulletin boards will usually hold essays, math problems, or other artifacts that represent a strong attention to mathematics and language instruction. Unfortunately, the same cannot be said for science. There are many reasons why science is less a focus in schools. We will describe some of these reasons as well as some of the frustrations teachers face as they attempt to implement quality science instruction in their classrooms. It is important to note that our descriptions of science teaching and learning may paint a picture of teachers as deficient when it comes to science instruction. We suggest, however, that it is not teachers who are deficient. In fact, in our experience we have found teachers to be incredibly capable of engaging in thoughtful scientific teaching and learning. Rather, due to lack of resources, the pressure from accountability mechanisms, or the absence of professional development opportunities, teachers find themselves struggling to implement quality science instruction. It is important to note that the lack of quality science instruction directly impacts the opportunities for elementary students to build the necessary foundational skills for achieving scientific literacy.

The following scenarios were developed using both the stories that teachers and preservice teachers told us as we engaged in professional development experiences with them and our own observations working as teachers, teacher educators, and researchers in elementary schools. While the scenarios are not all instructional, they do all speak to issues (pedagogical, logistical, and knowledge-based) that impact effective science instruction.

Scenario 1: Once-a-Week Science With the Expert

In this model, elementary classroom students may have science instruction once a week. The science is taught as a stand-alone "special area" where the special-area teacher typically focuses on "hands on" activities that are "cookbook" in nature. During most of these activities students are not asked to wonder, explore, "mess about" (Hawkins 1965), or work toward personal sense-making of the science. Rather, they are supplied with step-by-step procedures for activities with prescribed and predetermined results. During these experiences, students may be asked to memorize "the scientific method" and be erroneously asked to believe that scientists follow a lockstep process for problem solving. Most often, this type of instruction is not integrated into the overall curriculum and requires students to do little, if any, critical thinking or problem solving. The lack of real and personal inquiry makes this scenario incompatible with the reforms outlined by the National Research Council (NRC 1996, 2007).

Scenario 2: Meet Your Partner—Social Studies

Another common formula for determining when science instruction occurs is the sharing model that pairs science with another under-represented subject area (often social studies). In this scenario, science may be taught once or twice a week for a grading period (e.g., "first nine weeks") and then it is not taught at all the following grading period when the partner subject is taught. Not only does this scenario imply that neither science nor social studies is as important as reading and math; it also makes integration across the curriculum extremely difficult—if not impossible. When science is omitted from the curriculum, valuable opportunities for students to build scientific literacy skills are lost.

Scenario 3: Let's Read the Text

Reading, comprehending, and "mentally messing around" with nonfiction texts and resource materials are integral parts of strong science instruction. In fact, all subject areas rely on strong reading comprehension skills for personal "sense-making" and critical thinking. These are skills that are invaluable to students as they progress through middle school, high school, and college. They become vital as students graduate from college and enter the workforce.

In science, when resource materials are accessed as a way to help students make sense of relevant questions in which they are interested, the results can encourage dramatic learning and engagement and attract more interest in science careers. However, when science *is* taught in most elementary classrooms, the instruction—and use of critical reading material—is often teacher-driven and pedagogically ineffective. In many classrooms, science instruction starts with a vocabulary list of "key terms" which can be found in traditional textbooks often mandated by school district administrators. Students are expected, usually outside of any relevant context or personal curiosity, to memorize these terms. Following the memorization, students may be asked to engage in traditional activities that often have predetermined results. Usually, input from the students is an afterthought—if gathered at all; and, little, if any, time is spent generating questions or wondering about the science being taught.

Scenario 4: These Kids Can't Do Science

When schools and teachers adopt traditional behavior management systems, practitioners are often reluctant to offer student-driven activities. More often, teachers will work to maintain order in the classroom by controlling as much of the instruction as possible. Especially when schools are under pressure to raise test scores, environments are not typically conducive to rich learning experiences. To compound the situation, research shows that in classes where there are socioeconomic and linguistic disconnects between the teacher and the student population, strict behavior management systems tend to be more prevalent (Smith-Maddox and Solórzano 2002). Since the majority of elementary school teachers are White individuals from middle-class backgrounds (Zumwalt and Craig 2005), this translates to less efficacious science instruction for children of color and those living in poverty.

Why Might This Be the Case?

It is important to stress that the scenarios described above are not surprising given the traditional experiences of many elementary school teachers, fears related to teaching science (e.g., adequate content knowledge, sufficient resources, and sustained professional development). The failures are also noted with increased attention to accountability. In our experiences, preservice and inservice elementary teachers rarely identify science as their favorite subject to teach. Often for these teachers, their own science experiences have been unsatisfactory. These unsatisfactory experiences translate to teacher struggles in two main areas: science pedagogy and science content.

From a pedagogical perspective, science teaching reform initiatives over the past two decades have largely focused on an inquiry-based approach (Bybee 2010; NRC 1996, 2007). This pedagogical approach requires teachers to address several components that often make them uncomfortable. These include: a student-driven curriculum, open-ended questions, and overall flexibility in planning for and implementing instruction. Since this approach is not in line with the more traditional teacher-directed approach—where the teacher knows and chooses the activities, important vocabulary, and the curriculum structure before the students enter the classroom—teachers are often hesitant to embrace inquiry in any form. Teachers' discomfort with an inquiry-based approach can be connected to their own inexperience with both inquiry (Haefner and Zembal-Saul 2004) and issues connected to allowing students to make instructional decisions (Windschitl 2002).

In addition to the lack of experience with inquiry-based teaching, elementary grade teachers often feel underprepared with respect to their content knowledge of science (Buczynski and Hansen 2010). Like the issues around inquiry-based teaching, the dilemmas with content are complex. Simply requiring preservice teachers to "take more science" rarely results in the development of deep, complex scientific understanding; yet, this is often the mandate. Research in science education strongly supports an interactive curriculum that allows students time to develop and test ideas as they work toward personal meaning-making (NRC 2007). However, it has been well documented that high school and college science courses are typically taught from a teacher-directed perspective, which does not allow for the development of rich scientific understandings of science. Many preservice teacher preparation programs require several science courses, but these are usually at the 100 or 200 level and rarely provide the preservice teachers with time or resources to help them think critically about the science content.

Since the majority of elementary grade teachers have not been afforded the opportunity to develop a passion to learn science outside of school, the in-school experiences become even more critical. When these in-school experiences are unproductive, the future teachers are left underprepared. The disconnect becomes even more pronounced when we look at society's incorrect but simplistic view of elementary school teachers and the real meaning of doing science.

Clearly, the complicated process of teaching science using an inquiry approach requires teachers to understand complex science ideas and the ways in which students develop these ideas (Shulman 1986). Perhaps it means encouraging teachers to learn *with* their students. When teachers do not have access to quality science content—and the necessary pedagogy to guide children in scientific inquiry—the impact of science instruction decreases significantly. This affects students' ability to use science and scientific reasoning in their postschool life or to seek science and engineering careers.

Our Approach

Working with elementary teachers through a district-mandated professional development experience prompted us to develop a more collaborative approach where classroom teachers would be supported to develop experiences that supported students to engage in inquiry science. As we have described elsewhere (Magee and Flessner 2011) we see five main strategies that teachers can employ to facilitate authentic inquiry experiences in their classroom. These are:

1. Use "Thinking Starters."

2. Listen to Children's Ideas.

3. Use Standards as a Guide.

4. Develop Complex Questions.

5. Document and Reflect.

Use "Thinking Starters"

For teachers, it is often difficult to know where to start. We have had success with asking students to generate questions after they have engaged with interesting hands-on activities that have been purposefully selected. Knowing that inquiry is a long-term venture, students are most successful when teachers offer intriguing, contextually relevant tasks that lend themselves to real world connections and personal curiosity. One teacher with whom we worked used a homemade compost bin as a "thinking starter." The fourth grade students in her classroom were asked to observe and question. The compost bin (made in a small 9 in. × 6 in. × 2 in. plastic box) was left in the classroom, and students were encouraged to look at it during science time or any other time when they had a moment. This thinking starter generated many good questions and was a constant source of curiosity for the children. Additionally, many of the students had gardens at home and could make connections to that as well.

Another thinking starter a teacher used was paper airplanes. The teacher had a kit that she modified and used in an open and exploratory fashion. Instead of giving children a cookbook list of directions, her students were asked to design paper airplanes, make observations, and develop questions. From the observations and questions that the children supplied, the teacher was able to support the children's inquiry. Good thinking starters can be almost anything as long as the teacher maintains a focus on student ideas and questions and sees the thinking starter as a springboard for further exploration.

Listen to Children's Ideas

While it is tempting for teachers to plan ahead and make instructional decisions outside the presence of children, we have found that the most productive inquiries are built from children's own ideas. While these ideas may not always be—or perhaps only rarely the case—conceptually correct, they do represent the children's sense-making. Looking at these ideas as logical stepping stones in the learning process allows teachers to build from them instead of working to change them into something else (Driver and Easley 1978). For example, a first-grade teacher that we worked with led a discussion with her class about living and nonliving items. The children were discussing the question, "Is a rock living?" The children were divided into three different camps. The first group said that the rock was not living—it could not breathe or eat. The second group said that the rock was living since it could grow (there were clearly smaller rocks nearby). The third group was undecided and felt that there were good arguments from both the other groups. The teacher, instead of affirming that the first group was correct, honored all responses and asked the class how they might explore these ideas further. As a whole, the class devised an experiment to measure the rock, bury it, wait a specific amount of time and then remeasure it to see if it had grown. In addition to content, the teacher was teaching her students how to use evidence to check possible explanations. The teacher recognized that even though this method would take longer, the changes that her students would learn the content with efficacy in fact exemplified real learning. If she had not *listened* to the children, she would not have known what to do next.

Use Standards as a Guide

The teacher in the above story did use the Standards—as many teachers are required to do. While it is sometimes possible, teachers usually do not have the luxury to follow student suggestions for inquiry without some connection to state or national standards. However, connecting to the Standards does not mean that teachers need to abandon inquiry-based teaching or that students do not get the opportunity to learn in the same manner as scientists. In actuality, most scientists are hired to solve particular problems. Importantly, the ideas and decisions for how to *proceed* are often left up to the scientist, but the original problem or dilemma may be one that someone else has requested. We have found that teachers can use the Content Standards as a guide. When they intentionally choose strong thinking starters and listen to children's ideas, the Standards can be a strong framework instead of a constraint.

Develop Complex Questions

One of the things required for good science teaching is a thoughtfully complicated question. Rarely is a "good" question single-faceted. Rather, a series of related questions often emerge. These questions encourage children to dig deeper, make connections, and feel that the inquiry is relevant beyond the project at hand. Additionally, complex questions are rarely answered by finding answers online or in a textbook. In this way, they are much like the real questions that scientists pursue. Because the questions are complex, answering them requires critically thinking about information that is gathered and synthesized. Information is then seen as a way that is contextually relevant! We have found that these kinds of questions promote sustained inquiry where students are engaged for a longer period of time. In the compost bin experience, the students were able to formulate questions such as, "The soil looks darker, why?" It promoted all sorts of follow-up activities and readings.

Document and Reflect

Finally we have found that good science teaching requires documentation, documentation, and more documentation! When children engage in the documentation of their scientific inquiries, they reflect on what they have learned. Science journals provide students with an outlet to capture their thinking through writing or drawing; photography allows children to capture important details that allow for further careful observation at a later date. Responding to teacher prompts encourages children to focus their thinking and to communicate effectively with a specific audience. Each of these forms of documentation allows students to create trails of their thinking and learning that can be revisited throughout the inquiry process.

Sharing the Work—Have a Kids Inquiry Conference!

The teaching described above causes changes to the types of conversations that happen in elementary classrooms. In these classrooms, science becomes less about following a recipe and more about the real work of scientists. Because of this, educators need to engage in alternative ways—other than traditional science fairs—of showcasing the depth of their students' understanding. We have found that a Kids Inquiry Conference (KIC), as described by Saul at al. (2005), accomplishes this feat. Like conferences attended by those working in scientific fields, a KIC encourages children to develop inquiry questions, design projects to explore the answers to those questions, carry out inquiry-based projects, and share their knowledge publically. As university-based teacher educators, we have worked with many teachers in order to prepare for and present Kids Inquiry Conferences. The section that follows explores what we have learned about working collaboratively with teachers and students as we all worked to replace the image of a traditional science fair with that of a KIC.

Working Toward the Kids Inquiry Conference

First and foremost, we believe in trusting relationships that are built over time. In our roles as teacher educators, we have developed longstanding relationships with particular schools, individual teachers, and groups of students. These relationships have been solidified because everyone involved has been willing to commit time and energy to the relationship. This commitment to collaborate is essential to the success of a Kids Inquiry Conference.

As we began to envision the KIC, we worked with teachers to develop a yearlong professional development program that is related to inquiry-based teaching. We were fortunate in that several of the teachers with whom we worked had existing relationships with us from prior professional development work that we encouraged with the schools. This helped us delve deeply into identifying teacher strengths and their needs as we moved toward implementation of the KIC.

Knowing that the Kids Inquiry Conference was the culminating event helped all of us (teachers as well as teacher educators) sign on for a long-term professional development project. With a lofty goal in mind, we all understood the magnitude of the commitment. This also energized us as we set forth with the planning process.

The professional development program that we designed allowed all members of the collaboration to learn from one another. While university-based faculty members are often seen as the experts in relationships like the ones we are describing, we were quick to point out that we were learning just as much from the teachers and the students as they were learning from us. While we have had time to engage in in-depth study of inquiry-based teaching, we are not full-time teachers responsible for a classroom full of children and a host of curricular areas to address. Though we both have teaching experiences, we needed the teachers to remind us of the realities of the classroom, what was manageable, and how to progress in our work together.

To begin our work together, teachers expressed their interests and their needs. The teachers had different understandings of inquiry-based teaching as well as different comfort levels with this type of teaching and learning. Teachers had different expertise with science content, and they differed greatly in the amount of science they actually taught in their classrooms. These differences provided us with a great variety of challenges but also allowed us to structure conversations so teachers who were more comfortable and confident with inquiry-based teaching to share their expertise with those who were less familiar with these ideas. This allowed us to learn about implementation and feasibility from teacher experts, and it allowed other teachers to see their peers in leadership roles.

Teachers met with one of us every two to three weeks. The frequency of these meetings allowed teachers to try new ideas and gradually become more comfortable with the ideas and philosophies behind inquiry-based teaching. We offered support through e-mail and phone conversations; we co-taught lessons with teachers who expressed a need or interest; and we provided resources (books, materials) that teachers requested throughout the process. Because all of us had committed to participating in the Kids Inquiry Conference, we were all able to listen to children and co-construct thoughtful learning experiences that would facilitate the types of conversations, learning, and interactions that are necessary for encouraging careers in scientific fields.

Inquiry-Based Teaching Comes Alive

Because of the teachers' willingness to step outside of their comfort zones, amazing things began to occur. In this section we highlight several of the ways that inquiry-based teaching was manifested in the classrooms of the teachers with whom we worked. We hope that these vignettes allow the reader to understand the many different forms that inquiry-based learning can take and how the experiences support elementary students to envision a career as a scientist.

In one classroom where we worked, one teacher, Leslie*, allowed her children to explore any question that interested them. Students were asked to create a list of questions that were intriguing to them. After the class generated their list of questions, some students decided to work together in groups where there were common interests. Others chose to engage in individual research projects. One student seized the opportunity to explore questions that had arisen in her personal life. This child had been experiencing difficulty relating to a grandparent with Alzheimer's disease. Because the student was personally invested in the study of this disease, she saw purpose in her work, researched diligently, and went far beyond any assignment she would have been required to complete in a traditional classroom. Because of her inquiry, the child was able to ask specific questions based on her experiences interacting with her grandparent. Her diligence in her research allowed her to further interact with her relatives, ask new questions, and dig deeper to understand the struggles that those with Alzheimer's face. This example is a remarkable instance of a teacher facilitating academic growth by allowing students to make connections to their lives inside and outside of school. Often students actually learned more from other students—encouraging further input from them as well as in their own lives. The teacher and the student were also engaged in discussions about the scientists who work in laboratories and hospitals to learn more about diseases like Alzheimer's. According to the teacher "Jesse was so excited to consider that she might be able one day to work in a lab that cured diseases like Alzheimer's. The KIC project supported her seeing herself as a scientist."

Another teacher, Kathy, was able to use inquiry-based teaching to address State Standards in the area of science. Rather than beginning with the Standards and creating lessons that were disconnected from her students' lives and experiences, the teacher began by listening to her students. She realized that her students had an interest in worms. By engaging them in thoughtful dialogue, listening to their ideas, and *then* connecting these ideas to State Standards, the teacher was able to create a robust unit on "interconnectedness." In doing so, she was able to facilitate student learning as they answered questions such as, "How does the anatomy of a worm affect soil?" and "How are other animals living in the soil impacted by worms?" Student ideas were honored, standards were addressed, and inquiry-based teaching was validated as a way to build connections between the real world and academic content.

In one final example, Mary, a teacher in a kindergarten/first-grade multiage classroom, listened to her children's ideas surrounding the concept of recycling. As she listened, she began to wonder if students were confusing the concept of "reusing" with the concept of "recycling." Because of the discussions they were having, the teacher decided to introduce the concept of "reusing" in a class meeting. As the children engaged in conversation with the teacher, they identified times when objects should be recycled and when they could be reused. For example, the students quickly realized that objects such as cardboard boxes could be reused to create dollhouses for the play area or game boards for the math games which they were creating. In this classroom, deliberate conversations led young children to become aware of how waste was

---

* Teachers' and students' names have been changed throughout this chapter in order to ensure confidentiality.

managed in their classroom on a daily basis. These conversations linked to larger conversations in the school community about sustainability and showed that young children can understand complex topics that have an immediate impact on their lives and the world.

Alerting Teachers and Students to Conference Basics

From the beginning of our collaborations, we—along with the teachers—were clear with the students about the Kids Inquiry Conference and their role in the KIC. Initial conversations always lead children to ask about where the conference would be held and whether or not they would have to present in front of a "big group of people." Students become excited when they realize that they will be presenting on a university campus or that a group of students from another school will come to their building to engage in the Kids Inquiry Conference. They also relax their shoulders and begin to breathe more slowly when they realize they will not have to present in front of a huge group of adults! However, they also understand the importance of clearly documenting their learning in an effort to communicate effectively with their audience. In the classrooms where we worked, students and teachers together documented the process of inquiry-based learning. This was done through the use of science journals, research logs, photography, and posters that documented the learning that occurred in the room. Documentation helped students communicate their understanding to others; it also deepened their own understanding of their investigations. Rather than creating a typical science fair project (where a topic is chosen, a hypothesis is made, and students spend their time collecting data to support or refute the hypothesis), the Kids Inquiry Conference format allowed students to document their understanding of their work in progress and further their own questions. In this way, children developed presentations for the KIC that focused on continually challenging working explanations, engaging in dialogue with others, and asking new questions. We and the teachers also reminded the students that "real scientists" work in very similar ways. Since one of us (Paula Magee) had been a practicing research chemist, we were able to answer questions about what it was like to be a scientist working in the lab. The elementary students were extremely interested in those perspectives. We interpreted this as the development of a growing interest in science careers.

Preparing for the KIC

A few weeks prior to the Kids Inquiry Conference, teachers began to engage children in a discussion about how they would share their work. Most of the groups decided that they would use display boards to showcase their learning. One teacher asked children to work with her to create a list of items that should be on each child's or group's board. These items included:

1. a title for the project

2. "Big Questions" linked to photographs, illustrations, or other representations designed by the students

3. a clear timeline of the daily work from the start of the project

4. research and findings from books, the internet, and other sources

5. discoveries and observations from students' own personal activities

6. further questions that arose throughout the inquiry process

7. a final question to guide further inquiry

As students practiced their presentations for the big day, they were able to use these posters as visual aids and as a way to organize what they wanted to say to their audiences. Because few students had experience systematically documenting their learning or presenting that learning to others, the boards became a tool to organize their thinking in a way that facilitated communication with an audience.

Presenting the KIC

Kids Inquiry Conferences are where children have opportunities to engage with an audience but also with each other. Because of this, we deliberately structured times where teachers, university faculty, students, parents, and other visitors could interact. Regardless of the setting of the conference, the conferences we have helped to organize have always been kicked off with a gathering of everyone involved. These "opening ceremonies" allowed everyone to see the large numbers of people involved and interested in the work. In addition, this initial meeting allowed those leading the conference to explain how a Kids Inquiry Conference differs from a traditional science fair. At this meeting, the schedule of the day was reviewed. It is important to note that prior to this meeting, we recruited volunteers (teachers, preservice teachers from our university courses, parents) who understood the flow of the day, directed traffic, and answered questions throughout the conference. These volunteers are essential to a successful conference. And their value cannot be overstated.

After the opening meeting, students headed to different rooms (assigned prior to the start of the day). In each room, groups of students from different schools gathered to present their work. We purposely integrated children from similar grade levels but from different schools to encourage dialogue between and across schools. In these rooms, tables and chairs were available for children to use in setting up their displays.

Three 15-minute rotations were scheduled for students to present their work. Groups took turns presenting their projects to the other students in their room. Other visitors circulated amongst the rooms as children presented. During these presentations, children knew that their objective was to share, and listen to, understanding that was gained throughout the inquiry process. Students developed an appreciation for the work that scientists do and recognized that being a scientist required excellent communication skills. This was evidenced by students saying things such as "scientists do so many things" and "I like being a scientist!"

After the third rotation, a large-group discussion ensued. Chairs were gathered in the middle of the room and a circle was formed. An adult facilitator in each room engaged children in a discussion of what they had learned. Children noted ideas that intrigued them, questions that were left unanswered, and ways that others had helped them think about extensions for their work. Preservice teachers from the university were asked to prepare questions prior to this discussion if, in rare instances, children had nothing they wanted to discuss. In addition, these college students acted as time keepers to ensure that the discussion did not exceed the scheduled minutes.

After the discussion circles, students rotated through the other rooms of the Kids Inquiry Conference. Children took turns rotating to see the projects of their friends, their siblings, and students from other schools. Again, specific times were scheduled for group presentations, and other times were scheduled for each group to rotate through other rooms. With this schedule in place, students had the opportunity to engage with children outside of their assigned room, but movement among several rooms was organized and manageable.

What We Learned

Experience and Continuity Matter

Make a Kids Inquiry Conference an annual event and a way of teaching science. As we write this chapter, we have completed two Kids Inquiry Conferences. There is no doubt that participating in KICs has been extremely helpful for the teachers. We saw teachers willing to try different things and allowing kids to behave in ways that were much more congruent with the real work that scientists do.

For example, Stacey, an experienced fourth-grade teacher, participated in both conferences. During the first KIC, she was very attentive to "staying with the standards" and needing to control the choices that the students made. During our pre-KIC meetings she often expressed worry that the students might not be learning or that they would be out of control, behaviorally. After the first conference we met and she shared her thoughts on the children's learning, saying, "I cannot believe how much they learned. They didn't just memorize answers, but they actually *knew* the information about composting [the topic under investigation]. I know that they will retain this information and understand it with great depth." She also expressed great relief that, for the most part, the students remained on task and engaged. This original experience set the groundwork for Stacey to push herself and the students further during the second year of the project.

During the months leading up to the second conference, Stacey was much more willing to let her students make decisions about the project, this time concerning the concepts of force and motion. The students designed race cars and Stacey said, "I want them [the students] to make all the choices in the design. I know that the more they can make these choices the more they will learn." This narrative reminds us of two important things. First, the original experience gave the teachers an authentic opportunity to "mess around" with inquiry-based teaching and a student-directed curriculum. Teachers, like students, learn through the process of *doing and sense-making*. The original KIC and the professional conversations that led up to it supported the teachers to think about and challenge notions of teaching that they had. Second, knowing that a second KIC was going to definitely occur opened the space for teachers to go a little further with respect to student decision-making. During the second year the teachers were able to concentrate more on the inquiry itself since they already knew what to expect of the conference. Making a commitment to an annual event instead of a one-time shot increases the potential for meaningful experiences tremendously. At the time of this writing, we are preparing for our third KIC, and we are hoping to increase the number of participating teachers at the school from 6 to 12.

Inquiry-Based Teaching Encourages Student Independence

My students thrived with the hands-on and minds-on work of the flight investigations. They loved experimenting and making the paper airplanes. I could tell how much they learned about how and why planes fly. One student even told me that he wants to be an "airplane scientist."

—Kelly, fourth-grade teacher

In addition to being productive for teachers, the KIC and inquiry-based teaching are extremely beneficial for the students. The experience of preparing for and participating in a KIC encourages students to behave and think like practicing scientists. While they are working on their projects, students are generating questions, preparing "working explanations," and devising ways to make sense of their ideas. This sense-making includes setting up experimental activities, reading the work of experts, and thinking hard about what it all means. Students, like scientists, create opportunities for using evidence-based thinking in a real-world context.

Unlike a process-skills approach, where students might learn academic skills in isolation, the KIC supports students' work from the outside in—look at a problem, question, or curiosity and use scientific thinking to better understand it. This is the way that practicing scientists approach their work, and an inquiry-based approach supports elementary students to do the same. When students have opportunities to see themselves as capable learners and understand that science is not about memorizing answers but making sense of things using evidence and ingenuity, then we can expect students to develop the kind of scientific thinking skills that are in alignment with the National Research Council's (1996, 2007) Standards and the work of practicing scientists. This experience helps students develop self-efficacy that can lead to pursuing science careers. The KIC resulted in many student ideas about being a scientist; one of the major outcomes was more elementary school students liking the idea of being a practicing scientist!

References

Buczynski, S., and C. B. Hansen. 2010. Impact of professional development on teacher practice: Uncovering connections. *Teaching and Teacher Education* 26: 599–607.

Bybee, R. W. 2010. *The teaching of science: 21st century perspectives.* Arlington, VA: NSTA Press.

Driver, R., and J. Easley. 1978. Pupils and paradigms: A review of literature related to concept development in adolescent science students. *Studies in Science Education* 5: 61–84.

Haefner, L. A., and C. Zembal-Saul. 2004. Learning by doing? Prospective elementary teachers' developing understanding of scientific inquiry and science teaching and learning. *International Journal of Science Education* 26 (13): 1653–1674.

Hawkins, D. 1965. Messing about in science. *Science & Children* 2 (5): 5–9.

Magee, P. A., and R. Flessner. 2011. Five strategies to support all teachers: Suggestions for getting off the slippery slope of "cookbook" science teaching. *Science & Children* 48 (7): 34–36.

Marx, R. W., and C. J. Harris. 2006. No Child Left Behind and science education: Opportunities, challenges, and risks. *The Elementary School Journal* 106 (5): 467–478.

National Research Council (NRC). 1996. *National Science Education Standards.* Washington, DC: National Academies Press.

National Research Council (NRC). 2007. *Taking science to school: Learning and teaching science in grades K–8.* Washington, DC: National Academies Press.

Saul, W., D. Dieckman, C. Pearce, and D. Neutze. 2005. *Beyond the science fair: Creating a kids' inquiry conference.* Portsmouth, NH: Heinemann.

Shulman, L. 1986. Those who understand: Knowledge growth in teaching. *Educational Researcher* 15 (2): 4–14.

Smith-Maddox, R., and D. G. Solórzano. 2002. Using critical race theory, Paulo Freire's problem-posing method, and case study research to confront race and racism in education. *Qualitative Inquiry* 8 (1): 66–84.

Windschitl, M. 2002. Framing constructivism in practice as the negotiation of dilemmas: An analysis of the conceptual, pedagogical, cultural, and political challenges facing teachers. *Review of Educational Research* 72 (2): 131–175.

Zumwalt, K., and E. Craig. 2005. Teachers' characteristics: Research on the indicators of quality. In *Studying teacher education: The report of the AERA panel on research and teacher education,* ed. M. Cochran-Smith, and K. M. Zeichner, 111–156. Mahwah, NJ: Lawrence Erlbaum Associates.

NSTA's Efforts to Interest More K–12 Students in Pursuing STEM Careers

Alan J. McCormack
Past-President, NSTA

Francis Q. Eberle
Former Executive Director, NSTA

Setting

The National Science Teachers Association (NSTA) has inspired and coordinated science education in the United States for 64 years. As the largest professional organization in the world supporting excellence and innovation in science teaching and learning, NSTA is increasingly seen as the advisor to the nation on critical issues of importance related to science education.

In the past 15 years, many significant reports have identified and called for improving science education, with suggested solutions focusing on the state of science teaching. NSTA is uniquely positioned with the John Glenn Center for Science Education to address these national issues by leveraging its membership and encouraging use of current research and cutting-edge technologies. As the leading organization in science teaching, NSTA is positioned to fulfill this role of an expanded focus on science teaching as no government or quasigovernmental organization can do in our nation's capital.

Overview

The future appears bright for those who choose a career in the fields of science, technology, engineering, and mathematics (STEM). This is true for hundreds of different careers, in America and around the globe. We live in a technology-dominated world. Think of the impact of personal computers, the internet, smart phones, new medical developments, advances in forensic science, and space exploration: The list of STEM advances is exceedingly long! And, these changes affect each of us, everyday.

Not too long ago there was a prevalent stereotype of the "geek" scientist: an unkempt, spectacled, aging white man in a wrinkled white lab coat living a dull life in a cluttered laboratory. This image is rapidly being replaced by active, "with it," excited career devotees who are thrilled to explore the multitudinous dimensions of the natural universe. Some explore the stars, some the deep oceans, others the unseen worlds of microorganisms or atoms. Theirs is a world that is curiosity-driven, provoked by natural mysteries, and providing occasional great satisfaction as investigated problems are resolved. STEM careers can also provide a nice income, recognition from peers, and a wealth of highly interesting life experiences. It's also a common misconception that STEM explorers are loners (and somehow a little "weird"); most work in cooperative teams and enjoy quite normal social lives. Some even reach celebrity status—Carl Sagan, Stephen Hawking, or Albert Einstein.

Scientists and engineers make the breakthroughs that give America its competitive edge. Their careers require creativity, perseverance, and ingenuity. New technological and scientific breakthroughs will always be needed; there is no endpoint to science or historical place where it will become obsolete. STEM careers can be productive, enjoyable, intriguing—even glamorous.

Why Become a STEM Professional?

For those with curious personalities, a creative and problem-solving view of the world, and other scientific inclinations, a STEM career can be the best in the world. STEM specialists get to do what they truly enjoy, and at the same time contribute to the betterment of life for everyone.

Scientists, engineers, inventors, and mathematicians tend to be admired by society and can enjoy the accomplishment of discovering or inventing new ideas, while accomplishing a decent level of learning.

The U.S. Department of Commerce produced a recent study, *STEM: Good Jobs Now and for the Future*, providing evidence that STEM workers play a key role in economic growth and stability. Results of the study are encouraging:

- STEM occupations are projected to grow by 17% from 2008 to 2018, compared to 9.8% growth for non-STEM occupations.
- STEM workers command higher wages, earning 26% more than their non-STEM counterparts.
- More than two-thirds of STEM workers have at least a college degree, compared to less than one-third of non-STEM workers.
- STEM degree holders enjoy higher earnings regardless of whether they work in STEM or non-STEM occupations.

STEM careerists drive our nation's competiveness by generating and implementing new ideas, creating new products, and building new industries. Stem careers are the careers of the future. These professionals have the satisfaction of knowing their work helps other people. They discover new medicines, create new mechanical devices, and make breakthroughs in electronics that literally change the world. STEM professionals might work in a laboratory, genetically engineering bacteria to produce new antibiotics. Or they might work with an oil company, analyzing deep geologic rock strata. Perhaps the work takes place in a deep sea submersible, looking for new species of marine animals. There is an endless spectrum of career possibilities. Following is only part of the career spectrum:

Life Science Careers: Life scientists study living organisms. This division includes biology, botany, anatomy, physiology, agricultural science, and zoology.

Agricultural and Food Scientists
Conservation Scientists
Environmental Engineers
Botanists
Medical Scientists
Medical Doctors
Microbiologists
Molecular Biologists
Veterinarians
Ornithologists

Nurses
Entomologists
Marine Biologists
Biology Teachers or Professors
Biological Technicians
Laboratory Technicians
Neuroscientists
Geneticists
Zoologists
Fisheries Biologists

Physical Science Careers: Physical scientists study chemistry, physics, and astronomy. Scientists in these fields explore the atom, magnetic forces, all forms of energy, and stars and planets—all the nonliving parts of our universe.

Astronomers
Chemists
Biochemists
Geologists
Nuclear Physicists
Oceanographers
Archeologists
Physics Teachers or Professors

Planetarium Directors
Atmospheric Scientists
Meteorologists
Geophysicists
Space Scientists
Forensic Scientists
Physicists
Chemistry Teachers or Professors

Engineering: Engineers study scientific principles and put them to practical use. There are many engineering disciplines, including electrical, mechanical, aerospace, computer, and civil.

Aerospace Engineers
Agricultural Engineers
Geological Engineers
Biomedical Engineers
Chemical Engineers
Civil Engineers
Electrical and Electronic Engineers
Environmental Engineers
Marine Engineers
Engineering Teachers or Professors

Materials Engineers
Mining Engineers
Metallurgical Engineers
Mechanical Engineers
Nuclear Engineers
Petroleum Engineers
Engineering Technicians
Industrial Engineers
Surveyors

Computer and Mathematics Careers: Computer scientists design computer systems and software. Mathematicians design and apply statistical and mathematical operations for data analysis and engineering procedures.

Computer Scientists	Computer Programmers
Network Systems Analysts	Mathematicians
Computer Software Engineers	Computer Support Specialists
Operations Research Analysts	Statisticians
Database Administrators	Network Administrators
Mathematics Teachers or Professors	

How Can Students Be Enticed Into STEM Careers? Influences of NSTA

Students are most likely to become interested in entering STEM careers if they are exposed to exciting, dynamic school programs in science, technology, engineering, and mathematics. NSTA and many other professional organizations (AAAS, NSF, BSCS, NABT, ACS, APT) are actively involved in helping build great STEM curricula for schools and professional development for science teachers. Because our experience is with NSTA, we will limit our discussion to the contributions of that organization and how it can help influence students become interested in STEM careers.

The National Science Teachers Association, founded in 1944 and headquartered in Arlington, Virginia, is the largest organization in the world committed to promoting excellence and innovation in science teaching and learning for all. NSTA's current membership of more than 60,000 includes science teachers, science supervisors, administrators, scientists, business and industry representatives, and others involved in and committed to science education. The organization publishes four peer-reviewed member journals:

- *Science and Children,* for elementary school teachers
- *Science Scope*, for middle school teachers
- *The Science Teacher*, for high school teachers
- *Journal of College Science Teaching*, for professors of science at the college level.

NSTA also conducts a well-rounded publishing program to allow science teachers to share ideas with thousands of others who teach science. The content reflects the needs of its audience of classroom teachers, science supervisors and administrators, teacher educators, and parents. NSTA Press publishes 25 professional books each year, providing both scientific and pedagogical updating for teachers of science at all levels, from preK to college. One of the many benefits of the NSTA journals and books is that exciting science activities, the latest scientific information, and great teaching methodology become part of school science programs throughout the nation—thus capturing the interest of students who may aspire to STEM careers.

NSTA Conferences on Science Education

NSTA organizes multiple conferences for science educators each academic year. These conferences provide the latest in science content, teaching strategy, and research to enhance and expand teachers' professional growth.

NSTA conferences are jam-packed with innovative presentations and hands-on workshops as well as special invited speakers, educational field trips, short courses, NSTA symposia (which provide online follow-up after the conference), and exciting social events. The exhibition of science education materials is the largest of its kind and an invaluable source of curriculum and other products.

As an important addition to the national conference agenda, NSTA presents Professional Development Institutes—focused, content-based, partnered programs that explore key topics in significant depth. These daylong programs offer participants a unique learning opportunity that includes a personalized pathway through the full conference agenda. NSTA national conferences may also feature one-day topical research dissemination conferences on focused topics. In plenary sessions and multiple small-group workshops, speakers present findings from their NSF-funded research.

The NSTA Learning Center for Science Teachers

The Learning Center is NSTA's electronic professional development portal to help teachers meet their personal needs for learning science topics and finding innovative science lessons. The Center provides more than 6,500 different resources that cater to personal preferences for learning. Over 2,000 resources, such as journal articles, science objects, podcasts, and web seminars are available for free. Other resources include SciPacks, SciGuides, and Short Courses. All of these resources are highly useful for teachers in making science successful and enjoyable for students, thus directly making science appealing to students as a future career.

NSTA Awards

NSTA offers a number of awards to both teachers and students, intended to recognize accomplishments and entice students to consider STEM careers. Here are descriptions of just some of the relevant STEM-career influencing awards:

Angela Award

This award honors one female student in grades 5–8 who is involved in or has a strong connection to science. The award has been established in honor of Gerry Wheeler, Executive Director Emeritus, for his outstanding dedication to NSTA and lifelong commitment to science education.

The annual awardee is a female resident of the United States, U.S. Territories, or Canada, and is enrolled in full-time public, private, or home school. The winning student is judged on academic success in science and potential for future success in a STEM university major and a lifelong STEM career. The winner receives a $1,000 U.S. Savings Bond or Canadian Savings Bond, and is honored at the Teacher Awards Banquet at NSTA's national conference.

Informal Science Education Awards

Science education doesn't just happen in the classroom. It happens in museums, in magazines, on the web—even on TV. Since 2003, when the Discovery Channel teamed with NSTA to create the annual Faraday Science Communicator Award, NSTA has honored individuals who are not classroom teachers but who work in or have developed a compatible setting for science communication—e.g., museum, nature center, zoo, state park, aquarium, radio, television, internet, and other science-rich institutions or media.

NSTA administers two other award programs of interest to those engaged in informal science education. The Distinguished Informal Science Education Award honors NSTA members who are not classroom teachers and who have demonstrated their dedication to informal science education. And since 1993, the Anheuser-Busch Distinguished Service Award has recognized the outstanding efforts of K–12 students and teachers across the country working at the grassroots level to protect and preserve the environment. One teacher wins $5,000, an all-expenses-paid trip for two to a SeaWorld or Busch Gardens park for a special awards event, and an all-expenses-paid trip to the NSTA National Conference on Science Education.

Toyota Tapestry

Toyota TAPESTRY Awards recognizes outstanding science educators who are making a difference by demonstrating excellence and creativity in science teaching. Since 1991 the program has awarded more than $9.2 million to 1,147 teams of teachers for innovative science classroom projects. Thanks to these teachers' tireless efforts to improve their skills and increase their effectiveness, students nationwide are gaining a better understanding of science principles and methodologies. Toyota and NSTA sincerely hope these grants continue to inspire teachers and serve as a catalyst for lifetime science learning.

A partnership between Toyota Motor Sales, U.S.A., Inc. and NSTA, the Toyota TAPESTRY Grants for Science Teachers program offers grants to K–12 science teachers for innovative projects that enhance science education in the school and school district. Fifty grants totaling $500,000 are awarded each year.

Toshiba ExploraVision

The Toshiba/NSTA ExploraVision competition has been sponsored by Toshiba for 20 years. It is managed by NSTA as an enjoyable science competition that encourages students to work in groups of 2–4 within their grade range (K–3, 4–6, 7–9, and 10–12). Students are asked to identify a technology today and then imagine what science and technology might be like 20 years in the future that could solve a problem. They have to track and explain the history of the technology to illustrate how it came to be as it is today. They do this as background for their explanation of what scientific or technological advances need to occur for the vision of their solution to be viable in 20 years. This is all a part of the written aspect of the competition.

Students are required to provide additional information about their project. This includes possible societal impacts of their proposed idea. They must also provide any possible positive and negative impacts of their idea. They need to include a record of their brainstorming and design process to help judges determine if they have considered alternative designs for their idea. This might include fuel types such as electricity from the grid, solar-generated power, or even portable sources such as from batteries. The list of alternative design features clarifies the thinking processes of students as they developed their idea.

About 20,000 student applications are completed and submitted annually. Each year a total of about $200,000 is awarded to the regional and the national winners. From water fountains to hearing aids to nanotubes, school teams choose a technology that is relevant to the world today and then explore what it does; how it works; and how, when, and why it was invented. Then they imagine their chosen technology 20 years from now and prepare an in-depth report that conveys their vision to others. ExploraVision is a hands-on, minds-on project that simulates real research and development to inspire students and fuel imagination. The ExploraVision program has awarded $4,440,000 to more than 287,000 participants since its inception in 1992; up to $240,000 in savings bonds and Toshiba products are awarded each year. As a direct result of participation in the competition, many of the Toshiba/NSTA Exploravision competitors have chosen STEM-related university majors and careers. Let's hear stories from three competitors:

Story One

Anand Sarwate and two of his classmates won first place in the grades 10–12 category of the 1997 Toshiba/NSTA ExploraVision competition. The project, *The Artificial Vision Restoration System (AVReS)—Eye of the Future*, articulated a vision for a fully integrated artificial seeing device based on a combination of biotechnologies and signal-processing hardware. The proposed highly advanced prosthetic eye incorporated smart hydrogels, amorphous silicon photoreceptors, tissue scaffolding, and advanced signal processing chip technologies to mimic and replace the entire eye structure from the cornea to the optic nerve.

Sarwate seemed to have had an affinity toward science from an early age. Participating in ExploraVision not only helped to further solidify his interest in pursuing STEM education and a related career; it helped him to endure and succeed in his post-ExploraVision scientific endeavors. Sarwate acknowledges that he learned a great deal about science and technology from his ExploraVision project; he learned how to think big and stretch his imagination to envision a world of endless possibilities with science and technology from gene therapies and cholesterol treatments to miniscule sensors, monitors, and microphones, to reengineering our roads and highways. Most importantly, ExploraVision taught him that communication and collaboration are key and two of the most valuable skills for a scientist. Sarwate explained:

> ExploraVision taught me to communicate and collaborate. I had to communicate and collaborate with all kinds of people: my teammates, our ExploraVision coach, the experts we consulted, and the broader community. When I went to the Massachusetts Institute of Technology, these skills were invaluable in the projects I worked on in radar imaging, building robots, diagnosing cancer, and even teaching a computer to listen to music. All involved teamwork and presenting our discoveries and projections for the future both internally and to the outside world. It was the same kind of experience I had with ExploraVision and that boosted my confidence and ability to communicate effectively, realize the value in and importance of collaborating, and succeed in postsecondary STEM education. The same

has been true of my graduate work at Berkeley and my current postdoctoral work at the University of California in San Diego.

Sarwate credits his high school teacher, David Stone, for introducing him to ExploraVision. Stone still encourages his students to participate in ExploraVision today. Stone said, "For the past fifteen years, I have used the Toshiba/NSTA ExploraVision collaboration model in structuring our school's Extracurricular Research and Development Teams. The ExploraVision model encourages my students to take ownership in knowledge they've acquired and collaboratively apply that knowledge, combined with their creativity, to solve real-world problems."

Story Two

Dr. Arthur Desrosiers III won first place in the grades 10–12 category of the 1994 Toshiba/ NSTA ExploraVision competition before going on to pursue an M.D. and postgraduate work in general surgery, craniofacial plastic surgery, and plastic and reconstructive surgery. Desrosiers and his ExploraVision teammates tackled a problem that was close to home for them—how to build a tunnel connecting Cape Cod to the Massachusetts mainland. After brainstorming many possibilities, they devised a concept for a futuristic Laser Tunneling Machine (LTM).

Desrosiers remarks that even though a lot has changed since his ExploraVision days 17 years ago, the basic tenets of what Exploravision is about remain the same. Its winning ingredients, he says, include problem solving, creative thinking, teamwork, and communication. Desrosiers elaborates:

> From my own personal experience, I can offer this: ExploraVision participants are thinkers and doers. The program encourages young people to look at the world around them, find a problem they think should be addressed, and work as a team to analyze what had been done successfully and what needs improvement. In the process, students consider a myriad of possibilities using a creative approach and technology to develop an innovative solution and making a contribution to existing knowledge and the world's reliance in our ability to improve the quality of human life. Students are challenged in the process and open up opportunities for themselves and others. The unique aspect of ExploraVision—merging scientific thought to problem-solving and allowing the creative expression of ideas—is really analogous to how ExploraVision impacted my life, and has led me to be where I am today.

> I used my $10,000 ExploraVision award to pay for college. I wanted to research the human system and look at breakthroughs that could be used in the field of medicine. After starting medical school, I decided that I wanted to be a surgeon so I could learn the art and science of healing the human body. Now that I have focused my career on plastic surgery, I use the same problem-solving skills and creativity that I used with ExploraVision.

Desrosiers is faced every day with a new patient that has a unique problem, whether it is reconstruction after breast cancer or fixing a patient's face after trauma from a car accident, but skills nurtured through ExploraVision long before Desrosiers became a surgeon are commonly used in his daily work, he says:

I am using my problem-solving skills and creative thinking to devise a solution. Plastic surgeons actually have been innovators for decades. The recent face transplants emphasize that surgery can return psychological health and heal a person; in this fashion doctors use technology in a creative way to improve the quality of human life. The career path that I have chosen has definitely been influenced by ExploraVision.

Story Three

Dr. Eleanor Ross entered a student competition in science and technology in eighth grade and never looked back. In her own words:

> My experience with ExploraVision inspired me to remain curious and think critically about the world. It led to my interest in scientific research, from my simple project examining plant growth in high school, to my current study looking at predictors of surgical outcomes in infants with tetralogy of Fallot, a form of congenital heart disease.

Dr. Ross recalls an instance when one of her infant patients developed a dangerous abnormal heart rhythm:

> After being alerted of the problem by the patient's heart monitor, a team of physicians and nurses assembled and quickly worked together to put in a breathing tube, set up a special pacemaker, and give medications to help normalize the patient's heartbeat. Thanks to many innovative people—physicians, scientists, bioengineers—we had all of the technology available to help save this baby's life. I take time to appreciate the medical innovation that now allows infants and children born with heart problems to live longer, better lives. We also had the skill set to work together as a team to save the baby's life—a skill I developed as a young ExploraVision participant.

In her daily work today, Dr. Ross recognizes that there were additional skills learned through ExploraVision, including brainstorming ideas, developing action plans, and helping people. How is it that completing a competition had such a long-term impact leading Dr. Ross to pursue a STEM career more than a decade after her experience in the competition? Answering this question is not simple. There is little longitudinal data about K–12 student career decision making related to their learning or experiences in STEM. Most information is anecdotal and from individuals who have had some sort of defining moment. It may be more likely that there are many "defining" moments, but it is not clear. Trying to learn about and replicate these moments should be the goal of science educators. Because understanding them is so difficult and the data so slim we revert to what information we have.

Science and Engineering Festivals

A recent national trend—Science and Engineering Festivals—is likely to have profound effects in guiding students into scientific careers. The "granddaddy" of these was the USA Science and Engineering Festival held in Washington, D.C. and deemed the nation's first *national* science festival. This inaugural event was held from October 10, 2010, through October 24, 2010, and culminated with a two-day Expo on the National Mall that gave U.S. science and engineering organizations the opportunity to present interactive hands-on science activities with the goal of engaging the general public and generating scientific excitement and awareness. Over 550 organizations, including NSTA, partnered with the inaugural USA Science and Engineering Festival, with support from 125 universities and research institutes, 125 professional science societies, 50 government agencies, 30 high-tech and life science companies, and 150 informal science outreach organizations. The second USA Festival was held at the Washington, D.C. Convention Center in April, 2012. Other Science and Engineering Festivals are being planned for many larger cities across the United States.

Science Fairs

NSTA is a strong supporter of science fairs at all levels: individual school, district, state, national, and international. Science fairs challenge students to design an experiment, test a hypothesis, and present their results via a display board and oral presentation before judges. Winning projects can move up the line from local to regional to national and even international competitions. Research over many years indicates that science fairs have influenced science career choices by innumerable students.

The Intel International Science and Engineering Fair (Intel ISEF), the world's largest international precollege science competition, annually provides a forum for more than 1,500 high school students from over 65 countries, regions, and territories to showcase their independent research. There also is Siemens Competition and the new Goggle International Science Fair. NSTA has been supportive of all these events. The Intel ISEF is the premiere science competition in the world, exclusively for students in grades 9–12. It has grown from the National Science Fair, which was created by Society for Science and the Public in 1950. In 1958, the fair became international for the first time when Japan, Canada, and Germany joined the competition.

Today, millions of students worldwide compete each year in local and school-sponsored science fairs; the winners of these events go on to participate in Intel ISEF-affiliated regional and state fairs from which the best win the opportunity to attend the Intel ISEF. The Intel ISEF unites these top young scientific minds, showcasing their talent on an international stage, enabling them to submit their work to judging by doctoral-level scientists—and providing the opportunity to compete for over $4 million in prizes and scholarships.

Bring a Scientist or Engineer to Your School Program (National Lab Network)

Engaging and developmentally appropriate laboratory experiences are essential for all students, yet too often the labs they experience are boring and not truly reflective of the nature of science. Many schools are staffed with teachers who lack training in conducting discovery-oriented laboratories or inquiry-based science lessons. They frequently work with outdated lab equipment and materials, or, in many cases, no labs at all. A USA General Accounting Office report in 2000 found that approximately 40% of college students who dropped out of the sciences reported problems related to high school science preparation, including lack of sufficient preparation in math, laboratory experiences, and exposure to computers. The National Lab Network is an intensive, nationwide effort to remedy these deficiencies in the teaching of STEM disciplines (science, technology, engineering, and math) for middle and high schools across the country. The goals of National Lab Network are to:

1. Create an increased number of meaningful hands-on, discovery-based laboratory opportunities for teachers to use with middle and high school STEM students.

2. Increase the involvement of STEM professionals in K–12 education through volunteer efforts. A National Lab Day website (*www.nationallabnetwork.org*) is available where schools can request help and scientists and engineers can volunteer their services.

3. Provide schools with an opportunity to assess and upgrade their current lab facilities with a systematic, volunteer-based, effort.

"Lab" is defined quite broadly: A place where students can explore, experiment, test, and get their hands dirty and their minds engaged. It's not just test tubes and beakers. A lab could be a laptop to a software designer, a mountaintop to a geologist, a computer link to a distant particle accelerator to a physicist, or a factory floor to an industrial engineer. It's a place where hands-on lessons in science, engineering, and technology can be designed to happen, or where math can come alive, and could be anywhere in the physical or virtual world.

With support from teachers, parents, volunteers, professional societies, federal agencies, industry, and foundations, National Lab Network has the potential to transform STEM education, providing all of our students with truly exciting hands-on lab experiences. This effort is likely to have great payoff in seducing students into STEM careers

Science Matters Programs

Science Matters is NSTA's newest initiative, designed to spark a national sense of urgency and action among schools and families about the importance of science education. Science Matters volunteers host free community events for elementary teachers, parents, school officials, and students. Here we engage in exciting hands-on activities and discover new ways to bring science to life for students and children.

The pipeline for our next generation of career scientists, engineers, and technicians begins in the K–6 classroom. Quality elementary science lessons capture children's attention when they are most open, most curious, and most naturally disposed to asking questions about the world around them. Young children who receive a strong foundation in science during their elementary school years do better in science in later grades. Many students also make fundamental career decisions by the time they get to middle school, so engaging students in science at an early age provides them with more information about opportunities in STEM careers. NSTA maintains a Science Matters website (*www.nsta.org/sciencematters*), open free to all. At this website you can:

- Read reports and policy statements from key stakeholders on why science matters for everyone.

- Determine if your child is receiving a quality science education by using a Science Education Checklist.
- Find practical ideas to help children learn science at "Tips for Busy Parents."
- Learn how parents, teachers, informal science educators (museums, zoos, parks, and recreation centers), and community and business organizations can work together to foster better learning experiences in K–12 science at the "Teacher and Counselor Corner."
- Explore (and share) classroom and at-home hands-on science activities and experiments at the "Awesome Websites and More" section.
- Learn more about quality science education and the National Science Teachers Association.

The Latest Science Matters Community Event: "Science Rocks!"

At the 68th NSTA National Conference in Indianapolis, Indiana, NSTA launched *Science Rocks!* This innovative program brings middle school students, educators, and parents face-to-face with the nation's most accomplished scientists and engineers, with the objective of inspiring students and educators to consider science and engineering as exciting areas of study and potential career paths.

The morning portion included *Science Rocks in the Classroom*, where "rock stars" of science, math, and engineering visit several local middle school classrooms, allowing an up close and personal exchange between students and celebrated members of the science community—putting a face on science. Middle school students, with a particular focus on local Title I schools, were the target audience. This age group is considered the most appropriate for this sort of experience, as they are approaching more advanced concepts in science and math, and their minds are open to new and exciting possibilities for their futures.

The evening program concluded with a panel discussion of the award-winning scientists and engineers—open to the general public and the 12,000 educators attending the conference. Facilitating this meaningful interaction grants the general public exposure to positive role models and the ways that they overcame obstacles and made discoveries that have transformed the lives of Americans. It is paramount for both educators and students to develop and maintain a positive attitude toward science and to learn that the science community is made of a diverse group of vibrant and passionate individuals and offers exciting career opportunities, enabling students to aspire to become a "rock star" of science in their own community.

Some Key Elements for Programs Encouraging STEM Career Development

All STEM career-oriented programs need to explore the nature of science and the amazing discoveries resulting from scientific enterprises. Science can be a thrilling roller coaster ride for those willing to jump on and feel the thrills. Whether the coaster track runs through school programs, challenging competitions, informal science programs, or in doing actual scientific research, certain elements of science need to be part of the experience of potential STEM careerists. Some of the most important are the following:

Exploring the Nature of Science

Science can be an exciting enterprise. Scientists explore nature, form scientific explanations, organize knowledge, and form a distinct scientific culture. To decide on pursuing a career in science, students should first learn about the distinctive nature of the scientific enterprise. Here are some key characteristics of science:

1. *Scientists explore*

    - Scientists transform observations into questions for investigations.
    - Scientists' observations are influenced by their previous experiences and existing ideas.
    - Investigations conducted by scientists are influenced by communities they are part of (both scientific and nonscientific).
    - Scientists' predictions are influenced by their existing scientific knowledge.
    - Scientists design investigations to test their predictions.
    - Many different approaches, methods, and pathways are used in the conduct of scientific investigations.
    - Investigations are designed to collect relevant and accurate data.
    - Scientists aim to critically analyze and maintain open minds in consideration of experimentally collected data.

2. *Scientists derive scientific explanations*

    - Scientific observations often involve creative insights.
    - There may be competing explanations for the results of an investigation.
    - Scientists often pose models as part of their explanations.
    - When an explanation correctly predicts an event, confidence in the explanation is increased.
    - Scientific explanations are always tentative and subject to change as more information is collected.

3. *Scientists organize scientific knowledge*

    - Scientific explanations must withstand peer review before being accepted as scientific knowledge.
    - New scientific explanations frequently meet opposition.
    - Over time, the types of scientific knowledge that are valued tends to change.

4. *Science has established its own culture*

    - Open-mindedness is important to the culture of science.
    - Historically, however, the principle of open-mindedness has sometimes been violated.
    - Scientific progress comes from logical and systematic work, and also through creative insights.
    - Science interacts with other cultures, such as political, economic, and social science cultures.

No doubt about it, the best way to learn the nature of science is by being directly involved in hands-on inquiry in the manner of an actual scientist. By making direct observations, posing questions, framing hypotheses, designing and conducting investigations, and confronting data to determine its meaning—these are keys to understanding science and for understanding what a career in science would be like.

Examining Historical Episodes

Another way to interest students in a career in science is to examine the highlights of careers of great scientists. The history of science is laden with great stories of discovery, competition, brilliant insights, serendipity, and even misadventure. Many episodes are absolutely fascinating, and they reveal much about the excitement, drudgery, dead ends, and downright humanness of scientific exploration. Here are some interesting scientific characters prospective science careerists might investigate:

- *Luigi Galvani* was one of the first to investigate experimentally the phenomenon that came to be known as "bioelectrogenesis." Working around 1780 at the University of Bologna, Galvani found that electrical current could cause contraction in the legs of recently deceased frogs. A subsequent conflict of interpretation of this phenomenon with Alessandro Volta resulted in a long-term scientific feud. This, fortunately, was instrumental in leading Volta to the invention of the first electric cell (the Voltaic Pile), which was fundamental to the development of today's electronics.
- *Louis Pasteur* is among the greatest benefactors to humanity. He discovered causes for anthrax, cholera, and rabies, and contributed to the development of vaccines used for immunization to many diseases. He also debunked the then-accepted belief in spontaneous generation of organisms, thereby encouraging the development of modern biology, medicine, and biochemistry. He also found the scientific explanations for rising of bread, wine-making, and brewing of beer.
- *Marie Curie* discovered and explored the mysterious element radium. Her work opened doors to deep changes in the way scientists conceive matter and energy. She also led the way to a new era of medical knowledge and treatment of diseases such as cancer.

The history of science parallels the history of human development. Scientists and engineers were the first to design tools, make sense out of the motions of stars and planets in the sky, and to design great buildings.

Characteristics of Successful Scientists

There are many different types of scientists, but there are general personality characteristics that seem to contribute to success in scientific careers. Some of these are:

- *Curious.* Can you imagine an *uninterested* scientist? It seems to "go with the territory—scientists have well-developed curiosity about some aspects of the natural world. For some, it might be insects, for another, behavior of lasers, for another, distant planets. To be a scientist, you must yearn to learn!

- *Determined and persistent.* To be sure, science requires hard work. Solution of problems in science may take decades, or even many lifetimes. "Stick-to-it-ivity" is definitely desirable in working scientists.
- *Creative and innovative.* We tend to think of creativity as characteristic in the realms art and literature, but the ability to invent new ideas and devices is absolutely essential for STEM professionals. Creations of explanatory models for natural phenomena require thinking far outside of ordinary "boxes."
- *Open to new possibilities.* A good STEM worker needs to be flexible and willing to modify thought patterns in light of evidence. There is no room for forcing prejudgments on conflicting data. Open-mindedness is a valued scientific attitude.
- *Patient and detail-oriented.* Thomas Edison reported trying 1,004 different materials for his first lightbulb before he found one that wouldn't quickly burn out. That took months of trial-and-error experimentation. Sometimes, also, the smallest, seemingly insignificant observation turns out to be crucial, so note-taking and careful data collection are critical to research and invention.
- *Team-Oriented.* Most STEM work is now done in collaborative teams—this requires listening and cooperative social skills, and developed abilities in communication.

Conclusion

If we knew more about how our brains work and how we made decisions, helping more students select a STEM career would be much easier. Since we don't yet know how students make these decisions, we use more triangular analysis connection techniques such as considering program dimensions, factors from research, interviews, and observations of student behaviors. These give some picture of why K–12 students select certain careers. Interest in a career in engineering can be influenced by role models but also by how students perceive careers (Schunn 2009). Students also think about their own futures and choices they have for a career fairly early, as early as middle school. It appears that there is nothing that is more influential in STEM career development than actually *doing* science or engineering.

References

Barta, C. 2010. *Parents and 21st-century kids: A ExxonMobil survey of math and science attitudes.* Washington, DC: McLaughlin & Associates and Hart Research and Associates.

Carnevale, A. P., N. Smith, and M. Melton. 2011. *Help wanted: Projection of jobs and education requirements through 2018.* Washington, DC: Georgetown University Center on Education and the Workforce. Available online at *www9.georgetown.edu/grad/gppi/hpi/cew/pdfs/FullReport.pdf*

Harris Interactive. 2011. *Stem perceptions: Student and parent study.* Report commissioned by Microsoft Corporation. Available online at *www.microsoft.com/en-us/news/presskits/citizenship/docs/STEMPerceptionsReport.pdf*

Langdon, D., G. McKittrick, D. Beede, B. Khan, and M. Doms. 2009. *STEM: Good jobs now and for the future.* Washington, DC: U.S. Department of Commerce.

National Research Council (NRC). 2007. *Taking science to school: Learning and teaching science in grades K–8.* Washington DC: The National Academies Press.

Schunn, C. D. 2009. How kids learn engineering: The cognitive science perspective. *The Bridge* 39 (3): 32–37.

Creating a Pipeline to STEM Careers Through Service-Learning: The AFT Program

Anton Puvirajah and Lisa Martin-Hansen
Georgia State University

Geeta Verma
University of Colorado–Denver

Setting

The Academy for Future Teachers (AFT) is a STEM education and career recruitment program for Metro Atlanta high school students, hosted by Georgia State University in Atlanta, Georgia. This program was developed in response to the changing demographics of our students: shifting much more quickly than the demographics of our teacher populations in the United States. Minority students are increasing in number while the majority of teachers continue to be white and female. In Georgia, 83% of the teachers are female, and this percentage has been relatively stable over the years (Scafidi, Sjoquist, and Stinebrickner 2006). Research suggests a direct relationship between the lack of highly qualified minority science and mathematics teachers and the lack of minority students who choose science or mathematics careers (Toolin 2003). Additionally, the underrepresentation of racial and ethnic minority teachers (including mathematics and science teachers) and the underrepresentation in STEM and STEM-related careers leads to students having difficulties being able to relate and identify themselves in these STEM roles. Researchers and educators are trying different approaches to increase interest and competency in STEM with the intent of increasing the numbers of underrepresented populations in these fields, as well as recruiting future teachers from this pool.

AFT approaches the challenge of increasing underrepresented groups in STEM fields by creating supportive service-learning experiences for high school students, facilitated by exemplary high school science and mathematics teachers and college professors. The service-learning component consists of high school students teaching STEM content to preschool and middle school students. Scaffolding for this experience is provided within the three-week intensive summer experience, focusing on building participant capacities related to attitudes and knowledge in STEM areas. This is purposefully constructed with the goals of developing student long-term interest in STEM and STEM careers, including careers in STEM education. In the unique model of the AFT program, student capacities are built in their understanding of the nature of science and science learning and teaching, the nature of mathematics and mathematics learning and teaching, and the significant understanding of certain science and mathematical concepts. Additionally, this understanding is put into action as they apply what was learned by teaching mathematics and science lessons to preschool and middle school children in concurrently held summer programs. The AFT program provides a means to develop students' identity in thinking of themselves as scientists, mathematicians, or as science and mathematics educators. In addition, we have found that the experience gives students a sense of agency in that they feel that they can do science, do mathematics, and teach a child a lesson. They become empowered through the mathematics and science learning experiences they created for younger students.

Funding for the AFT Program

For several years (2004–2009), the AFT program received support from the National Science Foundation as it was included in a large Mathematics and Science Partnership in Georgia called PRISM (Partners in Reforms in Science and Mathematics). With that initiative, AFT focused strictly on recruitment of future science and mathematics educators with an additional goal of attracting students to STEM careers. The current AFT model has continued with that focus and has been supported through several state and private grants with no charge to the participants. Recent funding agents include The University System of Georgia Board of Regents (USG-BOR) through their Science, Technology, Engineering and Mathematics (STEM) funding and the American Honda Foundation. All individuals, instructors, mentors, and students received a stipend for their AFT involvement. The individuals overseeing the project forged partnerships with local metro Atlanta school districts, as the recruitment effort required school counselors to inform high school students of this summer opportunity and teachers to provide letters of reference.

Recruitment of Students Into the AFT Program

The AFT program recruits participants from Metro Atlanta by sending out informational flyers, brochures, and application kits to principals, counselors, and science and mathematics department heads throughout the area school districts. Because of the limited capacity of the program, during some years the AFT program only sent recruiting material to select school districts. Students applying to the program, in addition to completing a standard application form, were required to have a GPA of 2.5, submit an essay on why they wanted to participate in the AFT program, and submit two letters of recommendation from their high school teachers. Because of the limitations on the capacity of the AFT program, not all qualified applicants are chosen. Participants are chosen from the pool of applications based on GPA, the quality of the response to the essay prompt, and teacher recommendations. It should also be noted that in addition to the AFT program being offered free of charge to the participants, they are also provided passes for public transportation, money for lunch, and a stipend of $200 at the completion of the program.

In 2004, 34 high school students participated in AFT, and since then it has grown in capacity each year. In 2010, AFT served about 60 high school students. Since one of the goals of the AFT program is to encourage students belonging to underrepresented groups to consider STEM for their postsecondary studies and STEM-related occupations, the AFT program actively recruited in districts with large numbers of underrepresented groups. When AFT began in 2004, the program only recruited students from Atlanta Public Schools, and the first cohort of students were all African American. Now the AFT program recruits students from a number of school districts in the metro Atlanta area. Students in the most recent cohort represented 26 schools from nine school systems. In 2010, AFT received 131 complete student applications for 60 openings for the program. This created a rich pool of student candidates. Of the 60 students selected for the 2010 AFT program 13% identified themselves as non-African American, with females comprising 82% of applicants. While this high number of females is not surprising to us, we would like to see greater numbers of African American males participate in the program. Historically and at present, African American males are underrepresented in STEM professions.

The AFT Model

The summer AFT experience at Georgia State University is constructed by the director, the Associate Dean of School and Community Partnership, and the faculty from higher education and K–12 education. In the three-week AFT program students have weeklong mini content-pedagogy hybrid courses in secondary science, secondary mathematics, and elementary science and mathematics. The intent of the courses is to provide students experiences in authentic ways of learning science and mathematics through modeling and peer-teaching.

The Teaching and Support Staff

Teachers from local school districts were hired to co-teach in AFT with higher education faculty. The three teaching teams—elementary science/mathematics, secondary science, and secondary mathematics—work together to create engaging and authentic experiences for the students. The teaching teams have expertise in the particular content and pedagogy that they taught the AFT students. In addition, three GSU graduate students act as mentors to each cohort of AFT students, and also support the teaching staff. The mentors talk with students about career goals, assist the instructors with classroom management, and generally support students by clearing up questions related to assignments and being available as a contact for questions about the program and questions about Georgia State University. It should also be emphasized that much like the AFT students, the teaching and support staff are predominantly African American. For example, in our most recent year of the program, all K–12 teachers were African-American. One of the higher education faculty members was African American, while the second member was South Asian, and the third member was Caucasian. All GSU graduate student mentors were African American.

The Curriculum

The AFT model is organized into three discrete cohorts of students: two cohorts of first-year (Y1) AFT participants and typically another cohort of second-year (Y2) participants who progress through a series of one-week experiences with three different emphases (secondary science, secondary mathematics, and elementary mathematics/science). In each of the weeklong experiences, students learn science and mathematics content through engaging and inquiry-oriented activities. In addition, the students learn about philosophies and methods related to teaching and learning in K–12 settings. As students learn content, they also learn how to teach content and learn about the pedagogical rationale for teaching the content in a particular way. In each of the weeklong programs, the AFT students get opportunities to create reform-minded lessons, receive feedback on the lesson from instructors, and then teach (field experiences) these lessons to preK–8 students. The AFT students' in-class and out-of-class experiences are organized so that they experience both STEM learning and teaching in authentic and meaningful ways. In Table 8.1, a general description of what students learn in each week of experience is highlighted. The Y2 students are also provided with a curriculum focusing on mathematics and science content as well as pedagogical learning, which is similar to what is learned in Y1, but with more application in terms of teacher behaviors (questioning) and investigation into different types of lesson designs. We also present a detailed daily activity overview for the secondary science program in Table 8.2 (p. 116).

The innovative design of the AFT program is buttressed by the collaborative activities (team teaching) and a service-learning component that is found in each discrete experience in the program. AFT students also teach young students in other programs. The instructors team-teach while the participants are learning mathematics and science content as well as pedagogy. This is how one can construct experiences for others that make that content accessible and interesting. The participants knew that they would participate in the service learning portion, where they are responsible for teaching younger students a mathematics or science concept and doing so in an interesting and engaging way. This *need to know* helped to generate the intrinsic need to have an idea of how to communicate effectively beyond simply telling someone about a concept. By teaching students how people learn, AFT provide them with tools to be successful in their own future STEM learning experiences. Past participants have commented on how knowing their own preferred learning style has been helpful as they are often faced with learning situations that do not fit well with how they feel they learn best. AFT helps them to realize that they can use tools such as diagramming, drawing, working in a small group, or searching out online interactive tutorials to add visual or interactive ways of learning when those types of experiences were provided as part of a course that they are taking during the school year.

NSES Goals and Student Experiences in the AFT Program

The National Science Education Standards (NSES) listed four goals for school science (NRC 1996). The AFT program aligns closely with these goals of student engagement in a variety of rich STEM experiences (Table 8.3, p. 118). In many different ways these experiences help students move toward increased scientific literacy. Students experience STEM in contexts that are linked to everyday life issues. They are asked to communicate in several ways, with peers as well as younger students to express mathematics and science ideas as they discuss and make claims about evidence. It is the intent of this program to inspire students to pursue STEM careers, thereby "increasing their economic productivity through the use of knowledge, understanding, and skills of the scientifically literate person in their careers."

Table 8.1. Summary of Activities Within Each Weeklong Program

Program Structure	Students are divided into three groups or *cohorts*: two groups are Y1 participants and one group consists of Y2 participants Students cycle through three, weeklong experiences for a total of three weeks of AFT experience.
Elementary Mathematics, Science, and Pedagogy (1 week)	Mathematics and science content are addressed in the elementary section with specific emphases on the processes of science and mathematics (problem-solving, exploring scientific phenomenon, manipulating a variable). Students learn about the importance of exploration and curiosity involved with science and mathematics. Students also have experiences in learning through play, an appropriate pedagogical approach for elementary students. *Service learning component:* Students create and teach pedagogically and developmentally appropriate science and mathematics lessons to children (3–5 years old) at our college-run child development center. Students then share and reflect with each other their teaching experience and offer suggestions from improving and or modifying the lesson.
Secondary Mathematics and Pedagogy (1 week)	Students learn the importance of mathematics processes through explicit connections of mathematics concepts to real-life contexts. For example students apply technology for data gathering and analysis in real-life mathematics contexts. The students also learn how to plan and implement engaging mathematics lessons that teach both mathematics concepts and processes. *Service learning component:* As a culminating activity, the students create and teach a mathematics lesson to a group of middle school students attending a summer school program at a neighboring school. After teaching the mathematics lessons, students share their reflections on their experience and provide feedback to their peers.
Secondary Science and Pedagogy (1 week)	Students learn pedagogies and pedagogical content knowledge appropriate for teaching science to older children and young adults. They develop their understanding of nature of science and learning science as inquiry. The students also learn to develop science lessons using the 5E learning cycle model. *Service learning component:* As part of their week, the AFT students observe and provide feedback on science lessons taught by a cohort of preservice science teachers in the Master of Arts in Teaching program at our college. As a culminating activity, the AFT students prepare and teach a 5E-based science lesson to a class of middle school students attending a summer school program at a neighboring school. After teaching the science lessons, students share their reflections on their experience and provide feedback to their peers.

Table 8.2. AFT Daily Activity Overview for the Secondary Science Program

Activity/Lesson (Description Optional)	Why This Activity? (Rationale)	Goal(s) 1: Content, 2: Pedagogy, 3: Attitudes/Interests in STEM
Nature of Science: 1. Myths about NOS 2. Tricky Tracks 3. Nature of Science Tubes: Students in groups are given a mystery box; they are to determine what's in the box without opening it	• Through discussion of the activity students learn about the various tenets of nature of science. • Students learn about the importance of making observations in science and the difference between observation and inference.	1. Science Content: Nature of Science, Processes involved in science 2. Pedagogy through watching the teacher model the lesson 3. Increased interest in STEM
Physics (Force and Motion) 1. Choosing a safe vehicle 2. Speed and collisions 3. Mass and collisions	• Revisiting the physics concepts and linking them to everyday life. Students learn the importance of learning physics concepts and its importance of applying them in their real lives. This brings in the ideas of developing habits of mind and developing scientific literacy.	1. Science Content: Physics, Processes involved in science 2. Pedagogy through watching the teacher model the lesson 3. Increased interest in STEM
Earth Science (Topography) 1. Where should we build a house? 2. Making topographical maps 3. Studying topography 4. Making decisions based topographical maps	• Revising the Earth science concepts and linking them to everyday life. Students learn the importance of learning about topography and how that information can be useful and helpful in making decisions about new housing development. This brings in the ideas of developing habits of mind and developing scientific literacy.	1. Science Content: Earth Science, Processes involved in science 2. Pedagogy through watching the teacher model the lesson 3. Increased interest in STEM
Fundamentals of Teaching 1. Characteristics of "good" and "bad" teachers 2. Dispelling stereotypes of instruction 3. Importance of communication	• This activity requires the students to examine their preconceived notions of teaching and how they tend to label instructors as "good" or "bad." • Participants are faced with a challenge to "teach" their partner how to complete a task without using speaking and while their partner cannot see.	1. Science Content: Nature of Science; Science Inquiry 2. Pedagogy: Creative means to overcome instructional obstacles 3. Attitude and interest in STEM through problem solving

Activity/Lesson (Description Optional)	Why This Activity? (Rationale)	Goal(s) 1: Content, 2: Pedagogy, 3: Attitudes/Interests in STEM
Biology (Carrying Capacity) 1. "Look who's coming to dinner": Students participate in a competition based on density dependent factors and environmental resources. 2. Global Footprint Network: As a community, students calculate ecological footprint and consider different methods to reduce impact on the earth.	• As per Laurie's request to include eco-friendly lessons, this activity personalizes the limited availability of Earth's resources. • By participating in an activity that requires the students to compete for food and sacrifice members of their family for survival, students recognize the need to limit the consumption of resources and the production of waste.	1. Science Content: Biology/Ecology 2. Pedagogy: Teacher demonstration of lesson differentiation 3. Attitude and interest in STEM through critical thinking and discussion of a global concern
Biology (Enzymes) 1. Investigative lab to evaluate the role of enzymes in detergents and foods	• Students develop a lab protocol to test the influence of acids and bases on the activity of a specific enzyme. The activity represents research lab methods in that the directions for the experiment are not provided; students must determine which procedure would be most appropriate to meet the needs of the experiment.	1. Science Content: Biochemistry and Science Inquiry 2. Pedagogy: demonstrated through modeled instruction 3. Attitude and interest in STEM through problem solving and critical thinking
Differentiated Instruction 1. Bloom's Taxonomy and Multiple Intelligences 2. Gardner's Taboo: Students must have their partners guess the teaching activity using a specific learning style.	• Review of Bloom's taxonomy and Multiple Intelligences for instruction. • The activity encourages the students to use simple activities such as tying your shoe or teaching doubles.	1. Science Content: Nature of science 2. Pedagogy: Using various learning styles to address the needs of students 3. Attitude and interest in STEM through problem solving

Table 8.3. Goals for Science Education Within the National Science Education Standards Document (NRC 1996, p. 13) and Its Alignment With the AFT Program

NSES Goals ...Educate Students Who Are Able To	Student Experiences in the AFT Program
experience the richness and excitement of knowing about and understanding the natural world	Students in the AFT program learn through hands-on and minds-on experiences in various STEM topics. The students learn by both experiencing reform-based STEM lessons modeled by STEM educators and by developing and delivering their own STEM lessons to preschool and middle school students. Students explored topics associated with local geological and hydrological formations, pollution, and climate change.
use appropriate scientific processes and principles in making personal decisions	Students in the AFT program gain experience in using scientific process and principles in making personal decisions as they explore such topics like implications of local geological and hydrological formations to the availability and access to affordable drinking water and making decisions based on scientific evidence.
engage intelligently in public discourse and debate about matters of scientific and technological concern	Students in the AFT program use scientific evidence in supporting their claims. For example, AFT students debated about 'water wars' among Georgia, Alabama, and Florida using various artifacts and scientific evidence.
increase their economic productivity through the use of the knowledge, understanding, and skills of the scientifically literate person in their careers	Through their overall experience in the AFT program, capacity was built in the students to become economically productive citizens where they increasingly use their scientific knowledge to make personal and work-related decisions.

Summary

In AFT program design, all players actively create engaging, meaningful, and authentic learning experiences. Those creating learning experiences in the AFT program include the K–12 public school teachers, university faculty, MAT science students, and the AFT participants themselves. The teaching duos (higher education and K–12) plan and implement the summer experiences, modeling science and mathematics pedagogy through the teaching of science and mathematics content. AFT students learn content and pedagogy by doing as they create and teach engaging lessons for both preschool students (in the elementary section) and middle school students. Additionally, MAT Science students at GSU teach three lessons for AFT students, while AFT students provide the MAT students with verbal and written feedback on the lessons. This experience is mutually beneficial for both groups of students. MAT students are able to practice teaching "real" high school students and receive feedback from the same students. AFT students are able to learn science content, experience reform-based pedagogy, learn to provide constructive feedback, and have experience (although short) being in a Master's level methods course.

The AFT program addresses the need for reform when creating experiences that allow students to view themselves as mathematicians, scientists, and mathematics or science educators.

This is a novel take on recruitment for STEM and STEM careers. We have found that the most powerful component of the design is the active role students take in creating and implementing mathematics and science lessons for younger students. The lessons are implemented with pairs or small groups of AFT students as instructors, and the students (preschool or middle school) work in small groups with the instructors. The secondary science lessons, using the learning cycle format, focus on engaging students in hands-on and minds-on science experiences. In this case, the model promoted is a 5E learning cycle (engage, explore, explain, extend, and evaluate). The high school students then construct their own 5E science lessons and teach middle school students participating in a summer program. The AFT participants are encouraged to structure secondary mathematics lessons for middle school students with an emphasis on problem solving in algebra and number theory. The elementary lessons for preschool students focus heavily on engagement and exploration of science phenomenon through hands-on learning and learning through play.

Evidence for Success

As mentioned earlier, the intent of the AFT program is to inspire students to continue to learn STEM and to motivate them to pursue STEM and STEM-related careers. Special emphasis in the AFT program is to encourage and empower high school students to consider STEM as a career option. It comes from our understanding that appropriate decisions on career pathways can only be made by students when they get opportunities to explore STEM content in engaging and authentic contexts. With this in mind, we collect several types of qualitative and quantitative data to inform us on the nature and the experiences of the student participation in the AFT program.

The Program Evaluation Team

We (Anton and Lisa) were retained by the AFT program to provide data collection, analysis, program evaluation, and other research-related support. Three graduate research assistants, who are all PhD students in STEM education, assisted in our work. While the evaluation work is independent concerning the AFT program, we work closely with the program coordinator to manage data collection activities. The AFT model and its impacts have been shared at regional and national conferences. The program has received recognition through continued funding from government agencies, nonprofit foundations, and corporate donors.

Data Sources for AFT

- *Application forms.* Student demographic and academic data are obtained from the application forms for the AFT program. For example, we obtained information about student race, gender, school, grade level, and GPA from the application forms.
- *Science and mathematics attitude survey (SAM Survey).* We administer the SAM survey pre- and post-AFT experience. In the SAM survey, a four-level forced response 60-item (30 science and 30 mathematics) Likert survey is used to get students to rate their attitudes, motivations, identity, and future intentions within science and mathematics. The

presurvey is administered on the first morning of the AFT program during the student orientation. The postsurvey is administered the last day of the program.

- *AFT exit evaluation forms.* At the end of the three-week AFT experience, students complete a mostly open-ended/free response questionnaire concerning the AFT experiences and their future academic and career aspirations. More specifically, we ask in the evaluation form for students to comment about their: (a) overall experience in AFT, (b) AFT learning experiences, (c) perception of how well the instructors facilitated learning, and (d) future college and career plans regarding STEM and STEM education.
- *Science and mathematics content knowledge pre/posttest.* In an attempt to measure student learning of science or mathematics content, each teaching team is asked to construct a pre- and postassessment of expected learning goals. Learning goals include both science and mathematics content.
- *Individual interviews.* We also conduct a 15–20 minute semistructured individual interview with 45 students. In the interviews, the students are asked to describe and compare and contrast their high school science and mathematics experiences with their experiences in the AFT program. The researchers make several observation visits to various AFT classes and took notes concerning student engagement in the activities. These observations allow us to examine the aforementioned data with greater understanding of the context for student participation.
- *AFT instructor written reflections.* Two of us (Lisa and Geeta) offer our reflections on our experiences in teaching in the AFT program.

Findings

Science and Mathematics Content Understanding

When students' science and mathematics pre- and postassessments are compared, we found that they scored significantly higher on the postassessment than the preassessment ($p < 0.002$). In science, 89% of the students showed improvement from pre- to postassessment. In mathematics, 91% of the students also showed improvement from pre- to postassessment. One may think that the improvement may be obvious and expected. We agree. However, we note that from our experiences in looking at our preservice and inservice teachers' pre- and postassessments of science and mathematics content in the classroom, the pre-to-post improvement is normally observed to include about 55–75% of the students. The improvement in the AFT program is higher than this. The science and mathematics content that the students learn in the AFT program is based on the state standards. A majority of them have had at least some exposure to the content in the schools. The relatively high percentage in improvement is also indicative of high student disciplinary (science and mathematics) engagement in the cohort experiences. Although the content exams show significant growth, it should be noted that the secondary science section was the only set of instructors to use NAEP and TIMSS released test items in the construction of their pre- and posttests. The mathematics and elementary science and mathematics sections had purely instructor-created exams and thus may not have been as reliable. It is hoped that in the 2012 session, that the evaluators can play a more integral role in assisting in the construction of the pre- and posttests, allowing for more reliable data to be gathered.

Science and Mathematics Attitude and Affinity

While the pre/post SAM survey consisted of 60 items (30 science and 30 mathematics), we first share aggregate results relating to student attitude shift toward science and mathematics after participating in the AFT program. We then share results from some interesting individual items from the survey.

Students' positive attitudes about science and science careers increased (p < 0.001) at the end of the AFT program, with means changing from 14.26 (pre) to 17.26 (post) with a maximum possible score of 24. While students indicated increased (17.93 to 18.24) positive attitudes about mathematics and mathematics careers at the end of the AFT, this increase was not statistically significant. It should be noted that the students already had relatively high positive attitudes for mathematics and mathematics careers when they entered the AFT program. The pre/post SAM survey revealed that certain student notions about science and mathematics shifted by the time they completed the AFT program. Table 8.4 highlights this.

Table 8.4. Comparison of Select Pre/Post Item Scores From Science and Mathematics Attitude Survey: An Indication Affinity Toward STEM Careers (Maximum possible score 4. n = 42)

Item	Prescore	Postscore	Difference in Mean	Standard Deviation	*T*	*p*-value
Doing well in science is important for my future	2.88	3.24	−0.357	0.958	−2.416	0.020
Science is hard for me	3.00	2.67	0.333	0.954	2.264	0.029
Learning science requires special abilities that only some people possess	2.40	2.10	0.301	0.869	2.308	0.026
I am sure of myself when I do mathematics	3.05	3.26	−0.214	0.606	−2.291	0.027
Learning mathematics requires special abilities that only some people possess	2.43	2.07	0.357	0.850	2.722	0.009
Mathematics is an important life skill	1.40	3.52	−2.119	1.152	−11.922	< 0.000
I would like to avoid mathematics in college	3.17	2.98	0.190	0.594	2.007	0.044
Teaching is an easy career	2.14	1.69	0.452	1.041	2.817	0.007

From Table 8.4 we see that by the end of the AFT program students increasingly agreed that doing well in science is important for their future. Students indicated that science seemed less difficult for them after the AFT program. On the postsurvey, students agreed less with the idea that learning science or mathematics required special abilities that only some people possessed. Student confidence in doing mathematics also increased after the AFT program ("I am sure of myself when I do mathematics; I would like to avoid mathematics in college"). At the beginning of the AFT program, students largely felt that mathematics was not an important life skill (1.40), however, after the AFT program there was a relatively significant shift in this view (3.52). It is also important to note that after the AFT program, students agreed more with the notion that teaching mathematics and science was not as easy as they had initially thought. The results presented above reflect the nature of the students' mathematics and science experiences in the AFT program. Students learned science and mathematics through engaging and relevant activities. This enabled them to envision and experience science and mathematics in real and authentic ways. Incorporation of strategies to teach and learn science and mathematics into the AFT program and students' participation in teaching others science and mathematics also influenced their visions of science and mathematics. As students learned how to teach, learn, and find meaning in their experiences, they were able to have greater appreciation for the fields of science and mathematics and feel that they had greater access in the these fields. We also feel that greater appreciation for the fields of science and mathematics allows students to have greater affinity toward careers in STEM and that they need not fear that a career in STEM is inaccessible for them.

Choice of Major in College Affinity

Student evaluation forms revealed their preferred choices for an intended college major. While we do not know the degree of impact AFT had on student preferences for college majors since this was assessed only at the exit (and not upon entry), 46% of the students indicated that they would like to pursue some form of STEM major in college, indicating that these students are serious about following a STEM career path. Table 8.5 shows the percentage of students choosing a particular college major.

Interview Responses

When we conducted interviews with students, we focused upon several areas including their impressions about the program, suggestions to improve the experience, and the most beneficial experiences. Additionally, we asked the AFT students to compare their AFT experiences with their high school experiences.

It was found through one-on-one interviews that students had varying school experiences in learning science and mathematics in school. As the interviews took place near the end of the AFT experience, there are hints as to how the AFT experience affected the participants. Participants often commented on how the experience in AFT, steeped in active learning, resonated with them. They often reflected upon their high school learning experiences with a critical lens after participating in AFT. The responses below highlight some of the student ideas about their prior high school learning experiences.

Table 8.5. Frequency Distribution of College Majors as Indicator for Future Career Choice to be Pursued by AFT Participants

STEM Fields		Non-STEM Fields	
Major	**Percentage (%)**	**Major**	**Percentage (%)**
Education – Mathematics	8	Accounting	2
Education – Science	4	Art	4
Engineering	8	Business	8
Forensics	1	Education – Other	13
Mathematics	7	English	9
Medicine	4	Graphic Design	2
Physical Therapy	2	History	2
Physics	5	Journalism	2
Science	7	Law	2
		Music	6
		Social Work	1
		Sociology	1
		Undecided	2
Total Percentage (%)	46		54

Miley: The math that I took, we had a lot of umm activities that were following the lesson plans, like hands-on and using the graphing calculator, so it just wasn't paperwork. We had other work so we can get a further understanding of the umm activity. And in chemistry, we did a few experiments, too, and a lot of worksheets. It was alright.

Amina: I took analysis last year with Mr. Dawson and it was a very rigorous, very difficult class, but I enjoyed it because he challenged us a lot and he really ... he helped us but he didn't just give us the answers. He made us figure it out on our own. I definitely liked that about my analysis class.

An additional theme dealt with the challenging or lack of challenging expectations or coursework in their high school learning. Often, students saw worksheets and lectures as being boring and less engaging and saw active and interactive learning like group inquiry and problem solving activities as being fun, engaging, and meaningful. The AFT program enabled the students to critically examine, and communicate how they are taught science and mathematics.

Shiyara: Yeah it's [changed] more of how I interacted with my teachers. I kind of got to see their perspective of us because I taught here and I saw kids and I'm like ok this is how they see us. Like this is how difficult we are and so annoying we are. So I tried to become a better student more understanding, get my work done on time, don't talk too much in class and all that stuff.

Jacquelyn: I also have the same teacher I've had two years in a row, 10th and 11th grade. Uhm, we did a lot of lab experiments, lot of hands on things and I really enjoyed that. In 9th grade we really didn't do any labs and I was really bored so I appreciate the labs that we did.

Aisha: The last math class I took was statistics and it basically talked about the way surveys are taken and how to choose groups of people, the questions that they ask and stuff like that. We got to interview each other, it was fun. My last science class was chemistry and we talked about atom theory, reactions, we did a lot of worksheets.

Cordell: Um, well I have had the same math teacher my freshman year and sophomore year and what he does is lecture a lot. Like he would just stand at the board and go over the book. And he'll be just like if we need help, he'll be like "look at the examples in the book."

One of the interview questions asked AFT participants ways to think back to their learning in high school and to make suggestions about what teachers might do to improve the learning experiences. Often, students commented on how important they felt learner engagement was in the lesson. Additionally, the real-life connections, making science and mathematics more *real* and *accessible,* resonated with the students.

Markice: Especially with math, instead of coming in and just start talking … more hands-on activities, or like more practical real-life examples, you know, like how it relates to everyday life.

Amelia: I would tell them to basically ask a lot of questions and to get the students to think and analyze different things. Like why does this happen when we do this? Why is it when we balance out this side we have to change on this side of the chemical equation? And I will also have them encourage the students to ask questions, but don't always answer the students questions. Have the students go through a certain process so they can answer the question on their own.

Theo: I feel maybe [his former high school teacher] needs to get us to do like class activities or group activities where we can talk with each other and not just look at him write on the board the whole time.

Poly: I would say maybe more labs with groups because chemistry we didn't do a lot of labs and like we kinda got kinda jealous because other classes did labs every week and we did, we didn't do many; and in AP Biology we do a couple but they're not really interesting so maybe we can do more labs. That will help us with the things we're learning.

When reflecting upon the entire AFT experience, students shared their general AFT experience on the end-of-program evaluation forms. Comments were overwhelmingly positive. Students stated that the activities of the AFT program were engaging and rewarding and that their AFT experiences were enjoyable.

Terrel: I think [high school students] should take the AFT program because it helps your social skills as well as your learning skills, um it's really good for you and I really like this program, so yeah.

Tiara: AFT was full of life, fun, and creative. I truly enjoyed my teachers, peers, and advisors. They made a huge difference.

Rodrick: I'm more confident and prepared.

Ariel: I loved the program! And WILL be applying next year!

Bashu: It's fun. It's nothing like school.

Arthur: Pushed me outside my comfort zone and made me think critically.

The students in AFT felt that the experience provided active learning experiences that engaged them in science and math learning. Positive aspects included that they felt more confident and prepared for college learning.

Voice of Teachers

In the AFT model, the student participants are not the only ones who report learning from the experience. Two former instructors, also authors of this chapter, described their experiences from teaching in the AFT program.

Geeta Verma, Secondary Science

In AFT, Geeta was a university faculty instructor for the high school science team. She co-taught the 3-week session with a high school science teacher from Atlanta Public Schools. The two teachers planned their teaching together and took turns facilitating science learning experiences for the students. The AFT experience enabled her to implement the pedagogical strategies she uses in her methods courses (with preservice teachers) and with inservice teachers. The direct experience of working with students was beneficial to her professional growth. She wanted to explore if there was a shift from adult pedagogy to working with adolescents and what it would mean for her preservice teachers. Geeta also shared that her high school teaching partner, "did an excellent job of mediating this gap." The high school teacher truly was a partner in the teaching process with the university instructor.

Geeta reported that she chose to participate in AFT because, "I knew of the [AFT] at GSU and found it a great opportunity to work with underrepresented high school students at GSU. I wanted to participate in it to find out what it is to teach high school students coming from metro-Atlanta area on a university campus and how the students felt about it." She thought that it was a great opportunity to work with high school students, as it had been several years since she had taught students of that age.

When Geeta thought about how the AFT experience had affected others, she spoke about students she had worked with directly:

> It was really interesting to find out that they have a certain image of university professors and I think they enjoyed working with various professors during the program. For me, having the high school teacher was really helpful since she was able to "unfold" the university experience for the students and I (as the university professor) was able to add more to that information. I could tell that the students were really interested in university life (courses, programs, etc.). It was nice to hear many of them talk about pursuing a degree program on a university campus related to STEM areas.

Lisa Martin-Hansen, Elementary Science and Mathematics and Secondary Science

In AFT (2007), Lisa was a higher education faculty representative who co-taught with an elementary teacher from Atlanta Public Schools. Later, she also taught in the secondary science section (2009). Lisa was a former elementary and middle school teacher with 12 years of experience teaching in public schools (eight years in elementary grades). Lisa said that she chose to participate in AFT because she felt strongly about the need for greater representation of people from underrepresented groups in STEM careers and STEM education. By participating in this program, she hoped that AFT could convince young participants that science could be interesting, exciting, and important to them personally, and become a possible field to pursue in college and as a career.

Lisa felt that she would have many learning opportunities as she participated in AFT:

> By teaching in AFT, I've had the chance to learn from my students and from my co-teacher. Additionally, I received some reassurance that many of my teaching strategies also work well with students from underrepresented groups. I try to implement reform-based teaching strategies that include student-centered learning, which is definitely a good fit, as those strategies are often recommended in culturally relevant pedagogy.

Lisa said she had overheard an AFT participant say, "I wish science was taught like this at school. I would really like it then." That seemed very revealing, as Lisa and her colleague worked to use reform-based curricula (Science Education for Public Understanding Program) to model reform and standards-based pedagogy as well as to teach science content. Lisa thought that if the general experiences of students were not engaging and thoughtful, AFT then played an even more critical role in helping students to see how science and mathematics can be both interesting and challenging. Lisa shared that AFT was a "very rewarding teaching and learning experience" both for herself as a university faculty member and also for the way she saw students embracing the challenge to immerse themselves in learning about science and mathematics, becoming interested in science and mathematics, and reaching out to younger children in the process.

Next Steps

Our team still has hopes for a longitudinal perspective, where past, current, and future AFT students will be contacted after high school graduation to determine their postsecondary education and career choices. We have approval to locate graduates of the program and are delving into the process of finding them and inviting them to participate in an interview regarding their career choices and their perceptions of the effectiveness of AFT. One way that we've started to keep in touch with past AFT participants is through our AFT Facebook page.

Student interaction with the AFT program was short in duration (three weeks). It would be interesting to explore how more sustained (and more frequent) interactions in an AFT-like program throughout the school year may affect students' affinity for STEM-related careers, including science and mathematics teaching. In future iterations of the study, we hope to refine the nature of pedagogical and content experience the students receive by better aligning and complementing their secondary science, secondary mathematics, and elementary science and mathematics experiences with each other. Additionally, we hope to further develop the pre/post content quizzes for a better measure of student content learning. We have offered to assist the instructors with that particular task in order to help foster greater reliability and validity of the items.

Ties to Other Specific Reform Efforts

The AFT program aligns with other reform efforts as there is a concerted effort at the federal level to increase numbers of college students pursuing STEM majors in the United States (Business-Higher Education Forum 2010). Additionally, an NSF–funded project focusing on increasing the number of African American Males in STEM (QEM Network 2010) by increasing the number and retaining the numbers of minority males in those fields exists to bring together and support several institutions working toward these particular aims. In the state of Georgia, several universities were granted STEM funding from the USG-BOR for establishing programs similar to the AFT program at Georgia State University in order to generate interest in STEM and STEM education. Lastly, with the development of the Common Core Standards in the United States, there is a healthy emphasis on STEM, including new emphases on engineering and technology. The goals and aims of the AFT program are in concert with all the aforementioned initiatives.

Questions Raised From This Program

Several questions emerge from the existing program, which provide direction for future research. These include:

1. How has this program affected underrepresented students (positively or negatively) as they consider their options in a STEM career? What other ways might we explore student ideas and beliefs about their future careers?

2. What type of long-term effect does AFT have in increasing the number of underrepresented students pursuing STEM careers and teaching?

3. What are the influences of the partnership between the K–12 instructor and the university instructor as they partner in co-teaching to implement the model?

4. What does the innovative co-teaching partnership mean for students' experiences in the AFT program?

Additionally, as we consider the effectiveness of the program to meet the goals of the project, the following questions may be raised:

5. What might AFT do differently to capitalize and institutionalize the positive aspects of this program (that increase the STEM interest for underrepresented students) in either university courses or by taking ideas back to the high school?

6. Should there be even more of an emphasis on science and mathematics content within the AFT? If so, how should that take place?

Lastly, as we consider scaling up the model, we would need to think about what aspects are unique to Atlanta, Georgia, and what other models might be developed in other regions of the United States. Especially, we can ask the following question:

7. Can other universities replicate or modify this program to recruit underrepresented students successfully into STEM and STEM education careers? How might the model need to change based upon institutional and personnel needs?

Currently, this is a grant-supported program. If there is strong merit in the program, how could the state support this type of program at several locations? As this model results in an increase in positive attitudes among underrepresented groups of students regarding STEM, we propose that this model has promise and should be replicated at several locations. This will help to address the needs we have in STEM to increase the number of underrepresented students aspiring to STEM careers.

References

Business-Higher Education Forum (BHEF). 2010. *Increasing the number of STEM graduates: Insights from the U.S. STEM education & modeling project*. Washington, DC: BHEF.

National Science Teachers Association (NSTA). 2004. Position Statement: Science teacher preparation. *www.nsta.org/about/positions/preparation.aspx*

Scafidi, B., D. L. Sjoquist, and T. R. Stinebrickner. 2006. Do teachers really leave for higher paying jobs in alternative occupations? *The Berkeley Electronic Journal of Economic Analysis and Policy* 6 (1): 1–42.

Toolin, R. E. 2003. Learning what it takes to teach science: High school students as science teachers for middle school students. *Journal of Science Education and Technology* 12 (4): 457–469.

The Quality Education for Minorities (QEM) Network. (2010). *Quality education for minorities (QEM) network African American males workshop report*. Washington, DC: QEM.

Preparing Students for Careers That Do Not Yet Exist

Glenn "Max" McGee
Illinois Mathematics and Science Academy

Setting

The Illinois Mathematics and Science Academy (IMSA), as a self-described "teaching and learning laboratory for imagination and inquiry," has a history of pursuing innovations closely aligned with the vision and framework of the National Science Education Standards. Innovations include both methods and materials for inquiry-based student instruction as well as for delivering professional development for pre-service and practicing teachers. Instructional innovations described include yearlong student inquiry and research projects (SIR), self-paced physics instruction, student-driven energy and engineering projects, instruction in innovation and entrepreneurialism, and a host of student-led outreach activities to "ignite and nurture creative, ethical, scientific minds of students throughout Illinois and beyond." Highlighted practices for improving the effectiveness of current STEM teachers as well as training and inspiring prospective STEM teachers included IMSA's Teacher Candidate Institutes, Golden Apple Scholars and signature programs of Problem-Based Learning and IMSA FUSION.

In addition to describing these successful innovations, this chapter contains specific results and a constellation of evidence for each program, which serve to demonstrate the efficacy of IMSA's efforts in four areas: (1) improving students' deep conceptual understanding of critical STEM concepts; (2) promoting students' advanced studies and pursuit of STEM careers, including becoming mathematics and science educators; (3) changing teacher practices; and (4) developing a culture in which students not only become advanced "power users" of scientific principles but retain a commitment to IMSA's mission of "advancing the human condition" long after they leave school. The chapter concludes with recommendations for organizations and institutions seeking to replicate these and similar practices as well as advancing and scaling these practices through generative networks and pioneering technologies.

Context

The internationally recognized Illinois Mathematics and Science Academy was created by the State of Illinois in 1985 to provide a "uniquely challenging education" to Illinois' top mathematics and science students in grades 10–12. The Academy was also charged to serve as a "catalyst … to transform mathematics and science education" throughout the state. IMSA currently enrolls 650 academically talented Illinois students in its advanced, residential college preparatory program, and every year it serves hundreds of educators and thousands of students in Illinois and beyond through innovative instructional programs that foster imagination and inquiry. IMSA also advances education through research, groundbreaking ventures, and strategic partnerships. While career preparation programs in schools emphasize traditional skills, career preparation at IMSA adheres to a far different philosophy, based on constructivist learning principles, a bold mission, and standards that go far beyond learning specific skills and leave students well prepared for the 21st century, including attainment of the competencies and skills outlined in the work of Zhao (2009) and Wagner (2010).

Now, some 25 years later, IMSA still prepares students for careers that do not yet exist. The Academy's mission, belief statements, and core competencies are the foundation on which students first acquire the habits of mind to construct the advanced knowledge and skills and fashion the mindset of expert learners that will enable them to succeed in careers that they may end up creating for themselves. While novice learners may be adept at acquiring information, IMSA's graduates have learned how to learn, generate new knowledge, be self-directed learners, ask and answer challenging questions, and both find and solve problems that impede the healthy development of the human condition.

Ties to Standards and Reform Efforts

IMSA has historically listed its core competencies for teaching and learning as inquiry-based, problem-centered, integrative, and competency driven. While these competencies have been evident at IMSA for 25 years, along with an emphasis on collaborative learning practices in which students are required to engage in meaningful dialogue, group research, and healthy debate as they work in teams on assigned projects, weekly math assignments or generative performance assessments, they actually form much of the basis for the conceptual framework for the new science education standards: "The new framework specifies eight science and engineering practices that students should learn and use over the course of their schooling. Examples include asking questions and defining problems, analyzing and interpreting data, and engaging in arguments with evidence. The previous standards included practices in its model of 'inquiry-based learning,' but the new framework is more specific about the practices that students should learn and use" (NRC 2011).

As detailed in the next section, inquiry, modeling, and debate—the pillars of the new framework—are found in every IMSA science class and as such are exemplars for schools seeking to pursue the forthcoming standards. In fact, IMSA has long distinguished the importance of teaching *real* science as opposed to *school* science, as we believe that preparing students for STEM careers requires experiential learning. Real science involves students thinking, collaborating, experimenting, and even failing. IMSA students develop an uncommon resilience as well as the ability to learn from mistakes, ask the challenging questions, and identify the critical resources in solving the most challenging problems. Students are not only prepared for careers, but they are prepared to create careers and to succeed in jobs that may not yet exist. This concept of pursuing real science is echoed in the language of the National Academies framework: "The framework calls for a full integration of the practices of science with the ideas and concepts. That is, students should learn the ideas of science through actually doing science" (2011).

The chair of the committee that developed the standards framework, Dr. Helen Quinn, provides her own insight, as well as examples as to the importance of inquiry, debate, and modeling:

Quinn's committee, comprised of university scientists and education scholars from across the country, said educators should deemphasize "discrete facts" and refocus on "a limited number of core ideas and crosscutting concepts." Every student should have a chance to work with the ideas, make connections and experience how science is actually done. For kids to really understand an idea, they have to work with that idea. So what you need to do is have fewer facts and more development of ideas," she said (Kenrick 2011).

In an interview with Glenda Chui (2011), Quinn elaborates on the importance of inquiry:

The current national education standards push for science as inquiry... What the research on learning shows is that students learn better when they have a context in which to put those facts, where the facts are developed in a coherent fashion and where they get to understand what science is by engaging in scientific practices...

For example engaging students seriously in arguing from evidence—so students are the ones drawing the conclusions and saying how does this evidence support or not support a particular explanation that was given for what's going on. Another one is using models ... teach kids how to think about a problem rather than learning a lot of Latin names for parts of the cell. How to think about cells and how they function is more important. When we just memorize things we have no real understanding of, all of us tend to forget them. (Chui 2011)

Additionally, IMSA's curriculum is not textbook-driven. Rather it is driven by a small set of Standards of Significant Learning that emphasize students attaining deep conceptual understanding of key concepts. To attain this deep understanding, students develop habits of mind in which they learn how to learn, make connections among big concepts and ideas, develop thoughtful questions, and engage in healthy debate. Again, the idea of pursuing a few core ideas and integrating ("cross-cutting") them is both aligned with and precursor for the new framework:

We had a set of criteria for what constitutes a core idea for science learning. It's not just what are the core ideas of the discipline, but what are the core ideas of the discipline that are important for students to learn about in K–12? For example in physical science, the core ideas are matter and energy and forces and interactions; those are the ones everyone would expect. But then another one is waves and their relationship to information technology. That's for kids to understand that physics and chemistry have applications, and understand how these things play out in things they see in their everyday life (Chui 2011).

The National Academies report states, "One aspect of this coherence is the emphasis on deepening students' knowledge of core ideas systematically over multiple grade levels. Another aspect of coherence is the integration of a common set of practices and crosscutting concepts across the disciplines of science and across all of the grades" (2011).

Major Features of the IMSA Program

Inquiry-Based Collaborative Student Instruction

Arguably the best preparation for future careers is IMSA's instructional model. The core competencies of inquiry-based, problem-centered, integrative and competency driven teaching and learning are expected of all teachers and are a daily part of student instruction. Observations using the Power Walkthrough model and student surveys given at the end of every course have confirmed that these methods are both engaging and inspiring to the extent that they have shaped students aspirations, sparked their imagination, and taught them how to think critically and creatively.

Moreover, in most classes at IMSA students sit at tables with their peers and not in individual desks, because instruction is designed to engage students in meaningful, sustained collaboration with their classmates. Whether completing weekly "problem sets" in mathematics, preparing a presentation in a history class, or conducting a science experiment, students work in teams, and often their assessments are based both on their team's product and their individual contributions to it. Given that the ability to work in teams is frequently cited as a key 21st-century skill for career success (Partnership for 21st Century Skills 2003) this collaborative model assures students learn both the benefits and challenges of working in teams.

Student Research

Student research is a cornerstone of IMSA, beginning with Methods of Scientific Inquiry (MSI) as an introductory course sophomore year and extending to Student Inquiry and Research (SIR) junior and senior year. Given that developing habits of mind is the most important aspect of career preparation, in MSI students design and conduct hands-on experiments, make observations, analyze data, draw conclusions, and communicate evidence-based principles. These scientific ways of thinking and knowing become the foundation for their IMSA experience. MSI is a one-semester course that is required of all IMSA sophomores. The course explicitly addresses three broad areas encompassed by the nature of science: data acquisition and analysis, experimental design, and written and oral communication. Activities support the development of basic skills across the science disciplines and promote an understanding of scientific inquiry and the nature of research. Student learning objectives include:

- To enhance student learning and understanding in the following areas: data acquisition and analysis, experimental design, and written and oral communication.
- To develop students' skills and levels of understanding and proficiency in the following Standards of Significant Learning (SSLs):
  - Construct meaningful questions that advance learning
  - Observe precisely and record accurately
  - Critically evaluate information and reasoning

- Find and explain connections among things and ideas
- Construct and support judgments based on evidence
- Write and speak with power, economy, and elegance
- Recognize the parts that make up complex wholes

Students develop the skills necessary to conduct an inquiry project through a variety of learning activities that deepen with time. These activities support the development of research skills, as well as demonstrate discipline-appropriate scientific thinking. After building appropriate inquiry and research skills, students work with a partner to define and conduct their own inquiry investigations and report the results of that investigation in the form of research papers, poster presentation, and oral presentation. Students work with their partner to complete the poster and oral presentations, but the final research paper is written individually.

The Student Inquiry and Research (SIR) program is IMSA's flagship program. No classes are held on Wednesdays so students can pursue a yearlong annual research project of their choosing with a mentor in the field. In SIR we partner with distinguished researchers; hundreds of students are bused to prominent laboratories, universities and museums to conduct investigations on diagnostics, nanotechnology, particle physics and more. Each August, approximately 85% of IMSA's juniors and seniors have identified their mentor and their project. The vast majority of this research is in the hard sciences, whether working on quarks at Fermilab, researching congenative heart disease in premature infants at the Loyola University Medical Center or advanced chemistry in the laboratories at the University of Chicago. Other students pursue studies in mathematics or in the social, behavioral or economic sciences and a few explore challenging issues in the arts. SIR is a graded experience, with students being assessed on their proposal, abstract, their research log, final paper and capstone presentation to a group of peers, staff and professionals. The reflections of graduating seniors indicate how much they value their experience. For example, in a letter to his State Senator seeking continued funding for IMSA, P. J. Patel wrote: "They challenge us to think like the scientists and develop knowledge based on understanding and not on memorization. All of my science classes were coupled with extensive laboratory experiences, which have allowed me to participate in real-world research at Northwestern's Feinberg School of Medicine."

These titles of projects the past three years indicate both the diversity and complexity of SIR projects as well as students' commitment to achieving IMSA's mission of "advancing the human condition":

- Nanoparticle Silver-Applied Filters as Water Filtration Solutions
- Engineered NanoBio Conjugates for Brain Cancer Therapy
- BA-D1: A Novel Treatment for Type 2 Diabetes
- A Genome Wide Association Study of Carotid Artery Plaque
- A Western Legal Shift to Incorporate Indigenous Intellectual Knowledge
- Mass Incarceration and Its Effects in Society
- An Analysis of the Patient Protection and Affordable Care Act and Its Effect on Physician Compensation and Health Insurance Companies

- Design of Genetic Sequences Encoding a Matrix Metalloproteinase-2-Degradable Synthetic Recombinant Protein
- Density Functional Theory Study of the Influence of VOx Promotion on the Mechanism of Alcohol Synthesis on Rhodium Catalysts
- The Effect of *Egr2* on the Cell Markers Lag3, 41BB, and CRTAM in the Anergic carEGR2 flox/flox TH1 T-cell Clone

In keeping with the theme of preparing students for careers that do not yet exist, six IMSA students recently completed two yearlong SIR projects working with students in China and researchers at the Chinese Academy of Sciences, Beijing University of Astronautics and Aeronautics, and Peking University. One group pursued converting the grass *Miscanthus* to butanol and another explored the design of wind turbines for "gentle breeze" environments. Students met via videoconference every three or four weeks to share data, discuss findings, test prototypes, and the like. During the course of this international collaborative research they connected frequently outside the videoconferences and were not only successful in producing a final project but also in developing close cross-cultural relationships, another of Zhao's (2009) 21st-century skills. Given that global problems will require global solutions, these students are well positioned to become leaders in international research careers.

Self-Paced Physics

A faculty research project designed to identify why female students were far less likely to pursue electives than their male peers led to the development of an innovative introductory physics course. While the first year of Self-Paced Physics is just completed and no evidence is yet available of girls' persistence in physics, student survey results indicated that the self-paced experience was positive in terms of both student achievement and motivation for further study.

TALENT

Total Applied Learning for Entrepreneurs (TALENT) focuses on student entrepreneurship in a STEM context. It is truly career preparation for entrepreneurs and innovators. The program engages students in activities that include, but are not limited to, understanding intellectual property, developing a business plan, developing products, securing funding, networking, communicating ideas, and starting a business. Taught in an evening seminar format, instructors engage students not only in developing their ideas but also in interacting with successful entrepreneurs in an array of businesses from high tech to meal preparation. One of TALENT's highlights is its Power Pitch Contest where IMSA student entrepreneurs pitch their new business ideas to venture capital investors and entrepreneurial leaders. One of the judges, John Hoesley, a highly successful entrepreneur and IMSA alumnus noted, "The ability to clearly communicate the value of your product or service and its growth potential in its early stage of development is critical to venture capital funding or seed funding. This real-world experience for IMSA student entrepreneurs gives them a head start in understanding the competitive marketplace and in preparing answers to vital questions before they seek funding."

Applied Engineering and the IMSA Energy Center

Students who do not participate in SIR projects often opt to pursue the Wednesday Applied Engineering seminars and laboratories. Working in small groups, students explore branches of engineering and learn about the highly diverse opportunities within the field. They will learn to analyze given problems and through teamwork arrive at a solution. A requirement for completion is to design and build various functioning objects, ideally that will improve the quality of life. The innovative ideas and prototypes are again evidence of preparation for nonstandard and as yet nonexistent careers as well as for traditional engineering.

During past years many of the Applied Engineering projects have been in the field of energy and integrated with the IMSA Energy Center. Given the proliferation of careers in energy coupled with students' natural concerns for the environment, IMSA's mission and core belief that "we are all students of our planet," students and staff launched the Energy Center three years ago. Students authored both its powerful mission, "a collaborative pioneering endeavor to spark innovative student inquiry focused on sustainable energy sources, usage and policy," and its compelling vision, "to promote the conservation of global resources and the implementation of energy alternatives based on innovative and collaborative research within the IMSA community and beyond." To integrate the teaching of science, technology, engineering and mathematics, the IMSA Energy Center draws on students' natural concern for their environment and desire to advance the human condition. Students join engineering and research teams to work on energy issues of their own interests. Each team selects leaders and assigns roles to team members. Students learn academic science content as they encounter the need to solve problems for their respective teams. This educational process is fluid. Students are able to share their ideas by forming new teams or joining existing teams at almost any point during the school year. The energy center has specific goals, each with set of activities and deliverables. The goals are:

- Research, construct, and produce alternative energy sources and demonstrations;
- Create community awareness about energy sources, usage, and policy and the Energy Center's goals, projects, and demonstrations;
- Serve as an educational resource to school systems throughout Illinois and beyond;
- Build collaborative relationships with organizations in the private and public sectors to combine resources that lead to new bodies of knowledge, programs, and services; and
- Secure financial partners to seed and launch projects and prototypes.

Preparing Future Teachers: IMSA Allies

While the majority of IMSA students pursue STEM careers, IMSA realizes that some of its best teachers are its current students. While some high schools may still have Future Teacher Clubs or classes that involve students in observing teachers, IMSA's Kids Institute and Allies programs actually enlist and prepare high school age students to teach younger students important STEM lessons. IMSA Allies are students who work as teachers and group leaders for all Kids Institute programs throughout the year. Kids Institute's design is to have kids teaching kids. The first "Kids" being IMSA students and the second being the outside students in summer camps, Saturday FUNshops, and school assemblies. On Wednesdays, Allies meet to learn about teaching pedagogy and strategies about how to work with a diverse population of students. They learn how to introduce STEM concepts through demonstrations and activities and after this first quarter have the opportunity to teach or lead groups of middle school students who visit IMSA. Allies also assist in writing the curriculum for FUNshops, summer curriculum, assemblies, and field trips.

Allies first spend time observing experienced teachers and group leaders. They next work as assistant teachers or co-group leaders in order to work side-by-side with experienced Allies. After the Allies and Kids Institute staff are comfortable that the students can take charge of his or her own classroom or group, they "graduate" to experienced teachers or experienced group leaders. Allies teachers are responsible for facilitating the inquiry-based, hands-on learning experience and to guide the students in their learning process. In other words, they are expected to teach the IMSA way, the way they are taught. IMSA graduates who go on to become teachers have returned to IMSA to share both their successes and frustrations. While being well prepared to become inquiry-based teachers, they have also confronted the hard reality that many schools are not open to these approaches. By and large, however, the resilience and persistence they have acquired through their IMSA experience has sustained them in their careers as they continue to be the leaders in forging a transformative model of teaching.

Leadership and Ethics

While the phrase "career and college readiness" generally brings to mind the idea of skill development, two of the most important and generally neglected career preparation skills, leadership and ethics, are required monthly seminars at IMSA.

LEAD, IMSA's innovative, student-run leadership program, inspires its sophomore students through open classroom discussion, engaging and meaningful activities, real-life applications, and personal reflection to strive to become positive, ethical leaders who pursue their passions and use their individual capability to create the change they want to see in the world. IMSA believes that every student has the potential to lead and that leadership can be learned. Thus, this series of seminars is designed to take an intricate look at definitions, theories, models, and conceptualizations of leadership. Students will be challenged to think critically about leadership during peer-to-peer facilitated lectures, class discussions, hands-on exercises, and group work. Students are provided with a foundation of leadership, which includes topics such as understanding self, social justice/group dynamics, communication, and conflict resolution/negotiation.

Considerations in Ethics introduces IMSA juniors to the very real, yet often rejected notion of ethics as a field of philosophical study. At monthly seminars students are introduced to the ethical systems of philosophers including Aristotle, Kant, Confucius, Bentham, Hobbes, Rawls, and others. Following the presentations, juniors engage in activity-based breakout sessions led by senior facilitators. In addition, two presentations are given by speakers from various fields, including medicine, politics, advanced technology, pharmaceutical research, and law, so students learn that ethics are integral to career success and best learned early on.

Professional Development

When IMSA was founded in 1985, part of its legislative charge was to serve as a catalyst for transforming mathematics and science education. IMSA fulfills this charge by not only delivering professional development and coaching in teaching the IMSA way so other teachers can prepare their students for 21st-century careers but also helping them grow and succeed in their careers. While IMSA has a host of opportunities for teachers at all levels of their career, from preservice to veteran, three programs have proven to be the most effective in changing teaching behaviors and in impacting student learning: Problem-Based Learning (PBL) Network, IMSA FUSION, and Teacher Candidate Institutes (TCI).

PBL Network

Problem-based learning is focused experiential learning organized around the investigation and resolution of messy, real-world problems. PBL engages students as stakeholders immersed in an ill-structured, problematic situation and organizes curriculum around this holistic problem, enabling student learning in relevant and connected ways. PBL creates a learning environment in which teachers coach student thinking and guide student inquiry, facilitating learning toward deeper levels of understanding while entering the inquiry as a co-investigator.

To prepare teachers in the art and science of the collaborative inquiry of Problem Based Learning, IMSA has created a series of institutes for individuals, teams, schools, and districts. Teachers learn how to teach content as well as learning skills essential for students to thrive in the 21st century and developed criteria to gauge progress in those skills as identified by the North Central Regional Educational Laboratory and the Metiri Group (2003). These skills fall into four groups: (1) digital age literacy, (2) inventive thinking, (3) effective communication, and (4) high productivity. Specific skills include global awareness and multicultural literacy; self-direction, risk-taking and managing complexity; teaming and collaboration; and the ability to produce relevant, high-quality products.

IMSA FUSION

IMSA FUSION offers exciting, hands-on, minds-on STEM activities for 20–30 talented students in grades 5–8 who attend weekly program sessions at their school, taught by teachers in their school who were prepared by IMSA staff. In fact, the professional development of teachers is the primary focus of IMSA FUSION. Teacher workshops provide rich content background, quality curricular materials and lab kits, and extensive training and practice in inquiry-based instruction. FUSION employs IMSA's recognized core competency of developing and delivering curricular materials and teaching approaches that are competency-driven, problem-centered, inquiry-based, and integrative. The effect on teachers and their students is profound. Writes one of the FUSION teachers:

> I have seen students grow intellectually and become better thinkers over the past two years as a result of the FUSION program. FUSION students approach open inquiry with more success than students who are not in the FUSION program because they have more confidence in solving problems. FUSION has given me experience in inquiry-based teaching and learning which has carried over into my classroom teaching. I have used lessons from the FUSION program in my regular classroom. The program has increased the expectations of our students. FUSION has inspired me to pursue a Math and/or Science endorse-

ment. FUSION lessons have also given me ideas on how to incorporate math and science lessons together.

Teacher Candidate Institutes

Teacher Candidate Institutes (TCIs) are two-week (8–10 day) programs designed to offer preservice education candidates an opportunity to encounter a wide range of instructional activities from planning and design to implementation and assessment in a mentored environment. The TCIs focus on STEM content and are meant to increase the comfort level and facility of teacher candidates in the critical areas noted above. The TCIs also introduce candidates to IMSA's constructivist approach to pedagogy, with an emphasis on inquiry, problem-centeredness, and integrated ways of teaching and learning. Ideally, the participating candidates have completed classroom observations, but have not yet done student teaching.

Teacher Candidate Institutes are divided into two distinct phases. The first, or training, phase, lasts three to five days, and is taught either by IMSA faculty and staff alone or in collaboration with faculty and staff from the partnering college or university. Candidates are introduced to IMSA's approach to mathematics and science teaching and learning through study and discussion of the core attributes of the competency-driven, problem centered, inquiry-based, integrative curriculum during a POP (Pedagogy, Orientation and Planning) workshop. They are then familiarized with the content to be delivered to the students with whom they will work. Content instruction is delivered for candidates in the same way it is for experienced teachers who are involved with IMSA's outreach programming. Candidates work through all activities that will be taught to the students during the second phase of the Institute, debriefing as they go. They conclude the IMSA-led section of the training phase by planning the rollout of the instructional unit with students. If time permits, they practice-teach to each other under the guidance of IMSA mentors.

Evidence of Success

While most high schools measure success in terms of test scores, IMSA uses these as a secondary measure to an array of metrics including student awards, publications, and placement in national and international competitions; alumni's pursuit of STEM careers and contributions to "advancing the human condition;" and SIR projects. Also, given the Academy's legislative charge to serve teachers and students throughout Illinois, data are collected for PBL, IMSA FUSION and TCI Institutes.

Student Achievement

While test scores are not IMSA's most important metric, the students excel on standardized tests. Data for a recent graduating class show the following mean scores:

- ACT Composite: 31.5 (national average = 21.1)
- SAT Reading: 666 (national average = 501)
- SAT Math: 721 (national average = 515)
- SAT Writing: 663 (national average = 493)

Also, although IMSA does not offer AP courses, 85% of students who tested last year scored 3 or higher on examinations. AP examinations were administered to 292 students. 125 students took the Calculus BC AP examination and had a mean score of 4.53 out of 5. Moreover approximately 25% regularly are named National Merit Finalists.

Students regularly place highly in state, national, and international competitions as individuals and as teams. For example, students are regularly selected as semifinalists for the Intel and Siemens competitions; in the last three years, three students have been on the U.S. Physics and Chemistry teams; and several students have published papers of their SIR projects in distinguished publications such as *The Astrophysical Journal Letters, The Journal of Physical Chemistry, Learning and Leading with Technology, Nature, Neuroscience Research Communications* and *The Science Teacher.* Within the last two years, IMSA's math team has won the state mathematics contest and Scholastic Bowl championship and a team of four has placed first in the International Mathematical Modeling Competition.

Alumni Longitudinal Study

The Academy conducts regular surveys of graduates. Results show that more than 60% of IMSA's graduates pursue STEM careers. Several of these are high profile, as IMSA alumni were on the founding teams of PayPal and YouTube, lead authors in developing Microsoft Outlook and Explore, and literally the pioneers of the internet leading the development of Mosaic and Apache. Recently, two graduates were lauded for discovering new planets and exploring "waltzing black holes." All of these, and hundreds of others, are engaged in careers that did not exist when they entered IMSA their sophomore year and are a testament to the power and success of an inquiry-based education.

Quantitatively, 60% of IMSA graduates have earned degrees in STEM fields and are now scientists, doctors, engineers, researchers, teachers, and leaders in other fields. Approximately 25% of alumni are employed in technology, mathematics, and engineering; almost 20% in medicine and other sciences; and more than 10% in business and finance. IMSA alumni have founded more than 30 new companies and created countless jobs.

A current longitudinal study of STEM specialty schools (Subotnik, Tai, and Almarode 2011) examined survey data from IMSA graduates and gifted and talented students who did not attend IMSA. The results showed that students who had research experiences in high school (e.g., MSI), who undertook an apprenticed mentorship or internship (e.g., SIR), and whose teachers connected the content across different STEM courses were more likely to complete a STEM major than their peers who did not report these experiences.

Problem-Based Learning Network (PBL)

Data from multiple sources, including independent observations and surveys conducted by external reviewers have provided affirmative evidence for the following:

- PBL has a positive impact on student learning.

- IMSA's PBL model develops metacognitive strategies in students. (Pierce and Gerdes 2005) on IMSA's PBL drive Summer Sleuths program shows a significant increase in metacognitive statements initiated by students.
- Participants' students show a positive change in content knowledge, attitude and/or behavior (critical thinking, self-directed learning, collaboration). The independent evaluation study (Oyer 2005) on Fox Valley PBL Initiative shows that student impact increases (20–40 percentage points) as teachers gain more experience in PBL strategies.
- IMSA's introductory PBL workshops/institutes are effective in increasing teachers' knowledge and skills of PBL as well as increasing PBL teacher strategies in their classrooms.
- Educators trained in PBL implement PBL strategies and skills as part of their regular classroom practice and report that it makes a positive difference in student learning (Oyer 2006).

IMSA FUSION

In 10 years, IMSA FUSION has grown from a program serving 7 schools to more than 80 schools and in 2010–11, served over 200 teachers and 2,000 students. It was selected as one of the "Best Practice" K–12 STEM Education programs in the nation in September 2010, by the Bayer Corporation's Making Science Make Sense initiative for our proven track of helping girls and underrepresented minorities to participate and achieve in STEM. One reason this award was given is that IMSA FUSION is a data-driven and researched-based program that tracks program impact using the following tools:

1. Survey of Enacted Curriculum to measure teacher professional growth and impact

2. High School Transcript Study to measure long-term impact on students

3. Constituent Surveys to provide qualitative data of program impact

4. Site Performance Observations to measure program teaching and learning

Longitudinal program research demonstrates that the majority of FUSION alumni elect to take advanced coursework in math and science in high school and, in fact, attain above average grades in these courses. Data collected through the Survey of Enacted Curriculum show gains in FUSION teacher professional growth in the use of hands-on instructional strategies and approaches that develop student communication and demonstration of content understanding. In addition, teachers report that they are provided with the skills, support, and resources to use the best practices, inquiry-based, and real-world teaching that our students need to be 21st-century learners, bringing new, more effective instructional skills to their classrooms year after year. Program surveys taken by FUSION students, parents, teachers and principals indicate significantly strong perception of the benefits and value that FUSION brings to schools.

Data are tracked internally at the Illinois Mathematics and Science Academy as well, to show that IMSA FUSION has been a very significant pipeline for IMSA. Since 2005, 41 former FUSION students have graduated from IMSA. As of this past fall, 2010, more than 13% of the current students in IMSA's residential high school program participated in FUSION in their middle schools.

IMSA FUSION also increases access to STEM programs for underrepresented minorities and low-income students. Over the past five years, a little less than 50% of the FUSION participants were Caucasian, approximately 25–30% African American, and less than 20% Hispanic. The rate of participation by Asian students has increased from 2% to 10%. In this coming school year, 64% of the students in our new partner schools are underrepresented minorities. In 2010, the rate of students eligible for free and reduced lunch averaged 55%. For 2011–12 the average rate of low-income students in FUSION schools will increase to 62%. Twenty-one FUSION schools will have low-income student populations at or above 75%.

Needless to say, there is an abundance of anecdotal and testimonial data, but this reflection captures the gist of these by describing the impact of FUSION: Last year, an IMSA FUSION Site Support Specialist, Sharon Poynter, from the Springfield area was recognized by a young woman who had participated in the IMSA FUSION program at Grant Middle School in Springfield as a sixth grader. She was a FUSION student for one full year before she moved away for her seventh- and eighth-grade years. This student told Sharon that being chosen for the IMSA program "was the turning point" in her life because she realized she was intelligent and talented and that being part of the FUSION program instilled confidence that she never had. She worked harder in school and earned a scholarship to a Chicago area math and science high school. Currently in college, this FUSION alumna wants to continue her studies and become an optometrist. She had been raised by her mom and grandmother, and "had no college plans before her one year in the IMSA program."

Quantitative data exist that show the impact of the program on students and teachers as evidenced in the table below:

Table 9.1. Impact of IMSA Programs on Students and Teachers

Teacher-Reported Changes in Instructional Practice Due to Participation in IMSA FUSION	IMSA FUSION Graduates' Enrollment Patterns in Freshmen and Sophomore High School Mathematics and Science Courses
• *Competency-driven* (standards-influenced): 94% reported an increase in the application of math and science concepts. • *Inquiry-based* (student-led): 100% reported an increase in use of open-ended, student-driven, high level questioning. • *Integrative* (connected): 94% reported an increase in integrative learning experiences across disciplines. • *Problem-centered* (real-world focused): 100% reported an increase in the use of real-world problems in the classroom.	• 74% take advanced mathematics courses • 100% take advanced science courses* *Preliminary results based on FUSION graduates in five Illinois high school districts.

Teacher Candidate Institutes

Survey and observational data are collected for participants in IMSA's Teacher Candidate Institutes to identify if the targeted outcomes were met. The most recent evaluation plan showed:

- The indicator that "67% of participating teachers will increase their knowledge of inquiry-based practices" was met, with participants already holding some knowledge about inquiry-based practices before the program.
- The indicator that "100% of participating teacher candidates will practice their lesson presentation in phase one" was met as through observations of the participants' teaching.
- The indicator "100% of participating teacher candidates will reflect on learning in written journals in the debrief session" was demonstrated in their daily reflections in the first and/or second week.
- The indicator that "75% of teacher candidates will demonstrate inquiry-based strategies in teaching student participants" was seen in an analysis of the observation forms.
- The indicator that "75% of teacher candidates will note the use of inquiry-based teaching strategies during daily reflections" was met.

The large body of evidence of IMSA's success has been noted as IMSA regularly places among Newsweek's "best high schools in America," despite the fact that IMSA does not offer standard Advanced Placement (AP) courses because they are not yet inquiry-based. (Merrefield and Streib 2011) Also, in 2009, the Intel Foundation recognized IMSA as the Star Innovator Award Winner, its top award in the Schools of Distinction competition.

Conclusion

As "a teaching and learning laboratory for imagination and inquiry," IMSA has developed innovative programs, practices and services to prepare students for STEM careers and to train, coach, and support teachers in schools for preparing their students for future STEM careers. The "career preparation," is not traditional in just inculcating knowledge or teaching skills. Career preparation at IMSA is about teaching students to learn, to think, to collaborate, to challenge, to take risks, and to learn from failures. This basis of career preparation prepares them to be agile thinkers, ethical leaders, and individuals of vision, action, and commitment. The system has been effective, as IMSA has produced the visionary leaders who founded PayPal, YouTube, Netscape, and Yelp; astronomers recognized for discoveries; and medical doctors and researchers who have pioneered advances in their field.

While IMSA is in one sense a unique environment—a state-funded residential public school—but as a laboratory it is tops as a proving ground for best practices which can be replicated, with modifications, for an array of settings.

If we are educating tomorrow's students for today's careers, America will never retain its international leadership in innovation and invention, much less be able to thrive economically. Career preparation begins with identifying the mindset and habits of mind students will need to excel at careers that do not exist, to be ethical leaders, and to share mission and action that will advance the human condition.

References

Chui, G. 2011. New report lays out what kids should know about science. *SLAC News Center*, Stanford University. Available online at *https://news.slac.stanford.edu/ features/new-report-lays-out-what-kids-should-know-about-science*

Kenrick, C. 2011. Less memorizing, more engagement, Stanford physicist Quinn says. *Palo Alto Online* August 1. Available online at *www.paloaltoonline.com/news/show_story.php?id=22004*

Merrefield, C., and L. Streib. 2011. The best high schools in America. *The Daily Beast* June 19.

National Research Council (NRC). 2011. *A framework for K–12 science education.* Washington, DC: National Academies Press.

North Central Regional Educational Laboratory and the Metiri Group. 2003. *enGauge 21st century skills: Literacy in the digital age.* Naperville, IL: NCREL.

Oyer, E. J. 2005. Fox Valley problem-based learning initiative: Progress toward objectives 2004–2005. *Problem-based learning: Data matrix and report.* Aurora, IL: IMSA.

Oyer, E. J. 2006. Fox Valley problem-based learning network (PBLN): Summary of impact 1996–2006. *Problem-based learning: Data matrix and report.* Aurora, IL: IMSA.

Partnership for 21st Century Skills. 2003. *Learning for the 21st century.* Washington, DC: Author.

Pellegrino, J. W. 2006. *Rethinking and redesigning curriculum, instruction and assessment: What contemporary research and theory suggests.* Washington, DC: NCEE.

Pierce, J. W., and D. Gerdes. 2005. Problem-based learning of middle school students in the presence or absence of a teacher. Paper presented at the Midwest Educational Research Association Conference, Columbus, Ohio.

Subotnik, R. F., R. H. Tai, and J. Almarode. 2011. Study of the impact of selective SMT high schools: Reflections on learners gifted and motivated in science and mathematics. Unpublished paper submitted to the National Research Council committee exploring Highly Successful Schools or Programs for K–12 STEM Education.

Wagner, T. 2010. *The global achievement gap: Why even our best schools don't teach the new survival skills our children need—and what we can do about it.* New York: Basic Books.

Zhao, Y. 2009. *Catching up or leading the way: American education in the age of globalization.* Alexandria, VA: Association for Supervision and Curriculum Development.

The Steppingstone Magnetic Resonance Training Center: Opportunities for Students and Faculty in a True Research Laboratory Setting

Philip D. (Reef) Morse II
Steppingstone Magnetic Resonance Training Center

Kiyo Ann Morse
Steppingstone School for Gifted Education

Arthur Heiss
Bruker Bio-Spin

Setting

In response to the national call for more scientists, Steppingstone School for Gifted Education responded by establishing the Steppingstone Magnetic Resonance Training (SMART) Center, which will be described in this chapter. In collaboration with Bruker Bio-Spin and Scientific Software Services, the program was designed to attract gifted students, who are the most likely to pursue and excel in this type of scientific research. However, gifted students typically decide on their careers as young adolescents and well before they would have access to such a laboratory, which is usually available only in graduate school.

The attraction to gifted students is the uncertain, nonlinear, exhilarating process that is scientific research at its best. The SMART Center provides a true research experience for middle and high school students using magnetic resonance instrumentation. This training uses a Bruker ESP300 electron spin resonance spectrometer. Techniques for implementing the SMART Center concept in other venues will be discussed as well as the remarkable ability of young students to master advanced instrumentation and use it to develop and pursue their own research ideas at levels that interest the international scientific community and hopefully will inspire these students to make scientific research their chosen career.

The SMART Center is a fusion of educational methodology and scientific instrumentation that has involved over 50 students since June 2009. Students participate in four 6-hour sessions where they learn about resonance, spectroscopy, how to use the instrument, how to obtain and analyze data, and experimental design. Most importantly, students learn how to ask questions they can actually answer. Once they have completed the training course, they have access to the laboratory and instrumentation, where they pursue their research ideas and ultimately present their research not only to other students, but also to other audiences. Pre- and posttests show that students retain much of what they learn, including complex physical concepts like relaxation processes. Gifted students thrive and excel when doing research with no known answer. One project, antioxidant levels in green teas, has caught the attention of an internationally renown scientist. An eighth-grade student studying free radicals in coffee has presented her work at an international magnetic resonance conference.

The SMART Center model operates as a general means for knowledge transfer from the older, experienced generation, to the younger, excitable generation. Its motto "Exciting the New Generation" is not only a play on words that describes resonance processes, it is the ultimate purpose of its existence.

Introduction

Inquiry is defined as "a seeking for truth, information, or knowledge—seeking information by questioning." Individuals carry on the process of inquiry from the time they are born until they die. This is true even though they might not reflect upon the process. Infants begin to make sense of the world by inquiring. From birth, babies observe faces that come near, they grasp objects, they put things in their mouths, and they turn toward voices. The process of inquiring begins with gathering information and data through applying the human senses—seeing, hearing, touching, tasting, and smelling (EBC 2004).

The National Science Education Standards paraphrases the term *inquiry* as "active participation in the process of science" (NRC 1996). What is less clear is what "active participation" actually means in practice. Does it mean that students follow a set of directions in a laboratory environment? Does it mean that students sit under a tree and watch the clouds roll by? Does it mean learning about how a given method or instrument can be used to help understand our world? Does it mean all of these things and many, many more?

There is no one way to do science, just as there is no one way to solve a problem. If you think that the answer to 2 + 2 is 4, then you have not considered the problem in base 4 or base 3. The problem does not even exist in base 2; you would not have used those perspectives if you hadn't inquired about the basis for number systems and thought about what it means to count. Indeed the logic can be less obvious in the real world. What is the result of adding two drops of water to two drops of water? Fascinating problems exist all around us, often in answers we take for granted. What are the means by which students will learn to inquire about them? How do we as educators empower our students to develop truly inquiring minds?

One place to begin is to provide an environment where students participate in the processes of science as scientists. Perusal of NSTA LISTSERV messages shows a number of members with a solid working knowledge of science as practiced by scientists and a larger number of members with only cursory science experience. Even if all teachers could provide an appropriate science-learning environment, demands for "accountability" for basic standards named by administrators and legislatures far removed from the practice of science further constrain what can actually happen in the classroom. When teachers' jobs depend on their students' performance on written tests about factual information, it is little wonder that students faced with the real business of science—asking questions and figuring out how to answer them—do poorly. A typical student response indicates the problem with a focus on possible careers:

> In biology, we strictly devoted our time to content that was covered in the state content standards. It entails thoroughly knowing what will and won't be showing up on the state tests in the spring so we don't waste time on things that we know won't be on the test. In photosynthesis, photosystems and details of light and dark reactions [are] not necessary, but equation, location in cell, and role in ecosystems [are] necessary. It's a shame we have to leave out a lot that is not deemed important by the state, but that is how we had to narrow it down. (Hattie 2009)

Evaluating thought processes, problem-solving ability, ability to ask answerable questions, and laboratory skills are impossible to machine-grade. Yet these are the skills that successful practicing scientists use to ply their trade. How can we offer students the opportunity to learn these skills? To answer this question requires those traits that are important to the process of science—solving problems by thinking "outside the box," being willing to take risks, having the ability to move forward when the outcome is uncertain, permitting ourselves to fail and to learn from these failures, analyzing information, asking answerable questions, and realizing that there may well be no single answer. We must model that behavior when we wish to instill it in our students. This chapter tells the story of how the authors tackled this issue.

Relative to other chapters in this monograph, this chapter does not provide a detailed list of references. That is because the concepts and their implementation are new. To the authors' knowledge, no other facility like this exists in the United States and possibly, in the world. What we present here describes a work in progress. While it provides details about a specific application of advanced scientific instrumentation to student learning, it also provides a general template that can be used in many educational environments. Central to its implementation is the willingness of seasoned scientists to share their knowledge with others (Morse 2009, 2010). Details of how that happens are left as an exercise for the reader.

This chapter demonstrates principles in action. It is not a cure. It is not a recipe to follow. There are no guarantees of success. However, it provides a path toward and broadens the discussion of practical science education, how to achieve it, and how to know when you actually have achieved it. This chapter also describes steps to create a program that can be self-supporting if other avenues for implementation are not available. Independence brings freedom. It also brings additional tasks of creating revenue streams and attracting students. These tasks are discussed later.

We use the term *mentor* in this chapter to refer to the adults whose ultimate responsibility is the education of the students in their care. Ideally, the mentor is learning from the student as much as the student is learning from the mentor. The less the adults stand in front of the students and talk, the more the students take the responsibility for the learning process. Giving up the position at the front of the class is often the most difficult, and the most rewarding, action the mentor can take. Of course the adults still have the administrative responsibilities of student safety, proper use of the laboratory and its contents, and handling of necessary paper-work. However, these responsibilities should be subtle relative to active student learning in the physical environment.

Description of Project

The Steppingstone MAgnetic Resonance Training (SMART) Center arose out of conversations among Dr. Reef Morse, a retired physical biochemist and EPR (electron paramagnetic reso-nance—also known as ESR or electron spin resonance) spectroscopist and President of Scientific Software Services (a producer of software for data collection and analysis), Dr. Arthur Heiss of Bruker-BioSpin, the major manufacturer of EPR spectrometers in the world, and Kiyo Morse, Head of School at Steppingstone School for Gifted Education. Art and Reef were attending a magnetic resonance conference in Colorado and were discussing the possibilities of interesting students in the field of magnetic resonance. They both realized that students are exposed to chemistry, at least in the form of the interaction of baking soda and vinegar, at a relatively early age, but certainly are not exposed to magnetic resonance until late in their college careers; usually as advanced graduate students or postdoctoral fellows. It struck Reef that the way to interest students in magnetic resonance was to expose them to it as early as possible in their career plan-ning, even as early as middle and high school. This flies in the face of common dogma that deems no one ready to learn magnetic resonance until they have at least a year of physical chemistry and quantum mechanics! This was followed by a conversation with Kiyo Morse, who has over the last 30 years developed curriculum ideally suited for the development of gifted children. It was Reef's experience with this curriculum—which emphasizes education as a two-way street involving both teacher and student in a flexible learning environment—that finally brought the concept of the SMART Center into focus. Reef then asked Art if he had a used instrument that he would be willing to provide (new, these instruments cost around $200,000 or more). To Reef's complete and utter amazement, Art said, "Yes."

Once Reef had acquired the instrument and got it working, he applied for a grant from the Toyota Tapestry Foundation. He initially believed that a project with a visual component would be the most interesting to the potential participants and so the proposal was written to develop a magnetic resonance imaging project. In fact, this turned out to be a wrong assumption, as will be discussed later in this chapter.

The important lesson learned in this is: Ask for what you want. The only certainty is that if you don't ask, you won't get it. Since we are training students to think beyond their personal boundaries, we must think and act beyond our own as well.

What Was Our Purpose?

Science, as done by practicing scientists, is a messy, uncertain, and exhilarating process. It rarely follows the five (or seven) steps of the scientific method taught in school. How can a student form a hypothesis about something if he or she has no prior knowledge about the topic? The SMART Center provides an environment in which participants are allowed to experiment, ask questions (the answer to which is typically "See if you can figure it out."), and learn how to get answers. Its mission statement is the first document students see in their binder of class materials:

> The mission of the Steppingstone MAgnetic Resonance Training (SMART) Center is to provide an environment where participants can take part in an authentic science research experience including learning how to use advanced scientific instrumentation, designing experiments, collecting and analyzing data, and presenting their results to the general public.

> The SMART Center is an intellectually safe and nourishing facility where both students and staff celebrate learning. It is inclusive, supportive, and generative in all aspects of its operation.

It is the last paragraph of the mission statement that drives both long- and short-term operation of the facility. Every action, every document, every interaction takes place in the context of this mission statement.

Implementation

Besides the magnetic resonance spectrometer (the actual device is called an electron spin resonance, or ESR spectrometer), the laboratory is minimally equipped with a balance (0.1 mg resolution), automatic pipettes (2 mcl through 1 ml), heater-stirrer and magnetic stir bars, standard laboratory glassware (beakers, graduated cylinders, Erlenmeyer flasks), and specialty glassware specific to the ESR spectrometer (5 mm quartz tubes, 1 mm capillary tubes). Almost no chemicals are stocked, as students bring samples of interest with them and there is little formal preparation of these samples except to place them in the appropriate glassware for measurement.

Students receive a binder of materials and a notebook. They are instructed to write *everything* that has to do with the laboratory in their notebooks, which remain in the lab. Initially, no one writes much of anything in the notebook. This continues until someone tries to repeat an experiment, at which point they realize that they don't have sufficient information to do so. This is a critical teaching moment. This is handled by asking the student "Where would you find that information?" or "What do you think needs to happen now?" It is at this moment that students will decide to take, or not to take, responsibility for their work. This moment will crop up again and again as students learn how much information they need to record. The mentors suggest they write more, rather than less, immediately followed by the comment that they can, in the future, refer to this information and note changes from this protocol. The release of tension at this insight is palpable.

The binder contains all course material. In addition to teaching materials (theory of operation of the ESR spectrometer, an operations checklist, experimental protocols, and laboratory exercises), students read (along with the instructor) a document labeled "Rules of the Road." It contains the specifics of acceptable behavior in the laboratory. Both student and mentor sign this document. Failure to follow these rules results in dismissal from the lab (and, yes, we have dismissed students. The remaining students realize that the mentors mean business and that the rules apply to everyone).

1. Be respectful. Be respectful not only of the physical items in the laboratory such as instruments, glassware, and people, but also of ideas. Good ideas often come from unexpected sources. Keep your eyes and ears open.

2. Be aware that you are participating in a pilot program designed to develop curriculum and teaching methods. This has never been done before. Everything won't work all the time. The success or failure of this program is directly related to you; what you do and how you do it. If you think something can be improved, let us know. It's up to the SMART Center staff to make the decisions, but you provide the data.

3. If you make a mistake or break or damage something, let a staff member know immediately. We may not be happy to have to fix something you broke, but we'll be even more unhappy if we find it ourselves first. Take responsibility for your actions and act responsibly.

4. Follow the laboratory rules: Wear eye protection in the lab, do not mouth-pipette anything, no water-bottle fights, and so on. Use common sense and safety. You will be dismissed from the program if you cannot follow these rules.

5. Keep a notebook of everything you do. The original notebook will stay at the SMART Center but you may have a copy made for yourself. These notebooks are the property of the SMART Center and should be treated as such.

6. If you don't understand something, or aren't certain about what to do, ask.

7. It's OK to make honest mistakes as long as you learn from them. Self-analysis is an important part of research.

8. We don't have all the answers. You will be performing experiments and doing science for which there are no known answers. It's up to you to find out as much as you can about your subject and share that information with others. There is no textbook in this class. You are the textbook.

9. With the unbridled freedom that comes with pursuing your own ideas comes awesome responsibility; responsibility to be honest and straightforward in everything you do. Science only moves forward when everyone keeps this in mind.

10. Enjoy yourself. It's up to you to find the fun, joy, and excitement of the opportunities that the SMART Center can provide for you. If you are feeling bored, uninterested, or unhappy, look to yourself to fix these problems. If you are feeling happy, excited, and intensely interested, that is something you created. It works both ways.

Additionally, a problem-solving sheet is provided. If students see a problem, they should make a note of it and provide their idea for how the problem should be solved. Student ideas are always considered—some students have a better idea of what is actually in the training session than the mentors.

Writing Student-Oriented Materials (Or, How to Teach Quantum Mechanics Without Calculus)

The most difficult part of implementing the SMART center concept involved writing material that was appropriate for young (middle and high school) students about an advanced scientific topic. My (Reef's) years as a university professor and my experience working at Steppingstone with students in grades K–8 taught me that one of the most important aspects of communicating with young students is that you speak their language. If I start the course by saying, "In a magnetic field, the energy levels of electrons are split into high and low states" or "The longitudinal and transverse relaxation times of the resonance process provide information about the environment in which the electron resides," I can be assured that what I have accomplished is to reinforce the idea of science as a dry, boring, and unintelligible discipline. Nothing puts someone to sleep faster than a long lecture in a language they cannot understand. Hence, the trick is to have some knowledge about the life experiences of the students and the kinds of events with which they are most familiar. In short, make the material relevant to them.

For example, how do you teach a student about integration and differentiation if they had never had calculus? Certainly most students will have had experience riding in an automobile that has accelerated and decelerated, and they are most likely aware of the fact that the car has both a speedometer and odometer. Using this information, it is possible now to describe integration and differentiation in a way that the students can understand as shown in Figure 1.

Figure 10.1. Comparison of Motion of an Automobile Under Heavy Acceleration and Braking With Actual EPR Spectra

During heavy acceleration, the car moves forward until the throttle is released and the brake is pressed. The second and third panels show the readings of the speedometer and odometer at the same time. The first panel shows the usual presentation of EPR data from the spectrometer.

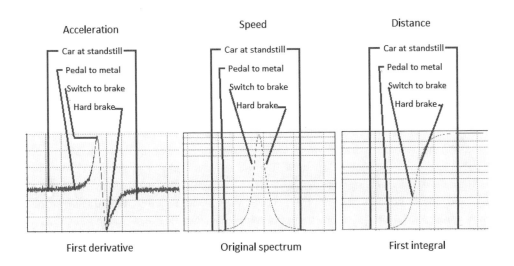

We began by offering three 5-day pilot training sessions. The program was advertised through distributed fliers and information to other schools (both public and private) and through newspaper articles. We received 136 applications for the 52 available slots and made our selections based on two major criteria: (1) a short essay that students wrote describing why they wanted to attend the training session and (2) geographical location. We also requested references in case we needed further information (family members were excluded as references). The intent was to get the best students with the widest distribution so that the students could return to their schools and discuss the program with their peers. Usually the interest of the student was quite clear from the essay. Applications with essays clearly not written by the students themselves were politely rejected. Students who participated in the pilot program ranged in age from 9 to 19.

Each five-day session included an introduction, a hands-on laboratory exploring the process of resonance, a theoretical and practical discussion of the use of the instrument and what kinds of experiments could be performed by the instrumentation, hands-on use of the instrument, and

a rotation where groups of students rotated among four tasks: (1) determining the presence of free-radicals in samples the students provided themselves; (2) a discussion of how various instrument parameters would affect their results; (3) data analysis; (4) presentation techniques. The session ended with a discussion of what did and did not work for them and the creation of a list of projects the students would like to pursue.

A pre- and posttest were given to evaluate what the students learned (when Reef Morse reported the data to his colleagues at an international conference, many commented that even their graduate students didn't know some of the concepts that the SMART Center students had learned).

The resonance experiment (available for download from *www.smart-center.org*) is written in such a way that there is a great deal of description of certain parts of the experiment and almost none about others. This is quite typical of a Materials and Methods in a scientific journal article. When the students ask for clarification, the mentor merely asks them what they think they should do, followed by the question "Do you think it's important? Why?" This allows students to take risks, to fail, and to devise ways of performing the experiment that are different from, and often better than, the path the mentor would take. It requires unusual self-control to watch a group of students go at something in a completely unintelligible way, but sometimes the outcomes are valuable and unexpected. Students also learn that there may be no right answer and that the answers they got were completely a result of how they did the experiment—there is also no such thing as wrong data. The data may not answer the question that was asked, but being able to analyze such data provides an important lesson for both student and mentor.

The students next use the instrumentation, under close supervision. This is about the only place in the lab where they must follow the directions. The consequences of a mistake at this task can result in loss of instrument use for quite a while if something important breaks. Hence, a detailed, step-by-step procedural outline is provided and the students are expected to follow it. Airline pilots with thousands of hours of experience still go through a checklist before every flight. We demand the same of the students. The safety and care of the instrument is ultimately the responsibility of the mentors and it is their duty to follow the students through the procedure. Students never run the instrument in the absence of someone experienced in instrument operation.

Once the machine is operating, students want to see results. We explain that the presence of free radicals in a sample will be indicated by the amplitude of the squiggly line that marches across the computer screen. Students are shown the spectra of some standard samples— coffee grounds, tea, burnt sugar, used engine oil, hair samples (Reef acts as the control as his hair is pure white). Immediately students start asking if coffee is bad for them because they have learned that free radicals are "bad." This apparent paradox can be explained by telling students that the free radicals we observe are very stable, otherwise we would not be able to see them. The "bad" free radicals are extremely short-lived and react so quickly that we would never see a signal from them. In this way students begin to deal with the contradictions between what they have believed as common knowledge and what the experiment actually shows. Students quickly start asking if "X" has free radicals. Our answer is always "I don't know, how would you find out?" At this point, the students start taking the responsibility for their experiments and their results. They are excited by the fact that they, themselves, can create new knowledge. They become the experts in an area. This is the transition to developing with the student an experimental protocol to answer the question(s) they ask. By asking "Why?" "What do you think?" and "How would you find out?" students can begin to participate in the scientific process as professionals.

Several points were elucidated by the pilot sessions. The most important was that students of a wide range of ages (9–19) can be taught to use advanced scientific instrumentation and that they recognize the instrument as a tool to be used to answer their questions. Even the youngest students learned a great deal from the experience (as evidenced by comparing performance on the pre- and posttests) even though most (with some notable exceptions) were not developmentally ready to handle highly abstract concepts such as molecular motion. This may arise from a lack of sufficient training in chemistry (few elementary or middle school science classes focus on the molecular nature of chemical and biochemical processes) although the students can, in fact, handle this material as evidenced by their ability to continue a discussion about molecular environments that had been sufficiently introduced by the mentor.

The most creative students were the middle school girls—they were refreshingly uninhibited in promoting their ideas and testing them. They had little fear of failure and saw results (or absence of results) as exciting. The high school students of both sexes were more reticent and needed to be sure that their ideas were "right" before testing them.

Given the intensely visual nature of most student interaction with their environment, we believed that students would be excited by the opportunity to build equipment that would modify the spectrometer so that it could be used for actual imaging. The grant to the Toyota Tapestry Foundation was based on this belief. However, students were much more interested in results that could be obtained quickly even if they were more abstract (interpretation of a squiggly line is a more abstract activity than presenting information as a recognizable image, for example, an image of a single coffee bean). Students were more excited by results that were the direct results of their actions (placing a sample of their choice in the instrument and observing that the squiggly line was bigger with one sample than another). A considerable amount of student material had to be discarded or rewritten to adjust to this realization. We learned that we could not predict what would interest students when they were introduced to a methodology of which they had no prior knowledge. We had to be ready to adapt quickly and to learn from what the students actually did rather than what we thought they would do.

Lastly, students wanted a hands-on experience. They were happiest when they were running experiments, discussing the results among themselves, and planning what to do next. The pilot program was continually adjusted to maximize actual practice and minimize lectures on theory. Currently there is almost no lecturing in the program unless it is clear that the entire class will benefit from a group discussion or if they request it.

In the fall of 2009, the SMART Center began offering the training course for a fee. Additional laboratory time also is also fee-based. Several frank discussions with the students in the pilot programs (which were free) concluded that the students understood that they needed to pay for continued use of the facility and that they were ready to do so. Again, this is one of the facts of science in the United States—someone has to pay for it. That the students themselves valued the experience to the degree that they were willing to fund their own efforts (or obtain the funds elsewhere) was gratifying and speaks to the intensity of the student's desire to continue their research at the SMART Center. However, for students of modest means the imposition of a fee raises a barrier that can be challenging. Students must now spend time raising money as well as participating in the course. The ideal situation is to seek funds to support these students rather than make them pay tuition themselves, even if the tuition is modest. Criteria for participation should not be compromised in any case.

Evidence of Success

Short Term

Short-term evaluations were performed by comparing student performance on the pre- and post-test (see Table 10.1, p. 156). Student achievement at this level was remarkable. Upon entrance, almost none of the students had any concept of the advanced terminology and methodology taught in the class. Upon finishing the class, students had an excellent working knowledge of such concepts as relaxation time and its relationship to line shape, the kinds of samples that were likely to contain unpaired electrons and hence produce a signal, and a better understanding of what constitutes a scientific experiment and how to analyze the data they obtained. Although not part of the written test, students all were able to operate the EPR spectrometer, prepare samples, and obtain data. Most importantly, students no longer thought of the instrument as an impediment but as a tool that they could use to pursue their scientific interests: The time spent in thinking about the instrument was replaced with time spent thinking about science. This was an unexpected and satisfying result.

Middle Term I

About 10% of the students who participated in the training class went on to pursue an independent-study project in the lab. We did not collect data on students who participated in the course but did not return to the SMART Center; but they may have pursued other scientific interests. Laboratory-based research was driven primarily by the desire to present at a science fair and less by a newfound love of electron spin resonance spectroscopy. Laboratory sessions were conducted in such a way that the student determined the research project (with some input from the mentor). This contrasts to research in other academic settings, where the research is usually driven by the person in charge of the laboratory. Students were allowed to pursue paths that were not optimal. In these situations, the mentor asked leading questions (Why are you doing this? What do you expect to find? Why? Does your experiment answer the question you are asking?) to bring the student to the realization that he or she may be able to pursue a more focused path, or to explain to the mentor that the student knew what he or she was doing. Two students placed first and third in their respective categories (chemistry and biochemistry) at the Detroit Science Fair with their work at the SMART Center.

Students quickly realize that good science is time-consuming. The SMART Center program, and any program like it, competes with sports, homework, and social activities for the attention of its students. Students' schedules are filled to the brim and finding time to develop a science project is difficult. This is a fact of life in these times and must be taken into consideration. Thus, scheduling flexibility is important in the first year or two of a student's participation. In addition, the program competes with activities that are easier, provide immediate rewards, and do not require the mental efforts that science demands. Hence, the student return rate is an important middle-term measure of success

Middle Term II

One eighth-grade student took considerable interest in the possibility of presenting her work at an international magnetic resonance conference. This student developed a project, planned and performed the experiments, worked with her mentor on the poster presentation, got her work accepted for presentation, and presented at the conference (Uppal and Morse 2011). During her presentation, professors, postdoctoral fellows, and graduate students talked with her about what she had done. In these discussions, the age and experience differences disappeared and what transpired was a conversation between two scientists interested in the data. This is a remarkable achievement for a 13-year-old; but it shows that even young students can participate in science at the same level as seasoned veterans. She confided that this was the most thrilling experience of her life!

Because scientific endeavors are of no benefit to society unless they are published and presented, an important goal and measure of success is the number of presentations and publications. Students rise to the occasion when they realize that the work they are doing may be worthy of this kind of formal public exposure. To date no student has published a scientific paper based on research done at the SMART Center; but it is very early in the game.

Table 10.1. Pre- and Posttest Performance of 13 High School Students Participating in the Smart Center Training Program

Under each test heading, the first column indicates the number of students attempting to answer the question and the second column indicates the number of correct answers. Material related to question 5 was not covered in class. This acts as an internal control. Questions 7–9 ask about material students should know prior to their participation in the class.

Questions	Pretest Attempts	Correct	Posttest Attempts	Correct
1. Define spectroscopy	13	1	13	7
2. What does EPR stand for?	9	0	13	11
3. List at least two common items that would give an EPR signal.	3	0.5	13	13
4. Compare and contrast T1 and T2.	3	0.5	13	13
5. Briefly, how would the following physical sample parameters affect an EPR spectrum:				
A. Sample viscosity	2	0	12	3
B. Probe concentration	3	0	12	1
C. Polarity (water vs oil, for example)	1	0	10	1
D. Oxygen concentration	1	0	11	2

Questions	Pretest Attempts Correct		Posttest Attempts Correct	
6. Briefly, how would the following instrumental settings affect an EPR spectrum:				
A. Modulation amplitude	3	0	13	8
B. Gain	1	1	13	6
C. Field Center	2	0	13	10
D. Sweep width	2	0	13	8.5
7. What steps are taken in designing and performing a scientific experiment? Explain the purpose and desired outcome of each step. Number each step for use in question 8.	13	13	13	13
8. What biases do you have that might affect each of the steps above? Use the step numbers from question 7.	13	13	9	7
9. Explain how you would organize and present your research to: your family, your school classmates, other students at the SMART Center, other scientists at the SMART Center, a group of scientists at a scientific conference, a newspaper reporter.	13	13	13	13
10. Draw the chemical structure of a stable free radical.	4	0.5	11	7.5

Long Term

Because the SMART Center's existence has been brief, the greatest long-term result—entrance of SMART Center participants in the realm of professional science—has not occurred. It will require at least another decade to evaluate the program at this level. However, it is the most important goal of all. This goal drives all aspects of the SMART Center program. Printed material, lectures, and all planned class experiences are evaluated in light of their ability to show the student a path toward a career in the scientific arena. Ultimately, the SMART Center will be judged by its success in developing future scientists.

Conclusion

Sustainable programs need a steady influx of students and money. Creating a means to provide both of these is just as important as running the program. Because the SMART Center operates independently it cannot depend on tuition payments or school budgets to support it. Developing a good marketing program becomes a critical step in developing the program. In addition, it is important that students who participate in the program tell others about their experiences. Word-of-mouth is one of the best sales tools. Students are usually willing to help someone from the program set up a presentation or a discussion session with their peers.

Currently, the SMART Center is run by volunteers. However, this is not a sustainable business model. Therefore it makes sense to develop collaborations with other organizations that have greater financial resources, such as industries and institutions of higher learning). Funding a program through grants is also an option, although many granting agencies will not allow payment of salaries (exceptions are the National Institutes of Health and the National Science Foundation). In a fully funded program, salaries and benefits become the largest expense. This cannot be overlooked in planning for sustainability.

An exact replication of the SMART Center is unlikely and unnecessary. What is important in creating a parallel learning environment is to engage the services of a scientist or scientists who have the time and resources to train younger students. As scientists retire, their knowledge base is lost to society unless they have a means to transfer their knowledge to others. The SMART Center concept provides such an opportunity. Many aging scientists have considerable experience mentoring younger students in a laboratory environment, and with proper facilities may be willing to participate at minimal cost while the program gets off the ground. Retiring scientists are an untapped educational resource. The SMART Center concept provides a means for them to contribute and excite the newest generation of scientific minds. The steps to follow are:

1. Find a scientist who is interested in teaching younger students. University cities and towns should have no trouble in finding older or retired scientists who would be willing to train middle and high school students.

2. Find and equip the laboratory. Sometimes when a university professor retires, his or her instrumentation is no longer wanted or needed by the institution. Arrange to transfer this equipment to the laboratory (sometimes heavy equipment is required). Make sure the facility has sufficient utilities for the instrumentation.

3. Get the little stuff. Beakers, balances, pH meters, small equipment, are vital tools. If specialty chemicals are required, obtain them as necessary (sometimes the scientist will have these chemicals available from their former laboratories).

4. Create a program. Write or obtain the student class materials. Run these materials by several colleagues who have a good understanding of how middle and high school students learn and what interests them.

5. Get people excited. We had a contest at our school where the winner got to be the first student to operate the EPR spectrometer. The newspapers loved it. Most students who participated in the first summer sessions at the SMART Center learned about it through newspaper articles.

6. Run the program. Allow for mistakes and plan carefully to prevent disaster.

7. Get feedback. Pre- and posttests are good evaluation documents if they are carefully written. You want the feedback to focus on the student's actual experience, not their feelings or emotions.

8. Make changes. Based on what you have learned on running your program a few times, tweak it so that it better reflects what it is you want to accomplish.

9. Go to number 5 and repeat.

While this may sound simplistic, it is a series of steps that will achieve the goal of this chapter—to pass the torch on to others so that they may learn from what we have done.

References

Educational Broadcasting Corporation (EBC). 2004. What is inquiry-based learning? Available online at *www.thirteen.org/edonline/concept2class/inquiry/index.html*

Hattie, J. A. C. 2009. *Visible learning*. New York: Routledge Press.

Morse, R. 2009. How scientists do science. Engaging students in a real-world science experience. *Michigan Alliance of Gifted Educators Newsletter*. Fall.

Morse, R. 2010. The authentic science experience: Student-directed research in a research laboratory. *Michigan Science Teachers Association Newsletter*. Spring.

National Research Council (NRC). 1996. *National science education standards*. Washington, DC: National Academies Press.

Uppal, S., and R. Morse. 2011. Formation of free radicals in coffee during roasting. Paper presented at the 53rd Rocky Mountain Conference on Analytical Chemistry.

The Promise of Service-Learning as an Instructional Approach to Motivate Interest in STEM Careers

Shelley H. Billig, Lyn E. Swackhamer, and Linda Fredericks
RMC Research Corporation

Setting

The challenge in motivating young people, especially those from disadvantaged backgrounds, to become interested and pursue careers in STEM-related fields is well documented. Public institutions, such as the National Science Foundation and the Committee on Science, Engineering, and Public Policy; and national policies, such as the America Competes Act of 2007, have established goals for increasing the overall numbers of individuals pursuing STEM-related careers and especially to increase the percentage of traditionally underrepresented populations, such as girls and women, African Americans, Latinos, Native Americans, and persons with disabilities.

Progress in increasing the interest of these populations has been relatively flat during the past decade. In 2004, for example, about 17% of all science and engineering degrees were awarded to students from these traditionally underrepresented backgrounds (Commission on Professionals in Science and Technology 2004, as cited in Byars-Winston, Estrada, and Howard 2008). In 2011, the percentage was roughly the same (NSF 2011).

Multiple factors have been found to serve as barriers to STEM interest. For example, individuals from underrepresented backgrounds are much more likely than their peers to report an unwelcoming climate in their classrooms (Cabrera, Colbeck, and Terenzini 2001, as cited in Byars-Winston, Estrada, and Howard 2008) and have negative perceptions of being in STEM-related fields because the fields are viewed as "masculine" (Byars-Winston, Estrada, and Howard 2008). Academic self-efficacy predicts interest and retention in STEM-related fields, but students from communities of color are less likely to feel academically efficacious than their peers (Byars-Winston, Estrada, and Howard 2008). Members of communities of color reported having fewer role models in STEM-related careers and often have little or no information from their families and communities about STEM-related career pathways (Davis-Lowe 2006).

One promising avenue for increasing interest in and pursuit of mathematics as a career is the practice of service-learning. Service-learning is an instructional approach that engages students in providing service to meet an authentic need by applying concepts learned in school. For example, students may apply learning from geometry to build a playground in a park. They may engage in multiple activities addressing environmental stewardship, such as measuring water quality in local drinking fountains or streams to assess their safety. They may track seat belt usage among teens and its relationship to percentages of injuries from car accidents, and then build a campaign among their peers for seat belt use. They may assist senior citizens in understanding their nutritional needs and graph the extent to which needs are being met through their current diets, recommending changes as needed. The types of projects students explore are limited only by their imaginations and the time and resources on-hand.

Service-learning as an instructional practice ideally has five components. First, students engage in an *investigation* of a community need. Students may conduct a community survey, research a problem on the internet, participate in a community walk, or otherwise identify a social problem that can be solved within a relatively short period of time, such as during a semester or yearlong project. Students then work to identify possible solutions to the challenge they identified. Typically this *planning* phase involves some brainstorming and researching the possibilities and their likely efficacy. Students decide on the solution to be pursued, and then plan the service they will provide. Once the plan is established, students decide responsibilities and timelines for their work and then implement their plan. This *action* phase involves the service that will theoretically meet the community need. Once service is completed, students develop and present a *demonstration* that shows the impact of their work. The demonstration can be for each other, for parents, or for interested community stakeholders. *Reflection* is the last component and an integral feature of all of the phases of service-learning. Reflection may be written, verbal, or nonlinguistic, and typically involves consideration of what is being done and why, predicted and real results for the community, and impact on self.

The research on service-learning shows its promise for increasing interest in mathematics. Recent studies show, for example, that service-learning is strongly associated with academic engagement (e.g., Billig 2010; Billig, Root, and Jesse 2005; Furco 2002); students' willingness to attend class and persist with challenging content (Billig 2009; Fredericks and Swackhamer, 2010; Northup 2010). Multiple studies have shown that students who participate in service-learning develop a stronger sense of self-efficacy for learning than their nonparticipating peers (e.g., Billig 2000; Billig 2009; Furco and Root 2010; Melchior 1998). In a few quasi-experimental studies, service-learning was also found to be associated with increases in academic performance on state assessments in reading/language arts, mathematics, and science (Billig, Jesse, and Brodersen 2008; Meyer, Billig, and Hofschire 2004).

Researchers who study service-learning have shown that service-learning is far more likely to produce impacts when it has specific program design characteristics: sufficient intensity and duration, explicit link to academic curriculum, meaningfulness to participants, youth voice, reciprocal partnerships with the community, attention to diversity, cognitively challenging reflection activities, and progress monitoring (Billig and Weah 2008). These characteristics were recently translated into a set of K–12 quality standards for the practice of service-learning (National Youth Leadership Council 2008).

The promise of service-learning as a vehicle for increasing interest in mathematics careers and achievement is supported by findings in the literature on effective mathematics programming. For example, Slavin, Lake, and Groff (2008) conducted a review of research on mathematics programs for students in middle and high school, including those studies that had randomized or matched comparison group designs, a duration of at least 12 weeks, and equivalence at the pretest. The meta-analysis performed for the 100 qualifying studies showed that effect sizes* were relatively small, with a weighted mean effect size of 0.03 for mathematics curriculum and 0.10 for computer-assisted instruction. However, programs that featured interactive processes, such as cooperative learning, had higher effect sizes, averaging about 0.42. Cooperative learning is built into each of the service-learning components. Students must engage in collaborative processes for investigation, planning, action, and demonstration.

A meta-analysis of studies of mathematics programs for students who were experiencing difficulties in mathematics also illuminates why service-learning may be associated with positive outcomes. In a meta-analysis reported by Gersten and Clarke (2007), researchers found that low-achieving students performed better when they experienced systematic and explicit instruction (0.58 effect size), engaged in structured peer-assisted learning activities involving heterogeneous ability groupings (0.62 effect size), and received formative assessment data (0.57 effect size). In particular, highest effects occurred when emphasis was placed on the steps and procedures for solving mathematical problems, students were allowed to ask questions, and students were asked to participate in "think-alouds," where they verbalized their thoughts or drew pictures of steps to take in solving problems, presumably because the verbalization helped to anchor the students behaviorally and mathematically. Sharing thinking with peers also appeared to be effective because it inhibits students who try to solve problems impulsively without devoting adequate time to thinking about mathematical principles required for solutions.

Each of the factors associated with degrees of success are a feature of high-quality service-learning activities. To perform each of the components associated with service-learning, teachers must offer explicit instruction, such as teaching how to develop blueprints and create structures for playgrounds, measure water quality, or graph nutritional intake. As previously discussed, students engage in heterogeneous group dialogues for learning activities. Formative assessments are a "natural" part of the experience since students experience the consequences of their efforts immediately. When done well, service-learning has explicit progress-monitoring components, whereby students collect baseline data and then document changes that have occurred as a result of their efforts.

Recent studies have also shown the value of other aspects of instruction related to service-learning that affect students' interest in mathematics and their mathematics achievement. Bittick and Chung (2011), for example, showed the value of narrative in affecting motivation. Narrative provides the context for learning and helps students to encode, recall, and apply their

---

* Effect sizes of 0.20 are considered small; 0.40 are considered moderate; and 0.6 and above are considered large. A small effect most likely would raise a student's score on a standardized test by about 8 percentile points, while a large effect would raise the score by about 25 percentile points.

learning to different types of situations. Narrative is a part of the service-learning experience since all mathematical actions are embedded within the service-learning experiences. Because students are engaged in meeting a community need, their mathematical work is immediately relevant and applied.

Bottge et al. (2007) found that embedding mathematics into solving real-world problems helps motivate middle school students to learn mathematics. Hidi and Renninger (2006) found that stimulating curiosity can serve as a "hook" for motivating both short- and long-term interest in mathematics. These factors are also present in service-learning since action (service) is driven by student investigation and planning of relevant community needs sparked by student curiosity and identification of solutions that they believe will make a difference in the community.

In addition, consistent with other factors found to be associated with interest and achievement in mathematics practice guide (Halpern et al. 2007), service-learning connects abstract ideas with concrete context, helps to convince students that their abilities in mathematics are not "fixed" but can be improved through effort or hard work, and highlights the importance of effort in succeeding in difficult tasks. Students are provided with prescriptive, informational feedback focused on strategy, effort, and the process of learning, and can immediately correct misunderstandings and learn from mistakes.

While the promise of service-learning for increasing interest and achievement in mathematics and pursuing mathematical careers is apparent, little research has been conducted to show that the promise can be reached. This chapter provides the results of one such study. In the next sections, the particular service-learning program design will be presented, followed by a description of the study itself, including design, methodology, and results. The chapter ends with a discussion of the factors within service-learning design that appear to be most relevant to increasing student interest in pursuing mathematical careers.

Service-Learning Program Design

STEMester of Service is a service-learning program developed by Youth Service America specifically to engage middle school students in service related to science, technology, engineering, and mathematics, with an emphasis on math and science. Most STEMester programs engage middle school students in a semester-long opportunity to address environmental issues connected to climate change, green space availability, health effects, and disaster management, with occasion to use technology to deepen and demonstrate the results of their learning.

Competitive grants of $5,000 are awarded annually to middle school teachers and service-learning coordinators for engaging up to 75 students in projects extending from Martin Luther King Day in January to the Global Youth Service Day in April and beyond. An additional $500 is given for collaboration of the grantee with a teacher, coordinator, or administrator to foster sustainability. Training is provided to all subgrantees through online sessions on project management and curricular connections, attendance at a Youth Service Institute, and personalized consultation and site visits.

The Youth Service Institute, held in October of each year, contains sessions on linking each of the eight quality service-learning standards to a middle school science/technology curriculum, and strengthening teachers' skills in incorporating the key aspects of quality service-learning.

Subgrantees in good standing are eligible to reapply for multiple years, and new grantees are also solicited. In the 2010–11 academic year, 12 of the 25 sites had participated previously in STEMester during the first round of grants in spring of 2010.

National YSA partners, including United Health professionals, State Farm agents, and National Wildlife Federation members, are available to assist STEMester sites in learning more about project areas as well as careers related to such areas as science, nature preservation, and disaster prevention. The Learn and Serve STEMester grant program through YSA provides funding annually to 25 middle schools situated in 12 states with the highest dropout rates. Funding is awarded to public urban and rural middle schools with large disadvantaged populations that typically have the least opportunity to serve.

Research Questions

The research was conducted to answer a large number of research questions, only two of which are considered here:

1. To what extent did participation in the YSA STEMester of Service influence students' academic engagement, academic competence, 21st-century skills related to teamwork and leadership, interest in STEM coursework, and interest in STEM careers?

2. What demographic and program characteristics served to mediate or moderate results?

Research Design and Sample

This study employed a quasi-experimental design, which included matched classrooms of service-learning and comparison middle school students. Classrooms of students were matched based upon grade level, course content, and student demographic and achievement profiles. Respondents included students in grades 6–8 who participated in service-learning programs, students in grades 6–8 comparison classrooms, classroom teachers who implemented service-learning, and representatives of community partner organizations. In 21 sites, classrooms were matched using different teachers from the same school and in four sites, the participating teacher instructed both the service-learning and comparison classrooms. The 25 schools in the study were located across the United States, as shown in Table 11.1.

Table 11.1. Locations of Participating Schools

Alton, Illinois	New York City, New York
Cheney, Washington	Paradis, Louisiana
Chicago, Illinois	Phoenix, Arizona
Chicago Heights, Illinois	Saginaw, Michigan
Concho, Arizona	South Gate, California
Detroit, Michigan	Tacoma, Washington
Fort Collins, Colorado	Tucson, Arizona
Gainesville, Georgia	Vancouver, Washington
Hawkinsville, Georgia	Washington D.C.
Indian River, Michigan	Westminster, California
Kapaau, Hawaii	

Participating and nonparticipating students completed pre- and postsurveys, with presurveys being administered in the late fall (typically in November or December), and postsurveys administered in late spring after service projects were completed. Classroom teachers also completed surveys in the spring.

A total of 1,054 STEMester students and 349 comparison students completed both pre- and postsurveys. The number of student survey respondents by group (service-learning or comparison) and grade level is presented in Table 2. In both groups, there were almost equal numbers of male and female respondents. In the service-learning group, the largest percentage of respondents (54%) were seventh graders, while in the comparison group almost two-thirds (65%) were eighth graders. Slightly more than one third of the service-learning students were Caucasian (36.7%) while almost half (48.8%) of the comparison students were. About 20% of both groups were Hispanic/Latino. The service-learning group contained a larger percentage of Black/African American respondents (17.3% vs. 8.3%) and Asian/Pacific Islander respondents (13% vs. 7.4%) than the comparison group.

Table 11.2. Student Survey Respondent Characteristics

	Service-Learning Students (N = 1,055)[*]		Comparison Students (N = 349)	
	Frequency	Percentage	Frequency	Percentage
Gender				
Male	532	50.4	181	51.9
Female	523	49.6	168	48.1
Grade				
6	259	24.6	80	22.9
7	572	54.3	39	11.2
8	223	21.1	227	65.0
Missing	1	0.1	3	0.9
Race/Ethnicity[a]				
White/Caucasian	387	36.7	170	48.8
Hispanic/Latino	211	20.0	80	22.9
Black/African American	182	17.3	29	8.3
Asian/Pacific Islander	137	13.0	26	7.4
American Indian/ Alaskan Native	11	1.0	6	1.7
Multiple	76	7.2	20	5.7
Other	35	3.3	15	4.3
Missing	16	1.5	3	0.9

[a] Percentages may not sum to 100 because respondents could select more than one category.

[*] N is the total number in a sample.

In the surveys, students were asked to provide information about their participation in volunteer and service activities during the 2010–2011 school year. Table 11.3 shows that participation in school was substantially higher for service-learning students than for comparison students. Participation with a group or organization outside of school was also higher for service-learning students than for comparison students. Service-learning students were also asked if they participated in service-learning activities in school before the 2010–2011 school year. Of the 964 students who responded, 61% indicated they had prior experience with service-learning; 39% reported no prior experience with service-learning. Previous participation might impact findings since it is possible that many of the effects of service-learning have already been accrued.

Table 11.3. Student Volunteer and Community Service Activities During the 2010–11 School Year

Activity Type	Service-Learning Students (N = 1,055)		Comparison Students (N = 349)	
	Frequency	Percentage[a]	Frequency	Percentage[a]
In school	284	26.9	103	29.5
With a group or organization outside of school	222	21.0	132	37.8
None	622	59.0	172	49.3

[a] Percentages may not sum to 100 because respondents could select more than one category.

Survey Measures

This study utilized survey subscales that were developed by the authors and colleagues at RMC Research, based on previous studies used in evaluations of Learn and Serve America programs. Students responded to survey items using a 4-point scale where 1 = strongly disagree, 2 = disagree, 3 = agree, and 4 = strongly agree. Reliability analyses (Cronbach's alpha)[*] were conducted for scaled student outcome measures for Grades 6–12 using data from the presurvey measures. All scaled items were approaching or at an acceptable level of Cronbach's alpha, near .7 or higher. In addition, the service-learning participant surveys included items that assessed students' perception of the quality of their service-learning program. These items were also measured on a 4-point agreement scale. The reliability analysis conducted on the service-learning program quality subscale was based on the service-learning participant postsurvey. The results of the subscale reliability analysis are presented in Table 11.4 (p. 168).

[*] Cronbach's alpha is a measure of the reliability or internal consistency of a composite measure or scale that is based on multiple survey items. Values range from 0 to 1.

Table 11.4. Student Survey Reliability Analysis

Subscale	Number of Items	Sample Item(s)	Cronbach's Alpha
Academic Engagement	9	I feel that the schoolwork I am assigned is meaningful and important. My classes are interesting to me.	.85
Academic Competence	6	I can get good grades if I try. I can do well in school if I want to.	.81
21st-Century Skills	14	I am good at working as part of a team. I am good at taking on different roles and responsibilities.	.90
Interest in STEM Coursework	9	I intend to take advanced courses in mathematics.	.86
Interest in STEM Careers	4	I am interested in careers that require engineering skills. I am interested in careers that require technology skills.	.75
Service-Learning Program Quality	9	I feel that my service-learning activities were meaningful. I helped come up with ideas for my service-learning activities.	.94

Twenty-one (53%) out of 40 service-learning teachers who participated in the study completed an online survey in spring 2011. Table 11.5 presents characteristics of teacher survey respondents. Approximately three-fourths (76%) of teachers were female. Only two of the teachers had less than six years of teaching experience in K–12 schools. The largest group (43%) had between 11 and 20 years of teaching background. Two-thirds of the teachers (66%) implemented service-learning for two or fewer years.

Table 11.5. Teacher Survey Respondent Characteristics (N = 21)

	Frequency	Percentage[a]
Gender		
Male	5	23.8
Female	16	76.2
Years Teaching in a K–12 School		
2 years or less	1	4.7
3 to 5 years	1	4.7
6 to 10 years	6	28.6
11 to 20 years	9	42.9
21 years or more	4	19.1
Years Implemented Service-Learning		
2 years or less	14	66.7
3 to 5 years	3	14.3
6 to 10 years	3	14.3
More than 10 years	1	4.7

[a] Percentages may not sum to 100 because respondents could select more than one category.

The survey asked teachers about the nature of their service-learning activities, perceptions of service-learning program quality in their classrooms, perceptions of impact on students, and teacher background information. RMC Research developed the 33-item measure of service-learning quality that included measures of link to curriculum, partnership quality, meaningful service, youth voice, diversity, reflection, and progress monitoring. Items were rated on a 4-point scale where 1 = strongly disagree and 4 = strongly agree. Table 11.6 presents results from reliability analyses of the service-learning program quality subscales. Coefficients for all scales indicated high internal consistency.

Table 11.6. Teacher Survey Reliability Analysis: Service-Learning Quality Indicators

Subscale	Number of Items	Sample Item(s)	Cronbach's Alpha
Link to Curriculum	4	Academic learning goals for service-learning activities were clearly articulated. Service-learning activities helped students learn how to transfer knowledge and skills from one setting to another.	.84
Partnerships	5	Service-learning partners collaborated to set common project goals. Service-learning involved an in-depth partnership with at least one community agency.	.73
Meaningful Service	4	Youth were interested in and engaged with the service-learning activities. Service-learning activities addressed issues that were personally relevant to the youth.	.87
Youth Voice	6	Service-learning activities helped youth develop their leadership skills. Service-learning activities were characterized by a climate in which youth were comfortable expressing their ideas.	.92
Diversity	4	Service-learning activities provided youth with an opportunity to develop their conflict resolution skills. Service-learning activities provided youth with an opportunity to recognize and overcome cultural stereotypes.	.78
Reflection	5	Reflection occurred before, during, and after the service experience. Reflection prompted youth to think about alternative solutions to complex community problems.	.84
Progress Monitoring	4	Evidence was discussed in the context of how to improve the service-learning process. Evidence of the quality of service-learning implementation was collected from multiple sources throughout the service-learning process.	.85

Data Analysis Procedures

Descriptive statistics, *t*-tests,[*] and analyses of variance (ANOVAs)[**] were used to analyze survey data. Repeated measures ANOVAs[***] were used to examine survey outcomes for service-learning and comparison students in Grades 6–8. The ANOVA models examined differences in scores, over time, for the two student groups.

To determine if the service-learning student responses were statistically similar to the comparison student responses on the presurvey, independent sample *t*-tests were conducted on each of the outcome subscales for the student surveys. Findings indicated no statistically significant differences between the service-learning group and comparison group for any of the subscales, so the groups were treated as equivalent. Difference tests were also conducted for the variables of gender, age, and ethnicity. Groups were not equivalent with regard to age so age was used as a covariate when conducting the repeated measures ANOVAs.

To examine moderating factors associated with student outcomes, additional analyses were conducted using student and teacher survey data. Student demographic variables, student ratings of service-learning quality, and teacher ratings of service-learning quality were linked with outcome data using multivariate analysis of variance (MANOVA).[****] Effect sizes, using Cohen's *d*,[*****] were calculated to determine the strength of the relationship between the moderators and outcomes. The larger the effect size, the stronger the relationship between the moderator and the associated outcome.

Study Limitations

The primary limitation of the study was in having fewer comparison surveys than anticipated. Eleven of the 25 STEMester grantees were unable to find a suitable comparison teacher; in some cases, the uniqueness of the program or geographical isolation of the study site made the identification of a comparison site unfeasible. Four comparison teachers whose classes had submitted presurveys did not complete any student postsurveys. While their characteristics at the time of the presurvey did not vary from others in the sample, it is not known whether their lack of participation influenced findings.

---

[*] A t-test is a statistical procedure that is commonly used to examine differences in mean values over time or across two groups.

[**] Analysis of variance (ANOVA) is a statistical procedure that examines differences in outcomes for two or more groups.

[***] Repeated measures analysis of variance (ANOVA) is a statistical procedure used to examine differences within and between groups when the same data are available for multiple points in time.

[****] Multivariate analysis of variance (MANOVA) is a statistical procedure that examines differences between two or more groups when there is more than one dependent, or outcome, variable.

[*****] Cohen's *d* is a measure of effect size, designed to measure the magnitude of treatment effect. Effect sizes (ES) can also be thought of as the average percentile standing of the average treated (or experimental) participant relative to the average untreated (or control) participant.

Findings

In this section, program implementation is discussed, followed by an analysis of overall results and factors that serve as mediators and moderators of outcomes. Implementation is presented first since the research is consistent in showing that only high-quality service-learning yields important impacts.

Table 11.7 shows the focus areas of service-learning projects as reported by students. More than half of the students (54%) reported engaging in projects that focused on environmental stewardship. Students also frequently reported helping animals and younger children as part of their service-learning activities.

Table 11.7. Service-Learning Project Focus, Reported by Students (*N* = 971)

Focus Areas	*N*	Percentage[a]
Helping the environment	753	53.6
Helping younger children	287	20.4
Working with senior citizens	137	9.8
Helping animals	428	30.5
Helping the homeless	179	12.7
Other	97	6.9
Did not do a service-learning project	113	8.0

[a] Percentages do not sum to 100 because many respondents selected more than one category.

Table 11.8 presents teachers' perceptions of service-learning quality in their classrooms. Teachers generally agreed that they aligned their practices to all of the standards measured. Highest ratings were given to providing opportunities for students to engage in meaningful service activities and establishing links between service activities and the curriculum. Lower ratings were given to the quality of partnerships and diversity efforts.

Table 11.8. Teacher Perceptions of Service-Learning Quality

Service-Learning Quality	*N*	Mean[2]	*SD*[3]
Link to Curriculum	20	3.54	.48
Partnerships	21	3.11	.70
Meaningful Service	21	3.55	.47
Youth Voice	21	3.49	.48
Diversity	21	3.23	.51
Reflection	21	3.38	.46
Progress Monitoring	21	3.29	.49

Note. Responses were rated on a 4-point scale where 1 = Strongly Disagree, 2 = Disagree, 3 = Agree, and 4 = Strongly Agree.

Students also rated the quality of their service-learning activities. As seen in Table 11.9, students assigned highest ratings to items about showing respect for other people's opinions (diversity) and gaining skills from service-learning activities that will be useful in the future. Items that were given the lowest scores related to coming up with ideas for and making decisions about service-learning activities (youth voice) and talking in class about ways to solve neighborhood or community problems. Generally, students and teachers agreed that service-learning activities were meaningful. Student ratings of youth voice were lower than those of teachers.

Table 11.9. Student Perceptions of Service-Learning Quality

Service-Learning Quality	N	Mean	SD
Overall quality	971	3.12	.58
I feel that my service-learning activities were meaningful.	906	3.15	.70
My teacher made sure we linked service-learning activities to classroom subjects such as English, math, and/or science.	894	3.18	.70
The skills that I learned from my service-learning activities will be useful to me in the future.	902	3.24	.70
My service-learning activities were important to me.	910	3.17	.71
I helped make decisions about my service-learning activities.	872	3.07	.73
I helped come up with ideas for my service-learning activities.	864	2.93	.78
During my service-learning activities, we were expected to show respect for other people's opinions.	905	3.25	.67
My class was asked to identify specific things we had learned during our service-learning activities.	864	3.14	.71
My class talked about several different ways to solve neighborhood or community problems.	856	3.07	.79

Note. Responses were rated on a 4-point scale where 1 = Strongly Disagree, 2 = Disagree, 3 = Agree, and 4 = Strongly Agree.

Duration and intensity were determined through teacher responses. Teachers were asked to estimate the number of weeks and the number of hours per week that their students were engaged in service-learning during the 2010–11 school year. Teachers reported that service-learning activities lasted between 14 and 20 weeks. While six teachers reported service-learning implementation of less than 14 weeks, the majority of teachers (15) reported implementation that exceeded 14 weeks, the approximate length of one semester. Almost half the teachers (48%) reported implementing service-learning activities three to five hours per week, while one-third (33%) of the teachers said that they implemented service-learning activities for two hours a week or less. The remaining four teachers said that service-learning was implemented for six hours or more per week. These data show that duration was fairly standard, but intensity varied across the sample.

Student Outcomes

Pre- and postsurvey measures were compared for service-learning and comparison students. Table 11.10 shows the results for both groups and reveals the service-learning students rated themselves significantly higher over time for the subscales of academic engagement, 21st century skills, interest in STEM courses and skills, and interest in STEM careers. The effect size was small for all four of the significant outcomes, but larger than the typical effect (.04) found in the literature.

Table 11.10. Differences Between Service-Learning Student Participants and Nonparticipating Peers on Survey Outcome Measures

| Measure | Service-Learning Students | | | Comparison Students | | | Significance | Effect Size (Cohen's *d*) |
	N	Presurvey Mean	Postsurvey Mean	*N*	Presurvey Mean	Postsurvey Mean		
Academic Engagement	1,049	2.95	2.99	348	2.86	2.82	.033*	.19
Academic Competence	1,048	3.45	3.46	348	3.42	3.40	.297	—
21st-Century Skills	1,030	3.09	3.14	343	3.09	3.07	.044*	.11
Interest in STEM Content	1,007	3.03	3.06	341	2.97	2.86	.000***	.18
Interest in STEM Careers	935	2.88	2.91	310	2.89	2.76	.000***	.18

Note. Responses were rated on a 4-point scale where 1 = Strongly Disagree, 2 = Disagree, 3 = Agree, and 4 = Strongly Agree.
*$p < .05$, ***$p < .001$.*

These findings were corroborated by independent assessments of the students regarding their acquisition of skills. When asked to indicate which of several areas of skill and experience (if any) they acquired as a result of participating in service-learning, students were most likely to identify skills in science (44%), mathematics (41%), writing (35%), and reading (34%) as primary areas of impact. These were followed by job, computer, and work experience skills.

Factors That Influenced Outcomes

A series of additional analyses was conducted to assess the impact of the following factors on service-learning student outcomes:

- Student gender and grade;
- Student perceptions of the quality of their service-learning experience;
- Student motivation to attend school on days when there was service-learning;
- Students' prior exposure to service-learning;

---

* The *p*-value is an indicator that represents the likelihood that observed results occurred by chance. In education research, values of $p < .05$ (i.e., values indicating that observed results had a less than 5% chance of occurring by chance) are typically used to identify results that are statistically significant. Lower *p*-values indicate a smaller likelihood that observed results occurred by chance and are therefore associated with statistically significant findings.

- Teacher perceptions of service-learning program quality, including whether or not there was enough time devoted to service-learning activities to achieve the intended project outcomes;
- Teacher reports of service-learning duration and intensity;
- Teachers' overall teaching experience in K–12 schools; and
- Teachers' experience implementing service-learning.

As shown in Table 11.11, there was a strong relationship ($d \geq .80$) at statistically significant levels between students' ratings of service-learning program quality and most outcome areas. As student ratings of the quality of programs increased, so did their ratings of academic engagement, academic competence, acquisition of 21st-century skills, and STEM academic and career interest.

Table 11.11. Factors that Influenced Student Outcomes: Student Ratings of Service-Learning Quality

Moderator	Outcomes Moderated	df[4]	F[5]	Significance	Effect Size (Cohen's d)
Student Ratings of Program Quality					
(Positive Moderator)	Academic Engagement	1, 945	243.162	.000***	1.04
(Positive Moderator)	Academic Competence	1, 945	178.891	.000***	.91
(Positive Moderator)	21st-Century Skills	1, 945	253.018	.000***	1.06
(Positive Moderator)	Interest in STEM Content	1, 928	162.123	.000***	.86
(Positive Moderator)	Interest in STEM Careers	1, 928	119.626	.000***	.72

***$p < .001$.

Gender and age also moderated outcomes, but as shown in Table 11.12, effect sizes were moderate ($d < .50$). Males reported higher outcomes in interest in STEM content and careers than females, and younger students had higher outcomes than older students.

Table 11.12. Moderators of Student Outcomes: Gender, Grade Level, and Age

Moderator	Outcomes Moderated	df	F	Significance	Effect Size (Cohen's d)
Grades 6–8					
Gender					
(Males higher)	Interest in STEM Content	1, 1,306	32.558	.000***	.32
(Males higher)	Interest in STEM Careers	1, 1,306	52.313	.000***	.40
Age					
(Negative Moderator)	Academic Engagement	1, 1,337	37.155	.000***	.33
(Negative Moderator)	Academic Competence	1, 1,337	15.739	.000***	.22
(Negative Moderator)	21st-Century Skills	1, 1,337	21.624	.000***	.25
(Negative Moderator)	Interest in STEM Content	1, 1,306	55.557	.000***	.41
(Negative Moderator)	Interest in STEM Careers	1, 1,306	5.598	.018*	.13

$*p < .05, ***p < .001.$

There were many statistically significant moderating effects of teacher ratings on student outcomes. As shown in Table 11.13, teacher ratings of service-learning quality had a significant influence on outcome.

Table 11.13. Moderators of Student Outcomes: Teachers' Perceptions of Service-Learning Quality, Partnerships, Time to Complete Activities

Moderator	Outcomes Moderated	df	F	Significance	Effect Size (Cohen's d)
Grantee Type					
First Year or Second Year					
(Negative Moderator)	Academic Engagement	1, 1,337	30.185	.000***	.30
(Negative Moderator)	Academic Competence	1, 1,337	13.911	.000***	.20
(Negative Moderator)	21st-Century Skills	1, 1,337	11.598	.001**	.19
(Negative Moderator)	Interest in STEM Content	1, 1,306	5.764	.016*	.13
(Negative Moderator)	Interest in STEM Careers	1, 1,306	7.540	.006**	.15

Moderator	Outcomes Moderated	df	F	Significance	Effect Size (Cohen's d)
Teacher Ratings of Program Quality					
Link to Curriculum					
(Positive Moderator)	Academic Engagement	1, 606	34.877	.000***	.50
(Positive Moderator)	Academic Competence	1, 606	16.256	.000***	.34
(Positive Moderator)	21st-Century Skills	1, 606	20.411	.000***	.39
(Positive Moderator)	Interest in STEM Content	1, 598	25.452	.000***	.42
(Positive Moderator)	Interest in STEM Careers	1, 598	14.062	.000***	.32
Partnerships					
(Positive Moderator)	Academic Engagement	1, 612	13.287	.000***	.29
(Positive Moderator)	Interest in STEM Content	1, 604	17.341	.000***	.34
(Positive Moderator)	Interest in STEM Careers	1, 604	17.058	.000***	.34
Meaningful Service					
(Positive Moderator)	Academic Engagement	1, 612	43.768	.000***	.55
(Positive Moderator)	Academic Competence	1, 612	18.460	.000***	.36
(Positive Moderator)	21st-Century Skills	1, 612	24.355	.000***	.41
(Positive Moderator)	Interest in STEM Content	1, 604	30.560	.000***	.46
(Positive Moderator)	Interest in STEM Careers	1, 604	17.933	.000***	.35
Youth Voice					
(Positive Moderator)	Academic Engagement	1, 612	53.047	.000***	.61
(Positive Moderator)	Academic Competence	1, 612	12.218	.001**	.29
(Positive Moderator)	21st-Century Skills	1, 612	29.598	.000***	.45
(Positive Moderator)	Interest in STEM Content	1, 604	47.460	.000***	.57
(Positive Moderator)	Interest in STEM Careers	1, 604	28.732	.000***	.45

Moderator	Outcomes Moderated	df	F	Significance	Effect Size (Cohen's d)
Diversity					
(Positive Moderator)	Academic Engagement	1, 612	40.420	.000***	.52
(Positive Moderator)	Academic Competence	1, 612	7.335	.007**	.22
(Positive Moderator)	21st-Century Skills	1, 612	20.162	.000***	.37
(Positive Moderator)	Interest in STEM Content	1, 604	26.966	.000***	.43
(Positive Moderator)	Interest in STEM Careers	1, 604	38.526	.000***	.51
Reflection					
(Positive Moderator)	Academic Engagement	1, 612	26.814	.000***	.42
(Positive Moderator)	21st-Century Skills	1, 612	13.341	.000***	.30
(Positive Moderator)	Interest in STEM Content	1, 604	21.902	.000***	.38
(Positive Moderator)	Interest in STEM Careers	1, 604	27.785	.000***	.43
Progress Monitoring					
(Positive Moderator)	Academic Engagement	1, 612	27.466	.000***	.42
(Positive Moderator)	Academic Competence	1, 612	9.707	.002**	.25
(Positive Moderator)	21st-Century Skills	1, 612	13.427	.000***	.30
(Positive Moderator)	Interest in STEM Content	1, 604	22.915	.000***	.39
(Positive Moderator)	Interest in STEM Careers	1, 604	24.804	.000***	.40
Teacher Ratings of Duration and Intensity					
(Positive Moderator)	Academic Engagement	1, 612	19.354	.000***	.38
(Positive Moderator)	Interest in STEM Content	1, 604	18.719	.000***	.38
(Positive Moderator)	Interest in STEM Careers	1, 604	19.860	.000***	.39

Moderator	Outcomes Moderated	df	F	Significance	Effect Size (Cohen's *d*)
Teacher Ratings of Enough Time for Service-Learning Activities					
(Positive Moderator)	Academic Engagement	1, 612	4.807	.029*	.18
(Positive Moderator)	Interest in STEM Content	1, 604	7.876	.005**	.23
(Positive Moderator)	Interest in STEM Careers	1, 604	22.719	.000***	.39
Teacher Years Teaching in K–12 School					
(Negative Moderator)	Academic Engagement	1, 612	24.720	.000***	.48
(Negative Moderator)	Academic Competence	1, 612	13.368	.000***	.36
(Negative Moderator)	21st-Century Skills	1, 612	18.396	.000***	.42
(Negative Moderator)	Interest in STEM Content	1, 604	38.588	.000***	.59
(Negative Moderator)	Interest in STEM Careers	1, 604	25.357	.000***	.48
Teacher Service-Learning Experience					
(Negative Moderator)	Interest in STEM Content	1, 604	17.711	.000***	.44
(Negative Moderator)	Interest in STEM Careers	1, 604	7.786	.005**	.29

1 *N* is the total number in a sample.

2 The mean or average value is a measure of central tendency computed by adding a set of values and dividing the sum by the total number of values.

3 The standard deviation (*SD*) is a measure of how spread out a set of values is. Higher standard deviations indicate greater variability in data across respondents.

4 Degrees of freedom (*df*) indicates the number of responses used in the final calculation of a statistic. This number is usually just slightly smaller than the overall sample size.

5 The *F* statistic provides a basis to test for statistical significance when used in analysis of variance (ANOVA).

Other moderators showed:

- Moderate positive effect sizes are associated with students' ratings of academic engagement when service-learning activities were viewed by teachers as linking to curriculum, engaging students in meaningful service, providing youth voice, and promoting understanding of diversity and respect among all participants.

- Students' ratings of acquisition of STEM knowledge increased as teacher ratings of youth voice increased. Student ratings of interest in STEM courses and skills increased when teacher ratings of promotion of diversity went up. Both of these findings were associated with moderate effect sizes.
- Teacher ratings of duration and intensity were significantly and positively related to student ratings of academic engagement and interest in STEM content and career.
- A positive relationship was found between teacher ratings of whether there was enough time for service-learning activities and student ratings of academic engagement and STEM. Student ratings for these areas increased the more that teachers felt there was enough time devoted to service-learning activities so project outcomes could be attained.

Teacher ratings of community partnerships, reflection activities, and progress monitoring were significantly related to student outcomes, but effect sizes were smaller than those listed above.

Discussion

This study shows that service-learning, particularly when it is of high quality as defined by the K–12 standards and indicators of quality (NYLC 2008) has significant promise in prompting middle school students from economically disadvantaged settings to become interested in STEM content and careers, particularly mathematics and science. While overall effect sizes of participation in service-learning are small, effects of participation in high-quality service-learning are moderate, and can account for a significant difference between participating and nonparticipating students.

Student findings show that impact is highest when there is significant duration and intensity of the experience, time to complete all activities, link to curriculum, youth voice, and promoting diversity and respect for others. Males and younger students benefitted more than females and older students.

The promise of service-learning for promoting interest in mathematics content and career is likely to be associated with several process factors that current research shows are related to interest in STEM. First, service-learning promotes confidence in one's ability to succeed in STEM-related fields. As Byars-Winston and colleagues (2008) showed, self-confidence is highly associated with positive mathematics interest and achievement outcomes at every level of education, elementary through college. Service-learning is an approach in which virtually no one fails; rather, confidence is gained in working with others to solve mathematical problems directly related to the service at hand. Immediate feedback (as mentioned previously, also connected to mathematics interest and achievement) is given to service-learning participants so that they can complete projects, and students develop a sense that they can make a difference in the world through their application of mathematical skills.

Second, service-learning is associated with the cluster of interactive, hands-on, inquiry-based learning opportunities that has been shown to be more effective than traditional instruction in promoting the interest of diverse students in STEM subjects (Clewell and Campbell 2002; Henderson and Dancy 2011; Moriarty 2007). Effective instructional approaches to stimulate involvement also include student-initiated experiments or research (Tsui 2007); the use of interactive displays or models (Rule et al. 2009); contextual learning projects (Davis-Lowe 2006); and project-based experiences to apply knowledge to real-world problems (Building Engineering and Science Talent 2004). Service-learning includes aspects of each of these types of instructional approaches.

Third, students in service-learning are exposed to mathematical mentors and role models. Multiple studies have shown that students from diverse backgrounds who are provided with mentors achieve more and persist longer in STEM-related courses than those who do not (Cohen 2006; Rule et al. 2009). Informal mentoring and naturally formed relationships, such as those present in service-learning, have shown to lead to better outcomes (Tsui 2007).

While the promise of service-learning for promoting interest in mathematics content and career is suggested in this study, it is clear that the practice of service-learning will need to be improved if the effects of service-learning are to be realized. Service-learning without high quality has modest effects at best. If service-learning is to maximize results, the practice must have stronger and more intentional links and explicit discussion about the role of mathematics in helping students to make a difference through their service. The investigation, planning, action, demonstration, and even reflection phases should be explicitly designed to incorporate mathematical thinking and activity, and debriefs should show students the ways in which their classroom learning has been applied in the service setting.

Further, students should be encouraged to teach others, perhaps through legacy service projects, that mathematics is important to success. For example, service-learning to address obesity concerns, now relatively prevalent, can easily be designed to have multiple phases, such as promoting exercise, developing nutrition plans, and helping conduct economic impact studies. Students who start these projects can work with other classes to engage in the learning and promote the use of mathematics for addressing this important issue.

The topics to be addressed within service-learning are nearly limitless. With teacher ingenuity and knowledge of what works best to engage students, service-learning has enormous potential to engage students and interest them in the STEM topics vital to our nation's future.

References

Beier, M. E., and A. D. Rittmayer. 2008. *Literature overview: Motivational factors in STEM: Interest and academic self-concept*. Houston, TX: SWE-AWE-CASEE ARP Resources.

Billig, S. H. 2000. Research on K–12 school-based service-learning: The evidence builds. *Phi Delta Kappan* 81 (9): 658–664.

Billig, S. H. 2009. Does quality really matter? Testing the new K–12 service-learning standards for quality practice. In *Advances in service-learning research: Vol. 9. Creating our identities in service-learning and community engagement*, ed. B. E. Moely, S. H. Billig, and B. A. Holland, 131–157. Charlotte, NC: Information Age.

Billig, S. H. 2010. Why is service-learning such a good idea? Explanations from the research. *Colleagues* 5 (1): 8–11.

Billig, S. H., D. Jesse, and R. M. Brodersen. 2008. Promoting secondary students' character development in schools through service-learning. In *Advances in service-learning: Vol. 8. Scholarship for sustaining service-learning and civic engagement*, ed. M. A. Bowdon, S. H. Billig, and B. A. Holland, 57–83. Charlotte, NC: Information Age.

Billig, S. H., and W. Weah. 2008. K–12 service-learning standards for quality practice. In *Growing to greatness 2008: The state of service-learning project*, ed. J. C. Kielsmeier, M. Neal, N. Schultz, and T. J. Leeper, 8–15. St. Paul, MN: National Youth Leadership Council.

Bittick, S., and G. Chung. 2011. *The use of narrative: Gender differences and implications for motivation and learning in a math game* (CRESST Report 804). Los Angeles: University of California National Center for Research on Evaluation, Standards, and Student Testing.

Bottge, B., E. Rueda, R. Serlin, Y. Hung, and J. Kwon. 2007. Shrinking achievement differences with anchored math problems: Challenges and possibilities. *The Journal of Special Education* 41 (1): 31–49.

Building Engineering and Science Talent. 2004. *What it takes: PreK–12 design principles to broaden participation in science, technology, engineering and mathematics*. San Diego, CA: Author.

Byars-Winston, A., Y. Estrada, and C. Howard. 2008. *Increasing STEM retention for underrepresented students: Factors that matter*. Madison: University of Wisconsin, The Center for Education and Work.

Clewell, B. C., and P. B. Campbell. 2002. Taking stock: Where we've been, where we are, where we're going. *Journal of Women Minorities in Science and Engineering* 8 (3/4): 255–284.

Cohen, C. C. 2006. *Building the nation's scientific capacity: Evidence from the Louis Stokes Alliances for Minority Participation Program*. Washington, DC: The Urban Institute.

Davis-Lowe, E. 2006. *Fostering STEM diversity*. Portland, OR: OPAS Initiative.

Fredericks, L., and L. Swackhamer. 2010. *Evaluation of YSA's STEMester of service*. Denver, CO: RMC Research Corporation.

Furco, A. 2002. Is service-learning really better than community service? A study of high school service program outcomes. In *Advances in service-learning research: Vol.1. Service-learning: The essence of the pedagogy*, ed. A. Furco and S. H. Billig, 23–50. Greenwich, CT: Information Age.

Furco, A., and S. Root. 2010. Research demonstrates the value of service-learning. *Phi Delta Kappan* 91 (5): 16–20.

Gersten, R., and B. Clarke. 2007. *Effective strategies for teaching students with difficulties in mathematics* (Research Brief). Reston, VA: National Council of Teachers of Mathematics.

Halpern, D., J. Aronson, N. Reimer, S. Simpkins, J. R. Star, and K. Wentzel. 2007. *Encouraging girls in math and science: IES Practice Guide* (NCER 2007-2003). Washington, DC: U.S. Department of Education, National Center for Education Research, Institute of Education Sciences.

Henderson, C., and M. H. Dancy. 2011. *Increasing the impact and diffusion of STEM education innovations*. White Paper commissioned for the 2011 Characterizing the Impact and Diffusion of Engineering Education Innovations Forum. Washington, DC.

Hidi, S., and K. Reddinger. 2006. The four-phase model of interest development. *Educational Psychologist* 41 (2): 111–127.

Melchior, A. 1998. *National evaluation of learn and serve America school and community-based programs: Final report*. Washington, DC: Corporation for National and Community Service.

Meyer, S. J., S. H. Billig, and L. Hofschire. 2004. The impact of K–12 school-based service-learning on academic achievement and student engagement in Michigan. In *Advances in service-learning research: Vol. 4. New perspectives in service-learning: Research to advance the field*, ed. M. Welch and S. H. Billig, 61–85. Greenwich, CT: Information Age.

Moriarty, M. A. 2007. Inclusive pedagogy: Teaching methodologies to reach diverse learners in science instruction. *Equity & Excellence in Education* 40: 252–265.

National Science Foundation (NSF), Division of Science Resources Statistics. 2011. *Women, minorities, and persons with disabilities in science and engineering: 2011* (Special Report NSF 11-309). Arlington, VA: NSF.

National Youth Leadership Council (NYLC). 2008. *K-12 service-learning standards for quality practice*. St. Paul, MN: NYLC.

Northup, J. 2010. *Evaluation of Illinois learn and serve*. Denver, CO: RMC Research Corporation.

Rule, A. C., G. P. Stefanich, C. W. Haselhuhn, and B. Peiffer. 2009. A working conference on students with disabilities in STEM coursework and careers. *Proceedings from the 2009 working conference on students with disabilities in STEM coursework and careers*. Cedar Falls, IA. (ERIC Document Reproduction Service No. ED505568)

Slavin, R., C. Lake, and C. Groff. 2008. *Effective programs in middle and high school mathematics: A best evidence synthesis*. Baltimore: The Johns Hopkins University, Best Evidence Encyclopedia.

Tsui, L. 2007. Effective strategies to increase diversity in STEM fields: A review of the research literature. *Journal of Negro Education* 76 (4): 555–581.

Real World Externships Exposing Students to Possible Careers in STEM Disciplines

Jeffrey Weld
Iowa Mathematics & Science Education Partnership

Ted Anthony Neal
University of Iowa

Disa Lubker Cornish and Isabel Montemayor
University of Northern Iowa

Setting

For secondary teachers of mathematics, science, and technology, Real World Externships help them answer the legitimate student query: "Why am I ever gonna need to know this?" with real challenges and problems encountered and solved in actual Iowa companies. Along with a modern background on how the discipline is used in the real world, teachers are equipped with a heavy dose of how 21st-century skills apply in their content areas. For business hosts, externs bring maturity, independence, and a strong knowledge base for making significant contributions over the course of a summer. Relationships

Waterloo Middle School teacher Shalia Moore, a teacher-extern, partnered with Hy-Vee's registered dietician and certified wellness coach to provide scientifically based, objective nutrition information to employees and customers. Nutrition became a focus area in Shalia's teaching.

are sustained over the academic year as teachers translate work experiences and career awareness to classroom lessons.

The Iowa Mathematics and Science Education Partnership (IMSEP), in collaboration with teachers and Iowa business/industry partners, have placed teachers of mathematics, science, and technology into local businesses and agencies throughout Iowa for six-week-long summer immersions in real projects as *externs*. Real World Externships for Teachers of Mathematics, Science, and Technology was piloted in 2009 to build bridges between the business and education worlds. The program has grown to be available across the state with over 30 Iowa business partners in 2011. This program provides Iowa's math and science teachers an opportunity to experience the latest real world application of their disciplines. Teachers bring back their experiences by designing hands-on, minds-on problem-solving activities for students in the classroom to spark interest in pursuing careers in STEM fields in Iowa. Businesses meanwhile, enjoy the contributions of autonomous, industrious, creative, and bright partners in solving challenges. The program's goals are:

1. Increase both teachers' and students' awareness of business and industry applications of mathematics, science, and technology;

2. Modernize the curriculum for teaching mathematics, science and technology;

3. Improve both teachers' and students' STEM career awareness;

4. Enhance and build school–industry relationships and partnerships; and

5. Improve retention of current mathematics, science, and technology teachers.

Some key points of the program are:

- Iowa businesses and industries are recruited into this program through promotion by partners including the Association of Business and Industry, the Iowa Business Council, Chambers of Commerce, service clubs, and other modes of communication.
- A call for applications is issued to qualified mathematics, science, or technology teachers for an externship opportunity in the geographic vicinity through the area education services and other teacher databases.
- Teachers are mentored throughout the six-week experience by university mentors for two graduate credits, resulting in products that include curriculum alignment, content learned, journaling experiences, and a poster for implementing new strategies and philosophies back at school in the fall.
- Teachers have participated from across Iowa in settings including a hospital, an architectural firm, an implement manufacturer, a nutraceutical plant, a wind turbine producer, and more.
- Real World Externships offer a launch point for permanent business-school partnerships. Businesses may assist teachers through the academic year via speaking engagements, tours, resources, and potential internships and jobs for students.

- Preliminary evaluation findings attest to strengthened inquiry philosophies and career promotion among teachers and positive feedback and performance reviews among business hosts.

Brief History of Real World Externships

Universities have welcomed teachers into laboratories as a means of professional development for years. The National Science Foundation has a special program for funding just such opportunities, called Research Experiences for Teachers (RET). One of the co-authors operated a RET here at the University of Northern Iowa (UNI) from 2006–2008 (funded by a Department of Education grant). Teachers who participated in the RET attested to increased understanding of the nature of science, of inquiry, and of their own subject matter. What the RET could not do though, is provide teachers with a rich professional development experience closer to home, tied to their community milieu, connecting to the private sector, ushering new career knowledge to be shared with students. Teachers are often blindsided by the question "When am I ever gonna need to know this?" Partnering with industry equips teachers to answer that question, and more.

In 2009, the Real World Externships Program was launched as a signature component of a state-funded initiative, the Iowa Mathematics and Science Education Partnership (IMSEP). Advantages to the externs concept over RET are that it is local; it connects schools and businesses; it enhances teachers' content knowledge as applied in industry; it enlightens teachers as to career opportunities to share with students; and it benefits the private sector by providing a conduit into helping shape the school curriculum while enjoying authentic expertise on the part of the teacher on-site. The program was designed through consultations with teachers, business leaders, and university professionals. Comparable programs were studied too in order to replicate best practices when possible. Vermeer Corporation in Pella, Iowa, for example, has offered three-week facility orientations to teachers for years. The Workplace Learning Connection in Cedar Rapids, Iowa, offers a 40-hour private sector job shadow to teachers. Other Iowa companies independently welcome teachers to the plant grounds or corporate offices for job shadows, plant tours, orientations, and other types of exposures to business. In other states, externshiplike experiences are provided by companies and consortia. The 3M corporation selects a partner school district within Minnesota or western Wisconsin each year for sending teachers to their St. Paul facility for six-week, company-paid work experiences. Operating since 1984, the 3M project termed TWIST (Teachers Working in Science and Technology) has reached over 200 teachers. In Vermont, the Employer-Teacher Work Experience Program is funded by the federal School-to-Work Initiative to place teachers in industries for hands-on experiences translatable to classrooms. Ohio secondary teachers can take part in authentic research experiences at NASA's Glenn Research Center in Cleveland for a 10-week duration under the guidance of a NASA mentor. Southern California teachers have available through a private sector consortium of aerospace companies the Industry Initiative for Science and Math Education (IISME). IISME offers full-time summer fellowships paid by companies, reaching over 2,000 teachers over the course of a 27-year history. These are but a few examples of the burgeoning crop of internshiplike opportunities available to teachers across the country. They have informed Real World Externships program designers in terms of key components as well as tripping points to avoid.

Externships inspire. Iowa needs inspired teachers of math, science and technology in order to inspire our youth to become STEM savvy citizens capable of entering higher education and the STEM workforce. Our state's outlook mirrors a national condition: declining interest, performance, and career awareness in the STEM fields among our students at the very time that opportunities in a techno-scientific economy burgeon. Three industry sectors of Iowa's new economy—bioscience, advanced manufacturing and information solutions—require energized mathematics, science, and technology education programs. Yet, only 34% of Iowa eighth graders were rated proficient on the 2009 National Assessment of Educational Progress mathematics. Only 25% of our high school graduates take physics or a computer course. And just 50% of Iowa ACT-tested students are on target to be ready for college algebra, a gateway course for mathematics, science, and technology majors. Never doubt, though, that Iowa students are perfectly capable. We face not an ability problem, but a motivation crisis among learners. If only their teachers could make the subject matter more appealing, more relevant, more related to the exciting work going on at Pella Corp., or Kemin Industries, or Principal Financial, or John Deere or any of the hundreds of companies that dot the Iowa landscape. Well, they can't. And that is because teachers rarely experience the private sector beyond a plant tour or career day guest speaker. Teachers in the STEM fields are excited to see how their subjects get used in industry. And most industry leaders are anxious to improve the way math, science, and technology is taught. Both can happen when teachers spend a summer out of school, in a business. They add value to operations. They create a private-public sector bridge. They take new teaching and career ideas back to school. Iowa businesses can and do host student interns for one-at-a-time exposure, but to do the same for a singular teacher means exponential impact—more than a hundred inspired, excited students *each year* of that teachers' career.

Research-based benefits of similar programs that bring teachers to universities for research include more teaching innovations, career awareness, and improved student learning. Counter-intuitive to common fears that such programs cause teachers to depart classrooms, they become *more* committed teachers. Our evaluation of this program backs those assertions, as detailed in a subsequent section.

Program Mechanics

The cycle begins with the identification of willing business and agency hosts. New partners are established through direct contacts and by advertising through trade groups and business clubs. Most of these partnerships get locked in by May of the year. Companies are coached by the mentor team on suitable projects for teacher participants. These project descriptions are used to advertise to teachers within a geographic range, and applications are sought. Company representatives are able to review applications, inviting their top choice(s) to the facility for a three-way orientation meeting (teacher, business representative, extern mentor representative). By early June we aspire to fill all slots across the state, then hold a pre-externship workshop by university mentors to define the experience for the externs. They and their hosts get surveyed prior to beginning. The businesses and teachers work out six-week summer experience and some a little longer, when agreed upon by the business and teacher.

A core of mentors administer this project, advertise and recruit both teachers and business sites, assist with the development of project/duty descriptions for the externships, supervise the faculty advisors, administer the graduate credit (through the University of Northern Iowa's STEM departments), and evaluate the project. Staffing requires one faculty mentor per 10 teacher externs. The faculty mentors are science, math, or technology education specialists from each of the three state universities. The faculty mentors are liaisons between businesses and teachers who make weekly in-person or virtual visits to every externship site, and monitor teachers during the following academic year. They are responsible for the facilitation of group discussions between externs to reflect and translate their externship to learner opportunities. Things asked of the teacher externs include:

1. Keep a journal documenting hours, activities, and things learned over the course of the externship;

2. Expose their students to careers in STEM-related fields;

3. Identify specific Iowa Core Curriculum content skills seen over the course of the externship and how students will see the real-world application of that skill in the classroom;

4. Identify specific 21st-century skills seen over the course of the externship and how students will see the real-world application of that skill in the classroom;

5. Create and present a paper and a poster documenting things learned with the experience;

6. Participate in a pre- and postexternship survey and interview process.

Each teacher extern earns a daily stipend of $150 over the course of the externship or $4,500 for a six-week externship. The teacher externs also earn 2 hours of graduate credit for a discount rate of $75/credit through UNI's Continuing Education program. Externs are able to receive credit in math education and science education. These credits then go toward their recertification for their teaching license. The externships typically run six weeks, starting in mid-June through early August—specific dates are determined between the teacher extern and his or her business placement partner. A standard 8:00 a.m.–5:00 p.m., 40-hour workweek for six weeks over the summer is expected. However, a more flexible work schedule may be negotiated with the business host. Breaks and vacations are also negotiated at the onset of the externship with the employer.

Costs to operate the Externship program include, in addition to the $4,500 stipend of each participant plus tuition, administrative expenses. For example, mentors (university supervisors) receive $600 per teacher, and the travel expense associated with visiting externs can amount to another $600 per teacher over the summer and into fall. In addition, teachers who complete the program are eligible for $250 minigrants to translate their experience back to school (typically software, books, or equipment is purchased). Other expenses include special compensation for attending pre- and postexternship workshops, and registrations to state teachers' conferences. This project is funded by a three-year Innovative Technology Experiences for Students (ITEST) grant from the National Science Foundation.

Business Partners: Who and How

Business and agency hosts typically have in common an interest in shaping the curriculum, a history (albeit in some cases nascent) of engaging with schools for relevant learning experiences, and a private-sector nature that incorporates science, mathematics, and technology in meaningful, fruitful, and stimulating ways. They offer externship projects that apply the mathematics, science, and technology concepts of the Iowa Core Curriculum 21st-Century skills. Ideally they draw their employee base at least in part from the school community that the teacher externs serve. Partners range in size from local "mom and pop" scale of operations to major regional or national manufacturing hubs. All share commitments to math, science, and technology education at the local level, and the capacity to provide a teacher with stimulating, meaningful project work in consultation with program mentors at the universities. The externship opportunities are found that best serve mathematics, science, and technology teachers, as well as their private sector partners. The following are logos of some of the businesses and agencies that have hosted in the past:

Teacher-Externs: Who and How

Every teacher in the state, whether rookie or veteran, male or female, large school or small, has been charged with building relevance, career awareness, and 21st-century skills into their teaching, as per the Iowa Core Curriculum. Yet, a tiny fraction of teachers have ever spent time in the private sector where math, science, and technology are used on a daily, applied basis. Thus our target population is broad and welcoming, expecting applicants who are seeking to improve their teaching and content skills to provide their students with a more concrete and activity-based classroom and laboratory experience. Qualified teachers (i.e., appropriate subject area, grade level) within the geographic region of an advertised business or agency opening, are sought. If selected by the business contact, a three-way meeting is arranged between teachers, business hosts, and mentors to arrange a working calendar to mutual satisfaction fulfilling the six-week requirement. A variety of assignments are asked of externs in addition to the project performed on-site. At the conclusion of the summer externship, teachers are aided in translating the experience into lessons by their university mentors. In Table 12.1 you will find a sampling of teachers, their externship sites, and brief descriptions for summer 2010.

Table 12.1. Iowa Externs FY2010

Business	Type of Business	Teacher Specialty	Summer Extern Experience
Abbe Hills Farm Mount Vernon	Sustainable & organic farm serving 100 families in Cedar Rapids, Mount Vernon and Lisbon	Biology/General Science	Learning sustainable farming techniques and the science of farming and land stewardship
Allen Hospital–Waterloo	Regional medical center	High School Mathematics	Assisting in the development of a process improvement strategy for different departments in Allen Hospital and the Greenhill Medical Group
Con Agra–Council Bluffs	Food packaging company	Chemistry and Physics	Standardizing work practices and process improvement within plant via statistical process controls and line studies
Diamond Vogel Paints–Orange City	Paint manufacturer	Biology, Chemistry, and Physics	Working as a lab tech in a powder coatings R&D lab
Diversified Industries/ Sudenga– George, IA	Feed and grain processing and delivery systems	Mathematics and PLTW	Compiling data and using math and data analyses for a series of projects and time studies to optimize workflow and automate raw material inventory
DNR–Sioux City	DNR Field Office– Onawa	Biology	Working on various projects around the Missouri River and Loess Hills such as habitat surveys for bird and butterflies; wildlife habitat exploration; invasive species management; and bird banding
Ellison Technologies Automation– Council Bluffs	Integrated advanced manufacturing technologies company	Mathematics	Completing burden absorption analysis and making recommendations for improved monthly financial planning
Genencor– Cedar Rapids	Industrial biotechnology company	Chemistry and Biology	Working as an analytical lab technician to develop a consistent method to accurately measure enzyme concentrations and gain exposure to chemical engineering functions within the organization
Kemin Industries– Des Moines	Biosciences—Health and nutraceuticals	Ninth-Grade Advanced Unified Science	Developing an efficient process of extracting and purifying nutraceuticals
		Biology, General Science	Working on media optimization for production of an enzyme via fermentation

Business	Type of Business	Teacher Specialty	Summer Extern Experience
Lee County Conservation–Montrose	Public access to areas that meet the conservation, education, recreation and wildlife needs for Lee County Iowa	Biology, Human A&P	Mapping and surveying the vertebrate wildlife found at the Heron Bend Wildlife Area
Monsanto–Ankeny	Multinational agricultural biotechnology corporation	Biology, Honors Biology	Ankeny Extern Project: Working in high throughput genotyping laboratory, learning a production-oriented PCR-based genotyping process
Monsanto–Muscatine		Science	Muscatine Extern Project: Working on research plot to measure corn's growth response to nitrogen
Principal Financial Group–Des Moines	Financial services/insurance	Technology	Working with IT professionals in IT application development; support, day-to-day infrastructure operations, financial management, IT security, and project management activities
Procter & Gamble–Cedar Rapids	Health, cosmetic, household care	Mathematics	Working on several manufacturing processes such as material transfer control, reliability modeling, fill weight variation and wastewater treatment
Rockwell Collins–Cedar Rapids	Aerospace and defense communications/aviation electronics	Chemistry, Physics, Algebra	Providing statistical analysis on a PCD work estimate tool to validate the correctness of the estimates/predictions being generated
		High School Mathematics	Working on fabrication methods and manufacturing processes of printed circuit boards

The Program Evolves

Real World Externships developers continue to work to improve the program. We now have a statewide database of businesses and many veteran businesses. These businesses are encouraged to get their "job proposals" figured out in early January so that teachers can be recruited from their area. This brings about the difficulty that anyone has: wondering where they will be in six months. However, this is a general framework with an understanding that changes often take place before the teacher actually walks in the door. This flexibility has proven to be beneficial because it is often the case where the teacher brings certain skills and goals to the table that the businesses are able to focus their objective to meet. The long-term goal is to have more businesses applying than we have the capacity to serve through our funding streams. That would make this a competitive environment where only the best ideas are presented to the teachers for summer opportunities.

From the teacher standpoint, several changes have been made. The most recent cycle incorporated online blogs for teachers to share their summer experiences. Teachers were required to answer the following prompts during their experience:

- Week 1: What concerns do you/did you have at the beginning of the externship? What did you do or what help did you have to overcome those concerns?
- Week 2: Now that you have been with the business for a few weeks engage them in a conversation of their concerns at the beginning of the externship. Share them, and what you have done to alleviate those concerns.
- Week 3: What are some of the connections you see between your externship and math or science essential concepts and skills? 21st-century Skills? Five Characteristics of Effective Instruction? Eight Standards for Mathematical Practice?
- Week 4: Now that you are one month in, how do you see this experience changing your classroom? Think in terms of relating your experience with careers that your students might explore in STEM fields. How can you involve students in the future opportunities from the classroom? Fieldtrips? Classroom visitors?
- Week 5: How can your business (or others) be more involved in your classroom? What can you or your school do to engage students with the real world? What can the real world (our externship hosts) do to engage students in their world?
- Week 6: Wrap Up. We have seen what you have been doing over the summer, here is your last chance to reflect on what the experience has meant to you, what you will take with you to the classroom and perhaps how the experience could be made better or more effective.

These blogs were helpful to share what was going on with fellow externs, businesses, mentors, students, teachers, and other interested constituents. Additionally, these blogs allowed students an opportunity to share what career opportunities they have discovered. They are a vehicle to share with students what a career in STEM would look like from the perspective of an employee, but through the lens of a teacher. Here are a few of the blog addresses to see what the teachers produced during their experience:

- *http://cgardnersafety.blogspot.com*
- *http://meekersteve.blogspot.com*
- *http://externships2011monsanto.blogspot.com*
- *http://jenmillermath.blogspot.com*

Additionally, teachers wrote a two-page reflective paper, met with mentors in person at the beginning and end of their experience, were in touch on a weekly basis, and participated in program evaluation activities. Also, mentors visited classrooms to see how the summer experience was translating back to the students.

Due to our increased numbers, we brought on board more mentors to maintain a 10 to 1 ratio of externs to mentor. Teachers were brought together in early June to learn about the expectations of the experience. A final meeting took place in early August where businesses and teachers were able to reflect on the summer and offer guidance for improvement.

Evidence of Success

An external evaluator, the Center for Social and Behavioral Research at the University of Northern Iowa, guides evaluation. Human Subjects approval of the Institutional Review Board of the University of Northern Iowa was gained for working with teachers, business hosts, and students on program evaluation. Each year, we improve how we measure impact of this program on teachers, students, and private sector hosts. During 2011, evaluation methods include pre- and postexperience surveys with teachers and business hosts, five assignments of teachers, end-of-summer debriefing forum, follow-up classroom interviews, and a student survey of STEM-related interest and awareness. For teachers and students, these are the measureable program objectives:

1. Teachers who participate in the externships will engage their students in activities that apply concepts in their field to real-world applications.

2. Teachers who participate in the externships will demonstrate curriculum changes that incorporate Iowa Core Curriculum 21st-Century skills such as employability skills, financial literacy, and technology literacy.

3. Students of teachers who participate in the externships will show improved understanding of content concepts and the Iowa Core Curriculum 21st-Century skills, and increased interest in STEM-related careers, through improved grades, higher standardized test scores, and positive growth in attitudes about STEM study through surveys.

For business hosts we also aspire to impact their notions of teachers, of schools, and how best to support the production of inspired, knowledgeable future career-seekers. Business hosts are encouraged to seek ways to have an impact on the curriculum that teachers use in their classroom; working to align it with their business needs. Businesses are also able to directly impact schools by providing equipment, providing guided tours, setting up internships for students, and encouraging employees to work with the local school districts. Additionally, we conduct pre-experience and postexperience questionnaires and interviews of business and agency hosts.

The evaluation examines the association between teachers' participation in the program and their students' STEM-related interest and awareness using pre- and postsurveys and Iowa Tests of Educational Development (ITED) score analysis. Students complete the presurvey at the beginning of the 2011–12 academic year. Student postsurveys are administered at the end of the fall semester. The student survey contains four demographic questions and 35 items related to students' interest and awareness in STEM topics and careers. Evidence of program impacts on students is yet to be determined fully, although data collection is ongoing.

Teaching Practices as Evidence of Success

Pre-experience and postexperience questionnaires are administered to teacher-externs, which focus on the following topics: participant teaching practices, participant attitudes and beliefs about teaching, and the externship experience. Both the pre-experience questionnaire and post-experience questionnaire are administered via self-administered paper-and-pencil format. The pre-experience questionnaire was administered at each pre-experience workshop. The post-experience questionnaire was administered at the postexperience forum.

Teacher-externs were asked about the emphasis they give to various goals or objectives as part of their teaching prior to the externship experience and plans for emphasis after their externship experience. Results show increases in the percent of teachers who said they will place major emphasis on the following:

1. Encouraging students to explore alternative explanations or methods for solving problems

2. Integrating the course curriculum with other subjects or fields of study

3. Understanding the theoretical concepts and ideas underlying scientific applications

4. Career opportunities and how their classroom will support exposing students to these options

Results show decreases in the percent of teachers who said they will place major emphasis on the following:

1. Preparing students for taking standardized tests in the subject

2. Fully covering the course curriculum as prescribed

3. Teaching facts, rules, or vocabulary

Teacher-externs also rate the frequency of student engagement in various learning activities pre-experience and their plans for student engagement postexperience. Results show increases in the percent of teachers who said they will *often* (almost every class or every class) engage students in the following:

1. Work on hands-on activities to design or implement their own scientific investigations

2. Investigate possible career opportunities in math or science

3. Work individually on written work or assignments in a workshop or textbook

In open-ended responses, many teachers report that they expected the externship experience to help make their class activities and content more relevant to industry and the real world. Teachers reported in postsurveys that the experience had indeed done this. Additionally, teachers expected that the externship would help them gain perspective of employee needs and expectations and could relay this information back to students and help build their skills in those areas. Again, postsurvey results showed that the externships met teacher expectations in gaining a better perspective of industry. Teachers also reported the experience impacted plans to build students' problem-solving and 21st-century skills. These findings regarding the externship's impact on teacher practices support teacher increases mentioned above.

Teachers also reported on how motivated they are in their teaching and the extent to which they feel they can motivate or influence their students. Results show increases in the percent of teachers who said they are *very* motivated in the following ways:

1. I consider preparing students for the kinds of expectations they will encounter in a work setting as an important part of my job.

2. I am motivated to use more technology in my main field of teaching.

3. I consider myself a "subject matter expert" in my main field of teaching.

In addition to gaining knowledge of STEM careers and ideas for real-world applications to bring to the classroom, teachers reported gaining connections with businesses and other teachers as a result of the externship experience. Teachers reported plans to bring experts to the classroom to talk with students as well as planning field trips to businesses. Teachers also reported gaining a better understanding of a business atmosphere and work/skill expectations for students in the future. Also, externs reported strengthening their content knowledge and learning new technology tools such as the blog as a result of the externship experience.

Teacher-externs reported that they participated in the program to gain real-world experiences to apply in the classroom. By gaining such experience, teachers are now more confident in their abilities to advise students about STEM careers and are more knowledgeable about real-world applications. Teachers plan to use the ideas gained from the externship experience to make class activities more relevant to students and to build student skills for future employment. Teacher-externs anticipate using the business and teacher connections established to bring additional expertise to the classroom. Finally, teachers anticipate that their increased knowledge of STEM careers and skills will lead to increased student interest and achievement in STEM areas.

Feedback from teachers included:

- "Working in a research facility has helped me discover the employer expectations in the private sector. I can bring this experience to the table with students and discuss how to improve those employability skills."
- "I have another experience that I can share with my students when I am trying to relate school work to life after high school. I have made contacts in the science world that I can use for collaborating ideas and improving my science knowledge. I have been reassured that I belong in education."
- "By far this experience has motivated me to look at my teaching in a different way and also motivated me to work with my students in a new way."
- "You have to connect the students to the real-world in some way and you have to encourage students to want to learn. This experience has taught me that math is always out there for students to find."
- "The value from this experience was building a partnership with a local business, seeing different ways to connect our curriculum with everyday use, and working more with the Iowa Core Curriculum, especially on the 21st-century skills."
- "I don't expect that a lot of my students are going to work at Con Agra in Council Bluffs, Iowa. But I do think that they will use my knowledge of the industry and those similar to it to apply their knowledge in the future. I think my students have a better understanding of why challenging yourself is important. We have also focused on what employers are looking for in an applicant and how that carries over to class."

Excerpted teacher reflections on the experience clarify their change and growth over the externship experience (listed below by name of the company where each teacher worked):

Genencor: The hardest part of this project actually occurred at the beginning. I never realized how difficult it was to design an experiment that would study and hopefully solve a specific problem. This experience forced me to think back to all my chemistry classes, and what I realized is that all of the labs we had done had a list of procedures to follow in order to show some concept or idea. At no time in my education were we expected to design a procedure that would study or solve a particular problem. So where do we go from here? I need to put students in position where they are required to design an experiment in order to solve a particular issue.

Kemin: One of the biggest traits that I could tell was looking for which industries demanded from their employees—namely the ability to problem-solve. This showed up in many situations, but I'm sure this is valued no matter what field you work in. It was great to see the persistence applied to problems. Of course there was motivation. You had to produce results or your job may be on the line, so you really didn't have too many choices except to push through problems and continue to improve on efficiency. Many times I saw students reach a problem and give up or wait for someone, a teacher or friend, to fix it for them or give up on it entirely. I need to be careful to not take away my students' chance to solve problems on their own and try to put them in situations where they are challenged. I think it really helps them to recognize that their decisions in situations of adversity really play a huge part in their success.

Procter and Gamble: This overall experience was great. I now can share a real experience and not something that is conjured up in my mind. One of the biggest things that I will bring to my classroom is emphasizing a work effort that is worthy of a good industry employee. Initiative, patience, endurance, and have no fear. Also, since Procter and Gamble is one of the largest local employers, I will be taking my students there for a field trip so they can see what STEM careers are available in the area. This is vital to keeping our local talent here in Iowa and it is increasingly important to expose students to these opportunities.

DNR and City of Carrol: My students need to share ideas clearly, both in spoken and written word. Teams are the norm in the workplace and so students need to develop their skills in sharing ideas and data in a timely and accurate manner. I already have students work in teams but emphasizing the rationale behind their significance is something I intend to stress more this year. They need to experience, as I have through this program, that learning is perpetual and often times uses mathematics in unexpected and imaginative ways!

Allen Hospital: I think it would be very meaningful for students to experience this problem-solving process because it is based in real life. This was one of the only experiences I have seen where both parties were mutually benefitted. I think it just enriches each other's situation. Additionally, Allen Hospital has a huge demand for STEM-educated students and it is important to show students career options at the local hospital.

Rockwell Collins: The main area I will be able to take back to my classroom, however, is the emphasis on 21st-century skills. We used technology almost constantly with much of our time on computers, using a graphing calculator, on the phone, and preparing and sharing ideas using presentation tools. Other aspects of the job that should be emphasized in the classroom are communication, adaptation to changing expectations and responsibilities, work ethic, collaboration, and self-directedness, especially in problem-solving pursuits. Seeking out help from others when necessary (and being allowed to do so) is essentially in the modern-day math classroom. This experience has reminded me of the importance of learning as a team and to not make it an individual effort. My classroom will be different this school year. A new emphasis on communication between students will improve the mathematical and real-word understanding my students need.

Boone DNR: Critical and logical thinking allows the DNR to make the relationships between evidence and explanations. The connection I would like to make with my classes is that the students can use the same inquiry skills such as identifying problems, measuring and collecting data, analyzing data, and proposing or revising solutions that the biologists and technicians of the DNR use.

Con Agra: There is no other time in a student's life where they will have the opportunity to build these skills in a controlled environment than in high school. It is important that students see the value of building these talents and transferring them to their life after high school. This experience gave me tools to use in my classroom, and in my life. I am excited to discuss my experience with my classes and help them understand why their years in high school are truly pivotal points in their lives. I also viewed this as a great way to answer the question, "When will I ever use this?" in the classroom. After a short time, I immediately saw the 21st-century skills needed to run a successful business, and how components of this experience would find their way into my classroom next fall.

Monsanto, Ankeny: The externship has been a meaningful experience for me. I have been a science teacher a long time, but I have very little real lab experience. Getting to be part of a cutting-edge, high throughput biotechnology lab—at least for a short time—was both interesting and fascinating. I was impressed with how everyone, including lab technicians and management, grasped the difficult genetics and biochemistry involved and their willingness and ability to share their knowledge with me in language I could understand. I also was impressed with the way everyone, and especially the technicians, were so skilled in all the hands-on aspects of the lab as well as in operating all the high-tech equipment. They are good communicators and problem solvers. They are also good at working together as part of a team. Being at ease with technology, communication, problem solving, and the ability to work as part of a team—these are all skills I hope to encourage and help my students to develop.

Business Host Findings as Evidence of Success

Pre-experience and postexperience questionnaires were administered to business hosts via e-mail. The questionnaires included primarily open-ended questions and focused on the following topics: (1) business host reasons for participating, (2) goals and expectations for teacher-extern, (3) learning and benefits gained from teacher-extern, (4) anticipated future engagement with teacher-extern, (5) business host interest in hosting a teacher-extern in the future, and (6) showing students future career opportunities in science and mathematics. The pre-experience survey was administered in June 2011. Thirty-one participating business hosts completed the pre-experience survey. The postexperience surveys were administered in August 2011. Twenty-six business hosts completed the postsurvey.

In general, business hosts reported that they were originally motivated to host a teacher-extern for the potential mutual benefit the program offered to the business and the teachers. The majority of business hosts said that the benefit to the business (cost or resource savings, new knowledge or completed projects) and the benefit to the teacher, students, or community were important motivating factors. In addition, most business hosts recognized the potential of the program to increase student interest in and awareness of STEM careers in Iowa, thereby enhancing the STEM employment pipeline in Iowa. The following were commonly cited by business hosts as reasons for involvement in the Externship program (listed in descending order by frequency of responses):

1. Externship program provided free labor and current staffing was too low to have completed the project without the extern

2. General benefits for teachers and students

3. Help company recruiting efforts and raise awareness of the company

4. Community involvement

5. Positive experience in the past

6. Strengthen STEM education in Iowa

7. Gain a new perspective on the business (from both the extern and the host sides)

8. Create partnerships with schools/education

9. Provide teachers and students with exposure to STEM careers

Business hosts were asked to list goals they had for the externs at the beginning of the summer. Most business hosts wanted to see the externs complete projects that would be mutually beneficial to both the host and the extern. The following were commonly cited goals:

1. Learn new skills related to research, computers, science, math

2. Complete a useful project or task for the business (provide useful assistance)

3. Gain real-world experience, see applications of math and science in the real world, and bring that experience back to the classroom

4. Learn about business, the balance between research and business, and the many integrated skills and concepts involved

5. Learn about the process of getting a project started and completed

6. Build the extern's curriculum and apply new concepts in class

7. Have an enjoyable experience

Business hosts did begin the experience with some concerns or reservations about the upcoming externship period. Hosts were concerned about the high level of commitment of resources that would be required in hosting an extern. Would that commitment of resources be worth it in the end? In addition, hosts reported being concerned about providing a good experience for the teacher-extern. These concerns for the business and the teacher can be distilled into concerns about whether the externship placement would be a good match. Business hosts that commit multiple resources toward a teacher-extern want a return on that investment, but also understand the importance of a positive experience for the participants. The following concerns or reservations were cited by business hosts:

1. High level of commitment of resources by the business (time, money, space, etc.)

2. Meeting the extern's expectations and providing a useful experience for the extern

3. Extern's level of preparation (having adequate skills), motivations (money or experience), ability to work with the company, ability to work independently

4. Safety and confidentiality

5. Not enough time to complete a project

At the end of the externship experience, most business hosts said they thought the teacher-externs had gained knowledge and valuable experiences over the summer. Hosts said that teachers gained a better understanding of how the classroom and real world are connected in the fields of science and math, as well as how interdisciplinary STEM careers operate. Business hosts reported that teacher-externs gained the following from the experience:

1. Learned about the research process, the business host, and the diversity of experiences available in math and science

2. Careers available for students who study in the STEM disciplines

3. Saw firsthand the ways that classroom concepts (in math, science, and other topics) are applied in the real world

4. Gained ideas for collaboration and networking in the future

Business hosts were asked to speculate about how students of the teacher-externs would benefit from the program. In general, hosts said they expected students to gain a heightened awareness of STEM careers in Iowa and a better understanding of the links and connections between the many topics they study in school. At the end of the externship, most business hosts reported that students would gain an understanding of the relevance of the things they learn in school to the real world. The following responses were shared by hosts:

1. See how classroom concepts apply to multiple real-world business/careers.

2. Understand that multiple topics and skills are needed in real-world jobs (interdisciplinary nature of the real world)

3. Better knowledge of the science, math, and business worlds

4. Exposure to the business host

5. Making mistakes as a part of the learning process

Business hosts reported learning from the teacher-externs, as well. Most hosts had limited knowledge of the educational system in Iowa, the curricular requirements in schools, and the challenges teachers face in the classroom. At the end of the summer, business hosts reported a greater awareness and understanding of these issues as well as an appreciation for the ways that businesses can be a partner with the educational system. After the experience, business hosts reported they had learned about the following from the externs (and from the externship experience in general):

1. The challenges teachers face in the classroom when conveying educational concepts and engaging students

2. How to engage students and communities in STEM

3. The difficulty of exposing students to STEM careers in a limited classroom if businesses don't take a more active role in opening their doors to teachers and students

4. There are excited, motivated people going into teaching in Iowa

5. The expectations and needs of youth/young learners

6. The educational system in Iowa (the core curriculum, "roadblocks" to educational progress, etc.)

7. A new perspective on their own company and job (new enthusiasm, management skills, etc.)

8. New knowledge from the extern's project

At the end of the externship period, business hosts were asked about perceived benefits to the company. The most often-cited benefit to the business from participating in the externship program was that the externs completed projects that were helpful to the company in terms of knowledge acquisition, management experience for staff, building community relationships, and others. The full-time staff was able to work on other projects, resources were used well, and the externs provided help during busy periods. Benefits included the following:

1. Completed helpful projects

2. Increased pipeline of STEM workforce

3. Made contacts with local schools

4. Can use the program as a promotional/public relations tool

In general, business hosts were positive about their experiences with the externship program and reported enthusiasm for hosting externs in the future. Their responses to the pre-experience and postexperience questionnaires reflect a desire for mutual benefit from the program. They valued both the benefits to the extern and the benefits to their businesses. Hosts were most satisfied when the experience was mutually beneficial and the extern was a good fit within the business. In general, expectations and goals that were set at the beginning of the experience were achieved by the end of the summer. It will be important in future externship sessions to work with business hosts and teachers to ensure a good placement match, ensure a shared understanding of expectations at the beginning of the program, and maintain open lines of communication between teacher-externs, business hosts, and program staff.

Finally, businesses were given a chance to share some direct quotes regarding their summer externship experience. Below are a few of these quotes:

- This program offers a lot of potential. We want the best new employees that can have long and impactful careers. The opportunity to engage in their education has enormous potential benefits.
- We really appreciate the assistance that this program has provided and we look forward to continuing a partnership with IMSEP. Thanks for all the help!
- I think this program will prepare teachers and enhance student achievement in STEM. It provides community partnerships that will continue after the program for ongoing support.
- Great Program, it really helps to bring the current business world into the classroom. It is a good program—we enjoy participating—the only part that doesn't work for us (and that is due to our distance) is attending the group meetings.
- This is a very beneficial program for everyone involved! The knowledge gained through this program should not have a price tag attached to it! Host businesses must have viable, challenging projects for the externs to work on during the program. I believe we have received more benefit from our externs than we have provided them. This is a very worthwhile program from a business perspective, but the long-term effect could mean a more prepared worker entering the workforce based on the extern's experience being transferred to the students.
- The Black Hawk County Conservation Board appreciates the opportunity to participate in this program and encourages the program to continue. It has been very beneficial in many ways to this agency over the past years. Thank You!
- This is a good program and everyone involved has provided a positive experience for us at Innovative Lighting. Bettina has been a model Extern participant. During her six weeks she has always been respectful, dependable and provided timely and detailed work. She proved to be a valuable team member and we all enjoyed having her here this summer. We wish Bettina the best in her future endeavors.

Teacher-Produced End Products

The following display is an example of the posters produced by teachers at the end of their experience, highlighting their summer into a condensed presentation. This poster is a useful tool for all involved to help promote the wonderful learning that takes place during an externship.

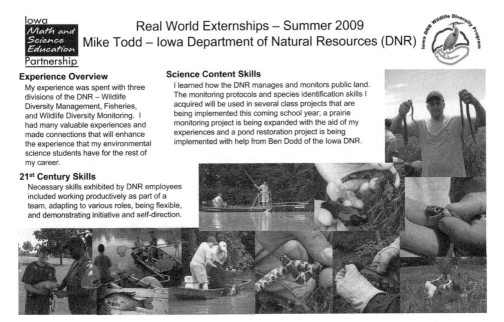

Real World Externships – Summer 2009
Mike Todd – Iowa Department of Natural Resources (DNR)

Experience Overview
My experience was spent with three divisions of the DNR – Wildlife Diversity Management, Fisheries, and Wildlife Diversity Monitoring. I had many valuable experiences and made connections that will enhance the experience that my environmental science students have for the rest of my career.

21st Century Skills
Necessary skills exhibited by DNR employees included working productively as part of a team, adapting to various roles, being flexible, and demonstrating initiative and self-direction.

Science Content Skills
I learned how the DNR manages and monitors public land. The monitoring protocols and species identification skills I acquired will be used in several class projects that are being implemented this coming school year; a prairie monitoring project is being expanded with the aid of my experiences and a pond restoration project is being implemented with help from Ben Dodd of the Iowa DNR.

This project was made possible by the Iowa Mathematics and Science Education Partnership and the Iowa Department of Natural Resources

Conclusions

Externships are not without their challenges. There are several that have been addressed and there are sure to be more to come. Perhaps the largest challenge that we face with externships is finding appropriate matches for businesses and teachers. The business world is not always able to articulate their needs far enough in advance for the right teacher to be found. Additionally, the right teacher often has little to no concept of what is needed or if they can actually do it. On top of that is the delicate balance of giving enough time for good work to be accomplished and for teachers to also enjoy their only vacation time of the year. To work through this, we have become better at helping businesses write a general description of their needs, specifically highlighting the skills they desire to accomplish their tasks. We try to get this general description out to teachers as early as possible to allow businesses the opportunity to interview and select the most appropriate teacher to work with them. Furthermore, we're overcoming this challenge by advertising more and getting more businesses and teachers involved than we can make placements for; making this a competitive environment where only the best matches are funded.

Another struggle that we have faced, although limited, is when a mismatch is made. Perhaps the teacher does not have the skill set to accomplish the job requested. Maybe the business is looking to fill a hole in their company, like a data entry person. We handle this by having open lines of communication and making sure both sides know that issues need to be dealt with at the beginning of the experience. We schedule meetings between all members within the first week or two of the experience to make sure that matches are appropriate. When they are not, which is rare, we work together to adjust the experience or find a new position for the teacher, perhaps with a different company altogether. We are sure there will be more challenges in the future but we will continue to address them as a team, keeping the mission of the program as our guiding force.

Future of Real World Externships

As a result of the investments on the part of the Iowa Department of Economic Development (IDED) and the National Science Foundation, Real World Externships for Math, Science, and Technology teachers has progressed from a modest ten-teacher professional development trial in 2009 to now a population of nearly 100 Iowa teachers having come through the project. More and more Iowa companies are opening their doors to teachers, and some are even cost-sharing. Provided we can continue to demonstrate gains on the parts of all three constituents—teachers, their students, and business hosts, the program may be primed for scale. Inevitably we hope to expand the number of business partners and teachers, to engage school administrators, to replicate the model, and to offer comparable programming at the preservice as well as community college level. This program and the lives it has touched thus far would not be possible without the valuable partnerships in addition to the IDED including the faculty in content departments at UNI who assess for graduate credit, the agencies that have helped connect businesses and schools including the Association for Business and Industry, the Iowa Business Council, the Technology Association of Iowa, the Iowa Biotechnology Association, School Administrators of Iowa, area education agencies, numerous school district administrators, Rotary clubs, Chambers of Commerce, and regional economic development groups. STEM education is an "all hands on deck" challenge for Iowa, for which all of these groups has answered the call. For additional information about this program, visit *www.iowamathscience.org/externships*. The Real World Externships program is funded by National Science Foundation grant #DRL-1031784.

APPENDIX I
SAMPLE MEDIA COVERAGE

CONTRIBUTED PHOTO

Muscatine High School science teacher Josh Hanna works on a project at Monsanto in Muscatine, as part of an externship with the Iowa Math and Science Education Partnership.

A hands-on approach

MHS science teacher gets first-hand look at science in the work world

CONTRIBUTED PHOTO

Muscatine High School science teacher Josh Hanna said working as an extern this summer at Muscatine's Monsanto Plant provided him with valuable information that he can take back to his classroom.

Cynthia Beaudette
563-262-0527
cynthia.beaudette@muscatinejournal.com

MUSCATINE, Iowa — It's one thing to teach students about science.

It's quite another to actually experience some of the ways those lessons can be applied in a science-related career.

Muscatine High School science teacher Josh Hanna had the chance to do just that this summer at Monsanto in Muscatine — and he's excited to tell his students what he learned.

"This brings a new level of relevance to my classroom," said Hanna.

Hanna, 28, of Muscatine, was accepted into the Iowa Math and Science Education Partnership, a state program that provides Iowa teachers with an opportunity to work in a local business or industry on an externship basis.

Externships are experience-based learning opportunities, similar to internships, offered by educational institutions to give teachers short, practical experiences in their field of study.

Hanna spent the past six weeks at Muscatine's Monsanto plant participating in regular workday tasks and projects.

Monsanto is a worldwide ag company that uses innovation and technology to advance conservation and help farmers increase their yield.

Hanna worked on a project measuring the effect of nitrogen on the growth of corn.

Monsanto plant manager David Penn said this is the first time his corporation participated in the program, and he and his staff are pleased with the results.

"Josh is so enthusiastic and energetic," said Penn. "He made it so easy for us. It's been great having him here and we'll definitely be participating again."

Hanna said part of the program's appeal is the fact that it's local.

Many times, continuing education programs for teachers involve workshops at major universities that require travel and time away from home.

That kind of commitment can be difficult for people like Hanna, who has a wife and young children.

ONLINE

Josh Hanna's blog about his summer experience at Monsanto
http://externships2010monsanto.blogspot.com/
Iowa Math and Science Education Partnership
http://www.iowamathscience.org/externships/

"At the end of the day, I get to go home to my family," he said.

Jeff Weld, director of the Iowa Mathematics and Science Education Partnership, said the externship program is available to all Iowa math and science teachers and it's growing.

"We had 10 teachers in the summer of 2009 and there were 33 this year," said Weld. "With luck, we'll have 50 next summer."

The Talent Marketplace: Where Science Careers Are Made

S. Anders Hedberg
President, Hedberg Consulting LLC

Setting

In this chapter, aspects of science career planning and development are discussed from a different perspective, which at first glance may seem remote and overly theoretical. However, it is the author's hope that, as the logic of the reasoning unfolds, the initial discussion about analogies between the worlds of education and business will prove to be pertinent for a discourse about how best to prepare our young generation for the science workplace.

Briefly, this is the premise of the discussion: PreK–12 education in general should prepare a young person for all the rigors of life and citizenship. A key element in life, liberty, and the pursuit of happiness is the individuals' success in gaining employment and developing a career that helps pay the bills for the individual and his or her family. Therefore it is fair to conclude that a key goal of education is to prepare the individual for a successful entry into the workforce.

Science education will help prepare some individuals for careers in the science workforce. More importantly, however, science education will help prepare *all* individuals for important requirements of *all* workplaces, by virtue of the unique skills that rigorous science education helps develop. Thus, problem solving, critical and analytical thinking, data processing and the ability to reason and draw correct conclusions from evidence are highly valued skills in all areas of the U.S. economy, including its government, public, private and nonprofit sectors.

In order to discuss this role of the education sector as a developer of a product (employable talent) intended to be used (employed and further developed) by a key customer, the workplace sector, I have chosen to draw on analogies from the world of business.

In the world of business, markets are made up of two essential elements, providers and consumers of goods and services. They exist in a productive relationship of interdependence which is usually relatively balanced and to a large extent self-regulated. When a need for a new service or product arises, a producer will provide for the need. If the need disappears, usually production stops, or an overage of unsold product will stack up, resulting in falling prices and loss of revenue for the producer. Conversely, if a consumer's need cannot be satisfied by one provider, the customer goes elsewhere for business. Competition for customers keep prices down and a lack of competition allows for price increases. The consumer who goes searching for a service provider may pay a premium.

In this chapter, we will look at the interdependence of developers and users of science talent, the product of good science education, from a perspective of market analysts—in this case, considering the dynamics of the talent marketplace. We will find, not surprisingly, that there is an imbalance in the US science talent market, and we will consider ways to correct this imbalance.

A Quick Look at the Status of Science Education One Decade Into the 21st Century

Looking back to the days of *A Nation at Risk* (NCEE 1983), we started off with a clear determination to not fall deeper into the abyss of science "uneducation" in the mid- to late-1980s. National education, business and science organizations such as the American Association for the Advancement of Science, the Business-Higher Education Forum, the Business Roundtable, the Council of Chief State School Officers, the National Governors Association, National Research Council, National Science Foundation, and the National Science Teachers Association contributed valuable leadership and collaborated to chart a course for improvement in K–12 science education over the decades that followed.

Clearly defined science education standards, inquiry-based science education (IBSE) by skilled teachers trained in the use of exemplary curriculum and pedagogy grounded in research, and periodic student assessment formed a core in our reform strategy.

The National Science Resources Center (NSRC), founded by the National Academies and the Smithsonian Institution in 1986, defined several critical elements for a strategic science education reform plan:

1. Learning and teaching through guided inquiry, to replace rote memorization of declarative textbook facts;

2. Teacher preparation to support inquiry-based science education (IBSE). This included inservice professional development as well as preservice instruction, with emphasis on the former, and still mostly faltering attempt to address the latter;

3. Development of curriculum tools designed to foster and support IBSE;

4. Materials Support Systems and Services necessitated by the kit-based curriculum units which contained both perishable live materials and breakable classroom equipment; and

5. Support from school district administrators, education policy makers and community stakeholders.

It is generally agreed that in order to succeed and become fully sustainable, science education reform must be designed as a systemic change project and ideally be embedded in a stakeholder community with strong leadership (ASSET 2009, AMSTI).

Twenty-eight years after *A Nation at Risk,* we have made important strides to better provide for our children through IBSE initiatives. More than a quarter of our nation's K–12 students are impacted by systemic change initiatives that better prepare them for science literacy and in a best case, continuing education and productive careers. Thus, in an absolute sense, we are doing better, even *much* better. But in a relative sense we are still slipping behind our contemporary developed countries. TIMSS and PISA jointly drive home this fact in alternating blows, every other year (IEA 1985; OECD 2000).

While the periodic international comparison can help inject a healthy dose of urgency into the education debate, it serves a more important role as a reminder of our role in the global talent marketplace. Why is this important? Because we must prepare our students to become productive citizens!

If we agree that the primary role of education is to prepare the individual for productive citizenry, involving gainful employment and acceptance of a responsible role in society, then it follows that education must involve skill-building and practice of how to apply factual knowledge in a range of different real-life situations. In the case of science education, we agree that many important abilities result from understanding and having practiced science inquiry in the process of learning. By incorporating scientific habits of mind in the daily processes of living, we are able to identify analyze and solve problems, regardless of their general nature. Having learned to distinguish facts from fiction, to recognize conjecture and hypothesis, and being able to understand and interpret evidence, we are better equipped to make critical decisions that can impact our future. This can involve decisions about our own and our family's health, safety, and economy, and it includes casting a vote for local, state, and national representatives in a democratic election. As had been said so many times before, a primary goal of effective science education is to build a scientifically literate citizenry.

However, it must be recognized that all these abilities are also universally important in the workplace. While scientific literacy is absolutely necessary in the scientific workplace, the ability to think critically; to recognize, analyze, and solve problems; and to make decisions based on facts and projected outcomes is highly valued in every workplace (Adult Literacy 2008; Lievens et al. 2001; Price and Turnbull 2007; Shaffer et al. 2006).

The following discussion uses the term *science* to define a broader field of learning, teaching, and practice that encompasses a range of excursions and extensions from pure science. While STEM is increasingly used to wrap together science, technology, engineering, and mathematics, this term includes four separate fields, each with defined standards, definitions, outcomes, and products. For the purposes of this chapter, *science* will be used to also include mathematical computations necessary for the practice of science, as well as technological and engineering solutions used both to practice science and to bring scientific concepts to the end user. In the discussion that follows, we will call the place where science is practiced the *science workplace*.

We will now place the science workplace, and in more general terms *the workplace*, in an appropriate relationship to the place where education happens, the education sector. Let us use some familiar concepts from our daily lives to help describe this situation:

As citizens, we move in and out of our roles as consumers. Most of us are also contributing in some way to a production supply line through our daily work. So, in that sense we are constantly helping to maintain a productive complex marketplace, with millions of products and services delivered and received daily. If we for a moment consider talent, and more specifically science talent, to be such a product, it will allow us to define the talent marketplace. We can then further define the supply chain that leads to the talent marketplace, and we can delve into some the talent consumer characteristics.

The Talent Marketplace

Viewed simplistically, there are producers of marketable talent and there are users/consumers of talent. Somewhere in between these two key drivers there is also a space and time for interaction between the two.

The Developers of Talent

Obviously, talent comes as raw material, unpolished flawless gems if you will, to the first station of refinement. The loving and nurturing care of parents and family has at this point already laid the groundwork for a finished product. Whether the professional polishing begins in day care, prekindergarten, or kindergarten, the process continues for at least another 12 years. The increasingly refined product—student learners—move from classroom to classroom, teacher to teacher, building to building (ideally with ongoing encouragement from parents, family, and friends), until finally talent preparation stage 1 is over on high school graduation day.

For some, this means entering stage 2, college, and maybe later a third stage of professional training or graduate school. For others this means finding a job. In either case, at this point the student needs to have incorporated a basic but solid understanding for how facts, concepts, and processes that have been learned over the past 12 years are actually used in real life. For those students who continue their education, their choice of specialization and career direction will hopefully be informed by experiences that add relevance of real-life science application and help validate the theoretical education. For those who choose to exit school, such experiences will add significant value to their preparation to enter the workforce.

All those education professionals who contribute their expertise to the polishing of the gem of talent up through stage 1 and beyond are part of the "talent development" sector. This is, for all intents and purposes, synonymous with the education sector.

The Users of Talent

Again, we are all consumers of science products and services. Behind all these goods and services is the talent that has contributed to discovery, research, innovation, development, and commercialization. This science talent spans a wide range of professions including lab technicians, machinists, process automation specialists, technology transfer managers, biologists, project planners, engineers, health care professionals, human resources and financial specialists, and many, many more. How does this science talent—remember our broad definition of science—find its way into these workplaces where products and services of science are prepared for all of us to use in order to better our lives?

Some of the talent is hired directly from high schools and community colleges into lower-level service functions. Entry-level professional track jobs might be populated with competitive bachelor degree college graduates, whereas highly specialized, advanced degree holders (masters and doctorate levels) are sought for the key manager and executive positions. Employees with special, highly valued competencies, "knowledge workers," (Jackson, Hitt, and DeNisi 2003) are sought after and targeted for career development, often involving international assignments (Bartlett and Ghoshal 2003; Caligiuri and Di Santo 2001; Morrison 2000; Stahl et al. 2007). Importantly, the workplace views the skills base of its employees as one of its main assets (Grindley 1991), closely linked to its core competencies (Garavan et al. 2001). Even when economic hardship leads to millions of unemployed workers, there is a shortage of talent, forcing the workplace sector to search feverishly for those who will make the difference between profit and loss (Athey 2005). When a corporate science workplace has defined the advanced level key job that needs to be filled, they will seek out and attract the best talent for that job, regardless of where the candidate may live. It is often understood that the cost of acquiring this talent may involve engaging a search firm, relocating the successful candidate from a distant country, managing the legal entry requirements (e.g., work permit, visa), and potentially also relocating a family with school-age children and helping to enroll these children in the desired school. Not infrequently, there is also a need for language training of the candidate in question (Manpower Group 2011). Taken together, the cost of finding and hiring this talent can be considerable (PWC 2010). What can we take away from this discussion? Two facts: (1) Workplaces value well-prepared talent extremely highly and (2) It would be considerably less expensive to find and hire talent within the home country.

The Talent Marketplace

This more or less virtual marketplace is where the developers and users of talent can meet and interact. However, a problem with the talent marketplace is that the two key players actually don't meet and interact as much as they could and should—with a few exceptions. Examples include:

1. Job fairs staged at the high school level, which primarily serve to let students get promotional snippets of facts about jobs they already have a preconceived notion about from television shows such as *CSI*.

2. Very high level interaction between education institutions and workplace representatives also take place at the professional and graduate schools of top universities. This represents a highly productive exchange that benefits both parties by trading support for world leading academic research against access to prime talent for top science positions.

As a marketplace, this one is otherwise unique. The "product" walks him- or herself from the place of final refinement to the door of the customer and conducts the full-scale marketing and sales at no cost for the developer.

So, with rare exceptions, the developer of talent (the education sector) is currently taking very little responsibility for the marketing and sale of its product. Or worse—the developer makes very little effort to understand whether the talent it prepared matches the needs of the customer.

Is This System a Seller's Market or a Buyer's Market— And Does It Matter Anyway?

Traditionally, (at least historically) the talent market as we have defined it in this paper behaves like a classical seller's market. Using the same analogy as earlier, the products/services marketplace, a seller's market is one where the producer/developer has the upper hand and able to set the terms of the transaction because there is little or no competition for customers. In this situation the buyer has little leverage and is left having to buy what is offered, maybe even if it does not exactly meet the need. A seller's market is also characterized by an overabundance of buyers in relation to the volume of goods and services offered.

Conversely, in a buyer's market, the relationship is reversed. A glut of goods and services (in this case talent) gives the buyer the upper hand in the trade. The producer/developer must pay close attention to the buyers' needs in designing the product, since the competition to make a sale is high. The buyer can always go elsewhere to get what he needs.

Neither of these two scenarios is ideal or beneficial for either party. A healthy market is one where the trade is balanced, where the offering of goods and services matches the customers' need and a fair price is asked. Changing product outflow or changing needs are gauged quickly and adjustments are made (Kardes 2001).

The education sector has traditionally decided how talent is to be developed, at least through high school. There are variances between states, and even between districts within states, but by and large, boards of education and political appointees such as chief state school officers set the curriculum and hire teachers for the public schools. National standards serve as guidelines and recommendations. Thus, the talent developer behaves as if he has the advantage in this marketplace. However, the problem is that this is an artificial marketplace, which lacks the constant contact and monitoring of buyer and seller needs, since the closure of the transaction is actually not made by the developer, rather by the finished product itself—at his or her own peril and cost. This brings us to the economy of the talent market.

Talent Economy

Altogether this is a poorly designed talent economy, since it lacks, to a large extent, the all-important feedback loop between developer and user. Operating in splendid isolation from each other, they will go about their business independently, leaving it to the product (graduating student/job seeker) to make the necessary adjustments. This design is thoroughly wasteful.

Valuable resources are squandered throughout the education sector as a result of the cyclic efforts to reform the system in synchronicity with changes of elected leaders. The start/stop periodicity of politically motivated initiatives, often going hand-in-hand with grant programs and a smattering of support from the corporate sector, gets in the way of sustainable improvement. As with good science, strategic improvement of education must be based on well-designed research. Because of the cycle time in K–12 education (it takes 12 years to develop each talent product), new initiatives must be given time to show their effectiveness before adjustments are made.

As discussed previously in this chapter, the talent user—the science workplace sector—will spend vast sums of money to find and acquire the special talent they need. Even if this high-level spending on nonnative talent is limited to a relatively narrow band of science leadership positions, there are significant costs associated with training new hires to qualify for specialized tasks and work environments, even when recruitment from the national talent pool is warranted (ASTD 2009).

Finally, the graduates/job seekers themselves carry, in addition to massive student loans, the additional cost of often multiple study majors and adjunct studies to qualify for jobs in an increasingly competitive job market (Surowiecki 2011). However, the primary cost burden inflicted by this system is the protracted job search and time spent as a nonearner, resulting from a poor match between talent preparation and workplace needs (OECD 2002).

Talent Market Dynamics

The discussion so far has focused on assessing today's situation, which is dynamic, not static. We are now going to consider what drives these dynamics and what they result in. The fact that certain elements in this composite framework have been changing rapidly over the past decades, and by all accounts will change even more (and faster in coming years), is a subject of intense study by organization development experts (Schuler, Jackson, and Tarique 2011; Tarique and Schuler 2010). Interestingly, this change dynamic, which is heavily biased toward the side of the talent user, drives the talent market to further imbalance and makes a correction more urgent that ever.

The Changing Science Workplace: Implications for the Talent Market

We will now explore how one of the two talent market drivers, the customer, adjusts to the circumstances under which it operates and how this adaptation to other pressures and influencing factors in turn drives further imbalance in the talent market. First, let us consider who belongs to the science workplace sector. With an admittedly broad definition, this sector includes all public, government, nongovernmental, and private organizations that use knowledge, competencies, and skills related to and derived from science. A few examples are the Departments of Energy, Homeland Security, Law Enforcement, Transportation, Education at every level, Health and Human Services, corporations working in the fields based on science (e.g., energy, aviation, aerospace, automotive, allied health, pharmaceuticals, IT, communication, mining, manufacturing), and also banking, finance, and insurance. Foundations and nonprofits are also members of this sector. In short, a science workplace is any place where work is performed in exchange for a salary, fee, or other compensation to use, produce, or support science-related products or services.

Most of these organizations work within wide networks that include both public and private sector representatives. Many of them also work both domestically and internationally. Some, particularly multinational enterprises (MNEs) work in formal partnerships and strategic alliances across organizational boundaries and national borders. This means that their missions, operational principles, standards of quality, ethics, and conduct are constantly influenced by other members of their networks. As business and operational norms change in these networks and partnerships, every member becomes aware and adjusts accordingly. This means that change happens quickly, and at some level change is continuously ongoing (Albrecht and Sack 2000).

While some operational styles may be idiosyncratic and prevalent in certain sectors, say governmental departments, others are more flexible and opportunistic. For example, private corporations are free to set their organizational structure, governance principles, size and financial objectives. The world of science business has experienced several such changes over the recent decades.

Studies of the impact of company size on productivity and growth gave rise to descriptors borrowed from the animal kingdom. Birch and Medoff (1994) labeled small (less than 20 employees) and large companies (more than 500 employees) as "mice" and "elephants." Neither of these two "species" generates significant new employment. Enterprises that grow quickly by acquiring their competitors may approach a plateau of productivity (Dickerson, Gibson, and Tsakalotos 1997) and find themselves in competition with "gazelles," companies that are neither small nor large, but often young, nimble, and quick to adapt to change (Birch and Medoff 1994; Acs and Mueller 2008).

Further, emerging technologies spurred the formation of innovation boutique businesses with few employees and even fewer products designed for niche markets, sometimes destined to become acquired by an "elephant." Today, symbiotic relationships between all three species can be found as strategic alliances and interactions that drive business evolution and promote innovation (Gabrielsson, Politis, and Galan 2011; Spilling and Steinsli 2004).

Internal organizational changes have led to new demands on the individual employee: The very large departments growing inside the elephant corporations, characterized by many layers of management, have been found to foster risk aversion, inertia, and slow decision-making. "Flattening" of organizational units have led to increased personal accountability, faster communication, and quicker decision-making deep down in the organization (Hammer and Champy 2003; Sheridan 1998; Malone 2004). Many businesses encourage employees to become "intrapreneurs" who engage their skill portfolio where it is best needed, and who are sought out by task teams in need of a specialist (Carrier 1994; Filion 2002; Wunderer 2001). These new business behaviors reward employees who are innovative, creative and good team contributors, leading to opportunities for personal and professional development, self-reliance, and accountability (Bassi and McMurrer 2004; Sheridan 1998). Through these experiences, the workplace sector has learned the importance and value of having skilled employees at the right place at the right time (Guthridge, Komm, and Lawson 2008; Rawlinson, McFarland, and Post 2008; Siegel 2008).

This represents only a tiny fraction of the changes that permeate the science workplace sector. Yet, armed with knowledge about these trends, educators would be able to help prepare students for the realities of the workplace while they are still in the classroom, helping them secure employment, and develop strong careers.

Problems With the Talent Market: What Can We Do About It?

A short action agenda would look like this:

1. Establish a dialog between the education and workplace sectors about the talent market.

2. Agree to stay connected to sustain these efforts.

3. Establish a "Win-Win" adaptable centerpiece program that meets the needs of both parties.

Let's discuss these action steps in some detail:

Establish a Dialog Between the Education and Workplace Sectors About the Talent Market

We will now discuss ways to establish a productive dialog about these critical issues between the two sectors, either by building on existing contacts or by starting from scratch. The past decades have seen several examples of initiatives that engaged educators and business people in collaborative projects. Achieve, Inc., the Business-Higher Education Forum, and the Business Roundtable are a few nongovernmental organizations that have brokered such collaboratives. Recently, Change the Equation set goals for establishing effective public-private initiatives in support of STEM education.

From these and several others like them, a list of truly exceptional best practice initiatives that have guided students onto strong STEM career tracks have emerged. While each of these has made a difference for cohorts, they rarely lead to sustainable long-term projects that grow and spread.

It is unlikely that any single organization will be able to harness all the combined corporate social responsibility potential for education in the United States and emerge as the leader of the business-education agenda. And while it is good to have hundreds, if not thousands of different but effective projects operating separately, as a vast collection of random acts of kindness, an important shared objective can be met if they all accomplish one thing: Focus both educators and workplace people on improving their own, local niche of the talent market.

The primary objective in every such local initiative is to initiate a productive discussion about the ever-changing needs and continuous adjustments in the science workplace. The workplace sector must share their insights and projections for future talent needs and the education sector must find ways to take this information to the classroom. This can be represented by Figure 13.1.

This schematic illustrates how the U.S. talent market might be strengthened by infusing existing, diverse school-workplace initiatives with a shared vision for a combined talent market built on continuous interaction. More effective and better aligned education-workplace partnerships can result from clear communication of challenges, opportunities and needs for the talent market.

Figure 13.1.

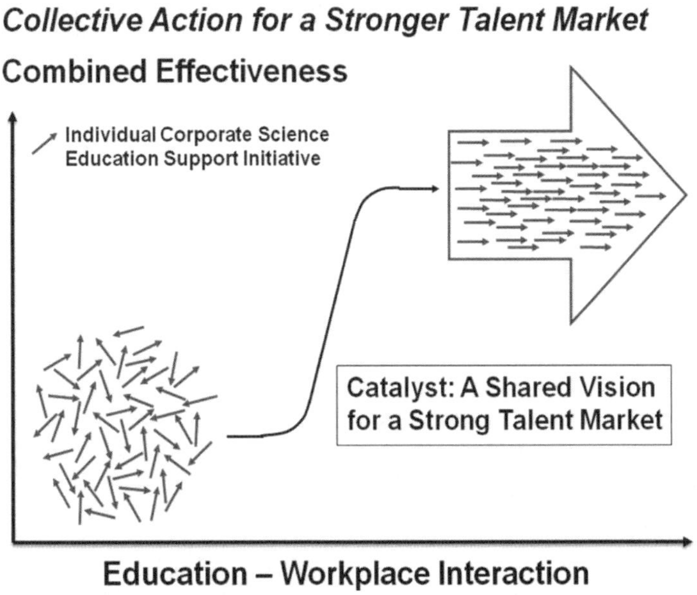

Collective Action for a Stronger Talent Market
Combined Effectiveness

Individual Corporate Science Education Support Initiative

Catalyst: A Shared Vision for a Strong Talent Market

Education – Workplace Interaction

Agree to Stay Connected to Sustain These Efforts

We must now build on the initial dialog to establish a lasting and sustainable relationship between the two sectors. Political winds will continue to change direction, giving newly elected officials opportunities to put their own brand of education to the test and causing instability to the talent market. It will therefore be absolutely necessary to build stability and sustainability into the core elements of the talent market through strategic long-range planning. To achieve the overarching objective of a stronger national talent market, it is necessary to recognize how local education agendas are connected to those driving the state and national talent markets.

Except for basic and entry-level jobs in the science workplace sector, the needs of the hiring organizations will continue to move talent across the U.S. map. Therefore, it will be the location of these science-based organizations that determines where the talent goes for employment. Competition for a good job in a specific location can come from any state and region. Therefore, the best way to level the playing field is to give every student the same benefit of workplace preparation.

As we have discussed earlier in this paper, the workplace dynamics will lead to ever-changing needs for new talent (Schuler, Jackson, and Tarique 2011; Tarique and Schuler 2010). Consequently, the exchange between the education and workplace sectors can never stop. We are constantly aiming at a moving target. There will always be a "tomorrow's workforce" sitting in a classroom, and those students must be given the benefit of understanding new trends in the workplace.

Establish a "Win-Win" Adaptable Centerpiece Program That Meets the Needs of Both Parties

In order for a productive and sustainable relationship between educators and workplace representatives to flourish, it will be essential to have a mutually beneficial program activity in place as a core element. Currently active local initiatives as those discussed above may have such programs in place. However, since many different types of workplaces are represented and economic circumstances vary between regions, a core program concept must be both flexible and adaptable in order to add the desired value.

What follows is a description of a curriculum-based program which specifically addresses the need to communicate science workplace operations and behaviors as well as future talent needs directly to classroom teachers.

R$_x$eSEARCH: An Educational Journey

This novel and innovative program is designed to help high school students develop skills and behaviors necessary for successful careers in the workplace. While the program makes direct reference to subject matter and processes commonplace in sectors based on science, a far broader range of occupations and vocations make use of the general skill portfolio, including critical thinking, teamwork, and communication that results from this program.

The program was created by Bristol-Myers Squibb in 2004 as a key element in the company's strategic education philanthropy portfolio. It was originally designed and implemented as a curriculum tool to be operated under a philanthropic partnership of healthcare-based organizations and corporations, dedicated to help improve science education and science workforce preparation. During the program development, the National Science Resources Center (NSRC), operating under the Smithsonian Institution, was engaged to specifically address the design of classroom lesson materials, as well as teachers and student's guides. In 2008, the program copyright was transferred by Bristol-Myers Squibb to the NSRC, based on the recipient's commitment to continue to support and further develop the program.

The original idea underpinning the program is that students seek relevance and real-world application in their education and that learning scientific and technical concepts is more effective when students are actively engaged in hands-on exploration and metacognitive activities directly connected to the subject matter. The program consists of two tracks that are interconnected and best taught interactively: The applied science classroom track and the workplace track.

The Applied Science Classroom Track

This curriculum component borrows the applied science and associated applications in technology, engineering, and mathematics from research and development in the pharmaceutical industry. The complete sequence of events and activities that commences with the emergence of a new unmet medical need and leads through discovery research, preclinical development and clinical R&D, up to readiness for commercialization of a new appropriately formulated drug, makes up the backbone for the short course.

In order to avoid any reference to existing brand products or disease scenarios that might lead to perceptions of bias on the part of the participating schools or teachers, the story line, which builds up a plausible scenario of complex problems and challenges for student to engage in and resolve, is entirely fictitious. However, as scientific, technological, ethical, and resource management issues arise along the way, students are guided through the process of problem solving and issues resolution based on factual considerations.

To give an example: The outbreak of a new infectious disease, High School Syndrome, presents the initial challenge for students, giving opportunities to discuss several aspects of general health: What is a disease? How are diseases classified, and what constitutes a cure? During the guided search for ways to attack the disease, students are faced with the problem of how to identify and test chemical leads derived from nature and challenged to use fact finding, critical analysis, and logical reasoning.

Interacting with pharmaceutical discovery research professionals, students address other key questions: How can we test agents for activity against the actual disease? What is the actual biochemical target, and how can a simple model system be developed that allows for high throughput screening?

Beyond the initial discovery phase, students encounter a whole range of new questions and challenges when they take on the roles as preclinical development scientists: "Could our lead molecule have toxic effects on the body? How can we find out? Now that we have identified a substance that will find and act on the biochemical target with the desired effect, how do we formulate the compound so that it survives the body's chemical breakdown defenses and get to the target intact? How can the test tube synthesis of a molecule in microgram quantities be scaled up for production of kilogram quantities? How much active drug can we package into a pill so that we get the positive effect we want?"

Students face different issues when the time comes to test the lead candidate in humans:

"Is the dose-effect relationship the same as for animal models? Can we get away with one daily dose, or is more needed to fight the infection? What happens when you take the drug for a long time?"

Ethical questions lead to rich discussions but also to difficult decisions when students must make a choice between drug candidates that are effective in treating the disease but have bad side effects and others with low positive effect potential and no side effects.

Additional critical decision challenges follow when the commercialization potential enters into the analysis: High costs of R&D have to be balanced against future revenues, which depend on global disease epidemiology, economy of affected populations, and health care policies. Students must argue for their decision to select the final drug candidate among several that have different indication characteristics, but also varying revenue potential.

Throughout the course, students will engage in interdisciplinary applications and use science, math, and technology concepts and processes to move the project along through team-based activities and discussions. They derive facts and insights through interaction with scientists, engineers, and other professionals, and teachers complement the core course materials with current related issues from media and historical records. Figure 13.2 schematically describes the translation of industry-specific R&D elements and corresponding course objectives.

Figure 13.2.

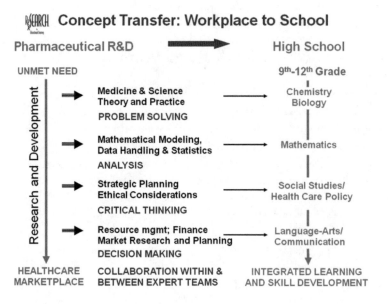

The course introduces students to workplace practices for planning and executing complex work tasks, such as project and strategic planning. It also places great emphasis on clear and precise communication between team members, a skill that will be further discussed under the program's workplace track. Table 13.1 shows an overview of the 11 lessons of the applied science classroom track's 11 lessons.

Table 13.1.

Course Overview

Lesson 1	Introduction	*Diseases and Their Impact*
Lesson 2	Discovery Research	*Targets and Magic Bullets*
Lesson 3	Discovery Research	*Screening for Solutions*
Lesson 4	Discovery Research	*The Power of Molecules*
Lesson 5	Preclinical Development	*Chromatography Separation*
Lesson 6	Preclinical Development	*Selecting the Best Molecule*
Lesson 7	Clinical R&D	*Investigational New Drug Application (IND) and Phase I Clinical Research*
Lesson 8	Clinical R&D	*Phase II Clinical Trials*
Lesson 9	Clinical R&D	*Phase III Clinical Trials and New Drug Application (NDA)*
Lesson 10	Commercialization	*Exploring the Business of Science and Medicine*
Lesson 11	Marketing	*Where Business & Science Overlap*

This program element provides a scaffold for the paired element, the workplace track.

The Workplace Track

This element differs from the applied science classroom track in that it aims to help students understand and practice the behaviors and skills they need to include in their repertoire in order to effectively meld into the workplace.

Many of the skills and abilities highlighted in this program are also found on the roster posted by the Partnership for 21st-Century Skills (*www.p21.org*), and for a good reason. A key objective of this program is to provide teachers and students with tools for learning in direct alignment with prevailing standards. Hence, the design of the workplace track was guided by the new Core Curriculum Content Standards number 9 for the state of New Jersey (State of New Jersey Department of Education 2011). This standards document, entitled *21st-Century Life and Career Skills*, outlines six skill areas needed to be addressed in New Jersey elementary, middle, and high school classrooms (Table 13.2, p. 218).

Table 13.2.

New Jersey Core Curriculum Content Standard #9
21st Century Life and Career Skills

Framework for 21st Century Learning

- Critical Thinking and Problem Solving
- Creativity and Innovation
- Collaboration, Teamwork, and Leadership
- Cross-Cultural Understanding and Interpersonal Communication
- Communication and Media Fluency
- Accountability, Productivity, and Ethics

While several of these skills and behaviors might (and *should*) be practiced in daily classroom learning and teaching, significant additional value is added by emphasizing the importance of these as essential abilities in the practice of science in the workplace. This is accomplished both by providing teachers with a tool kit, "Practicing Workplace Skills: A Teacher's Guide" and access to R&D professionals, including scientists, engineers, veterinarians, physicians, technicians, project managers, and financial and marketing specialists. The teacher's guide contains clear definitions and descriptions of how these skills and behaviors are developed and used in the workplace and provides exercises used in the workplace to teach and practice these skills, but adapted for learners at the high school level.

The professionals who participate both in teacher professional development and in the classroom interacting with students receive specific training for these tasks. They are informed about their role as assistants to the teacher, invited to enrich course elements that are parts of the standards-driven curriculum. They receive training to understand basic aspects of classroom management and age-appropriate pedagogy.

However, the primary emphasis of training is on the professionals' role as practitioners of science in an integrated and complex workplace where the individual performer is valued for his or her contributions and ability to adapt to prevailing circumstances and help lead productive change. These individuals describe their roles in the process of drug discovery, development, and commercialization and provide concrete examples of how each of the six skills and behaviors listed in Table 2 are practiced in a wide range of situations. They describe case examples from their professional careers that illustrate both successful and nonproductive behaviors as well as results and consequences of both. Most importantly, they share with teachers and students how they constantly learn and adapt new skills that help them navigate the workplace environment, collaborate with colleagues and specialists they never expected to work with, and become entrepreneurs both on behalf of their employer and themselves.

The professionals also describe how they themselves first experienced the unique culture of the workplace as they transitioned out of the education environment, how access to mentors have helped them find their way, and how they now assist other workplace newcomers. Through integration of the two program tracks students have the opportunity to practice all the critical workplace skills in the context of drug development. Again, the all-important relevance becomes a key element in the process of learning and teaching.

R$_x$eSEARCH: An Educational Journey as a Model—Telling Your Own Workplace Story

This program was developed by a corporate representative for the workplace sector. Like other science workplaces, it operates in a highly specialized domain of science with a clearly defined mission, vision, and objectives. As it happens, this area both draws from, and delivers to, the field of health care. Its primary expertise is in the area of life science but, as every other workplace, it depends on the expertise of professionals from nearly every profession in the U.S. economy. This highly integrated matrix of specialists, internal service providers, customers, supply lines, coordinators, and external alliance partners, which is sometimes spread over several continents, has validity for workplaces in both the private and public sectors. Hence, R$_x$eSEARCH: An Educational Journey is a model for close and productive interaction between the education and workplace sectors that can be viewed as largely universal.

The key principle is that the workplace sector can assist educators simply by telling its own story. So, whether the curriculum describes how sea wind and wave energy can fuel a power grid, how a larger more fuel-efficient airframe is designed, how artificial intelligence assists homeland security, or how disease can be fought through innovative medicines, the model is equally powerful. Success drivers include:

- Workplace professionals are invited to bring to the classroom the story they are passionate about and love to tell: how they do their work.
- Teachers and students get firsthand information about how science knowledge is applied to generate products and services.
- Workplace talent managers gain access to education strategists and policy makers and can share their needs for knowledge and skills.
- Educators get their finger on the pulse of the workplace and can open a career window for students to their future.

Back at the local level, the outcomes are as strategic and powerful as for any other educator-workplace program:

- Recruitment of new talented workers becomes closely tied to the future educational goals. Young professional families considering relocating to the area still ask: "How good are the schools where you want me to live?"
- School boards gain leadership from access to discerning community members who help them rise to their full potential and are able to attract the best trained teachers.

- Communities can grow based on strong tax revenue from both corporate and individual prosperity.

Taken together, the model has the potential to add value at local, regional, and national levels. Most importantly, it offers unlimited opportunities for educators and workplace representatives to explore current and future needs for knowledge, competencies, and skills and engage students in active learning, and practice for successful careers.

Conclusion

It is the author's hope that this chapter will inspire readers to study and better understand the forces that are at play in the talent marketplace. In so doing, it behooves us to consider both domestic and international aspects of this market, since we are now inextricably linked to people everywhere through economics, trade, and information traffic. It is the responsibility of educators to make every effort to prepare our next generation for the realities of global citizenship, regardless of where the home and workplace may be situated. Further, it makes good sense for workplace representatives, both from standpoints of human resource management, organizational development, and social responsibility, to actively assist educators in workforce preparation. Finally, as parents and community members, we all are stakeholders of education and have a shared responsibility to support professional educators in their work.

By offering a suggested action agenda and a case example of a flexible and adaptable core program, the author hopes to facilitate the first steps toward a stronger science talent market based on productive interaction between the education and workplace sectors.

References

Acs, Z. J., and P. Mueller. 2008. Employment effects of business dynamics: Mice, gazelles and elephants. *Small Business Economics* 30 (1): 85–100.

Adult Literacy. 2008. *Reach higher America: Overcoming crisis in the U.S. workforce*. Washington, DC: National Commission on Adult Literacy.

Alabama Math, Science and Technology Initiative (AMSTI). 2010. Summary of longitudinal evaluation of the AMSTI program: 2006–2009 standardized test results of the AMSTI adopters versus controls. Available online at *www.amsti.org/LinkClick.aspx?fileticket=MiemTIWEL_8%3d&tabid=133&mid=464*

Albrecht, W. S., and R. J. Sack. 2000, Accounting education: Charting the course through a perilous future. Sarasota, FL: American Accounting Association.

American Society for Training and Development (ASTD). 2009. State of the industry report. Alexandria, VA: ASTD.

Athey, R. 2005. It's 2008: Do you know where your talent is? Why acquisition and retention strategies don't work. A Deloitte research study. London, UK: Deloitte Development.

Bartlett, C., and S. Ghoshal. 2003. What is a global manager? *Harvard Business Review* 81 (8): 101–108.

Bassi, L., and D. McMurrer. 2004. How's your return on people? *Harvard Business Review* 82 (3): 18.

Birch, D. L., and J. Medoff. 1994. Gazelles. In *Labor markets, employment policy, and job creation*, ed. L. C. Solmon and A. R. Levenson, 159–167. Boulder, CO: Westview.

Caligiuri, P., and V. Di Santo. 2001. Global competence: What is it, and can it be developed through global assignments? *Human Resource Planning* 3: 27–38.

Carrier, C. 1994. *Intrepreneurship in large firms and SMEs: A comparative study*. Champaign, IL: Academy for Entrepreneurial Leadership.

Dickerson, A. P., H. D. Gibson, and E. Tsakalotos. 1997. The impact of acquisitions on company performance: Evidence from a large panel of UK firms. *Oxford Economic Papers* 49 (3): 344–361.

Filion, L. 2002. From employees to entrepreneurs. In *The dynamics of entrepreneurship: Growth and strategy*, ed. T. W. Liang, 158–178. Singapore: Prentice Hall.

Gabrielsson, J., D. Politis, and N. Galan, N. 2011. *Does rapid growth coincide with innovation? An examination of gazelles in Sweden*. Lund, Sweden: Lund University.

Garavan, T., M. Morley, P. Gunnigle, and E. Collins. 2001. Human capital accumulation: The role of human resource development. *Journal of European Industrial Training* 25 (2): 48–68.

Grindley, P. 1991. Turning technology into competitive advantage. *Business Strategy Review* Spring: 35–47.

Guthridge, M., A. Komm, and E. Lawson. 2008. Making talent management a strategic priority. *The McKinsey Quarterly* January: 49–59.

Hammer, M., and J. Champy. 2003. *Reengineering the corporation: A manifesto for business revolution*. New York: HarperBusiness Essentials.

Horizon Research. 2009, Examining the impact of ASSET membership on student achievement. Chapel Hill, NC: Horizon Research.

International Association for the Evaluation of Educational Achievement (IEA). 1985. *Trends in international mathematics and science study*. Amsterdam, Netherlands: IEA.

Jackson, S., M. Hitt, and A. DeNisi. 2003. *Managing knowledge for sustained competitive advantage*. San Francisco: Jossey-Bass.

Kardes, F. R. 2001. *Consumer behavior and managerial decision making*. 2nd ed. New York: Prentice Hall.

Lievens, F., C. Decaesteker, P. Coetsier, and J. Geirnaert. 2001. Organizational attractiveness for prospective applicants: A person-organization fit perspective. *Applied Psychology* 50: 81–108.

Malone, T. W. 2004. *The future of work: How the new order of business will shape your organization, your management style, and your life*. Boston, MA: Harvard Business School Press.

ManpowerGroup. 2011, The borderless workforce 2011 research results. Available online at *www.manpower.com.au/documents/White-Papers/2011_The-Borderless-Workforce-2011_Research-Results.pdf*

Morrison, A. 2000. Developing a global leadership model. *Human Resource Management* 39: 117–131.

National Commission on Excellence in Education (NCEE). 1983. *A nation at risk: The imperative for educational reform*. Washington, DC: U.S. Department of Education.

Organisation for Economic Co-operation and Development (OECD). 2002. OECD Employment Outlook 2002.

Organisation for Economic Co-operation and Development (OECD). 2000. Programme for International Student Assessment (PISA). *www.pisa.oecd.org*.

Price, C., and D. Turnbull. 2007. The organizational challenges of global trends: A McKinsey global survey. *McKinsey Quarterly*. May.

PricewaterhouseCoopers (PWC). 2010. Talent Mobility 2020: The next generation of international assignments. Available online at *www.pwc.com/gx/en/managing-tomorrows-people/future-of-work/pdf/talent-mobility-2020.pdf*

Rawlinson, R., W. McFarland, and L. Post. 2008. A talent for talent. *Strategy + Business* Autumn: 21–24.

Schuler R. S., S. E. Jackson, and I. Tarique. 2011. Global talent management and global talent challenges: Strategic opportunities for IHRM. *Journal of World Business* 46 (4): 506–516.

Seigel, J. 2008. *Global talent management at Novartis*. Harvard Business School case 9-708-486.

Shaffer, M., D. Harrison, H. Gregersen, J. Black, and L. Ferzandi. 2006. You can take it with you: Individual differences and expatriate effectiveness. *Journal of Applied Psychology* 91: 109–125.

Sheridan, J. H. 1998. Tale of a "maverick." How Ken Iverson built Nucor into the nation's no. 2 steelmaker. *IndustryWeek* 247 (11): 22.

Spilling, O. R., and J. Steinsli. 2004. On the role of high-technology small firms in cluster evolution. In *New technology based firms in the new millennium*, ed. I. R. Oakey, W. During, and S. Kauser, 3. Oxford, UK: Elsevier.

Stahl, G., I. Bjorkman, E. Farndale, S. Morris, J. Paauwe, and P. Stiles. 2007. Global talent management: How leading multinationals build and sustain their talent pipeline. *INSEAD Working Papers*, No. 2007/34/OB. Fontainebleau: INSEAD.

State of New Jersey Department of Education. *Core curriculum content standards*. 2011. Available online at *www.state.nj.us/education/cccs*

Surowiecki, J., 2011. Debt by degrees, *The New Yorker*, Nov. 21.

Tarique, I., and R. S. Schuler. 2010. Global talent management: Literature review, integrative framework, and suggestions for further research. *Journal of World Business* 45: 122–133.

Wunderer, R. 2001. Employees as "co-intrapreneurs"—a transformation concept. *Leadership & Organization Development Journal* 22 (5): 193–211.

Scientists as Partners in K–12 Science: Engineering, Science, and Technology Careers

Craig Johnson
Iowa Academy of Science

Setting

Attracting students to science careers requires the cooperation of many stakeholders. From local school systems to public and private colleges and universities, youth organizations, government agencies, business, and industry, there are many interests seeking to advance science and related disciplines. Students and their families need positive science experiences beginning at an early age and continuing through high school.

The Iowa Academy of Science (IAS) is an organization designed to bring together many science related interests. Given specialization in scientific-, technology-, engineering-, and mathematics-related disciplines it is often difficult to organize all of these stakeholders under one roof. While we agree on the broad need to advance common goals, such as increasing the number of science teachers or students entering science-related careers, actually accomplishing these goals requires collaboration. It is much easier to collaborate when those involved already have solid working relationships.

Membership

While scientific specialization has been responsible for many remarkable and rapid advances within scientific disciplines, this strength becomes a weakness when it comes time for members of various disciplines to cooperate. The Iowa Academy of Science fosters cooperation and encourages K–12 students to pursue careers in science and science-related fields through its membership, mission, and organizational structure. The membership of the Iowa Academy of Science includes scientists, science educators, graduate and undergraduate students, academic institutions, science-related organizations, and corporations. Through sponsorship of the Iowa Junior Academy of Science, middle and high school students are brought into the Academy. Encouraging more students to pursue careers in science or science related disciplines thrives on cooperation among scientists and science interests in the public and private sectors. Having a strong state academy of science provides a natural environment for cooperation among all disciplines and is an excellent resource for the state.

Mission

The Iowa Academy of Science was organized on August 27, 1875, at State University (now the University of Iowa) by 13 individuals. They recognized the need to bring scientists together for the advancement of science in the State of Iowa. The Academy was patterned after the American Association for the Advancement of Science (AAAS), which was organized almost 30 years earlier in 1848. Today the mission of the Iowa Academy of Science is to further scientific research, science education, the public understanding of science, and the recognition of excellence in these endeavors. The Academy is the only organization in Iowa chartered to work for the promotion of all sciences and related disciplines.

Mission and membership place the Academy in the midst of numerous scientific interests within the state. IAS members contribute to the success of the organization by serving on committees and in leadership roles. As a member-driven volunteer organization, the Academy draws upon the expertise of its membership to serve the citizens of Iowa. When the Iowa Academy of Science received a grant from the National Fish and Wildlife Foundation to develop a series of audio files featuring national wildlife refuges in Iowa, it was the membership that volunteered to write and record the audio files. These files are available for download online and may be played while visiting the national wildlife refuges. The natural history, geology, ecology, and conservation history of each refuge are featured on each download. The target audiences for the files range from children to adult. This is an example of how the Academy is able to bring together members from different disciplines to create an enjoyable and educational experience for the public. This cooperative effort is easily organized because expertise on many scientific topics already exists within the organization.

Organization

The Academy is organized under a nine-member board of directors with nine standing committees and 12 sections. The office staff includes an executive director, program director, executive assistant, and temporary student workers. The board, which includes the president, president-elect, past-president and six directors, are elected by the membership. Each section of the Academy elects a chair and vice-chair annually. Academy members may join up to four sections within the Academy. The sections include:

- Anthropology
- Cellular, Molecular & Microbiology
- Chemistry
- Community College Biologists
- Ecology & Conservation
- Engineering
- Environmental Science & Health
- Geology

- Iowa Science Teaching
- Organismal Biology
- Physics, Atmospheric & Space Sciences
- Physiology & Health Sciences

A variety of membership options are available for anyone interested in promoting science in Iowa. Whether individuals are in government, business, industry, K–12 education, at the college or university level, or in other related fields or occupations, the Iowa Academy of Science welcomes their membership.

The Academy structure encourages participation in decision making by the membership and welcomes the inclusion of new ideas and projects. While section membership supports the specialized fields of science the broader organization encourages communication across these disciplines by allowing members to join four sections and to attend research presentations outside of their main areas of interest. This arrangement has positive implications for the encouragement of K–12 students to pursue interests in science.

Iowa Junior Academy of Science

The Iowa Junior Academy of Science (IJAS) is the primary way the Academy promotes science to K–12 students. The IJAS was established by the Academy in 1931 and held its first meeting in 1932 after members recognized the need to involve students and their teachers in science research. The objective of the Junior Academy is to promote the study of and participation in science by middle and secondary students and teachers. IJAS programs are developed to

- promote an understanding of the importance of science and scientific research to meet many essential needs of society;
- encourage students with interest and aptitude in science to participate in science research;
- promote formal and informal discussions of science and scientific research by student groups, including teachers and members of the senior Academy, as appropriate; and
- help students explore career opportunities in science.

These four objectives are achieved through the volunteer participation of IAS members and the involvement of IJAS member schools, their teachers, and individual students.

Membership in the Iowa Junior Academy of Science is offered through schools or as individual memberships. When a school, such as a middle school or a high school, joins the Iowa Junior Academy of Science, all students within that school who are organized for extracurricular experience in science automatically become members. Each IJAS school maintains a science club with at least one teacher mentor. The Junior Academy also offers individual memberships to encourage participation by students whose school is not an IJAS member.

All Junior Academy members receive access to the Iowa Junior Academy of Science Wiki-Handbook (*www.ijas.pbworks.com*); an internet site with information for participation in all of the Iowa Academy of Science's IJAS Programs. This includes how to apply for research grants through the Junior Academy, tips for science fair projects, the visiting scientist program, the IJAS Annual Meeting Competition, and other programs.

The Academy encourages students to be aware of and to participate in science fairs and competitions and provides a list of more than 40 events with schedules, deadlines, and participation information to all IJAS members. Students also learn about research project ideas, judging criteria, scholarships, college visits, and out-of-state opportunities including National Youth Science Camp (*www.nysc.org*).

The Academy works with the Iowa Governor's office, the Iowa Department of Education, and the Iowa Mathematics and Science Education Partnership to advertise and select Iowa's delegates to National Youth Science Camp. The National Youth Science Camp originated in 1963 as a part of West Virginia's Centennial Celebration. It annually hosts 100 highly talented science students, two from each state in the nation. Iowa high school principals are encouraged to nominate their top students. The IAS Student Programs Committee selects two delegates and four alternates to represent Iowa. Iowa's two delegates travel to the National Youth Science Camp as guests of the state of West Virginia to spend three weeks with scientists from across the nation. Students are not required to be members of the Iowa Junior Academy of Science to participate in the science camp. This is another example of how the Academy is able to work with other scientific interests for the benefit of Iowa's students.

At the core of the IJAS experience is the opportunity to participate in science fairs. As part of the IJAS membership students are eligible to apply for Starr Student Research Grants and receive tips on how to develop a science fair project. The application process requires students to explain their project, develop a budget, and submit the request for review. The Student Programs Committee of the Iowa Academy of Science reviews the grant requests. The committee consists of scientists and science educators who provide feedback to the students and determine if a student may receive up to $200 to defray the cost of specific items in their budget. The purpose of the process is to encourage students to learn how to plan their projects and to improve their work in subsequent years. Students in grades 6–12 are eligible to participate. Many students report the judges' comments are as valuable as or more valuable than the funding they receive. Two years ago, by request of IJAS members, the Academy added the option for students to submit a grant proposal for comment only. One-third of the 2010–11 grants were only for comment. This illustrates the value students place on feedback from their senior academy peers.

Students receiving Starr Student Research Grants are required to present at either the State Science or Technology Fair of Iowa held every March at Iowa State University or at another regional science fair. Then they present at the Iowa Junior Academy of Science competition in April held in conjunction with the Iowa Academy of Science Annual Meeting. At the IJAS competition oral and poster presentations are judged by Iowa Academy of Science member volunteers in a supportive and encouraging atmosphere.

The students are encouraged to attend as much of the two-day Academy Annual Meeting as possible to meet Iowa scientists and to experience a professional meeting. The Academy makes a special effort to schedule a general session of interest to Junior Academy students. For example at our 2011 Annual Meeting we scheduled a presentation from the Jet Propulsion Laboratory about the Mars Rover Exploration Program. The presentation by Mr. Scott Lever combined robotics and space exploration, which are topics of interest to students. Mr. Lever used the opportunity to demonstrate to middle and high school students how science, technology, engineering, and mathematics are woven together in career applications.

The Academy also encourages the host academic institution of our Annual Meeting to provide opportunities for Junior Academy attendees. At our 2010 meeting, Graceland University hosted a 90-minute Lab Encounter, giving students hands-on opportunities to explore forensics, robotics, ecology, physiology, chemistry, and rocket science. In 2009, Des Moines University opened the DMU Surgery Laboratories and their Medical Simulation Laboratory. Students were able to experience the college-level learning environment and see exciting career opportunities that are available to them.

Iowa Junior Academy of Science members compete for two college scholarships, and two students in grades 9–11 are selected to serve as the Iowa delegates to the American Junior Academy of Science (AJAS) Annual Meeting, where they present their research in a poster session and participate in activities tailored to the interests of high school-age scientists. This event is planned by National Association of Academies of Science (NAAS) volunteers and is held in conjunction with the AAAS Annual Meeting in February.

The opportunity is made possible through several partnerships between the Iowa Academy of Science, three other general science organizations (AJAS, NAAS, and AAAS), and funding from the Iowa Space Grant Consortium, which is part of the NASA National Space Grant College and Fellowship Program. All expenses are paid for the students and a chaperone. This demonstrates how the Iowa Academy of Science and other state academies are able to successfully work with various science interests for the benefit of science education

Student and Teacher Experiences

Science teachers and students are willing to talk about the effectiveness of the Iowa Junior Academy of Science programs. DeAnna Tibben teaches Earth Science and Honors Earth and Space Science at Ames High School in central Iowa. The Ames community school district is one of Iowa's larger districts with an enrollment of over 4,000 students:

> As a requirement for the Honors Earth and space science class, students were to do a year-long research project. I found the IJAS sources not only helpful for me as the teacher, but as a valuable resource for the students. Sample projects, how to write a proposal, and having "real, professional" scientists read the student proposals and provide feedback was very, very helpful! My students did very well with their projects. Many took the feedback from the Starr grant reviewers and made changes. We had many winners at the Iowa State Science and Technology Fair. We had many category and special topic winners, best of show, and two groups went to the Intel International Science Fair—one as competitor and another as observers. (e-mail to Craig Johnson, October 5, 2011)

Ms. Tibben continued:

> Having IAS members work with my students is a definite plus! When I would send out an "all call" or "help/advice needed" e-mail to the membership, I would always get replies back from folks willing to work with the students. It is very powerful for 14-year-old students

to know that a professional scientist is reading their proposals, interested in talking and working with them and to get confirmation that they are on the "right track" or "doing really interesting projects." Students come away with the realization that they CAN do science! With a lot of the feedback we received, my students' perceptions were changed; scientists aren't stuffy, nerdy folks stuck in a lab somewhere, but instead are everyday folks, have a sense of humor, and are willing to make time for them.

An enthusiastic comment came from one of DeAnna Tibben's female students, "I have always enjoyed science classes. I never really thought of myself as a scientist before. But now I know what I want to do for the rest of my life! I want to study the stars."

Kelen Panec teaches physical science and human anatomy at West High School in Waterloo, Iowa. As the Chair of the Student Programs Committee that oversees the Iowa Junior Academy of Science Ms. Panec observed, "Seeing the expressions on the faces of the young people as they are preparing to present their research projects is always an exciting time for me. I know they are both scared and excited, but the enthusiasm they share in their presentations is the highlight of the Iowa Junior Academy of Science meeting" (e-mail to Craig Johnson, October 7, 2011).

Ms. Panec has served as the chaperone for the Iowa delegates to the American Junior Academy of Science (AJAS) meeting held in conjunction with the American Association for the Advancement of Science (AAAS) Annual Meeting. As a leader on the trip she has witnessed the transformation in students as they have new experiences. She says, "The opportunity to meet other students from other states who share a love of science is an incredible experience for our young scientists. When I see our young scientists leave the 'Breakfast with a Scientist' with such excitement, it makes me know that we are doing it right. That young person may have just spent an hour with an adult scientist who just may be a Nobel Prize winner in their field. Their life has been touched by the generosity of that adult who has been willing to spend time with a young scientist."

Nadine Weirather teaches sixth-grade science, language arts, reading, and is the middle school science fair coordinator at Central Lee Middle School at Donnellson in southeast Iowa. Central Lee is a rural school district serving 1,100 preK–12 students. Commenting on the effectiveness of the Junior Academy she says,

> The Iowa Junior Academy of Science has served my students well over the years. Students are supported in their science research. The Junior Academy provides a wiki that gives feedback, and helps students find mentors. Students in grades 7–12 have the opportunity to apply for grants in the fall and in the spring. My students receive valuable real-life feedback regarding their writing skills and their scientific thinking from comments made by the judges on these grant applications. My students often win grant money to help encourage and support them. (e-mail to Craig Johnson, October 5, 2011)

She goes on to say,

> The Iowa Junior Academy of Science also listens to the needs of grade 7–12 students. I had a student whose parents would not allow him to apply for a grant because he (they) didn't need the money and thought someone else should get it. The Academy listened to his needs

and made a category for submissions of research with no funding. In that way students are still able to get feedback and see the process that most scientists must go through. When any other school districts ask me about beginning a science research program, I tell them to start by joining the Iowa Junior Academy of Science.

Alicia Schiller-Holland was a member of the Iowa Junior Academy of Science as a student and has been a high school science teacher at Central Lee High School for eight years. On the value of the Iowa Junior Academy of Science she says,

> As a student involved with the Iowa Junior Academy of Science I was able to have opportunities and experiences that other student researchers did not get the chance to experience. I had the opportunity to learn how to write student research grants, have my research funded for three years and advance my presentation skills through the IJAS seminar and poster competition. Now as a science educator I have been able to translate many of the learned skills from the IJAS onto my students and my current profession. I have had the honor of receiving numerous grants to fund advancements in my science curriculum, and the success of receiving these grants I can directly attribute to my early grant-writing experiences in high school provided by the IJAS. I have also been able to give my current science students the opportunity to write grants of their own to fund their science research, and I have been able to watch them mold and develop their presentation skills through the IJAS poster and seminar competition each spring. My students' as well as my own experiences with the IJAS program has been a major asset to the success science has at Central Lee High School. (e-mail to Craig Johnson, October 6, 2011)

Cory Millmeier, a recent member of the Iowa Junior Academy of Science, is now in college majoring in accounting and finance:

> I appreciate the support IJAS provided for my research and interest in science as a middle school and high school student. Although I did not go on to pursue a science related field during college, the skills I gained from competing at IJAS competitions benefited me greatly. I had the opportunity to strengthen my oral and written communication skills by presenting my project through poster and PowerPoint presentations. I fielded questions from experts in my project area and was challenged to support my experimental findings as any professional scientist would be expected to do. Through the trips I was awarded, I enjoyed travelling with my teachers to national events where I not only had the chance to compete with other top-notch students, but attend amazing informational sessions from some of the great leaders in the industry. I appreciated the kindness and the support of the IJAS committee and hope that other young scientists can reap the long-term benefits this organization has to offer. (e-mail to Craig Johnson, January 4, 2012)

Cory Millmeier is an example of a student who excelled in science but has chosen a different career path in college. On the surface this could be looked at as a disappointment. However his experiences in the Iowa Junior Academy of Science will benefit him throughout his life and he will carry an appreciation for science and related careers wherever his future takes him. A science-literate society is a necessity for the future improvements in science and science education.

These testimonies provide a glimpse into what the Iowa Junior Academy of Science has been doing since 1932 to positively impact science education in Iowa. They also illustrate how the Iowa Academy of Science seeks to promote science and science education. Through member volunteers and the IAS staff the Academy collaborates with schools and other science organizations to benefit K–12 education.

There are other opportunities through the Iowa Junior Academy of Science. The Visiting Scientist Program allows any Iowa Junior Academy member, student, or teacher, or any teacher who is a member of the Iowa Science Teaching Section of the Academy, the opportunity to request a visit from an Iowa scientist. The Iowa Academy of Science staff matches educator requests with the appropriate IAS member-scientist. The scientist visits the school free of charge and meets with students in small or large groups. The Academy provides a travel stipend to the scientist. More than 250 Academy member scientists have volunteered to share their specialties with other Iowans. This is how the Iowa Academy of Science Visiting Scientist Program was born.

High schools joining the Iowa Junior Academy of Science are eligible to offer the Outstanding Science Student Award (OSSA) to one of their graduating students. Each OSSA winner receives an Outstanding Science Student medallion engraved with his or her name and a certificate. IJAS member schools may nominate one or more senior students for the OSSA. If only one student is nominated the student will be awarded the OSSA for that school. If more than one student is nominated the IAS Student Programs Committee reviews all nominations from the school and selects one student as the winner. Outstanding Science Student Awards are presented at school assemblies providing recognition for their science achievements outside the Junior Academy. Examples are students starting a schoolwide science tutoring program or serving as captain of the school's Canon Envirothon team.

Student researchers and their adult mentors are recognized by the Academy membership at the Iowa Academy of Science annual meeting's Junior Academy Awards Luncheon. Offering recognition is another way the Academy cultivates student interest in science careers.

Iowa Science Teaching Section (ISTS)

An important strength of the Iowa Academy of Science is the Iowa Science Teaching Section (ISTS). It advocates for excellence in science education by promoting professionalism, influencing policy, and enhancing learning. Teachers play an integral role in cultivating and encouraging student interest in the sciences. ISTS is committed to enhance student learning by exploring effective avenues for learning, promotion of elementary science, and serving as an information clearinghouse for science education.

ISTS is the equivalent of a state science teachers association in other states. Because of this unique arrangement, the Iowa Academy of Science is especially suited to blend the expertise of ISTS with other science sections within the Academy to encourage K–12 student interest in science. As one example, ISTS members serve with members of other sections on the Student Programs Committee, which advises the Iowa Junior Academy of Science.

Science teachers on a field trip at the annual ISTS Fall Conference

Tom Ervin is retired from teaching at Davenport North High School and is currently the president-elect of the Iowa Academy of Science. Mr. Ervin is a longtime member of the Academy and ISTS and taught Earth materials, meteorology, climate, and space at North High School in Davenport, Iowa:

> The largest section in the IAS is the ISTS. I joined both with my first paycheck in 1967. Over the years, I have found that the ISTS provides more than ample avenues for the professional who wishes to serve in a leadership role. Additionally, its annual Fall Science Teaching Section Fall Conference provides an excellent opportunity for the science educator to stay abreast of the many advancements and teaching methodologies which are constantly being developed. By participating in the Fall Conference, the classroom teacher can beat back the feeling of isolation that occurs when secluded in the classroom, and replace it with a feeling of collegiality that tells the teacher that they are an important part of an even bigger picture. Perhaps just as importantly, when a teacher returns to the classroom from the ISTS Fall Conference, their refreshed enthusiasm does touch and influence their students, hopefully encouraging them toward science as a career path. (e-mail to Craig Johnson, October 7, 2011)

ISTS sponsors the annual ISTS Fall Conference every October. This meeting attracts approximately 400 science teachers for an evening of learning followed by a full day of inspiring new ideas, sharing, and professional rejuvenation. Activities at this conference encourage teachers to expand their knowledge by making presentations to their colleagues, attending presentations, and hearing from keynote and featured speakers. They also meet with over 40 corporate and nonprofit exhibitors with new ideas for enhancing the science curriculum.

Community Colleges

Community colleges play an important role for science and technology education. Many students graduating from high school attend community colleges and attain associate degrees in technical fields. No program encouraging K–12 students to pursue science-related careers can ignore the importance of associate degrees for science-related careers. It is vital that students who are not going to be research scientists or science educators understand that there are many opportunities for them in science-related fields.

One of the Academy sections is the Community College Biologists. This section meets to exchange ideas and research that impacts students seeking associate degrees or who are working on four-year science degrees by beginning their work at community colleges. Community colleges supply trained employees to vital businesses and industries needing personnel able to handle the technical needs of society. Community colleges are institutional members of the Academy and have the opportunity to host IAS Annual Meetings. The Annual Meeting exposes their students to a professional science meeting and provides Academy members the opportunity to see the importance of community colleges in the context of science education. This is another way the Academy brings together professionals from various science-related fields for the benefit of society.

Teaching Awards

The Academy recognizes the winners of several awards at our Annual Meeting. The Excellence in Science Teaching Awards (ESTA) offers recognition in six areas: Earth/space science/environmental science, elementary science, general/multiple science, life science, middle school/junior high science, and physical science. Teachers are honored at the Iowa Academy of Science annual meeting in April with a plaque and cash award and at the ISTS fall conference in October. Recognizing excellence in science teaching is an important part of the Academy's mission.

The Academy also honors Iowa's Presidential Award for Excellence in Mathematics and Science Teaching (PAEMST) winners and nominees annually. PAEMST Awards are the Nation's highest honors for teachers of mathematics and science. Awardees serve as models for their colleagues, inspiration to their communities, and leaders in the improvement of mathematics and science education. Iowa winners and nominees are recognized at the Iowa Science Teachers Section (ISTS) Fall Conference held in October.

GLOBE

The Academy employs a full-time program director to facilitate educational outreach in both formal and informal settings. Educational programs are directed to students and teachers. In 1999, the Iowa Academy of Science began statewide sponsorship of the GLOBE Program and Project WET. These programs, directed by the Academy Program Director, are the Academy's first sustained effort to provide ongoing science education professional development to Iowa educators.

GLOBE is Global Learning and Observations to Benefit the Environment, an international hands-on science education program. GLOBE is funded by the National Aeronautics and Space Administration (NASA), National Oceanic and Atmospheric Administration (NOAA) and National Science Foundation (NSF) and by country/state/regional partners in all 50 US states and 110 countries worldwide. The Academy's partnership was originally funded through a grant from the Roy J. Carver Charitable Trust, Muscatine, Iowa and has continued through a variety of grants including the current partnership Title II MSP grant with the University of Northern Iowa (UNI).

The Academy GLOBE partnership offers GLOBE certification workshops to Iowa K–12 formal and informal educators. During a GLOBE workshop educators are introduced to and practice collecting data about their local air, water, soil, land cover, and seasons through the strict use of protocols designed by the GLOBE scientists. They meet, face to face or by video conference, with GLOBE or Iowa scientists to learn how scientists use the GLOBE data.

GLOBE could simply become a student service project with students and teachers collecting data for scientists. However, workshop participants also experience content and pedagogy activities designed to help them fit GLOBE into their classrooms and utilize the GLOBE database of more than 20 million points of GLOBE student data to allow their students to answer their own scientific questions. Students begin collecting data for the scientists. As they collect data they make observations and develop their own questions. The GLOBE database allows them to pursue these questions. GLOBE students have opportunities to complete their authentic science experience by sharing their research results with others through local and international events and activities. Through GLOBE, the Academy is able to provide educators with professional development and support to offer their students authentic science experiences.

For example, several years ago Mrs. Heidi Meyer's third-grade class at MFL MarMac Elementary School in Monona, Iowa, developed their own extension to the GLOBE phenology Green Down protocol. Phenology is the study of seasonal change. The GLOBE Green Down protocol measurement is a biweekly collection of the color change of four leaves at the end of a south-facing branch of a native tree. Mrs. Meyer and some of her students wondered why the GLOBE scientists requested all observations be taken on south-facing branches.

Partially to answer this question and partially to give all of the students in the class more ownership over the project, Mrs. Meyer divided her students into four groups and each group followed the GLOBE Protocol on one of four branches of their selected tree, each facing a different cardinal direction. The students made predictions about which branch would begin changing color first, which would change color the most, and when the leaves would fall from the tree.

The first-year students presented their project results to the Academy's Program Director and UNI faculty who visited the school as a part of Mrs. Meyer's original GLOBE professional development. Each year since, her class has presented at the University of Northern Iowa Spotlight Day, an event that highlights innovative classroom projects. Mrs. Meyer's students develop science, reading, writing, and technology skills as they research, complete, and communicate their project. Mrs. Meyer and two other Iowa GLOBE class projects are highlighted on the GLOBE Program website as GLOBE Stars for June 2011 (*http://globe.gov/stars/archive/2011/6*). Mrs. Meyer's project provides an example of how the GLOBE program facilitates inquiry-based science research.

The IAS Program Director has been involved in the GLOBE Program at the international level, serving on conference panels about teacher recruitment, retention, and support and implementation measurement. The Academy partnership was also selected to pilot Global Learning Communities concept through a special project called GLOBE ONE. To date, the Iowa Academy of Science GLOBE partnership has provided professional development for more than 400 educators. Iowa schools that have adopted GLOBE have been prolific in their data collection.

The Academy's GLOBE partnership has benefits to all aspects of the Academy's mission including science research (over 1% of data in the international GLOBE database is from Iowa), science education (GLOBE students are better than non-GLOBE students at many science skills), public understanding of science (involvement of community members in the GLOBE ONE project) and recognition of excellence in these endeavors (several Iowa schools have become GLOBE Stars; IAS Program Director Marcy Seavey was awarded the 2005 Educators Environmental Excellences Award by Region 7 of the EPA).

Project WET

Project WET is a science-based interdisciplinary professional development program with a mission of reaching children, parents, teachers, and community members of the world with water education. The Academy's Project WET partnership is primarily funded through state of Iowa grants from the Resource Enhancement and Protection-Conservation Education Program (REAP-CEP). The Academy offers a wide variety of Project WET workshops covering many water themes including water quality, watershed management, and water in Earth system cycles. The majority of Project WET workshops in Iowa are directed at preservice education majors in Iowa's teaching institutions.

The Academy reaches approximately 300 preservice teachers annually. The preservice workshop is conducted in conjunction with a science or social studies methods course and covers general water topics. It allows these new educators to enter the classroom ready to implement field-tested, hands-on, science-based activities. A follow-up survey of preservice participants found that 58% of respondents had begun using Project WET activities in their first three years of teaching. Also, 52% of respondents had integrated Project WET into their curriculum and were implementing activities beyond those presented in their workshop. As with GLOBE, the Academy's program director is active in the Project WET Network, presenting about the Iowa program at more than 10 national Project WET conferences and at the fifth World Water Forum, Istanbul Turkey, 2010, and serving on the writing team for several of the Project WET publications.

Other Educational Programs

Occasionally the Academy has sponsored other professional development opportunities for Iowa educators, most recently sponsoring two Inventing Flight (physics of flight) workshops with the Putnam Museum of History and Natural Sciences, ALCOA, and the Academy of Model Aeronautics. All of these opportunities have given the Academy a vehicle through which to directly support Iowa educators and influence classroom practice.

These educational programs are examples of how the Academy as an independent science organization is able to work with K–12 schools and teachers, students, universities, government agencies, business and industry to deliver hands-on programs for the benefit of students.

Other Opportunities

The Iowa Academy of Science has had a relationship with the Army Corps of Engineers at Saylorville Lake near Des Moines for many years, where the Academy operates the gift shop in the Visitor Center. Four years ago we agreed to establish the Iowa Academy of Science Speaker Series at Saylorville. Each summer, Academy members volunteer to make presentations to the public at the Visitor Center. This informal education opportunity is designed for both children and adult audiences. Attendance at these family-friendly programs ranges from 10 to 30, creating a one-on-one atmosphere. Topics have included dinosaur digs, Iowa wildflowers, water quality in Iowa's rivers and streams, weather, Iowa wildlife, and more. Many programs include hands-on activities for participants.

A child enjoys hands-on activities during the Iowa Academy of Science Speaker Series at the Saylorville Lake Visitor Center.

As an outgrowth of our experience at Saylorville, the Academy was approached in the spring of 2011 to provide speakers for the Army Corps of Engineers at Coralville Lake near Iowa City. Presentations were made in the campground amphitheater on Saturday evenings. Academy members volunteered their time and expertise to provide a positive science experience. Iowans learn their state is a place where science happens.

A general science organization like the Iowa Academy of Science is readily able to find scientists to speak on wide-ranging topics of interest to the public. The scientists are passionate about their work and it shows as they reach out to the public. Through contact with Iowa scientists, attendees see that science careers are not only attainable but are interesting and valuable to society.

Reflections

The Iowa Academy of Science is a valuable resource for the state. Like other state academies, it is uniquely suited at the state level to facilitate communication between scientific disciplines and the many science interests in the state. Representatives of government, academia, business, industry, schools and other interested groups are encouraged to join the Academy.

The Academy is a nonprofit organization existing for the benefit of the public. As an independent organization it is able to support formal and informal science education and facilitate statewide conferences and activities that promote the advancement of science, technology, engineering, and mathematics education. The Academy provides excellent opportunities for cooperation across science-related disciplines.

The National Academies of Science has recognized the value of state academies in science education. "State academies also can play a prominent role in science, technology, engineering, and mathematics education, both by influencing state education standards and funding and by supporting individual students. Many future science and engineering leaders presented papers or projects at state academies when they were high school or college students" (NAS 2008, p. 25). The same report addressed the importance of coalitions at the state level. "[S]tate academies can be particularly adept at putting together coalitions of state organizations to advocate for particular policies." This is recognition by the National Academies of Science that state academies are in a unique position to be effective advocates for science and science education within their states. Academy staff and members are able to efficiently design and implement programs to encourage science participation by K–12 students and to support collaboration among diverse science-related interests.

Specialization in science has created rapid scientific advancements with many benefits for society. However specialization has created a more difficult climate in which general science organizations such as the Iowa Academy of Science must operate. Sometimes different science interests may hesitate to cooperate because of a perception that they are in competition. State academies are able to help bridge these gaps. On the other side of the coin national specialized societies are not adept at bringing together the many scientific interests found at the state level. State academies such as the Iowa Academy of Science are equipped to create short- and long-term partnerships for the benefit of K–12 science education.

Reference

National Academies of Science (NAS). 2008. *State science and technology advice: Issues, opportunities, and challenges: Summary of a national convocation.* Washington, DC: National Academies Press.

Science Olympiad: Inspiring the Next Generation of Scientists

Gerard Putz
President and Cofounder of Science Olympiad

Jennifer L. Wirt
New Jersey Science Olympiad State Director

Setting

Any person opening a newspaper, reading *Education Week*, or scanning daily education blogs, knows there is a crisis in science education. In spite of decades of reform efforts, storms have been gathering since the afterglow of Sputnik wore off, and no amount of reporting will solve the problems faced in recent years: decreasing interest in science, technology, engineering, and math (STEM) courses and teaching, an ever-shrinking pool of qualified STEM workers in an ever-expanding global economy, and dropping test scores in critical areas. Science Olympiad, a national nonprofit organization dedicated to improving the quality of K–12 STEM education through competition and professional development, tackles these problems head-on and provides inspired solutions.

For the past 28 years, Science Olympiad has been a leader in science education, providing rigorous, standards-based challenges to more than 6,200 secondary school teams and 10,000 elementary schools in all 50 states. Science Olympiad's ever-changing lineup of events in all STEM disciplines provides a variety of career choices and exposure to practicing scientists and mentors. Recognized as a model program by the National Governors Association Center for Best Practices, Science Olympiad is committed to increasing competitiveness for the next generation of scientists.

Studies analyzing the perceptions of Science Olympiad competitors, in terms of science learning and interest, 21st-century skills and abilities, perceived influence on careers, and the overall benefits of being involved in Science Olympiad, have clearly shown that the program has a strong impact on the career choices of participants (Wirt 2011). In addition, anecdotal data underscores the positive emotional, social and real-world aspects of Science Olympiad.

> My participation in Science Olympiad foretold my future. My events were always the Earth science events—and "Write It Do It." The time I spent learning rocks and minerals for Science Olympiad prepared me for years of mineralogy and engineering geology courses,

and now field reconnaissance all over the Pacific Northwest. In retrospect, I realize that "Write It Do It" was the Science Olympiad version of developing construction plans and specifications, which is something else I often do at work. I feel particularly fortunate that I discovered my passion for geosciences in eighth grade, and have successfully pursued it for 19 years. Science Olympiad is an amazing opportunity for students because it merges teamwork and competition with science, technology and engineering. It sets the stage for what careers in science, technology, and engineering look like—design teams, aggressive project schedules, creative problem-solving and communication.

—*Tova Peltz, Geotechnical Engineer, Oregon Department of Transportation*

Science Olympiad Mission and Goals

Science Olympiad is a national nonprofit organization founded in 1984 and dedicated to improving the quality of K–12 science education, increasing interest in science among all students, creating a technologically literate workforce and providing recognition for outstanding achievement by both students and teachers. These goals are achieved by participating in Science Olympiad tournaments and noncompetitive events, incorporating Science Olympiad into classroom curriculum, and attending professional development institutes.

Science Olympiad has enjoyed a history of influencing the lives of students and teachers who found an outlet for their love of science. What started out as a grassroots assembly of science teachers who met at a National Science Teachers Association conference in the late 1970s has grown to become one of the premiere science competitions in the United States, changing the educational landscape and inspiring new science and technology leaders.

Science Olympiad is modeled after successful Science Olympiad tournaments held in Delaware and Michigan introduced by Dr. Gerard J. Putz, who served as the Regional Science Center Director, Macomb Intermediate School District in Michigan, and Jack Cairns, who was Science Supervisor for the Delaware Department of Public Instruction. The founders set the following goals for Science Olympiad:

1. To create a passion for learning science by supporting elementary and secondary Science Olympiad tournaments at building, district, county, state and national levels with an emphasis on teamwork and a commitment to excellence.

2. To improve the quality of K–12 science education throughout the nation by changing the way science is perceived and the way it is taught, placing emphasis on problem solving and hands-on, minds-on constructivist learning practices). This goal is accomplished through in-depth core curriculum training workshops and the distribution of curriculum materials.

3. To celebrate and recognize the outstanding achievement of both students and teachers in STEM disciplines by awarding certificates, medals, trophies, and scholarships.

4. To promote partnerships among community, businesses, industry, government and education leaders.

After participating in Science Olympiad and winning two medals at the regional tournament, I decided I wanted to major in science. This fall I will be attending Northeastern Illinois University majoring in biology.

—*Brittany Firszt, Steinmetz High School, Chicago Public Schools*

Science Olympiad Competition Structure

Modeling athletic teams, Science Olympiad teams prepare throughout the year for tournaments. There are three divisions of competition, Division A (Grades K–6), Division B (Grades 6–9) and Division C (Grades 9–12). The structure of Elementary Science Olympiad teams varies widely, but at the B and C level, each team is allowed to bring 15 students, though the club includes many more. Science Olympiad tournaments are often referred to as academic track meets, made up of 23 team events that rotate annually and are 100% aligned to the National Science Education Standards (NSES). (See Appendix A and Appendix B , pp. 253–254, for alignment of 2012 Science Olympiad events).

By combining events from multiple science, engineering, and technology disciplines, Science Olympiad encourages students with diverse interests to get involved in active, hands-on activities. Science Olympiad events follow a developmental sequence of age-appropriate science concepts from elementary to middle school to high school. For instance, in elementary school, a student might explore chemical substances in Mystery Powders, which accelerates to Science Crime Busters (add in solving a crime) in middle school, then cycles up to more complex chemistry in the Division C Forensics event. The same ramping up of skills can be found in the Structures category, where Pasta Bridge becomes Bridge Building, then Boomilever, in which sophisticated cantilevers are constructed.

Currently, more than 320 invitational, regional, state, and national Science Olympiad tournaments are held across the United States. Science Olympiad creates an exciting atmosphere of head-to-head competition coupled with recognition (awards, trophies, scholarships) for academic success. The goals of Science Olympiad tournaments are:

1. To bring science to life, to show how science works, to emphasize problem-solving aspects of science and the understanding of science concepts.

2. To develop teamwork and cooperative-learning strategies among students.

3. To make science education more exciting so more students will enroll in science courses and engage in other science activities like science reading, fairs, meetings, and field trips.

4. To promote high levels of achievement and a commitment to excellence, and to demonstrate that American students can perform at high levels.

5. To attract more students, particularly females and underserved populations, to professional and technical careers in science, technology, and science teaching.

Professional Development and Science Olympiad Event Design

Across the United States, 48 Science Olympiad chapters function as satellite organizations to the national office. The Science Olympiad State Director, tournament directors, advisory boards, and small armies of volunteers do the work of the local programs, providing intensive teacher training seminars in the fall and running invitational, regional, and state Science Olympiad tournaments in the spring.

The events of Science Olympiad are carefully chosen each year by a group of educators and professionals who serve as Rules Committee Chairs in the following standards-aligned areas: life, personal, and social science; Earth and space science; physical science and chemistry; technology and engineering; and inquiry and nature of science. These groups work via e-mail, professional conferences, Science Olympiad Annual Meetings each May, and the Summer Institute each July to develop Science Olympiad events, commonly known as "the rules," which are published at the outset of each school year. Each of the 6,200 teams across the nation must follow the 23 rules and participate in events that require a variety of skills from research and study, to lab work and experimentation, to design and construction of devices. While the major content areas remain constant, the rules are rotated annually to allow for new areas of science exploration, such as nanotechnology, materials science, protein modeling, and epidemiology. These events are carefully selected to model real-world applications of science and the STEM careers offered on each path.

Since 1999, Science Olympiad has worked with the Centers for Disease Control and Prevention (CDC) on the Disease Detectives event. Within the CDC, scientists were charged with creating K–12 workforce development outreach programs that would add to the pool of eligible STEM professionals. Covering topics like pandemics, disease outbreaks, food-borne illness, and the resulting effects on population, CDC found that the Science Olympiad Disease Detectives event is an effective way to motivate students to investigate careers in epidemiology. Similarly, the Milwaukee School of Engineering's Center for BioMolecular Modeling worked with Science Olympiad to develop the cutting-edge Protein Modeling event for high school participants. In this event, students use computer visualization and online resources to guide them in constructing physical models of proteins and learn about how protein structure determines function.

Students are often motivated to follow a career path once they've interacted with Science Olympiad events. Emily Briskin, a freshman at Yale University, was a gold medalist on her Centerville High School Science Olympiad team and attended President Obama's White House Science Fair in October 2010:

> Right now, I am studying Molecular, Cellular and Developmental Biology as well as French at Yale. I am interested in Global Health (Disease Detectives!) and Microbial Disease (Microbe Mission!), and I hope to eventually get my masters in public health and perhaps

work at the CDC. I am involved in Community Health Educators, a group that goes into middle school classrooms to discuss important public health topics.

A teacher can use Science Olympiad events as extensions of the standard curriculum and direct the most interested students to those events suited to particular areas of study, like forensics (Science Crime Busters) or aeronautical engineering (Wright Stuff; Bottle Rocket).

Likewise, teachers find Science Olympiad to be a useful classroom tool. Meredith Morgan, a middle school math and science teacher from Ames, Iowa, states:

> I have used parts of Science Olympiad events to engage students more enjoyably in K–8 classroom activities. Science Olympiad has not only been valuable in the science classroom, but also in teaching other subjects. For instance, I adapted Write It Do It for a middle school language arts lesson about including appropriate details in technical writing. Also, while student-teaching, I used Road Scholar to teach fourth grade students about reading road maps.

Sandra Yarema, a faculty instructor at St. Dennis School in Michigan, said, "Science Olympiad helps me connect students to science in a meaningful way. Their learning is self-motivated; they retain knowledge; they work cooperatively; and they return to the competition until high school graduation."

Early Research Used as the Backbone of Science Olympiad

In the 1980s, the Science Olympiad Steering Committee based much of its development on research done by David and Roger Johnson, Madeline Hunter, Benjamin Bloom, and Harry Wong. They asserted that cooperation and teamwork, practicing toward an objective, improving skills through competition, and making learning exciting through motivational activities are essential ingredients in attaining academic excellence. In an article titled *Talent Development vs. Schooling*, Bloom and Sosniak (1981) described the process by which individuals reached extremely high levels of accomplishment. One of his conclusions was that competitions played a major role in the success of each talent area participant. "In each talent field there are frequent events (recitals, contests, concerts) in which the child's special capabilities are displayed publicly, and there are significant rewards and approval for meritorious accomplishments." He said children are spurred to greater learning efforts in anticipation of the  public event and that such public events are a means of making the child's progress and development real and important. Bloom concluded that such events also bring participants into direct contact with one another and provide opportunities to exchange experiences and to observe and get to know outstanding peer and adult models of the talent.

Other research conducted by Calvin W. Taylor of the University of Utah concluded, "Extracurricular training experiences and accomplishments do show noticeable predictive power of later adult performance, achievement, and accomplishments." The value and implication of being involved in such extracurricular activities as Science Olympiad is apparent for developing productive high-performing adults. With regard to predicting college success other than via SAT scores and school grades, Educational Testing Service observed that "productive follow-through," defined as "persistent and successful extra-curricular accomplishment," indeed was the strongest predictor of leadership and significant independent accomplishment and clearly useful in predicting most overall college success.

Historical Background of Science Education

The launch of Sputnik in 1957 marked the beginning of intense focus on science education and curriculum reform (Bybee 2006; Price 2008; Stohr-Hunt 1996). The United States was in a heated competition with the Soviet Union. The goal was more than just a race to space; it was a race to prove overall superiority. Financial support was provided to science, technology, engineering, and math programs. Congress passed the National Defense Education Act (NDEA) in 1958 in an effort to produce highly trained people in the scientific and technical fields. One of the major ways the NDEA planned to do this was to improve K–12 science and math education (U.S. Department of Education 2011). Focus on science was expanding rapidly at this time, as President Eisenhower established the National Aeronautics and Space Administration (NASA), as well as the Office of Special Assistant to the President for Science and Technology (Price 2008).

Although the launch of Sputnik seems to be the starting point for the United States' focus on science, there was concern in the 1940s as well. During that time the presidential science advisor stated that reliance on other countries' scientific knowledge would result in a weakening of our own progress and competitive position in world trade. Both the President's Scientific Research Board in 1948 and the Labor Department in 1952 reported concern over the shortage of trained scientists and technical experts (Price 2008). As the years have progressed, the United States has focused more on comparative testing (Bybee 2006) and the need to thrive in an expanding global economy in which the population is STEM literate, as well as having the skills to solve problems, think critically, and work cooperatively.

The concern over a skilled and scientific workforce continues today. A committee including representatives from the Committee on Prospering in the Global Economy of the 21st Century, the National Academy of Sciences, the National Academy of Engineering, and the Institute

of Medicine created a document entitled, *Rising Above the Gathering Storm: Energizing and Employing America for a Brighter Economic Future (n.d.)*. The document stated that the committee was concerned about the eroding of our nation's "scientific and technological building blocks" (NAS 2007, p. 3). In 2009, President Barack Obama started the Educate to Innovate campaign. In his speech, President Obama, echoed the statements that were set forth in the 20th century. The United States must take steps to secure a stronger scientific and technological core of innovation and discovery. The president also noted that the government, students, parents, communities, organizations, and business must all work together to make this a reality (Wirt 2011).

Science Olympiad not only enhances students' knowledge of science, technology, and engineering, but it allows for tangential experiences into the wider community.

A productive citizen is scientifically literate. The National Science Education Standards (NRC 1996) outlines the qualities that make a person scientifically literate: someone who is versed in the ways of science and can ask, find, question, describe, explain, predict, and evaluate phenomena and methods. Such a person can engage in issues debated in a range of forums from the local to the international stage. A scientifically literate person will continuously build their knowledge base throughout their lifetime.

Effective science learning is an active process in which students are engaged in the world of science. Part of this engagement in science is inquiry. Inquiry is not just engaging in open-ended labs, but emulates scientific investigation, including performing research, observing, questioning, experimenting, collecting and analyzing data, and communicating results.

The events of Science Olympiad involve both inquiry and scientific literacy components. The NSES acknowledge that classrooms alone cannot provide a complete science education, and the resources of the greater community are vital. Science Olympiad does just that, by offering a variety of events, ranging widely in topic. Students and teams seek resources both within their schools and in the larger community. Professors, engineers, scientists and technical experts often serve as judges for events. Colleges and universities host Science Olympiad tournaments. All of these resources come together to allow students to expand their scientific understanding, and to interact with professionals in STEM fields.

Selected Science Olympiad Research

Past research yields supporting evidence that Science Olympiad develops vital 21st-century skills like collaboration, problem solving, and real-world experience. McGee-Brown, Martin, Monsaas, and Stomber (2003) conducted a three-year NSF-grant-funded longitudinal study on Science Olympiad. Wirt (2011) wrote a dissertation on the perceptions of Science Olympiad participants regarding their science learning and interest, 21st-century skills and abilities, and influence on careers, as well as the overall benefits of being involved in Science Olympiad. The study sought to determine if there were any differences of perception when gender was viewed as a factor. Hounsell (2001) also wrote a dissertation on Delaware science students and scientists.

McGee-Brown and colleagues (2003) also noted the variety of ways that Science Olympiad teams are organized. Some teams were organized as extracurricular activities, some were integrated into the curriculum, and others were a specific class during the day. Independence increased as students moved from middle school to high school, with middle school students needing more guidance from parents and coaches and high school students working more independently. According to McGee-Brown, "Science Olympiad is a model of collaboration and competition and students should be involved in the program" (Wirt 2011).

McGee-Brown (2003) found that various constituency groups associated with Science Olympiad thought the benefits of participation included increase in knowledge, exposure to collaboration, problem solving, creativity, and the chance to gain recognition. The participants thought the work was challenging and fun; they also saw scientists collaborate, not work in isolation. Students learned not only content specific to their event, but acquired skills such as organization, measurement, engineering, experimental design, and logical thinking. The students indicated that science was fun, but also hard work that involves experimentation, repetition, and precision. Participants enjoyed science more and learned both science content and skills.

Wirt (2011) found that Science Olympiad had an impact on the career choices of participants, and that they gained an increased level of learning and interest in science and STEM areas and 21st-century skills, and experienced overall positive benefits.

Similar research by Hounsell (2001) on Science Olympiad found that the participants benefited in a variety of ways: from the increase of knowledge and confidence to the development of problem-solving skills. Participants also garnered medals and trophies. Hounsell's (2001) study included Science Olympiad participants as well as nonparticipants, teachers, coaches, and judges. When surveyed, these groups all indicated that the top characteristics of successful science students included: intelligence, collaboration, creativity, problem solving, motivation, and communication. Hounsell then specifically surveyed people who were familiar with Science Olympiad. They felt that the "rewards for participation included medals, self-confidence, problem solving experience, knowledge, real-life experiences, hands-on science, and interaction with the scientific community" (Wirt 2011).

Extracurricular Activities and Student Motivation

I like the competitiveness of Science Olympiad; it makes science so much more fun. In fact, Science Olympiad makes a sport out of science without having the "jock" atmosphere surrounding. Being an athlete as well, I sincerely appreciated this 'other side' to competition. Science Olympiad was a major force in our family. I came from a family of 10 kids, and most of us did Science Olympiad. My brother competed for five years, got his PhD in Chemical Biology from Columbia University, and is now a professor at the University of Chicago. Although he was a football champion, my mother remembers that he took more pride in his Science Olympiad medals than the athletic awards.

—*Matthew Althoff, Pharmaceutical Sales, TAP Pharmaceuticals, seven-time letter winner in track/cross country at Notre Dame, NCAA championship competitor*

Extracurricular and co-curricular activities are one of the highlights of the day for many students. Approximately 25% of middle school and 52% of high school students participate in an academic club (Bucknavage and Worrell 2005). Structured, challenging activities can help a student develop many skills including interpersonal competence and educational success. Several studies, including one by Mahoney, Cairns, and Farmer (2003) and another by Logan and Scarborough (2008) found that participation in clubs allows students to interact in a positive way with not only their peers, but also with their teachers. According to Darling-Hammond (2007), effective schools create an atmosphere where students are able to work closely with adults. Juliana and Andrews (2005) found that passionate learning occurs when teachers and students are collaborative co-learners, talking and sharing knowledge with each other. They also found that teachers push students to think and allow students to direct their own learning which is both flexible and fits students' individual needs. This is how most Science Olympiad teams operate. Students are given events to work on and with the help of the coach as a guide, the student then works with her teammates to learn, research, create, and practice.

The Mahoney, Cairns, and Farmer (2003) group found that students who participate in extracurricular activities learn to set goals and use their experiences and skills later in life. According to Schroth (2007), students who were involved in extracurricular activities learn high-order and creative-thinking skills as well as problem-solving skills. The recognition and rewards that go along with success in extracurricular involvement is an essential component for students to develop their talents.

Research has found that science and math competitions increase student interest in those subject areas (Christie 2008). Students can't assess their own skills without comparison to others (Ozturk and Debelak 2008), and without competition, they may not fulfill their complete potential (Subotnik, Miserandino and Olszewski-Kubilius 1996). Whether a student wins or loses a competition, she can walk away with valuable learning. Science Olympiad is just this type of competition. According to researchers Logan and Scarborough (2008) and Ozturnk and Debelak (2008), student involvement in competitive experiences is truly valuable when working with an adult who helps them prepare for competition. This is the exact model that Science Olympiad teams follow (Wirt 2011).

According to Ozturk and Debelak (2008), academic competitions benefit students when people outside of the classroom are involved. People who work in a particular field, such as a STEM field, can help judge student work as well as break stereotypes. When female STEM employees are involved in academic competitions, both boys and girls see that STEM fields are accessible to either gender.

Science Olympiad and Career Choice: Research Results

I definitely feel that my early involvement in Science Olympiad had an impact on my career choices. The preparation helped me immensely throughout my college and post-college career.

—Jeffrey Silverman, PhD Student, Astrophysics, University of California, Berkeley

Dr. Jennifer Wirt's dissertation posed a specific question: What are the participants' perceptions of Science Olympiad's impact on their career choice? This research question analyzed data from an alumni survey. One of Science Olympiad's goals is "To attract more students particularly females and minorities to professional and technical careers in science, technology and science teaching" (website of Science Olympiad, n.d.). Work by Mahoney, Cairns, and Farmer (2003) found an increase in educational aspiration and positive plans for the future for students who engage in extracurricular activities. The Programme for International Student Assessment (PISA) 2006 reported that only 37% of students surveyed were interested in a career in science (Wirt 2011). A 1998 Bayer study found that out of the scientists surveyed, 61% first became interested in science before the age of eleven. In addition, over 90% of the scientists said that if given a chance to select a career again, they would choose science (Bayer Corporation 1998).

The question is whether Science Olympiad has an impact that increases students' interest in pursuing a career in the STEM field. The findings are impressive: Science Olympiad participants are extremely interested in working in a STEM field.

The National Center on Education and the Economy (2007) found that employers are looking for competent, creative, and innovative people. Employees will have to have a strong foundation in the core subject areas and be organized, self-disciplined, flexible, and be able to work as part of a team to innovate, analyze, and synthesize.

The Wirt (2011) study used surveys completed by former Science Olympiad participants found that the majority credited Science Olympiad with leading them to a career. "Seventy-eight percent of all college students and adults said that Science Olympiad did in fact lead them to a career and 61.3% were either majoring in or working in a STEM field as a result of participation in Science Olympiad."

The percentage included those respondents who were teaching science, math, engineering, or technology. Teaching in a STEM field was included in the calculation because even though teaching is not a STEM field per se, the subject area the teacher was engaged in was STEM-related. The anecdotal evidence provided numerous accounts of Science Olympiad participants becoming teachers because of their Science Olympiad experience. Some people credited the chance to work with their teachers after school in a different way than in the classroom, some said it was their desire to bring Science Olympiad to other students, and for some it was just their love of learning science (Wirt 2011). Fredricks and Eccles (2005) noted that the chance to work with adults is an important aspect of extracurricular activities.

When teaching in a STEM field was removed, the percentage of former Science Olympiad participants who were engaged in STEM fields was 49.1%. This is still well above the PISA report of 37% of students being interest in STEM careers (Wirt 2011). Science Olympiad is making an impact.

Children who had positive experiences with science and the STEM fields are subsequently interested in these fields as a career (Tindall and Hamil 2004). The quantitative data compiled from the surveys supported the fact that Science Olympiad was a positive experience for the participants and led them to make certain career decisions. The majority of the participants chose to work with some aspect of science, technology, engineering, or math (Wirt 2011).

When teaching STEM is removed, just slightly over half of those that credited Science Olympiad with their career choice did not choose a STEM field. There are two important findings to note here. First, these data may be skewed, as Dr. Wirt often had to determine a respondent's college major or career based on the participant's statements when they did not state it explicitly. Second, many of the participants that credited Science Olympiad with a career choice but did not pursue a STEM field noted that they learned skills that helped them in the career they did choose. Some of these skills included teamwork, problem solving, and critical thinking.

The data were also disaggregated by gender. Differences in career choices became evident. The number of males and females who pursued careers in science showed that a little over half of the scientists were female. There was more of a disparity in other STEM fields. Males dominated the engineering fields, as evidenced by a percentage differential of 69.1% male to 30.9% female. Although there is a substantial disparity between males and females going into engineering, female Science Olympiad participants still go into the field in greater number than as noted by other research (Wirt 2011). The current research data on engineering careers and gender disaggregation states that females are granted only 18% of the awarded engineering degrees (Tindall and Hamil 2004).

It is clear that Science Olympiad impacted the future careers of those who were involved. For many, their career of choice involved science, technology, engineering, or math. For others who did not choose to go into a STEM area, but still credited Science Olympiad with their careers, it was clear that they learned valuable work and 21st-century skills (Wirt 2011).

Science Olympiad and the STEM Workforce Pipeline

In February of 2007, the National Governors Association Center for Best Practices released the report, *Innovation America: Building a Science, Technology, Engineering and Math Agenda*. Contained within the document were several thought-provoking ideas for state education systems, such as the recommendation to "examine and increase the state's capacity to implement a rigorous aligned STEM education system statewide to improve teaching and learning." One implementation strategy, "to support STEM education outside the classroom via expanded learning opportunities that develop and maintain student interest," specifically mentioned Science Olympiad:

> States have also focused on increasing students' access to real world experiences in STEM through support for design and innovation competitions such as … Science Olympiad. These competitions provide students with real world STEM challenges and allow students to build, tinker, design and problem solve while learning deep content understanding of the problem at hand. Governors can look to these models to gain knowledge into alternate evaluation methods and for guidance in creating relevant, interesting STEM programs, and can offer incentives to encourage districts to participate in these activities. (p. 17)

Science Olympiad gives teachers access to dynamic content that brings regular science curriculum to life, inspiring both the teacher and student to think outside the box. Toren Stearns, valedictorian of Tokay High School in Lodi, California, traces his success in medical school at the University of Michigan back to a pivotal experience: "What really got me interested in medicine was being so involved with Science Olympiad. Mr. Porter's AP Biology class was the hardest class I took in high school, and because it was so difficult, I studied for it a lot and really grew to love the material" (Lodi News Sentinel Staff 2011).

According to the Bureau of Labor Statistics, by 2014 employers are expected to hire 2.5 million new STEM workers. In light of this pressing need, programs such as Science Olympiad are being increasingly recognized as sources of excellent career awareness, exploration and prepara-

tion. In the State of Illinois, a P-20 Council has been formed to "strengthen this State's economic competitiveness by producing a highly skilled workforce" (Public Act 95-626, establishing the P-20 Council). Science Olympiad has been serving on the College and Career Readiness and Work-based Learning Committees since 2010, providing insight into the development of a new "public policy framework for state leaders that increases collaboration across the systems and makes the pipeline more responsive to the diverse needs of students" (P-20 Council Mission Statement).

Tom Degnan is Chairman of the New Jersey Research and Development Council, which provides funding, volunteers, and mentors to Science Olympiad teams and tournaments. He said, "Science Olympiad is an exceptional program for students to fully appreciate how important and exciting science and technology can be, especially in an age where technology is an inextricable part of our daily life" (NJRDC website). With FORTUNE 500, government agency, and top STEM association partners like Lockheed Martin, DuPont, the Centers for Disease Control, Texas Instruments, U.S. Army, Society for Neuroscience, U.S. Air Force, and Google, Science Olympiad exposes students and teachers to practicing scientists and cutting-edge technology.

Science Olympiad: Generation Next

> Science Olympiad focused my plans in college and life to science. I love science, and knew I would go that way throughout life. Science Olympiad allowed me to see a broad range of scientific fields at any given time and allowed me to hone in on what I truly liked—not to mention the friendships, relationships, and common bonds that I have with former teammates and coaches. Science Olympiad ranks as one of the top experiences in my life!
>
> —*Mark Tourre, Forensic DNA Analyst, U.S. Army Criminal Investigation Lab*

As our nation faces a decline in homegrown scientists and engineers, Science Olympiad continues to provide content and experiences that motivate teachers and students to become (and remain) passionate about STEM. Science Olympiad events provide a wealth of opportunities for scientific exploration and discovery, from a kindergartener learning about the natural environment in the Tree ID event to a junior in high school designing his first Gravity Vehicle. The evidence linking Science Olympiad events to student interest in STEM careers is solid; perhaps even more exciting is the effect it has had on teachers over the past three decades. Krista Damery, a science educator from Madison, Michigan, was a Science Olympiad competitor from 1987 to 1995. She emphasizes, "Coaching a Science Olympiad team is what kept me teaching on several occasions. When the rigors of the career wear me down, the inspiration given by my team makes it all worthwhile. When I decided to go into education, I knew I wanted to be involved in Science Olympiad." By giving teachers an outlet to challenge students, and by giving students a platform to display their talents, Science Olympiad strives to create the next generation of STEM leaders.

> The impact of Science Olympiad on my resulting career path is nearly beyond words. The excitement of competing and excelling in an educational activity led me to choose science for my livelihood. I feel that one of the often-overlooked components of Science Olympiad is the fact that its goals combine education and scientific learning with competition. The competitive aspect of science is pervasive and is one of the major driving forces of scientific advancement.
> —*Brent Summerlin, Chemistry Professor, Southern Methodist University*

Exploring the World of Science

References

Bayer Corporation. 1998. Making science make sense. Bayer facts of science education survey. The Bayer facts of science education IV—By gender. Available online at *www.bayerus.com/msms/msms_education_resources_activities/ResourcesSTP/Survey/summary98.aspx*

Bloom, B. S., and L. A. Sosniak. 1981. Talent Development vs. Schooling. *Educational Leadership* (Nov): 86–94.

Bucknavage, L. B., and F. C. Worrell. 2005. A study of academically talented students' in extracurricular activities. *The Journal of Secondary Gifted Education* 16 (2/3): 74–86, 134–135.

Bybee, R. W. 2006. The science curriculum: Trends and issues. In *Teaching science in the 21st century*, ed. J. Rhoton and P. Shane, 21–37. Arlington, VA: NSTA Press.

Christie, K. 2008. Middle and high schoolers get hands-on STEM experiences. *Phi Delta Kappan* 90 (1): 5–6.

Darling-Hammond, L. 2007. The flat Earth and education: How America's commitment to equity will determine our future. *Educational Researcher* 36 (6): 318–334.

Fredricks, J., and J. Eccles. 2005. Developmental benefits of extracurricular involvement: Do peer characteristics mediate the link between activities and youth outcomes? *Journal of Youth and Adolescence* 34 (6): 507–520.

Hounsell, T. S. 2001. An examination of perceived characteristics of career scientists and Delaware science students who do and do not participate in the Science Olympiad. Doctoral dissertation. Wilmington, DE: Wilmington College.

Illinois P-20 Council. 2011. Education for our future: First report and recommendations of the Illinois P-20 council to the governor, the general assembly, and the people of Illinois. Available online at *www2.illinois.gov/gov/P20/Pages/Reports.aspx*

Juliana, M., and S. E. Andrews. 2005. Creating a climate for passionate learning. *Thinking Classroom* 6 (1): 21–26.

Lodi News-Sentinel Staff. 2011. Toren Stearns credits science competition for success. *Lodi News-Sentinel*. Sept. 19.

Logan, W. L., and J. L. Scarborough. 2008. Connections through clubs: Collaboration and coordination of a schoolwide program. *Professional School Counseling* 12 (2): 157–161.

Mahoney, J. L., B. D. Cairns, and T. W. Farmer. 2003. Promoting interpersonal competence and educational success through extracurricular activity participation. *Journal of Educational Psychology* 95 (2): 409–418.

McGee-Brown, M. J. n.d. Science Olympiad: The role of competition in collaborative science inquiry. Unpublished Manuscript.

McGee-Brown, M. J., C. Martin, J. Monsaas, and M. Stombler. 2003. What scientists do: Science Olympiad enhancing science inquiry through student collaboration, problem-solving, and creativity. Paper presented at the Annual National Science Teachers Association Meeting, Philadelphia, PA.

National Academy of Sciences (NAS). 2007. *Rising above the gathering storm: Energizing and employing America for a brighter economic future*. Washington, DC: National Academies Press.

National Center on Education and the Economy. 2007. *Tough choices or tough times: The report of the new commission on the skills of the American workforce*. San Francisco, CA: Jossey-Bass.

National Governors Association (NGA). 2007. *Innovation America: Building a science, technology, engineering and math agenda*. Washington, DC: NGA.

National Research Council (NRC). 1996. *National science education standards*. Washington, DC: National Academies Press.

New Jersey Research and Development Council. Press release. *www.rdnj.org*

Ozturk, M., and C. Debelak. 2008. Affective benefits from academic competitions for middle school gifted students. *Gifted Child Today* 31 (2): 48–53.

Price, T. 2008. Science in America. *CQ Researcher* 18 (2): 25–48.

Programme for International Student Assessment (PISA). 2006. Science competencies for tomorrow's world. Executive summary. Available online at *www.pisa.oecd.org/dataoecd/15/13/39725224.pdf*

Schroth, S. T. 2007. Selecting after-school programs. A Guide for parents. *Parenting for High Potential* 30: 18–21.

Science Olympiad. *www.soinc.org*

Stohr-Hunt, P. M. 1996. An analysis of frequency of hands-on experience and science achievement. *Journal of Research in Science Teaching* 33 (1): 101–109.

Subotnik, R., A. Miserandino, P. Olszewski-Kubilius. 1996. Implications for the Olympiad studies for the development of mathematical talent in schools. *International Journal of Educational Research* 25 (6).

Taylor, C. W. 1986. Cultivating simultaneous student growth in both multiple creative talents and knowledge. In *Systems and models for developing programs for the gifted and talented,* ed. J. S. Renzulli, 307–350. Mansfield Center, CT: Creative Learning Press.

Terrell, N. 2007. STEM occupations. *Occupational Outlook Quarterly* 26–33.

Tindall, T., and B. Hamil. 2004. Gender disparity in science education: The causes, consequences, and solutions. *Education* 125 (2): 282–295.

U.S. Department of Education. 2011. *The federal role in education*. Available online at *www2.ed.gov/about/overview/fed/role.html*

Willingham, W. W., J. W. Young, and M. Morris. 1985. *Success in college: The role of personal qualities and academic ability*. New York: College Entrance Examination Board.

Wirt, J. L. 2011. An analysis of science Olympiad participants' perceptions regarding their experience with the science and engineering academic competition. Doctoral Dissertation. South Orange, NJ: Seton Hall University.

Appendix A

2012 National Science Olympiad—National Science Standards Alignment

B (Middle School) Division

B Events	National Standard
Anatomy: Students are tested on their knowledge of anatomy and health concepts of the respiratory and digestive systems.	M.C.1: Structure and function in living systems M.F.1: Personal Health
Awesome Aquifers: Students construct an aquifer and answer questions about groundwater concepts; includes a presentation.	M.D.1: Structure of the Earth system M.U.2: Evidence, models, and explanation
Bottle Rockets: Prior to the tournament, students construct up to two rockets designed to stay aloft the greatest amount of time.	M.E.1: Abilities of technological design
Compute This: Students are given a problem that requires quantitative data capture from the internet and the presentation of data in a graphical format.	M.A.1: Abilities necessary to do scientific inquiry
Crime Busters: Students identify the perpetrators of crimes using paper chromatography and analysis of unknown solids, liquids, and plastics found at the scene of a crime.	M.A.1: Abilities necessary to do scientific inquiry M.B.1: Properties and changes of properties in matter
Disease Detectives: This event requires students to apply principles of epidemiology to a real-life health problem with a focus on food-borne illness.	H.F.1: Personal and community health H.G.1: Science as a human endeavor
Dynamic Planet: Students use process skills to complete tasks related to Earth's fresh water.	M.B.1: Properties and changes of properties in matter
Experimental Design: Given a set of objects, students design, conduct, analyze, and write up an experiment.	M.A.1: Abilities necessary to do scientific inquiry
Food Science: Students use their understanding of the chemistry of baking ingredients to answer questions at a series of stations.	M.B.1: Properties and changes of properties in matter
Forestry: This event tests students' knowledge of North American trees on the official list.	H.C.3 Biological evolution
Keep the Heat: Students construct a device to retain heat.	M.E.1: Abilities of technological design

B Events	National Standard
Meteorology: Students demonstrate a multidisciplinary understanding of climates on Earth.	M.B.1: Properties and changes of properties in matter
Microbe Mission: Students answer questions, solve problems, and analyze data pertaining to microbes.	H.C.1: The cell
Mission Possible: Students design, build, and test one Rube Goldberg–like device that completes a required task.	M.E.1: Abilities of technological design
Mousetrap Vehicle: Students construct a vehicle that uses one mousetrap as its sole means of propulsion to reach a target as close as possible to their predicted time.	M.E.1: Abilities of technological design
Optics: Students compete in activities and answer questions related to geometric and physical optics.	M.B.3: Transfer of energy H.B.6: Interactions of energy and matter
Road Scholar: Students interpret various map features using a variety of road and topographic maps.	M.U.2: Evidence, models, and explanation
Rocks and Minerals: Students identify, describe, and classify various specimens.	M.B.1: Properties and changes of properties in matter
Reach for the Stars: Students demonstrate knowledge of properties and evolution of stars, open and globular clusters, and star-forming galaxies.	H.D.4: Origin and evolution of the universe
Storm the Castle: Prior to the tournament, students design, construct, and calibrate a device that uses only the energy of a falling counterweight to launch a projectile as far and as accurately as possible.	M.E.1: Abilities of technological design
Towers: Students design and build the most efficient tower.	M.E.1: Abilities of technological design
Water Quality: Students evaluate aquatic environments.	M.A.1: Abilities necessary to do scientific inquiry
Write It/Do It: Students perform a technical writing exercise by describing a contraption while other students attempt to build it using only the written description.	M.E.1: Abilities of technological design

Appendix B

2012 National Science Olympiad—National Science Standards Alignment

C (High School) Division

C Events	National Standard
Anatomy and Physiology: This event covers the anatomy and physiology of selected body systems, this year limited to respiratory, excretory, and digestive systems.	M.C.1: Structure and function of living systems H.F.1: Personal and community health
Astronomy: Students demonstrate an understanding of the basic concepts of math and physics relating to stellar evolution and Type Ia supernovas.	H.D.4: Origin and evolution of the universe
Chemistry Lab: Students demonstrate chemistry laboratory skills related to periodicity and oxidation/reduction.	H.B.3: Chemical reactions H.B.2: Structure and properties of matter
Disease Detectives: Students apply principles of epidemiology to a real-life problem, with a focus on food-borne illness.	H.F.1: Personal and community health H.G.1: Science as a human endeavor
Dynamic Planet: Students use process skills to complete tasks related to Earth's fresh water.	M.D.1: Structure of the Earth system
Experimental Design: Given a set of objects, students design, conduct, analyze, and write up an experiment.	H.A.1: Abilities necessary to do scientific inquiry
Fermi Questions: Students estimate quantities that are difficult or impossible to measure.	H.A.1: Abilities necessary to do scientific inquiry
Forensics: Students identify polymers, solids, fibers, and other materials in a crime scene scenario.	H.A.1: Abilities necessary to do scientific inquiry H.U.2: Evidence, models, and explanations
Forestry: This event tests students' knowledge of North American trees on the official list.	H.C.3: Biological evolution
Gravity vehicle: Students design, build, and test a vehicle that uses gravitational potential energy as the sole propulsion energy source to reach a target point.	H.E.1: Abilities of technological design
Helicopters: Prior to the tournament, students construct and test free-flight rubber band-powered helicopters to achieve maximum flight times.	H.E.1: Abilities of technological design
Microbe Mission: Students answer questions, solve problems, and analyze data pertaining to microbes.	H.C.1: The cell

C Events	National Standard
Optics: Students compete in activities and answer questions related to geometric and physical optics.	H.B.6: Interactions of energy and matter H.B.3: Transfer of energy
Protein Modeling: Students use computer visualization and online resources to guide them in constructing physical models of proteins.	H.C.1: The cell H.U.2: Evidence, models, and explanations
Remote Sensing: Students use maps and remote sensing technology to explain human impact on the Earth.	H.C.4: Interdependence of organisms H.U.2: Evidence, models, and explanations
Robot Arm: Students design and build a robot that will move objects	H.E.1: Abilities of technological design
Rocks and Minerals: Students identify, describe, and classify various specimens.	M.D.1: Structure of the Earth system
Sounds of Music: Prior to the competition, students build one wind instrument and one percussion instrument based on a 12-tone tempered scale, describe the principles behind their operation, and perform a major scale, a required melody, and a chosen melody with each.	H.E.1: Abilities of technological design
Technical Problem Solving: Students gather and process data to solve problems.	H.A.1: Abilities necessary to do scientific inquiry
Thermodynamics: Students design and build a device to retain heat.	H.E.1: Abilities of technological design
Towers: Students design and build the most efficient tower.	H.E.1: Abilities of technological design
Water Quality: Students evaluate aquatic environments.	H.A.1: Abilities necessary to do scientific inquiry
Write It/Do It: Students perform a technical writing exercise by describing a contraption while other students attempt to build it using only the written description.	H.E.1: Abilities of technological design

Active Learning as a Way to Interest More Students in Science Careers

Claudia Khourey-Bowers
Kent State University at Stark

Tracy Saho and Vicki McCamon
Welty Middle School

Setting

I n this chapter, the experiences of a science educator and two technology education (TE) classroom teachers are offered. The school is a rural middle school in a Midwestern state where authors collaborated to promote active learning environments, which can encourage students to consider careers in Science, Technology, Engineering, and Mathematics (STEM). Ten different types of active learning strategies are explored in the context of STEM classrooms. Specific vignettes are provided from the two TE classrooms. Readers are invited to think about the following challenges, which are central to our chapter:

- How do students benefit from active learning strategies?
- What aspects of your curriculum can be re-designed to incorporate active learning?
- How can active learning strategies enhance the classroom environment?
- How can active learning strategies help prepare more students for STEM careers?

Evidence of the effectiveness of TE participation in promoting STEM careers is provided.

Active Learning for Encouraging Students to Consider STEM Careers

On a rainy day in May, middle school students entered Welty Middle School. They were not thinking so much of the approaching summer vacation, but more about time trials and robotic elevators. Completed in 1926, Welty Middle School in New Philadelphia, Ohio,

Welty Middle School, New Philadelphia, Ohio

serves a community dating back to the late 1700s. But despite the history of the community and its school building, the classrooms, students, and teachers are engaged in active learning strategies for the 21st century.

What Is Active Learning?

Active learning is an inquiry-based approach to teaching science. Students begin with questions about the world around them. They then analyze their observations using various tools and communicate their findings to peers and teachers (NRC 1996). In this process of active learning, students reflect on their assumptions about the natural world. By questioning their assumptions, students are able to reconsider connections between ideas and events. Using critical thinking skills, they can propose alternative solutions to scientific or technological problems.

Active learning strategies are typically student-centered or student-directed approaches (Blank and Alas 2009). When given the independence of active learning, students also are charged with expectations to create and manipulate knowledge, and ultimately constructing understandings that are consistent with scientific conceptions and real-world scenarios. Active learning can, and should be, part of every STEM classroom.

In this chapter, we will consider ways to transform every STEM classroom into an active learning environment. You are invited to think about the following challenges:

- How do students benefit from active learning strategies?
- What aspects of your curriculum can be re-designed to incorporate active learning?
- How can active learning strategies enhance the classroom environment?
- How do active learning strategies help prepare students for STEM careers?

How Active Learning Supports Goal 4 of NSES and More Emphasis Conditions

Goal 4 of the National Science Education Standards (NSES) is "to educate students who are able to … increase their economic productivity through the use of the knowledge, understanding, and skills of the scientifically literate person in their careers" (NRC 1996, p. 13). From a study of European students' attitudes toward school science, Osborne and Dillon (2008) concluded that science curriculum should be designed to prepare students to become critically aware citizens, living in a world shaped by technology and scientific accomplishments. Active learning, through the framework of STEM curricula, has the capacity to encourage students to have a more positive outlook on STEM careers.

In order to meet Goal 4 of the NSES, new emphases in *teaching*, *assessment*, as well as *content and inquiry* standards should be addressed. This chapter focuses on shifting emphases in three key areas.

- *Teaching standards* should shift emphasis from simply "focusing on student acquisition of information" such as memorization of facts, to "focusing on student understanding and use of scientific knowledge, ideas, and inquiry processes" (NRC 1996, p. 52). This new emphasis requires that learners go beyond memorization, by using content knowledge to understand relationships among concepts and to solve problems.

- *Assessment standards* should not rely strictly on "end of term assessments by teachers," but should value "students being engaged in ongoing assessments of their work and that of others" (NRC 1996, p. 100). Active learning strategies foster dialogue between teachers and their students, as well as among the students. Questioning of tentative knowledge can help students rethink their ideas and designs.

- *Content and inquiry standards* should shift emphases from "studying subject matter disciplines (physical, life, earth sciences) for their own sake" to "learning subject matter disciplines in the context of inquiry, technology, science in personal and social perspectives, and history and nature of science" (NRC 1996, p. 113). STEM and other integrated approaches to science curricula emphasize application of content knowledge, skills, and sociocultural contexts of scientific knowledge.

Welty Middle School: Exemplary Practices in Technology Education

Three middle school science teachers, sixth-grade teacher Ms. Tracy Saho, seventh-grade teacher Ms. Vicki McCamon, and eighth-grade teacher Ms. Debra Burkhart, have taken on the challenge of implementing active learning through a technology education (TE) curriculum. TE is one way to implement active learning strategies. Tracy, Vicki, and Debra guide their students in the middle school curriculum, Gateway to Technology (GTT) (Project Lead the Way 2010), which was adopted by the New Philadelphia School District. The teachers and the district have invested time, effort, and resources into the implementation of the GTT program. For example, the TE students have a dedicated computer lab that was specifically funded by the local community just for the GTT program.

The Technology Education curriculum is built from an integrated perspective, blending four domains of knowledge: conceptual, procedural, technical, and societal (Turnbull 2006). These four domains, as described by Moreland, Jones, and Chambers (2001), are part of an active learning cycle, which comprises theoretical and applied forms of knowledge. *Conceptual knowledge* is the understanding of relevant technological concepts and procedures; *procedural knowledge* is characterized by how, what, and when to do something; *societal knowledge* is the understanding of the relationships between technology and its effects on specific groups of people; and *technical knowledge* is the set of skills related to practical techniques. These four integrated domains of knowledge can be especially effective in engaging and challenging middle school students.

TE is not only guided by four domains of knowledge, but also by an iterative design. According to van Niekerk, Ankiewicz, and Swardt (2010), the design process has 10 stages:

- Stage 1: Problem statement (What is the problem?)
- Stage 2: Design brief (What is the plan for solving the problem?)
- Stage 3: Investigation (What data will be collected to help solve the problem?)
- Stage 4: Proposal (Prepare oral and written presentations of what needs to be done to solve the problem.)
- Stage 5: Initial idea generation (Brainstorm various ideas, then analyze them and select the best one.)
- Stage 6: Research (Find out more about the background of the problem.)

- Stage 7: Developing the selected idea to a final idea (Add more detail to the selected idea.)
- Stage 8: Planning (What plan do you have for making the product?)
- Stage 9: Making the product (Handiwork and design criteria are both important.)
- Stage 10: Evaluation of the final product based on stated criteria (Were all the criteria met?)

Students at Welty Middle School not only know these stages, but apply them every day in their TE classes. Introduced over a three-year period, the district first implemented GTT in the eighth grade. During the inaugural year, Vicki and Debra co-taught the eighth-grade program. During the second year of implementation, Vicki taught the seventh-grade modules. Tracy initiated the sixth-grade module in the third year.

In sixth grade, one module of GTT, Energy and the Environment (Project Lead the Way 2010), is offered in a nine-week exploratory course. Tracy describes the Energy module as focusing on renewable energy resources, alternative sources of energy, and environmental issues. The TE curriculum reinforces the Ohio sixth-grade science curriculum content standards dealing with energy and environmental issues. Within the time frame of a nine-week course, Tracy believes that a single module is a wonderful introduction to active learning, through the TE domains (conceptual, technical, procedural, and societal).

The seventh-grade curriculum comprises two modules (Magic of Electrons, Automation and Robotics) taught over a full semester. According to Vicki, the seventh-grade curriculum begins as student-centered and ends as a student-directed learning experience. The first quarter is primarily skill-building and understanding electric circuits. For example, students learn how to solder, how to fill each of the design roles in the curriculum (computer engineer, electrical engineer, and mechanical engineer), and how to make a DC motor. The first half of the course is student-centered, but mostly teacher-directed. The roles and responsibilities shift during the second part of the course. The second nine weeks focuses on computer programming and hands-on designs. At this point, the seventh graders are able and expected to work independently.

A visit to the GTT classes at Welty Middle School can provide many examples of active learning. Whether students are building, testing, or revising their plans, the TE students are mindful of their work, interacting with each other and with their teachers in positive and productive ways.

Earlier in this chapter, we invited you to think about four challenges:

- How can you engage your students through active learning strategies?
- What aspects of your curriculum can be re-designed to incorporate active learning?
- How can active learning strategies enhance the classroom environment?
- How can active learning strategies help prepare students for STEM careers?

To help answer these questions, we would like to share our top 10 ideas for using active learning in STEM courses. As you read about the active learning strategies, you will find out how Tracy and Vicki use them in their TE classes.

Top 10 Active Learning Strategies

Number 10. Watch Your Language!

Sometimes, multiple definitions of common words affect students' understanding of fundamental scientific concepts including such terms as *work, energy, size, shape,* and *growth.* Help your students distinguish scientific meanings from everyday meanings of words. Word walls, student-illustrated vocabulary cards, and science notebooks all can help create a working vocabulary while also developing understanding.

Instead of routine laboratory reports, students are urged to use reflective laboratory reports. In reflective reports, students still include purpose, hypotheses, procedures, data, and discussion but supplement each stage by including *why, what, who, when, where,* and *how* they arrived at each step. As students write reflective reports, and as we teachers read them, the connections between formal knowledge and personal knowledge become apparent. We can begin to understand how our students are thinking, as they themselves think about the scientific words and the meanings behind them.

In Tracy's classroom, students work in design teams of three on building wind turbines. Students conduct trials on the power of each team's wind turbine, measuring time to raise a cup of variable mass. Tracy reminded students to record the times and to measure the mass of the cup and the vertical height that the cup was lifted. Students calculated the power of their turbines, using a standard formula. In addition to doing the calculations, the sixth graders were able to connect abstract concepts such as mass and power with the machines they designed and built.

Number 9. Go for the Long Haul!

Design longitudinal studies where students collect data over an extended period of days, weeks, or months. Grow yeast colonies and make daily measurements of population growth and collapse. Raise fast-growing plants such as radishes and have students make observations over a period of several weeks of plant height, leaf number, length, and width. Have students select an independent variable to change conditions. Make seasonal observations of ecosystems such as pond conditions, ground cover, light levels, and animal tracks.

When using the TE process, students are engaged in a repetitive cycle of design, redesign, build, test, and rebuild. The sixth-grade students conducted three time trials on their wind turbines. As students continually reevaluate their work over an extended period of time, they are better able to step back from their original thinking and come up with new designs. When given time to think and act, students are better able to consider new designs, hypotheses, choices of materials, and the significance of variables.

As the seventh graders progressed through the Automation and Robotics module, they designed and built progressively more complex machines. With each task, they acquired specific knowledge and procedures that they were then expected to apply to meeting the challenges of the final project, a Fishertechniks model elevator.

Number 8. Use Discrepant Events to Awaken Curiosity and Inspire Questioning.

Dynamic models such as the drinking bird, happy and sad balls, and wind-up cars are surefire ways to get students asking questions about motion. Alternatively, put a static model such as a center of mass demonstration in a corner of the classroom for the students to discover. Wait until

Students construct an original design using Fishertechniks.

they start asking you questions about what it is and how it works. Predictions and hypotheses generation follow, as intrigued students are challenged to apply scientific knowledge to explain the "unbelievable."

GTT presents project-based scenarios, with specific criteria that both restrain and spark imagination. As students become engaged in the design challenge, they ask questions about the project goals, constraints, and real-world uses. Simply accepting information is not an option! Although the projects are predetermined, the solutions are not.

By the latter part of the semester, Vicki's seventh-grade students work independently, with the teacher facilitating only as needed. If student teams are uncertain about how to proceed, Vicki guides them through a line of questioning, rather than simply answering their questions. By the end of the module, all teams successfully complete the final project of the unit, an elevator that stops and starts at each of three floors.

Number 7. Use Novel Associations to Explore Concepts.

Rather than using textbook examples to study important concepts, unique examples are used. Does every motion problem involve trains? Study the physics of motion by observing the family pet. Explore Newton's laws by building and launching model rockets. Does every food web consist of grass, a rabbit, and a fox? Consider instead the food web of a rotting log. Why not use bacteria to convey concepts of population and abiotic factors? Encourage students to construct their own ecosystems or food webs by observing the school grounds or their backyards. Have students apply content knowledge and methods of scientific inquiry to investigate product claims, such UV light–sterilizing toothbrushes and fat-free potato chips.

Draw upon students' everyday experiences to authentically capture "real-world" problems. When one of Vicki's seventh-grade teams finished its project packet days before the other teams, she encouraged them to design a computer program that synced music from one boy's iPod to LED lights. As the team worked, other students gathered around periodically to watch and cheer their progress.

Number 6. Demystify Diagrams!

The most familiar diagrams—such as food webs, the water cycle, and chemical equations—attempt to convey complex relationships simply, using words, pictures, numbers, and symbols. But how many students really understand what the "shorthand" images represent? For example, in a food web, arrows point to the higher-order consumer. Why isn't the arrow pointing toward the organism that is consumed? How can we make sure that our students

Students design a light show to music.

understand that matter and energy are both moving from producers through consumers? Similarly, the water cycle typically pairs specific processes with specific parts of the Earth. For example, evaporation is shown over the ocean, while transpiration is shown over plants. Doesn't water both evaporate and transpire from plants? Doesn't water evaporate from roads, parking lots, and puddles as well as from the ocean? Chemical equations, symbolic of types and ratios of matter, present further problems. Do arrows in chemical equations mean the same thing as arrows in food webs? Are the products consuming the reactants?

In an effort to simplify, some diagrams can lead to incomplete understanding. Replace stereotypical thinking by giving students opportunities to create their own images, before relying

on standard diagrams. Have students make drawings and diagrams that depict their interpretations of the concept. As instruction proceeds, the drawings should become more complete and more consistent with standard representations.

TE provides many opportunities for students to create their own 2-D images of proposed 3-D objects. One sixth grader, still learning about formal depictions, draws a model with a wind turbine complete with measurements.

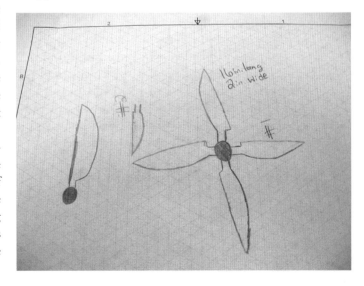

In Design Stage 5, students are expected to make isometric and orthographic sketches of their model. As students sketch the model, details and functionality become clearer.

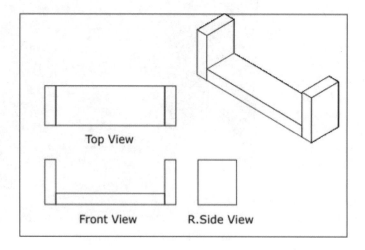

From Introduction to Designing Integrated Systems (CDLI 2007)

Number 5. Measure Twice, Lecture Once!

Just like the carpenter's adage of "measure twice and cut once," the suggestion here is to spend time with quantitative observations to develop understanding of fundamental concepts. Measurement can be used in the study of physical and chemical changes. Start with measuring matter involved in physical changes, such as mixtures or solutions. When working with chemical changes (especially when gases play a role), use closed system designs, such as reactions in freezer bags. Measurement can help students realize that in both chemical and physical changes, matter is conserved. Measurement can help develop the concepts of particulate nature of matter and conservation of matter.

In TE, measurement is crucial to successful use of the design process. Measurement develops proportional thinking, reinforces the importance of observation and inference, teaches the use of tools, and the importance of following directions. All of these conceptual and procedural tasks help to clarify the laws of the natural world for students.

The turbine trial consisted of timing the ascent of the cup as the blades whirled when a rotating fan was placed one meter away. Students repeated each trial three times, determining the best run as well as average values for power and work.

Number 4. Say It With Flowers!

And say it with pictures, words, and mathematical symbols! Every concept can be represented with concrete examples (flowers and models), images and diagrams (sketches and blueprints), words (descriptions), and symbols (equation for photosynthesis). We sometimes assume that middle school and high school students are abstract thinkers. But, in some domains, they may still be thinking concretely. For example, students tend to think that individual atoms demonstrate all the same properties as macro-amounts of substances, or that scale models of robotics have the same properties as a working automaton. Students need time to talk or write about their perceptions before being introduced to abstract theories. Then they can scaffold their own progress through multiple levels of representation by specifically addressing their current understanding. It is good for you and your students to discuss different models that are used to explain phenomena. Students can begin to understand that each model has strengths and limitations.

In TE, multiple representations of phenomena, including drawings, blueprints, 3-D objects, and computer animations, can help students develop an understanding of forces, dynamics, and materials.

Number 3. Create Concept Maps.

Concept maps are versatile learning tools. Concept maps can be used as pretests to determine students' prior knowledge or posttests to assess learning after given experiences. More importantly, concept maps can

Mrs. Saho works with students on their wind turbine.

Students work on an elevator simulation.

help build understanding as students actively construct meaning through recognizing associations between concepts. These relationships between concepts, called "propositions," can reveal how students organize their ideas. The process of concept mapping should begin with a focus question that serves as a guide to organization of concepts. Provide students with a "parking lot" of key terms and a skeleton template for the concept map (Novak and Canas 2008). The template should provide enough structure so that the primary divisions are suggested, yet it should be

Vicki assists students with their designs.

open enough for students to incorporate their own associations. In TE, good concept maps should show connections across the four domains of conceptual, procedural, technical, and societal knowledge.

Students' cognitive connections can be determined with oral and procedural tasks as well. When sixth graders were asked how wind turbines were used in real life, most responded that wind turbines are used to make energy, by connecting the output to a generator. As seventh graders wrote computer programs to direct their automated elevators, they demonstrated understanding of how electronic inputs can produce mechanical outputs.

Number 2. Write to Learn.

Use of structured writing tasks, such as observations, reflective lab reports, and science notebooks, can improve conceptual understanding by generating metacognitive thought. Thus metacognition, or knowing *how* you learn, is itself a form of learning produced by writing. At the same time, it is a catalyst for content learning (Wallace, Hand, and Prain 2007).

Writing can be used for knowledge-telling and knowledge-transforming (Wallace, Hand, and Prain 2007). Knowledge-telling focuses on the recall of information, such as observations, reading summaries, vocabulary reviews, and lecture notes. To encourage students to transform knowledge, teachers should have their students interpret and represent knowledge in new ways, such as reflective lab reports, creative writing, (including poetry and rap), and group writing. Ask students to write a rap about mitosis or a haiku about solutions. In group writing, students begin by anonymously writing one important idea about a specific topic, such as the rock cycle, on a piece of paper. They then pass their papers on to one or two other students, who in turn, add a new concept or clarification. This process encourages students to think more deeply or broadly about their current knowledge.

In the GTT program, summative grading rubrics are composed of 12 criteria: design briefs, design process notes, research results, design sketches, decision-making matrix, working drawing, assembly drawing, prototypes, test and record results, design changes, solution presentation, and teamwork. Of these 12, four are heavily dependent on the writing process (design brief, design process notes, research, and solution presentation). Students soon learn that writing is as important as the design process itself in TE.

Number 1. Talk the (STEM) Talk.

Teacher-student and student-student dialogue should be encouraged in the classroom. Time should be taken to ask questions that require students to think, use evidence, and listen to others. Discussion, by its nature, assumes that the discussants integrate knowledge from others into their own understandings. Students should be encouraged to work in small groups that can be accountable for learning. Groups can share their ideas orally, write brief reports, or include their findings in lab reports or on tests. Just as we learn as we teach, our students learn as they talk about concepts, events, and procedures. Concept development and language development are interrelated, so the more our students talk about the lesson, the more opportunities they have to refine their understandings of important concepts.

Dialogue is critical in TE, as students work in cooperative teams to design and build products. Much of TE is student-directed, so student-student dialogue is a key learning strategy. As individuals talk with their peers, new ideas and understandings can emerge.

The cooperative teams at Welty Middle School collaborate on developing designs and understanding. As students work to revise their models, they are able to justify the hows and whys of their design changes. Some students change their designs because the model did not work, or it performed at lower levels than those of other teams. During class, student teams work collaboratively, rather than being dependent on the teacher. Teams realized that as they made further design revisions, they need to change one variable at a time. Subsequent trials give students the positive feedback they need when their designs works!

Evidence of Effectiveness

We began this chapter with four challenge questions. What do Tracy and Vicki think about the effectiveness of GTT? What does the research tell us about the value of active learning in technology education?

How Do Students Benefit From Active Learning Strategies?

Tracy believes that the GTT program builds upon the sixth-grade energy and natural resource standards, allowing students to extend science content knowledge while developing inquiry skills. The most helpful parts of the curriculum are the truly "hands-on" problem-solving activities. The students are very engaged and work together to solve challenges.

Vicki believes that the most important skill is independent problem-solving, where students rely on each other and themselves. Initially, the independence is a little frustrating for the students, but they learn to become independent thinkers and doers. Vicki also noted that GTT encourages design improvement and supports technical skills such as measurement, mathematical calculation, and manipulation of materials by building products. It improves computer skills and communication skills as students create brochures and PowerPoint productions.

Findings reported by Yager and Akcay (2010) compared the effectiveness of textbook-based teaching with inquiry teaching. Their results indicated that inquiry teaching resulted in significant improvement in six domains of science instruction: conceptual, process (skills), application, creativity, attitudes (careers and interest), and worldview (including both nature of science and history of science). Textbook-based instruction enhanced only the conceptual domain. Without inclusion of active learning strategies, student understanding, problem-solving, and application skills are not developed. These research findings support the anecdotal knowledge from Welty Middle School about students' improvement in academic, procedural, and motivational areas by participation in GTT.

What Aspects of Your Curriculum Can Be Redesigned to Incorporate Active Learning?

In talking about the differences between the sixth-grade science and GTT curricula, Tracy described the differences as a continuum. She said that the GTT curriculum includes more of what she likes to do in her regular science class—more inquiry and more use of hands-on approaches. She believes that having the tangible support of ready-to-use materials and the computer laboratory provides students with wonderful opportunities to have frequent hands-on experiences that would not otherwise be afforded to them. By using the design process, the TE program guides the students through actual experimentation and manipulation of variables.

Active learning strategies integrate processes with conceptual knowledge. To make the most of that integration, classrooms need to promote creativity, intellectual safety (Khourey-Bowers 2005), and ongoing assessment. In Stage 5 of the design process, students are expected to generate multiple possible solutions to the problem. Peterson and Harrison (2005) assert that a classroom culture of creativity must be developed and nurtured in technology education classrooms. Characteristics of a creative classroom environment include a challenging curriculum, sufficient resources, organized and inviting physical facility, usefulness of tools, and adult support.

Both students and teachers should be involved in ongoing assessments of active learning processes. Van Niekerk, Ankiewicz, and Swardt (2010) developed an assessment rubric aligned with the stages of the design process. Tufte (2005) created a simple rubric for student self-assessment in which they rate their degree of success in participation, appearance of the final product, cleanup, engineering, and safety. Both of these rubrics can be adapted for use in any active STEM classroom.

How Can Active Learning Strategies Enhance the Classroom Environment?

Vicki sees the major difference between TE and science classrooms in terms of the degree of structure. A typical science classroom is much more teacher-directed and regimented, whereas TE classes tend to be more student-centered or student-directed. Because of the student-focus in the TE classroom, Vicki believes that "TE is a place for self-discovery of strengths."

Tracy has also found that all students do better in TE, as compared to a science classroom, especially students who tend to misbehave a little. For students who need extra academic help, TE gives them many opportunities to practice measurement and mathematical calculations. Within the TE environment, Tracy thinks the students are much more motivated to really care about doing their work correctly!

Cerezo (2004) studied the effect of problem-based learning (PBL) on "at-risk" female middle school students. At-risk was broadly defined in the study as girls who: (1) had very low grades in math or science, (2) said they disliked math or science, (3) performed below grade-level, (4) were diagnosed with learning disabilities, or (5) met criteria of low socioeconomic status. Results indicate that the girls' perceptions of PBL were very positive. They said that learning through PBL helped them be better organized, pay attention in class, learn from others, process information, and use problem-solving in real life. In addition, PBL seemed to help them complete their assignments in other, non-related classes. Cerezo's findings are consistent with those of Tracy's, who noted that her students are more motivated in GTT than in their regular science class, and with Vicki's, who saw the GTT classroom as a place of self-discovery.

How Can Active Learning Strategies Help Prepare Students for STEM Careers?

Tracy's goals for her students encompass all four of the domains of TE, including the societal domain: (1) become aware of different types of engineers, (2) learn what engineers do on a daily basis, and (3) learn the kinds of skills necessary in order to become an engineer. For the energy module, conceptual and societal goals focus on the importance of alternative energy and hands-on experience with renewable energy resources, so that students gain a better understanding of how work is done and energy is produced.

In terms of motivating students to pursue STEM careers, Tracy and Vicki agree that students who come into their classes with some interest in STEM careers are convinced by the end of the course that the STEM fields are right for them. Students with strengths in math and science and those who enjoy design challenges, actively consider careers in engineering. Through GTT, students begin to see the relevance in what they are learning in content area classes.

Participation in TE has been shown to result in a majority of students pursuing STEM careers. An evaluation of a yearlong program, designed to build interest in STEM careers among middle school children on Learning Disability (LD)–related IEPs, was conducted by Lam, Doverspike, Zhao, Zhe, and Menzemer (2008). The purpose of the program was to build technical self-confidence, with the eventual goal of increasing the number of students on LD-IEPs to consider STEM majors in college and STEM careers. Middle school students with LD–IEPs and without LD–IEPs actually participated in the program. The results showed a statistically significant increase in interest in STEM careers in both groups of children. The children's content knowledge also increased through participation in the program.

In a similar study, Zhe, Doverspike, Zhao, Lam, and Menzemer (2010) analyzed the results of a 10-week-long summer program designed to build interest in STEM careers among high school students. The goal of the program was to expose high school students to challenging engineering problems and to increase their self-confidence in academic areas. Of the participating students who subsequently attended college, 86% chose a STEM major.

When is the best time to expose precollege students to active learning or to TE in particular to promote STEM careers? According to Swift and Watkins (2004), K–4 is a good place to start. Curricular standards reflect the importance of technical literacy in society. While elementary education begins with facts, terminology, and other foundational knowledge, the inclusion of advanced concepts and higher-level thinking skills are also mandated. Of course, grade-level content, projects, and materials must be developed.

Most importantly, if we want students and future STEM professionals and technicians to be well-educated, the active learning approaches of TE curricula must actually be implemented in the schools. As Turnbull (2006) notes, assessment of TE principles and processes should be in context of enacted TE, not merely through administration of a mandated standardized test. Assessment of TE without immersion will not prepare students for STEM careers. Professional development and preservice education programs must prepare STEM teachers for student-centered and student-directed approaches. Additionally, assessment of TE should be designed to show progress in all four domains: conceptual, procedural, technical, and societal (Moreland, Jones, and Chambers 2001).

What can teachers do in their STEM classrooms to encourage more students to pursue STEM careers? All involved teachers should become colleagues and collaborators, as did Tracy and Vicki as they lead their students in STEM inquiries.

References

Blank, R., and N. Alas. 2009. Effects of teacher professional development on gains in student achievement. Available online at *www.ccsso.org/Documents/2009/Effects_of_Teacher_Professional_2009.pdf*

Centre for Distance Learning and Innovation (CDLI). 2007. *Introduction to designing integrated systems. Fabrication part 1: Planning and layout.* Available online at *http://gander.cdli.ca/es3205/unit03/section01/lesson03/1-learn-a.htm*

Cerezo, N. 2004. Problem-based learning in the middle school: A Research case study of the perceptions of at-risk females. *Research in Middle Level Education Online* 27 (1): 20–42.

Khourey-Bowers, C. 2005. Cultivating positive attitudes and higher achievement in middle-level mathematics and science. *Middle School Journal* 36 (3): 50–56.

Lam, P. C., D. Doverspike, J. Zhao, J. Zhe, and C. Menzemer. 2008. An evaluation of a STEM program for middle school students on learning disability related IEPs *Journal of STEM Education* 9 (1): 21–29.

Moreland, J., A. Jones, and M. Chambers. 2001. *Enhancing student learning in technology through teacher technological literacy.* Hamilton, New Zealand: University of Waikato.

National Research Council (NRC). 1996. *National science education standards.* Washington, DC: National Academies Press.

Novak, J. D., and A. J. Cañas. 2008. *The theory underlying concept maps and how to construct and use them.* Pensacola, FL: Florida Institute for Human and Machine Cognition.

Osborne, J., and J. Dillon. 2008. *Science education in Europe: Critical reflections.* London: The Nuffield Foundation.

Peterson, R., and H. Harrison. 2005. The Created environment: An Assessment tool for technology education teachers. *The Technology Teacher* 64 (6): 7–10.

Project Lead the Way. 2010. *www.pltw.org*

Swift, T., and S. Watkins. 2004. An engineering primer for outreach to K–4 education. *Journal of STEM Education* 5: (3 & 4): 67–76.

Tufte, R. 2005. The P.A.C.E.S. grading rubric: Creating a student-owned assessment tool for projects. *The Technology Teacher* 64 (5): 21–22.

Turnbull, W. 2006. The Influence of teacher knowledge and authentic formative assessment on student learning in technology education. *International Journal of Technology and Design Education* 16: 53–77.

Van Niekerk, E., P. Ankiewicz, and E. Swardt. 2010. A Process-based assessment framework for technology education: A case study. *International Journal of Technology and Design Education* 20: 191–215.

Yager, R. E., and H. Akcay. 2010. The advantages of an inquiry approach for science instruction in middle grades. *School Science and Mathematics* 110: (1): 5–12.

Zhe, J., D. Doverspike, J. Zhao, P. Lam, and C. Menzemer. 2010. High school bridge program: A multidisciplinary STEM research program. *Journal of STEM Education* 11 (1 & 2): 61–67.

Encouraging More Students to Pursue STEM Careers: Success Stories

Robert E. Yager
University of Iowa

The chapters that comprise our eighth Exemplary Science Program (ESP) series describe 16 exciting programs that encourage more K–16 students to aspire to science, technology, engineering, and mathematics (STEM) careers. The actions proposed to improve the numbers of students who are more positive about STEM careers. The plans offered by the authors of these chapters provide ideas for others to emulate.

Some propose using practicing STEM professionals to work in schools, to help with specific curriculum projects, and to provide parameters for indicating "reform" teaching. Many involve students with community leaders and often beyond the school itself. The involvement of researchers and their direct interactions with students is exciting. The ideas often result in students developing interest in careers that may not even currently exist. New ideas, too, often call for more changes for 2020 (a decade later) that could provide ideas and specific experiences with specific problems as they unfold. Again, many of the ideas include ways of involving students directly in problem-solving and issue-oriented discussions and actions. These conditions more easily lead to career interests as well! The whole process is exciting. Curious minds encourage students to promote and use actions that match course requirements and "reform" curricula. Students are important parts of the learning process.

Projects and plans to work with camp inventions, service-learning projects, academies of science, partners with technology and engineering projects, and special kids inquiry conferences all provide specific ideas and projects that are exciting and designed to alter the negative student attitudes about typical school science experiences. They help alleviate our failure to identify specific projects and activities to meet the career goal included in the Standards. The chapter authors are diverse and illustrate how all science (and technology) teaching can more openly and promptly move to ways that can assist students and classes to meet Goal Four of the National Science Education Standards (NSES).

Too often reforms—like the current focus on STEM efforts embraces—are harder to develop than merely the typical teacher-directed plans. Instead, change is slow (mostly because of teacher, administrator, and parent varying expectations). Science is *not* what is considered in science textbooks or what is included as test items on standardized tests. Most testing companies do not start with knowing what items should be included in such tests. They usually state, however, that since most science teachers use textbooks 90% of the time, all they need to do is to find which textbooks are used and develop the tests by examining these textbooks! This problem also exists because 17 states control the curriculum by specifying the textbooks that must be used in that state. However, many exciting programs are not bound by the use of textbooks. Also, some do not advocate or use standardized tests to indicate quality of teaching and evidence of student learning successes. Too many schools and teachers merely attempt to meet Standards, which may be the cause for the declining number of science teachers with specific plans for students to use in considering STEM careers.

Hopefully the current focus on STEM will improve the general outline of how new standards will be structured for 2013. Will they not include "topics" that merely relate to each of the four STEM "disciplines" instead of what a coordinated whole world believes? We do not need four sets of Standards for each of the four disciplines. The examples chosen for this monograph have included discipline experts and school staff members who view science more broadly and not as separate facets of more typical science courses. This makes integration of the STEM efforts seem unnecessary and unimportant. This was a failure of the 1996 Standards, as they considered the inclusion of physical science as a curriculum organizer. It resulted in no real change in the two discipline content fields, namely physics and chemistry courses. No one dropped physics and chemistry; both continued to be identified and required as high school "offerings" if students wanted to enroll at Harvard University after high school graduation. Disciplines seem to have a solid place in terms of the organization of college science departments *and* high school courses. The needed reforms may need to be organized around problems—not a new outline of content topics with the old disciplines with subheadings as Science, Technology, Engineering, and Mathematics (STEM).

The 16 chapters included should be used as the new Standards develop. Hopefully they will result in changing both the way science is taught and the science content needed. The chapter authors were asked to comment on the new ideas that could define school science for 2013. Evidence of success is needed (and provided) as indicators of real and useful learning in classrooms as even more reforms are visualized. If current efforts are to succeed, we need to improve teachers, teacher education, and professional development efforts in clearer and more exciting ways. Changes in teaching and curriculum describe results in greater numbers of students interested in STEM careers. In real science, answers are not known in advance; every idea needs to be tested and associated with real evidence to support it. Science is a collaborative enterprise, unlike art and literature. It requires ideas and evidence (many forms and many examples) before it is accepted by professional scientists.

The emergence of technology and engineering as central parts of STEM is clear and illustrates differences from typical science curricula. But this inclusion does remind many that similar efforts for moves to technology were offered as important additions to a focus on the natural world 40 years ago with major funding from NSF! It added much to what was or could be done in school classrooms. *The Man Made World* (ECCP) was published in 1971, after trial use was finalized, and offered as a textbook for general use. The plan was to offer such a course that included technology (and engineering) as examples of applications and real-life experiences. But the course did not succeed in terms of trials and textbook purchases. This often occurs with new courses and new ideas. Too often they are seen as not fitting into the typical program. *The Man Made World* was not seen by teachers and curriculum experts as appropriate or necessary for all students. In a sense, it was viewed as a distraction! Often the most innovative reforms often fail because teachers, schools, and the public are not experienced with such ideas in terms of why or how they were developed for use. Change too often is difficult to accomplish!

The ideas in this monograph point to creative and exciting opportunities for students, teachers, and the communities from where they come. Readers are invited to use their understanding and support for ensuring that the 2013 efforts with new Standards will result in real reforms! They need to respond to all four goals included in the 1996 Standards. The leaders for 2013 reforms indicate that the goals would not be altered as the plans for the 1996 efforts emerged; they remain important; it is only the definition of STEM content that needs to be reconsidered. It is an exciting time! We hope the ideas in this book will be useful as the deliberations continue.

Reference

Engineering Concepts Curriculum Project (ECCP). 1971. *The man made world: A high school course.* New York: Polytechnic Institute of Brooklyn. Available online at *www.eric.ed.gov/PDFS/ED019243.pdf*

Contributors

Bruce Alberts, author of *Changes Needed in Science Education for Attracting More Students to STEM Careers,* is Editor-in-Chief of *Science,* published by the American Association for the Advancement of Science (AAAS) in Washington, D.C.

Louise Archer, coauthor of *Educating Students About Careers in Science: Why It Matters,* is a professor of sociology education at King's College London in the United Kingdom.

Shelley H. Billig, coauthor of *The Promise of Service-Learning as an Instructional Approach to Motivate Interest in STEM Careers,* is vice president of RMC Research Corporation, Denver, Colorado.

Jayme Cellitioci, coauthor of *Designed to Invent: Camp Invention, A 21st Century Program,* is the curriculum designer of Invent Now, Inc. in North Canton, Ohio.

Karen Charles, coauthor of *Why STEM? Why Now? The Challenge for U.S. Education to Promote STEM Careers,* is a research education analyst at RTI International in Research Triangle Park, North Carolina.

Stephanie Claussen, coauthor of *Educating Students About Careers in Science: Why It Matters,* is a PhD candidate at Stanford University, Stanford, California.

Disa Lubker Cornish, coauthor of *Real World Externships Exposing Students to Possible Careers in STEM Disciplines,* is a program evaluator at the University of Northern Iowa Center for Social and Behavioral Research, Cedar Falls, Iowa.

Jennifer DeWitt, coauthor of *Educating Students About Careers in Science: Why It Matters,* is a researcher in the department of education and professional studies at King's College London in the United Kingdom.

Justin Dillon, coauthor of *Educating Students About Careers in Science: Why It Matters,* is head of the science and technology education group at King's College London in the United Kingdom.

Francis Q. Eberle, coauthor of *NSTA Efforts to Interest More K–12 Students in Pursuing STEM Careers,* is former executive director of the National Science Teachers Association, Arlington, Virginia.

Ryan Flessner, coauthor of *Utilizing Inquiry-Based Teaching and Kids Inquiry Conferences to Strengthen Elementary Science Instruction and to Encourage More Students to Pursue Science Careers,* is an assistant professor of teacher education at Butler University, Indianapolis, Indiana.

Linda Fredericks, coauthor of *The Promise of Service-Learning as an Instructional Approach to Motivate Interest in STEM Careers,* is a research associate at RMC Research Corporation, Denver, Colorado.

S. Anders Hedberg, author of *The Talent Marketplace: Where Science Careers Are Made,* is president of Hedberg Consulting, LLC in Ottsville, Pennsylvania.

Arthur Heiss, coauthor of *The Steppingstone Magnetic Resonance Training Center Opportunities for Students and Faculty in a True Research Laboratory Setting,* is vice president of Bruker BioSpin Corporation, EPR Division in Billerica, Massachusetts.

Craig Johnson, coauthor of *Scientists as Partners in K–12 Science: Engineering, Science, and Technology Careers,* is the executive director of the Iowa Academy of Science in Cedar Falls, Iowa.

Claudia Khourey-Bowers, coauthor of *Active Learning as a Way to Interest More Students in Science Careers,* is an assistant professor in the school of teaching, learning, and curriculum studies at Kent State University at Stark in North Canton, Ohio.

Paula A. Magee, coauthor of *Utilizing Inquiry-Based Teaching and Kids Inquiry Conferences to Strengthen Elementary Science Instruction and to Encourage More Students to Pursue Science Careers,* is a clinical associate professor at Indiana University in Indianapolis, Indiana.

Lisa Martin-Hansen, coauthor of *Creating Pipeline to STEM Careers through Service Learning: The AFT Program,* is an associate professor at Georgia State University in Atlanta, Georgia.

Vicki McCamon, coauthor of *Active Learning as a Way to Interest More Students in Science Careers,* is a middle childhood education teacher at Joseph Welty Middle School in New Philadelphia, Ohio.

Melissa McCartney, coauthor of *Science Beyond the Laboratory: The Intriguing Career Paths of Fourteen Scientists and Engineers,* is an editorial fellow at *Science,* published by the American Association for the Advancement of Science (AAAS) in Washington, D.C.

Alan J. McCormack, coauthor of *NSTA Efforts to Interest More K–12 Students in Pursuing STEM Careers,* is a professor of science education at San Diego State University, San Diego, California.

Glenn "Max" Mcgee, author of *Preparing Students for Careers That Do Not Yet Exist,* is president of the Illinois Mathematics and Science Academy in Aurora, Illinois.

Isabel Montemayor, coauthor of *Real World Externships Exposing Students to Possible Careers in STEM Disciplines,* is a program assistant at the Center for Social and Behavioral Research, University of Northern Iowa, Cedar Falls, Iowa.

Kiyo Ann Morse, coauthor of *The Steppingstone Magnetic Resonance Training Center Opportunities for Students and Faculty in a True Research Laboratory Setting,* is head of the Steppingstone School for Gifted Education in Farmington Hills, Michigan.

Philip D. (Reef) Morse II, coauthor of *The Steppingstone Magnetic Resonance Training Center Opportunities for Students and Faculty in a True Research Laboratory Setting,* is the administrator of Steppingstone Magnetic Resonance Training Center in Farmington Hills, Michigan.

Ted Anthony Neal, coauthor of *Real World Externships Exposing Students to Possible Careers in STEM Disciplines,* is a science education clinical instructor at the University of Iowa, Iowa City, Iowa.

Jonathan Osborne, coauthor of *Educating Students About Careers in Science: Why It Matters,* is a Shriram Family professor of science education at Stanford University, Stanford, California.

Anne Poduska, coauthor of *Science Beyond the Laboratory: The Intriguing Career Paths of Fourteen Scientists and Engineers,* is a senior program associate of the Research Competitiveness Program at the American Association for the Advancement of Science (AAAS) in Washington, D.C.

Gerard Putz, coauthor of *Science Olympiad: Inspiring the Next Generation of Scientists,* is president and cofounder of Science Olympiad in Oakbrook Terrace, Illinois.

Anton Puvirajah, coauthor of *Creating a Pipeline to STEM Careers Through Service Learning: The AFT Program,* is an assistant professor at Georgia State University, Atlanta, Georgia.

Alaina Rutledge, coauthor of *Designed to Invent: Camp Invention, A 21st Century Program,* is core curriculum and programs extension manager at Invent Now, Inc., in North Canton, Ohio.

Tracy Saho, coauthor of *Active Learning as a Way to Interest More Students in Science Careers,* is a teacher at Welty Middle School in New Philadelphia, Ohio.

Lyn E. Swackhamer, is coauthor of *The Promise of Service-Learning as an Instructional Approach to Motivate Interest in STEM Careers,* is a research associate at the RMC Research Corporation in Denver, Colorado.

Geeta Verma, coauthor of *Creating a Pipeline to STEM Careers Through Service Learning: The AFT Program,* is an associate professor at the University of Colorado–Denver, Denver, Colorado.

T. Georgeanne Warnock, coauthor of *Why STEM? Why Now? The Challenge for U.S. Education to Promote STEM Careers,* principal of R. L. Turner High School in Carrollton, Texas.

Richard Weibl, coauthor of *Science Beyond the Laboratory: The Intriguing Career Paths of Fourteen Scientists and Engineers,* is director of Center for Careers in Science and Technology at the American Association for the Advancement of Science (AAAS) in Washington, DC.

Jeffrey Weld, author of *Real World Externships Exposing Students to Possible Careers in STEM Disciplines,* is director of the Iowa Mathematics and Science Education Partnership at the University of Northern Iowa, Cedar Falls, Iowa.

Jennifer L. Wirt, coauthor of *Science Olympiad: Inspiring the Next Generation of Scientists,* is director of N. J. Science Olympiad in Paramus, New Jersey.

Brenda Wojnowski, coauthor of *Why STEM? Why Now? The Challenge for U.S. Education to Promote STEM Careers,* is president of Wojnowski and Associates, Inc. in Dallas, Texas.

Maryann Wolowiec, coauthor of *Designed to Invent: Camp Invention, A 21st Century Program,* is President of IEL Educational Consulting in Hudson, Ohio.

Billy Wong, coauthor of *Educating Students About Careers in Science: Why It Matters,* is a PhD candidate in the department of education and professional studies at King's College London in the United Kingdom.

Rieko Yajima, coauthor of *Science Beyond the Laboratory: The Intriguing Career Paths of Fourteen Scientists and Engineers,* is project director with the Research competitiveness Program at the American Association for the Advancement of Science (AAAS) in Washington, D.C.

Index

National Science Teachers Association